Dickinson

DICKINSON

Strategies of Limitation

Jane Donahue Eberwein

The University of Massachusetts Press

Amherst

Copyright © 1985 by The University of Massachusetts Press
All rights reserved
Printed in the United States of America
FIRST PAPERBACK EDITION, 1987
Library of Congress Cataloging in Publication Data

Eberwein, Jane Donahue, 1943–
Dickinson, strategies of limitation.

Bibliography: p.
Includes indexes.
1. Dickinson, Emily, 1830–1886—Criticism and inter-
pretation. 2. Dickinson, Emily, 1830–1886—Technique.
I. Title.
PS1541.Z5E34   1985   811'.4   84–16335
ISBN 0–87023–473–0; 0–87023–549–4 (pbk.)

Publication of this book was assisted by the American Council of Learned
Societies under a grant from the Andrew W. Mellon Foundation.

Acknowledgment is made to the following for material reprinted with
permission:

Harvard University Press, for material reprinted by permission of the
publishers and the Trustees of Amherst College from *The Poems of Emily
Dickinson*, edited by Thomas H. Johnson, Cambridge, Mass.: The Belknap Press
of Harvard University Press, Copyright 1951, © 1955, 1979, 1983 by the
President and Fellows of Harvard College; and for material reprinted by
permission of the publishers from *The Letters of Emily Dickinson*, edited by
Thomas H. Johnson, Cambridge, Mass.: The Belknap Press of Harvard
University Press, Copyright © 1958 by the President and Fellows of Harvard
College, © Copyright 1914, 1924, 1932 by Martha Dickinson Bianchi.

Houghton Mifflin Company, for material from *Life and Letters of Emily
Dickinson* by Martha D. Bianchi. Copyright 1924 by Martha Dickinson Bianchi;
copyright renewed 1952 by Alfred Leete Hampson. Reprinted by permission of
Houghton Mifflin Company.

Little, Brown and Company for material reprinted from *The Complete Poems
of Emily Dickinson*, edited by Thomas H. Johnson. Copyright 1914, 1929, 1935,
1942 by Martha Dickinson Bianchi; copyright renewed © 1957, 1963 by Mary
L. Hampson. By permission of Little, Brown and Company.

The Trustees of Amherst College for permission to reprint the 1848
daguerreotype of Emily Dickinson.

Earlier versions of chapters 2 and 6 appeared in "Doing Without: Dickinson as
Yankee Woman Poet," in *Critical Essays on Emily Dickinson*, ed. Paul J. Ferlazzo
(Boston: G. K. Hall, 1984) and are reprinted here by permission of the publisher.

That Such have died enable Us
The tranquiller to die—
That Such have lived,
Certificate for Immortality.
(P 1030)

Contents

Preface   ix

Part I: The Problem of Limitation

Chapter 1: "Could You Believe Me—Without?": A
Minimizing Self-Portrait   3
Chapter 2: "The Wildest Word": The Habit of Renunciation   21
Chapter 3: "An Enlarged Ability for Missing": Artistic
Exploitation of Limits   47

Part II: Literary Strategies for Growth

Chapter 4: "The Precious Words": Literary Sources of
Support   73
Chapter 5: "I Play at Riches": Acting Alternative Roles   94
Chapter 6: "My Little Force Explodes": The Poetics of
Distillation   128

Part III: Pushing against Circumference

Chapter 7: "Out upon Circumference": Testing Barriers   159
Chapter 8: "Dying in Drama": Death as Circumference   198
Chapter 9: "A Prognostic's Push": Premonitions of
Immortality   225
Chapter 10: "His Diameters": The Unbounded Circle   264

Notes   273

Index of First Lines   289

Index   301

Preface

To READ Emily Dickinson is an exhilarating experience; to write about her a humbling one. No analytic prose can do justice to those hidden nuggets of wisdom and exploding atoms of wit that startle us in her writing; yet characteristics of that writing (in prose as well as poetry) seem to demand explanation if only in response to the questions readers inevitably raise about the whys and wherefores of her remarkable sayings.

It is impossible to look at Dickinson's poems in any typical collection, whether chronologically or topically organized, without wondering about the connections that link them and the mind that produced them. How could the timid little girl who apparently tries to hide herself in many of these poems muster courage to assail the sublimest topics accessible to human imagination? Why do the often fragmented remarks of this provincial, even peculiar, person speak so compellingly and convincingly to almost everyone—general readers as well as scholars? There is something happening in these poems and letters that goes beyond autobiographical revelation and confronts us with a driving purpose that motivated Dickinson to advance "by Processes of Size" from awareness of her own smallness to recognition of God's "Diameters" (P 802).

This book emerges from a decade's teaching of Dickinson's poems and from repeated attempts to articulate what she was doing in those virtual nursery rhymes that confront us, surprisingly but insistently, with overwhelming issues of finitude and faith. It takes into consideration the chosen and stylized aspects of Emily Dickinson's life as well as her literary designs and treats her as a figure more comfortably situated than many of our contemporaries choose to acknowledge in her own time and place. It emphasizes her aspiration to look beyond the circumference of consciousness and mortality and examines her unique strategies for intensifying and making use of limitations.

The voice that I hope dominates the pages that follow is Emily Dickinson's. I have quoted her extensively throughout, stressing her earlier writings in the first part of this study and later ones toward the end without actually trying to chart a biographical course. I have copied her actual language, with all the orthographic and mechanical quirks that testify to its unedited origin, and I have tried to examine her poems in the contexts she herself provided both in her letters and in the fascicles recently made available in facsimile by R. W. Franklin. To him and to Dickinson's earlier editors I owe a profound debt of gratitude, as I do to the many biographers, critics, and commentators who have shaped my understanding while occasionally quickening my dissent.

It is a pleasure to extend particular thanks here to friends and colleagues who have contributed to the making of this book in many different ways: my friend and "preceptor" Hyatt Waggoner; counselors Everett Emerson of the University of North Carolina at Chapel Hill and Barton Levi St. Armand of Brown University; my Oakland University colleagues William White and Ronald Sudol; and Anne Lalas, who provided welcome editorial guidance. The gratitude I feel to my family is only partially acknowledged in the dedication. My greatest debt, yet again, is to Robert Eberwein for the scholarly support and stimulus that add their distinctive joy to our collegial marriage.

PART ONE

The Problem of Limitation

I

"Could You Believe Me—Without?"

A Minimizing Self-Portrait

EMILY DICKINSON lived a deliberately secluded life in the company of neighbors and close friends—most of them known to her through her family. Seldom as an adult did she have occasion to present herself to a stranger. In 1862, however, she ventured to introduce herself to Thomas Wentworth Higginson, the Worcester, Massachusetts, man of letters from whom she sought evaluation of her verse and confirmation of her poetic identity.[1] The description of herself that she offered him proves invaluable to modern readers trying to understand this elusive woman. For the most part, we must rely on descriptions of Dickinson based on recollections of her last years, when she had attained her quaint status as "the *character* of Amherst."[2] Most of these memories were immature impressions gleaned by Mabel Loomis Todd, the poet's first editor, from persons who had seen Emily Dickinson in their youth. Mrs. Todd, while describing herself as the poet's friend, had never laid eyes on her (though her daughter Millicent enjoyed this privilege of Amherst childhood).[3] Austin and Lavinia Dickinson spoke more openly of what their sister had not been than of what she was; her brother and sister knew their Emily too well and valued her privacy too highly to describe her publicly. For these reasons, Dickinson's description of herself to Higginson in the letter of July 1862, when she was at the height of her creative power, proves indispensable to those who wish to know her.

Three months before, Dickinson had opened her correspondence with Higginson by asking him, "Are you too deeply occupied to say if my Verse is alive?" (L 260). Despite the onslaught of manuscripts he was then receiving from hopeful authors in response to his "Letter to a Young Contributor" in the April *Atlantic Monthly*, Higginson replied and over the next few months prompted further correspondence from Amherst by raising questions about Miss Dickinson's age ("I made no verse—but one or two—until this winter—Sir—"), reading habits ("For Poets—I have Keats—and Mr and Mrs Browning"), and companions ("Hills—Sir—and the Sundown—and a Dog—") (L 261).

After three letters, he evidently asked for a photograph in the hope of gaining a flesh-and-blood impression of his gnomic correspondent. Dickinson's response merits close attention as a key to her self-image and as a reflection of her relationship to this "Preceptor": "Could you believe me—without? I had no portrait, now, but am small, like the Wren, and my Hair is bold, like the Chestnut Bur—and my eyes, like the Sherry in the Glass, that the Guest leaves—Would this do just as well?" Of course, it had to do "just as well," given her reluctance to provide conventional descriptive information. Evidently Higginson did believe her to be without a photograph, especially since she rationalized the lack of one of those daguerreotypes already in common circulation around her New England: "It often alarms Father—He says Death might occur, and he has Molds of all the rest—but has no Mold of me, but I noticed the Quick wore off those things, in a few days, and forestall the dishonor—You will think no caprice of me—." Whether Higginson suspected caprice we may never know, but those of us familiar with the commonly reproduced Dickinson daguerreotype of 1847 or 1848 have reason for suspicion—and for consequent wondering about the verbal portrait she substituted. The history of that photograph contradicts the poet's claims.

Dickinson represents herself in this letter as the lone holdout against paternal pressure for conformity. She claims that her father wanted her picture and that she refused to have it taken. But their motives were the same: to cheat death. She explains that Edward Dickinson looked on photography as a means of retaining some vestige of life after death for family use, but his daughter saw the photograph itself as an anticipatory dying—a rigidification of once mobile features without "the Quick" of breath: a "Mold" or form in the parlor while the body moldered. Had Higginson recalled her first letter at this point, with its promise of "quick gratitude" for his judgment on the life of her verse, his thoughts on whether "it breathed," he might have observed a substitution on her part of poetry for photography as a preservative.

Nevertheless, she did have a daguerreotype that was presumably available for mailing. Sometime before her death in 1886 she is reported to have given it to Maggie Maher, who joined the Dickinson household as a servant in 1869. A photographic copy of the daguerreotype graced the Homestead's parlor cabinet in the 1890s.[4] Perhaps she had in fact sat for her portrait in deference to her father's will: The picture was taken close to his birthday.

Whether Edward Dickinson influenced her decision or not, posing for a daguerreotype definitely put his daughter, then a student at Mount Holyoke Female Seminary, into near conflict with Mary Lyon, the formidable headmistress of that school.[5] In Susan Tolman's *Mount Holyoke Journal* for 1848, Jay Leyda has located interesting information about the daguerreotype enthusiasm that struck the young ladies that winter, right in the midst of a religious revival that featured a fast day on Christmas Eve, special conversion sessions for "all who were willing thus to give up their hearts to the influences of the Holy Spirit," and a Sabbath sermon for 26 December 1847 on the text: "Whoever he be of you that forsaketh not all that he hath, cannot be my disciple."[6] In the midst of such piety came an itinerant photographer, who established himself in South Hadley directly across from the seminary and distracted its pupils with distinctly worldly temptations. Some young ladies had even been "tardy or absent from exercises"; all were wasting the money their instructors were teaching them to budget. Late in December Miss Lyon felt constrained to advise her excited young charges that "if one was sure she had money enough, if she would not have to diminish her missionary contribution in consequence of it, there was perhaps no objection, to it." She advised, however, "that it had better be done elsewhere." Her counsel misfired, and Miss Tolman reported that since her discussion the photography sessions had "increased very much," to the point that Miss Lyon restricted the privilege eventually only to those who had already engaged a sitting, *"no others."* No wonder Emily Dickinson's photograph looks so sober, even a little scared! One wonders when she sat for it, whether before or after Miss Lyon's directives. In any event, she found herself a rebel and no doubt convicted herself yet again of that love for the world that she found impossible to reject in that spiritually pressured year at Mount Holyoke. Perhaps as a diligent student under her new "Preceptor," she preferred to smooth over her defiance of the headmistress and located the drama of her life instead in a filial conflict.

It is also possible that Dickinson withheld the photograph from her mentor because it was out-of-date: At thirty-one years of age she could hardly have felt like the collegian of seventeen. In 1852 she had had her hair cut considerably and wore it in a curly style that may also have characterized her in 1862 rather than the severe look of the daguerreotype.[7] She might also have found it an un-flattering likeness, as Lavinia found the daguerreotype of herself that she sent to Austin in 1852: "I will send you my picture, but I dont like it at all & should be sorry to have you or any one else think I look just like it. I dont think my real face is quite so stupid as the picture, perhaps I'm mistaken however."[8] Austin himself consistently refused to allow publication of his photograph in col-lege or town histories and was fond of repeating an old schoolboy couplet remembered by his daughter: "Fools' names and fools' faces / Only appear in public places."[9] Even Edward Dickinson seems to glower toward the camera in his daguerreotype.

The excuse Dickinson actually offered, that "the Quick wore off those things," seems the least compelling unless she demanded a far stronger impression of lasting vitality for herself than for others. She enjoyed photographs and once thanked her friend Elizabeth Holland for one in words that nearly contradicted the 1862 statement: "Your sweet Face alighted in the Rain, with it's Smile unharmed—All was there but Breath, and even that seemed optional" (L 542).[10] In the winter of 1862, a month or two before the poet first wrote to the *Atlantic* editor, an editor closer to home, Samuel Bowles, had reported to Susan Dickinson, Austin's wife and Emily's closest literary confidante, that he had been frustrated in two errands for Sue: a search for a Whittier volume then out of print and for a Higginson photograph.[11] He reported, "Higginson has not been done in photograph—so all said—& yet I have a memory of it I think, months ago." Was Susan scouting in ad-vance for Emily, looking for the sort of image of Higginson that she would soon refuse to send to him? In the next letter after this refusal she offered him a photograph of Elizabeth Barrett Brown-ing: "Persons sent me three—If you had none, will you have mine?" (L 271). In her late years photographs of Thomas Carlyle,

Daguerreotype of 1847 or 1848 (courtesy of Amherst College Library)

Mrs. Browning, and George Eliot graced her bedroom wall although she commented about Eliot, "God chooses repellant settings, dont he, for his best Gems?" (L 692). [12]

Millicent Todd Bingham's account of her mother's frustrated efforts to illustrate her 1894 edition of Dickinson's letters with a picture of the already popular poet provides evidence that the South Hadley daguerreotype presented Amherst's gem in a setting repellant to those who knew her. [13] The daguerreotype itself was missing, supposedly in the possession of Maggie Maher, although Mrs. Todd learned eventually that around 1892 Lavinia had given it to an Amherst collegian, Wallace Keep, who sent it to the editor many years later; it has become the normative depiction of Emily Dickinson since its first publication in 1931. [14] But the poet's brother and sister rejected a photographic reproduction of the daguerreotype as an illustration for the letters. They found it "too solemn, too heavy," lacking "the play of light and shade in Emily's face." They condemned it also for making her look too plain. An artist attempted a composite sketch uniting the face from the photograph with a cousin's hair style that Lavinia and Austin thought more characteristic of Emily, but neither was satisfied that the sketch resembled their sister. Later, Lavinia commissioned a Boston portrait painter to modify the daguerreotype impression by softening the hair and rearranging the neckline in a way that made Lavinia respond, "It really seems as if Emily was here." She looked forward to having a miniature painted with "some fluffy finish for the neck": probably the picture Martha Dickinson Bianchi published in *The Life and Letters of Emily Dickinson* (1924).

With only the photograph of the daguerreotype, two silhouettes cut in Emily's teens, and a primitive childhood portrait of the three Dickinson children to choose from when the letters went to press, Austin Dickinson preferred the stylized picture of Emily as a little girl, taken from the composite painting and given a modified background. It could hardly have projected an accurate sense of the "interesting & startling face" her sister remembered, but neither perhaps did the daguerreotype Dickinson herself withheld from Higginson.

The verbal self-portrait she substituted is more revealing in psychological ways and as an index of her imaginative process. It is surely both interesting and startling—most so, perhaps, to those who actually knew the woman. Her niece, Martha, described her in quite different terms, remembering her aunt in maturity as "of medium height, decisive in manner, not frail nor ever suggestive of ill health."[15] She emphasized the "dark, expressive eyes with their tint of bronze, and Titian hair set off by her white skin" and noted that, "Indeed, the richness of her hair and eyes were her salient points, oftenest commented on. She had regular features, and her upper lip, a trifle long, gave her face a slightly ascetic expression." This is certainly a kinder evaluation than Higginson's famous report after his first visit to the Homestead in 1870, when he described his timid hostess as "a little plain woman with two smooth bands of reddish hair" and a face "with no good feature" (L 342a). Amherst neighbors remembered Miss Dickinson's auburn curls, chestnut hair and eyes, very white skin, medium height, and good weight, although at least one visitor found her an ethereal presence, "a touch-me-not of purest quality."[16] Her self-portrait, however, undermines the vitality of these images and accentuates the "touch-me-not" impression. Every detail she offers distorts the facts of her appearance, yet each reveals something about her way of seeing.

She begins by referring to her stature, which she calls "small, like the Wren." The whimsical simile warns the reader not to accept her statement literally. If a dress from her final years can be taken as indicative of her adult size, she stood close to five feet, five inches—not an inconsiderable height.[17] In her teens, she had written to her closest schoolgirl-friend, Abiah Root, "I am now very tall & wear long dresses near[l]y" (L 13). Perhaps the smallness related to girth. Family correspondence suggests that Emily was the slimmer sister, less sturdy than Lavinia. She joked about the contrast in a letter to her brother when he was teaching in Boston, urging him to be careful of his health for the sake of loved ones at home: "I know *my* sake a'nt much, but Vinnie's is considerab[l]e—it weighs a good many pounds—when *skin and bones* may plead, I will become a *persuasion*, but you have *other* friends who are much more substantial" (L 45). Lavinia wrote shortly thereafter that Emily "has really grown *fat*, if youll believe it," as a consequence of a new medical regimen in which "I am very strict with her & I shouldnt wonder if she should come out bright some time after all."[18] Still, Dickinson always spoke of herself in diminutive terms to Higginson, confessing in her second letter that "I could not weigh myself—Myself—/ My size felt small—to me"

(L 261) and promising that her "little shape . . . would not crowd your Desk" in the next (L 265). Sometimes she spoke dolefully of her fragile form, as in the third letter to her unidentified "Master" when she wrote, "Wonder wastes my pound, you said I had no size to spare" (L 248); but at other times she emphasized comic potential, as when she expressed elation by fantasizing that "I could mount a grasshopper, and gallop around the *world*, and not fatigue him any!" (L 82).

Whatever her actual measurements, the letters and poems suggest a distinctively small self-image. In minimizing her size, Dickinson may have referred to her poetic rather than physical stature. That, at any rate, is what she asked Higginson to measure. The little-girl persona she so often adopted comports with associations she liked to draw between herself and tiny beings: the arbutus, a grass, a mouse, and the wren chosen for this simile.[19] Small, shrinking creatures aroused her empathy. So did rejected ones like the rat, spider, worm, and bat; and this identification with despised life reveals important aspects of the poet's approach to life that I shall try to explain in the course of this study. There was, of course, a theological basis for her self-abnegation in the Christian sense of man's nothingness before God—a doctrine often expounded from Connecticut Valley pulpits. Dickinson echoed orthodox language when she wrote to a pious friend in 1850 after the death of their near contemporary, Leonard Humphrey, that "We are very small, Abiah—I think we grow still smaller—this tiny, insect life the portal to another" (L 39), but she reacted against such constriction of her worth in an 1858 letter to Susan Dickinson: "Presume if I met with my 'deserts,' I should receive nothing. Was informed to that effect today by a 'dear pastor.' What a privilege it is to be so insignificant! Thought of intimating that the 'Atonement' was'nt needed for such atomies!" (L 194).

There is a sarcastic ring here to her talk of "privilege," but Dickinson's readers must be alert to her tendency to exploit whatever limitations she encountered—often to intensify those limitations in order to exploit them more. Even the self-pitying poem "I was the slightest in the House—" (P 486) includes the statement that the diminutive and overlooked speaker stationed herself where she "could catch the Mint / That never ceased to fall—" in a strategic position of paradoxical openness to wealth or grace. To be tiny was not necessarily to be negligible, or lacking in vital power.

Writing to a sick friend, Dickinson once wrote, "I hope you may be a hale Mattie before you go away—vast as Vinnie and I, who tower like Acorns" (L 654). A nut with the capacity to grow into an oak, she may have towered like an acorn over Higginson even while likening herself to the wren.

I have stressed Dickinson's attention to smallness here because of the centrality of the theme to her imagination. The Rosenbaum concordance to her 1,775 poems lists 58 references to the word *small*, 13 to *smaller*, 12 to *smallest*, 3 to *slight*, 1 to *slightest*, 37 to *least*, 27 to *less*, and 8 to *lesser*.[20] Even granting that many of these citations refer to impersonal lyrics, there is an obvious concentration of usage here, especially in tandem with all the references to children and little beings. Smallness, with its consequent facilitation of hiding and impulse toward growth, proved a surprisingly fruitful point of departure for this poet's imagination.

The other things Dickinson told her preceptor about her appearance compel attention also by their vivid expression, their contradiction of reality as we know it through the memories of her visitors, and their apparent appeal for pity. She undervalued every good feature. The hair, which her friends highlighted in their descriptions and which remained a rich auburn throughout her life, was likened to the "Chestnut Bur"—not the lustrous nut but its prickly and comparatively dingy envelope. Her eyes, variously remembered as brown or hazel, were compared to sherry—not the warm-toned liquor in the decanter but the dregs rejected in the glass. Her similes linked both hair and eyes to serviceable objects to be discarded. Later in the same letter, she called herself "the only Kangaroo among the Beauty" in a grotesquely self-mocking comment, although, to be sure, the kangaroo outleaps more shapely animals and, like the acorn and the wren, can be interpreted as a metaphor for ascension.

The wren seems to have been one of Emily Dickinson's favorite birds, one she often likened to herself or to women she regarded as small such as Mrs. Holland, to whom she wrote, "You always were a Wren, you know, the tenant of a Twig—" (L 950). When her cousin, Louise Norcross, recovered from sickness, Dickinson rejoiced "that my wren can rise and touch the sky again" (L 337). It seems to have been the tiny creature's force and courage that delighted the poet, its capacity to challenge the heavens and its melodious song. "The Wren will prevail," Dickinson assured another "little Friend" who had been thrown from her carriage by a shying horse (L 564). And she told Samuel Bowles in reference to bird songs that she never doubted that "at the last each Wren shall bear it's 'Palm'—" even, probably, each metaphorical wren (L 242). Regarding the wren as shy in a poem like "A Mien to move a Queen—" (P 283) and vulnerable to injury or scorn, she recognized its unimpressive qualities in her whimsical reply to the 1849 valentine she had all but commissioned from her cousin William Cowper Dickinson—an early identification with the bird and a more explicitly humorous one than her letter to Higginson suggested: "A little condescending, & sarcastic, your Valentine to me, I thought; a little like an Eagle, stooping to salute a Wren, & I concluded once, I dared not answer it, for it seemed to me not quite becoming—in a bird so lowly as myself—to claim admittance to an Eyrie, & conversation with it's King" (L 27). But she reconsidered, and the wren prevailed.

Perhaps Dickinson's most memorable and revealing development of her wren image appears in "For every Bird a Nest—" (P 143), a charming poem composed several years before her comment to Higginson. In this she shows the wren as "little" and "timid" yet still a questing pilgrim—a character in a celestial romance. The poet questions the cause of all this seeking. Wherefore, when nature assures us of a nest for every bird, does this one somewhat ridiculous being remain unsettled in the sky? The answer comes in the rhyme words linking the ends of stanzas three and four: "desires" and "aspires." Looking from the ground like a foolish little flutterer, the wren proves herself an aristocrat who refuses to settle for the "households" available on every tree but attempts to select the most rarefied lodging—a finer than usual brace to support her nest, superfine components to weave into it. She is restless, selective, ambitious—enclosing the pride of an eagle within her minuscule frame. A wren, indeed, by virtue of its very smallness and its tuneful charm, has more opportunity for discrimination than larger birds, being wooed by elaborate birdhouses of human artifice as well as by natural inducements of dainty twigs. Elsewhere, Dickinson observed that "Sir Christopher Wren is here prospecting for his nest—I suppose it will have a Dome and Aisles—."[21]

The lark, by contrast, settles instinctively on the ground, building her "modest house" with less fanfare, an action Dickinson described in a stanza notably less tuneful than those accorded the wren. This contrasting bird earns her stability and comfort by ignoring unattainable or even challenging alternatives. In likening herself to a wren, therefore, Dickinson capriciously alerted Higginson to her poetic aspiration even while discounting her personal stature.

The final stanza of "For every Bird a Nest—" can be applied to either the lark or the wren. Given the sequence of the poem, the former seems more probable. Yet this is an American lark (presumably a horned lark or possibly the eastern meadowlark), not the soaring, singing skylark of Shelley's poem or the songster whose tune rivaled the nightingale's in *Romeo and Juliet*. A much more settled, earthbound bird, it would be less likely than the questing, vaulting wren to rejoice among "the throng / Dancing around the sun." The wren seems here triumphant, like the towering acorn. That which was small could rise, especially if nurturing sublime ambitions.

R. W. Franklin's recent publication of Dickinson's *Manuscript Books* in facsimile allows us to examine the text of this poem as she copied it down in 1859 and to look at it within the context of other poems recorded at the same time.[22] Thematic, imagistic, or emotional correspondences often appear within such groupings, encouraging supposition about the poet's intentions as she copied her working drafts into more polished booklets. "For every Bird a Nest—" appears in fascicle 4 with fifteen other poems. The poem deals with choice—the difficulty of making choices in the face of multiple possibilities and discriminating tastes.

The next poem, the only one copied by Dickinson on the same manuscript sheet, appears earlier in Johnson's arrangement and has never been juxtaposed with it by critics. "'They have not chosen me,' he said," (P 85) is, however, another poem about choices and serves as the obverse to "For every Bird a Nest—." As often happened, Dickinson departed here at several points from her biblical source, chapter 15 of the Gospel of John. Rather than uttering these pained words in Bethlehem, scene of his infancy, Jesus spoke them at the end of his ministry, in the upper room in Jerusalem just after eating the Last Supper and immediately before his Passion. Nor did he remark about an impersonal "they" who had rejected him but about "ye," the friends surrounding him. And (as all Christians know) despite their sleeping in the garden, their running from the soldiers, and Peter's triple denial of his master, all but one of the Apostles eventually confirmed their choice of Jesus and remained loyal to death. Christ's statement that Dickinson repeats here is truly an anguished one—likely to remain in her memory in unconsciously altered form and applicable to less awesome human choices. The speaker of the poem, in this case the Daisy whom Dickinson used as her persona in her second and third "Master" letters (but not in the first, the only one apparently composed before this poem), identifies with Jesus in his capacity as rejected lover. She shares in his dishonor. Does she anticipate sharing in his eventual triumph? In addressing him as "Sovreign," may she not link her queen role with his as well as her Daisy role? The Calvinist theory of conversion that formed the basis of her religious training had informed her that Christ *must* choose a person in order for that person ultimately to choose him. In likening herself to the Savior, for whose election she had been taught to wait expectantly, she need not have been mortifying her pride any more than Benjamin Franklin did in cultivating the appearance of humility by imitating Jesus and Socrates; teen-aged Emily had, in fact, assigned the role of Socrates to herself when she and her school friends assumed classical identities as members of an informal club (L 5).[23]

The searching but soaring wren and the Christlike Daisy exemplify Dickinson's tendency to exalt the small beings with which she identified, often by indirect means. She habitually conceived of smallness as the starting point of her quest, the initial condition beyond which only progress was possible. She aspired to growth and observed its signs with mixed feelings. After one of Lavinia's visits with Dr. and Mrs. Josiah Gilbert Holland, Dickinson wrote, "I think Vinnie has grown since the interview, certainly intellectually, which is the only Bone whose Expanse we woo—" (L 888). Emotional growth could be more painful, especially when it turned out to be disproportionate to physical and intellectual capacities. In the second letter she drafted for her "Master," Dickinson complained that God "built the heart in me—Bye and bye it outgrew me—and like the little mother—with the big child—I got tired holding him" (L 233). Despite the pain, she measured life by growth and sought ways to expand the bone. By 1862 when she wrote to Higginson, she had determined on poetry as her secret of expansion. If the poems were alive—as she asked her preceptor to judge—they would compensate for her personal insufficiency. Why else did she inquire of an editor, "Could you tell me how to grow—or is it unconveyed—like Melody—or Witchcraft?" (L 261). She knew that the mystery was unconveyed, that Higginson had no way of directing her, but she appointed him from that time until well beyond her death as the literary world's prime observer of her artistic life process.

This Emersonian organic metaphor introduced Dickinson's first letter to Worcester in April 1862—"Mr. Higginson, / Are you too deeply occupied to say if my Verse is alive?" (L 260)—and expanded into an inquiry about whether he thought "it breathed." She ascribed more life to the verses she sent him than she did to herself in the devitalized self-portrait of the July letter. Yet even after having presented her inadequacies with such exaggeration, she still insisted on his aiding her expansion. He was to concentrate attention on "the growth of me" and imitate a surgeon in the painful struggle to set the internal fractures she apprehended in her art (L 268). We know from the rest of their correspondence and from his reminiscences after her death that she never followed her surgeon's prescriptions; yet she told him six years later that he had saved her life (L 330).

Her verbal self-portrait and even her deception about the photograph demonstrate that Emily Dickinson presented herself to her mentor as a kind of imaginative creation rather than as a flesh-and-blood woman. She acknowledged as much about the poems, warning in the July letter that "When I state myself, as the Representative of the Verse—it does not mean—me—but a supposed person." This was a well-placed caution and is still a helpful one for readers who try to read autobiography into lyric poetry. We are only beginning to identify the various personae who speak in Dickinson's poems. What she did not confide to him but what he must have guessed is that she adopted roles even in her correspondence and that the "Scholar" who described herself to him with such engaging humility was another construct of a poet's fertile imagination, based in autobiography, to be sure, but expanding by an imaginative process into a fanciful creature. Austin, when he read the letters Higginson published in his *Atlantic Monthly* introduction of Emily Dickinson in 1891, felt uncomfortable about their being printed because they put his sister in a false position, though admittedly of her own contrivance.[24] He warned Mabel

Loomis Todd that "Emily definitely posed in those letters." One of his friends, E. Winchester Donald, rector of Boston's Trinity Church, reacted to the *Letters* published in 1894 by commenting to Mrs. Todd that Dickinson had always played a role for at least one spectator—herself, that "she did attitudinize for her own pleasure."[25]

Such posing expressed a bountiful imagination even while it provided an antidote for the painful shyness that increasingly caused Dickinson to shrink from outside observation and assume an eccentric role within her small community. She confided once to visitors whom she had refused to see in person, the parents of Mrs. Todd, that "In all the circumference of Expression, those guileless words of Adam and Eve never were surpassed, 'I was afraid and hid Myself'" (L 946). She hid herself from Higginson also but offered suggestive glimpses, mainly through figurative language.

As Richard Sewall has observed, "Poets like Emily Dickinson may 'lie' in their hyperbole and exaggerated rhetoric. They may strike poses and don masks and speak through personae. But in their basic structures, where they begin, where they end, and how they got there, they do not lie. Certainly it was Emily Dickinson's constant aim, her life action, to make her 'truth' clear."[26] That basic structure of Dickinson's "life action" is the subject of this book. The July 1862 letter to Higginson serves as a paradigm of this larger metaphor that invested her poetry and even the details of her quiet life with astonishing significance and with an overriding unity. The design of her life was a process of movement from her smallness, a haunting sense of primal inadequacy, to circumference or the point of ultimate boundary between the finite and the infinite, the known and the mysterious, the human and the divine. It was an unorthodox religious quest, and she chose as her escort an unchurchly minister who shared her impulse to make language a vehicle as well as a record of spiritual growth. Because the quest was so central to her artistic identity, she could use this wren letter to ask (in a gracious way, demand) that he put aside "much business" to attend to her business, which she designated by her numinous word "Circumference."

When Dickinson introduced this term to Higginson, she wrote, "Perhaps you smile at me. I could not stop for that—My Business is Circumference." Presumably he *was* smiling; it would be hard not to do so in the aftermath of the wren, the chestnut bur, the driblets of sherry, and the kangaroo that framed this pronouncement. The humor and the appeals to sympathy may have protected him at first from understanding the enormity of the quest and the arrogance of the ambition. Having exaggerated her helplessness in this ironic self-study, she now proposed to fling herself against the cosmos, to soar beyond the eagle in the body of a wren. She recognized the challenge. Had Higginson been "perfectly powerful" as she suggested, it would scarcely be enough to serve as mentor to such a scholar as she signed herself. Little did he suspect that his wren would identify herself with the valiant bird she elsewhere celebrated, who "staked her Feathers—Gained an Arc—/ Debated—Rose again—" only to sail serenely "among Circumference," her proper element (P 798).

My thesis in this book concurs with several recent studies of Dickinson's work in assuming an overarching metaphor of quest, spanning the cavernous gap between limitation and boundlessness and in recognizing this quest as an implicitly religious action.[27] Because Dickinson seems to have used poetry as the major thrust of a broader personal quest, I mean to emphasize the poems without detaching them from her letters and life. My interest is not in biographical facts, as such, but in the metaphorical shape of what Sewall calls life action. In reading Sewall's *Life of Emily Dickinson*, Leyda's *Years and Hours of Emily Dickinson*, the three-volume Johnson and Ward edition of her *Letters*, and the reminiscences of persons who knew her, I find an inviolable unity of art and life. This is especially true of those aspects of her life that Emily Dickinson chose and shaped—even though the choices that formed her life into an artistic structure were chiefly negative ones. The givens of her life (ancestry, formal education, the limitations of her friends, the "War" between the two Dickinson houses, the Civil War, and her family's public role) interest me much less than the pattern of symbolic behavior the poet spun out through her actions and renunciations.

This poet restricted her life to a narrow compass within which she could substantially control it, and she assigned other people roles in her private drama. Higginson, for example, may have imagined himself a detached and superior observer in that famous first visit with her correspondent, and presumably she seemed at his mercy with her pattering step, childlike manner, and breathless voice. But from the time she placed two day lilies into his hand on entry, she put him in a comically disadvantageous position behind the flowering spikes. From all the aphorisms he recorded in that conversation, one gathers which person dominated the encounter. No wonder Higginson exclaimed, "I never was with any one who drained my nerve power so much. Without touching her, she drew from me. I am glad not to live near her" (L 342a-b). It is this artistic and symbolic behavior that I mean to examine here, noting its correspondence to the metaphorical quest enacted in the poetry across the entire span of her creative life.

As a romantic quester, Dickinson confronted awesome and various challenges along her route to infinity and never for more than ecstatic instants reached the goal. The essence of the metaphor, then, becomes the process of growth itself or, as she put it, the "Processes of Size" by which the mortal pilgrim, confined within time and space and limited in imagination by sensory capacity, expands toward the eternity, infinity, and empowerment that lie so teasingly just beyond circumference:

> Time feels so vast that were it not
> For an Eternity—
> I fear me this Circumference
> Engross my Finity—
>
> To His exclusion, who prepare
> By Processes of Size
> For the Stupendous Vision
> Of His Diameters—
> (P 802)

God, in this poem, directs these processes—being more "perfectly powerful" than Mr. Higginson, but God remains on the other side of circumference and is presumably unreachable until the expansive processes of growth impel the quester beyond mortal boundaries.

Several poems Dickinson grouped with this one in fascicle 38 echo her theme of growth and attentiveness to size—including "She staked her Feathers—Gained an Arc—" (P 798), in which the aspiring bird goes out "among Circumference" though not beyond it. Notable among these is "Who Giants know, with lesser Men" (P 796), which contrasts the gnat's imperturbable self-confidence with the timidity of those acquainted with giants. It is the gnat, however insignificant, who soars while giants lumber along the ground. As Dickinson noted in the poem directly following "Time feels so vast . . ." (P 802), "Poverty of Monarchy / Is an interior thing—" (P 803).

One of the paradoxes of Dickinson's approach to this theme of growth, this sensitivity to processes of size, is that she looked upon smallness as a kind of blessing, an ironic asset in the quest for circumference. The wren, the gnat, the slightest figure in the house, are all positioned for ascent. They have a flexibility denied to their more substantial comrades. And they experience the impelling force of greater need for empowerment. Where other writers interested in the theme of growth, therefore, might deny limitations, as Emerson and Whitman did, or inveigh against them with Margaret Fuller, Emily Dickinson tended to exaggerate those limitations, appropriate them for herself, identify with them. It is as if she drew tightly in upon herself until the very energy of her contraction exploded her, like a poetic atomic bomb, toward the margins of the universe. The July 1862 letter to Higginson serves as a model for a process she tended to follow in her life and in her poetry: an exaggerated sense of limitation that somehow impelled her toward the infinite. As the letter indicates, she knew that such growth required sacrifice, personal and artistic discipline, and occasional help from external powers. If she were to grow, she would do so by pressing in upon limitations and then devising those strategies for expansion that poetry encouraged. One of these strategies was role playing, imaginative identification with apparently stronger or more exciting lives in order to experience an amazing range of human fates vicariously. Another was that intense fixation on boundaries of every sort and watchfulness for cracks in the walls by which she tested circumference and speculated on what might lie beyond it. A third strategy involved play with language as a source of vision. Later sections of this book investigate these strategies of growth, which characterized Dickinson's artistic quest.

Forecasting the direction of critical interest in Emily Dickinson, Richard Sewall hoped that attentiveness to the design of her poetry would put to rest all misplaced pity so that "far from the little figure of frustrations and renunciations and regrets, we will come to see her as a poet of great strength, courage, and singleness of purpose."[28] What I would like to add, by way of qualification, is that we need not make an either-or choice between the sad little figure of Amherst myth and the valiant poet, between the pathetic and the sublime. As I interpret the private myth reflected in Dickinson's poems, letters, and life, pathos was for her a necessary precondition for sublimity, and limitation an essential corollary to growth. The "Stupendous Vision" followed upon an elaborate process that took as its starting point blindness and one of the most drastic senses of personal insignificance in world literature. Could Higginson believe her—without a photograph? Could she believe herself—without everything? The facts of her life are less pertinent here than the drive of Emily Dickinson's imagination toward nothingness because, in her experience, the wren positioned herself more strategically for circumference than the giant.

2

"The Wildest Word"

The Habit of Renunciation

"DONT YOU know you are happiest while I withhold and not confer—dont you know that 'No' is the wildest word we consign to Language?" (L 562). Dickinson posed these questions in an 1878 letter to Judge Otis Phillips Lord at an early stage in her autumnal romance with the widowed Salem jurist, her father's friend and ally in Massachusetts Whig politics. They exemplify a pattern of thinking that had come to characterize her over the years: a habit of renunciation, an excitement in denial, a preference for restrictions. Notions about Emily Dickinson's pitifully deprived life originated in her biography itself; the deprivation was there (mostly of her own choosing) though the pity is misplaced if it presumes her preference for normal domestic routine over an artistically chiseled existence. In a comment to Higginson that accompanied a memoir of George Eliot, the poet clearly recognized the chasm between life as written and life as lived: "Biography first convinces us of the fleeing of the Biographied—" (L 972). But it is inevitable that her readers take the same sort of personal interest in her that she took in Eliot and the Brownings and natural that we should look to biography for insight into the metaphorical design that governed her writing. The well-circulated myths about Emily Dickinson that originated in Amherst and the relatively prosaic facts of her existence as detailed by scholarly biographers display a pattern of constriction within her life (a tendency to intensify every limiting factor she confronted) and a habit of exploiting those constrictions for artistic growth.

The romantic myths started early and provide the most imaginative examples of this pattern. Best of all, in terms of comprehensiveness, is the story published by Genevieve Taggard in *The Life and Mind of Emily Dickinson* (1930); the tale reached Taggard through Mary Lee Hall, who got it from Mrs. Aurelia Hinsdale Davis, who may have picked it up from Lavinia Dickinson in her old age.[1] Quite probably, this is a version of the legend Mrs. Todd began to hear when she and her husband reached Amherst in 1881. The story is that Emily Dickinson, recently returned from Mount Holyoke, fell in love with George Gould, who was Austin's fraternity brother and Amherst College classmate. Gould was a prominent member of the class of 1850: an oratorical star and editor of a new literary journal, the *Indicator*. Their courtship, however, proved ill-fated, running afoul of Edward Dickinson's judgment of the suitor, who, as a ministerial candidate, might never be able to support Edward's daughter adequately. He forbade Gould further access to their home and required that Emily give him up. On the evening of commencement exercises, following the annual reception given by Mr. Dickinson as treasurer of the college, Emily is said to have met Gould on her father's lawn, dressed all in white, to pledge filial obedience and renounce her lover. She is said to have told him "that love was too vital a flower to be crushed so cruelly" and to have signified her stifled will by withdrawing into spinsterish seclusion and wearing nothing but white. This makes a good story in that it offers a complete (if hackneyed) narrative with a touching climax, character conflict, and foreshadowing. But there seems to be no substance to the report.

Certainly Dickinson's 1850 prose valentine to Gould, which he published in the February *Indicator*, shows little sign of serious commitment—especially in view of the verse valentine she dispatched a few weeks later to her father's law partner, Elbridge Bowdoin (P 1). The missive to Gould, a tour de force of sprightly wit that begins "Magnum bonum, 'harum scarum,' zounds et zounds, et war alarum, man reformam, life perfectum, mundum changum, all things flarum?" hardly reads like one of Dickinson's eventual love poems.[2]

Nor was Gould denied access to Edward Dickinson's home, which he visited occasionally after his graduation before undertaking his ministerial career. Nor did Emily retreat to her father's house for over a decade, nor bleach her dresses. Still, it is a good story in the sentimental vein and most likely quite typical of what her neighbors whispered.

The family's retaliation for such talk about patriarchal cruelty came in another story, promulgated by Mrs. Bianchi to explain how her aunt had reached "the end of peace" during her 1855 visit to her father, then a congressman in Washington.[3] While visiting friends in Philadelphia, Dickinson "met the fate she had instinctively shunned" and which she supposedly confided during her lifetime only to "Sister Sue." Bianchi describes the crisis with the most tactful suggestiveness: "Certainly in that first witchery of an undreamed Southern springtime Emily was overtaken—doomed once and forever by her own heart. It was instantaneous, overwhelming, impossible. There is no doubt that two predestined souls were kept apart only by her high sense of duty, and the necessity for preserving love untarnished by the inevitable destruction of another woman's life." The Yankee heroine fled to her home for refuge, only to be pursued there within days by the impassioned lover. Bianchi narrates how Lavinia raced to Susan Gilbert, crying "Sue, come! That man is here!—Father and Mother are away, and I am afraid Emily will go away with him!" But, of course, Emily held fast to duty and another woman's right. Her disappointed lover left his profession and home, withdrawing "to a remote city, a continent's width remote," and died prematurely, "the spell unbroken," while "Emily went on alone in the old house under the pines." This, too, makes a touching sentimental tale, paralleling the Hall story in its theme of love, renunciation, and enduring sorrow. The main distinction, however, is that Dickinson herself emerges as the focal will of this narrative and the source of renunciation. She seems a stronger though sadder figure, in charge of her own tragic destiny.

Again, it proves difficult to confirm this tale by recourse to poems, since Dickinson's 1855 visit to Washington and Philadelphia preceded the love poems by at least three years, generally six or seven. Yet the lyrics themselves seem to preserve moments in a narrative that follows the same curve of passion, renunciation, and elegiac remembrance evident in both the Hall and Bianchi stories. Poems of 1861 and 1862, in particular, offer a compelling if shadowy impression of disappointed love. If one reads them autobiographically (often a misleading approach to Dickinson's work but always tempting), one can discover an intense commitment to one man as the central figure of the poet's universe, a competitor with God for her devotion. She avows that she has elected one "Atom" from among "all the Souls that stand create" as an object of adoration (P 664). Yet the reader finds no promise of beholding this fascinating atom until eternity brings its revelation. Speculation naturally ensues. The lover remains a faceless figure in the poems, with no distinguishing characteristics to help biographers choose from among the names (Wadsworth, Bowles, Lord, or Mr. X) they want to offer as "That portion of the Vision / The Word applied to fill" (P 1126).

This romance, whether real or imaginary, had its passionate moments and climaxed in an encounter such as Hall and Bianchi fantasized. The most famous poem commemorating this communion of loving souls moves from a sense of elated possession through acceptance of parting to a hope of celestial marriage.

> There came a Day at Summer's full,
> Entirely for me—
> I thought that such were for the Saints,
> Where Resurrections—be—
>
> The Sun, as common, went abroad,
> The flowers, accustomed, blew,
> As if no soul the solstice passed
> That maketh all things new—
>
> The time was scarce profaned, by speech—
> The symbol of a word
> Was needless, as at Sacrament,
> The Wardrobe—of our Lord—
>
> Each was to each The Sealed Church,
> Permitted to commune this—time—
> Lest we too awkward show
> At Supper of the Lamb.
>
> The Hours slid fast—as Hours will,
> Clutched tight, by greedy hands—
> So faces on two Decks, look back,
> Bound to opposing lands—
>
> And so when all the time had leaked,

> Without external sound
> Each bound the Other's Crucifix—
> We gave no other Bond—
>
> Sufficient troth, that we shall rise—
> Deposed—at length, the Grave—
> To that new Marriage,
> Justified—through Calvaries of Love—
> (P 322)

The darkening tone of this initially jubilant poem reflects the general pattern of romance within Dickinson's work. The pledge of love and mutual commitment occurs in an hour, creating an anniversary to be recalled through life and a point from which subsequent change is measured.

Such an anniversary sets the occasion for "One Year ago—jots what?" (P 296) in which the speaker recalls the "Glory" of the previous year, whose "Anniversary shall be—/ Sometimes—not often—in Eternity." She says she tasted the "Wine" of this private communion "careless—then—," ignorant that it "Came once a World" and wondering whether the lover—larger and older—had recognized the uniqueness of that day. In the intervening year, however, she feels herself to have grown. He had spoken then of her "Acorn's Breast" and claimed greater capacity for fondness in his "Shaggier Vest" of mature masculinity. But her suffering has developed the acorn and aged the young sweetheart so that she claims to be "As old as thee" now through experience of pain. This passionate love that cannot be expressed except in a memorable hour turns out to be one of those limitations fostering growth—one of the circumstances that allow the wren to soar, if the lover chooses, to be "Great" or "Small" at his behest (P 738). Clearly the speaker of this and similar poems responds appreciatively to the enhanced self-image bestowed by her lover, by the sense of infinite possibility he conveys to her, even though the greatness arises from pain.

The aftermath of romantic ecstasy is misery and a desperate attempt to recover self-possession without the lover's continued presence to sustain her.

> I got so I could hear his name—
> Without—Tremendous gain—

That Stop-sensation—on my Soul—
And Thunder—in the Room—

I got so I could walk across
That Angle in the floor,
Where he turned so, and I turned—how—
And all our Sinew tore—

I got so I could stir the Box—
In which his letters grew
Without that forcing, in my breath—
As Staples—driven through—

Could dimly recollect a Grace—
I think, they call it "God"—
Renowned to ease Extremity—
When Formula, had failed—

And shape my Hands—
Petition's way,
Tho' ignorant of a word
That Ordination—utters—

My Business, with the Cloud,
If any Power behind it, be,
Not subject to Despair—
It care, in some remoter way,
For so minute affair
As Misery—
Itself, too great, for interrupting—more—
(P 293)

The tight parallel organization with which this agonized poem begins breaks down in syntactic confusion. The speaker can neither voice a prayer when unsure whether any person or power will hear it nor completely articulate even to herself her own final sentence, in which the subordinate "if" clause dangles helplessly to express her stammering and skeptical wishfulness.

Occasionally Dickinson refers to the nature of this union as a kind of implicit marriage, recognized as binding by the lovers but not to be revealed until heaven (should there turn out to be marriage or giving in marriage above for earth's hopeless lovers). With its humble, reverent expression of gratitude for the hidden gift of the lover's name, "The World—stands—solemner—to me—" (P 493) articulates the complexity of her response. The "Dream" of the lovers' mutual choice proves here "Too beautiful—for Shape to prove—," and Dickinson's longest poem mourns the frustration of one who can live neither with nor without her lover: who can neither die with him nor rise with him for fear "Your Face / Would put out Jesus'—" yet who yearns to be with him for eternity, whether in heaven or hell (P 640). She concludes by describing their apparently fixed earthly situation.

> So We must meet apart—
> You there—I—here—
> With just the Door ajar
> That Oceans are—and Prayer—
> And that White Sustenance—
> Despair—

In "The face I carry with me—last—" (P 336), the speaker looks for heavenly coronation "As one that bore her Master's name—/ Sufficient Royalty!" On earth, however, this love story ends in renunciation. She writes elsewhere that she must be content with honor foregone "With one long 'Nay'—/ Bliss' early shape / Deforming—Dwindling—Gulphing up—/ Time's possibility" (P 349). This "one long 'Nay'" of inevitable renunciation may be "the wildest word we consign to Language," but it hurts her nonetheless. "Renunciation," she found through this implicit story underlying her romantic poems, "is a piercing Virtue—" (P 745).

If Emily Dickinson's love lyrics assume any narrative shape, this is its design: mutually avowed passionate love climaxed in one or perhaps two brief, intense, profoundly troubled meetings; a commitment amounting to secret marriage; a lifetime's renunciation; a resultant yearning for recognition of this love (perhaps even its consummation) in an afterlife beyond the circumference of this. This narrative clearly reflects a reader's ordering of the lyrics, chiefly those Johnson dates to 1861 and 1862, and presumes that the poems express their author directly rather than one of the imagined persons discernible in many other poems. Quite probably no such specific sequence occurred in Dickinson's own life; yet it is fair to say that this pattern of avowal, renunciation, and expectancy existed within her imagination and shaped her perception of such courtship as required "No" to be "the wildest word."

Her readers and biographers have displayed remarkable ingenuity in their efforts to name the lover whom the poet identified only as "Master" and "Sir," making the strongest arguments for the Reverend Charles Wadsworth,[4] Samuel Bowles,[5] and Otis Lord.[6] The biographical narratives her readers have constructed to account for her relationships with Wadsworth and Bowles (both of them married) follow the design articulated above, with passion leading to inevitable renunciation. The eventual courtship with her father's widowed friend (better documented than the others though far too late in life to account for the love poems discussed above) traced a somewhat different curve toward a similar result.

As Mary Lee Hall cautioned Mrs. Todd, however, "The poems cannot be interpreted solely by Emily's love affairs, the *shadows* drove her into herself. She found much elation in the men who came into her horizon, and they seemed to be the matches that ignited her mental oil tanks."[7] The oil was already there, ready to explode. Neither Lavinia nor Austin believed there had been any one great love of their sister's life. As Lavinia put it, Emily "was always watching for the rewarding person to come,"[8] and the reward she derived from her friendships was largely an artistic one. She relished friendships while they stayed strong (sometimes defeating them herself by the sheer force of her possessive passion, as seems to have happened with school friends) but discovered early the fragility of love. In January of 1855, she wrote first to Susan Gilbert (then engaged to Austin) and later to her cousin, John L. Graves, essentially the same statement of habitual renunciation: "If it is finished, tell me, and I will raise the lid to my box of Phantoms, and lay one more love in" (L 177; 186). Certainly, she held onto the box of outgrown love and relied on its contents, hidden in her drawer, as a precious emotional investment (P 887). Recognizing limitation even to the force of love, Dickinson intensified that limitation by restricting her affection to fewer and fewer people and renouncing all but epistolary involvement even with most of the chosen. Still, the phantoms in her box and the lost loves in her drawer took on new life in poems that bespeak a depth of passion she probably never experienced directly and derive a startlingly universal insight into human emotions from drastically limited resources.

This tendency to devote herself to unreachable men whom she idealized and to court romantic disaster, if only unconsciously, for the sake of renunciation and its fruits naturally militated against the romantic and even marital attachments Dickinson could have formed in a college town with its annual influx of bachelors and in a family headed by lawyers who introduced her to young men of their profession. Although most of Dickinson's friends married, she cultivated instead a habit of exclusion in emotionally vulnerable relationships. From textual evidence, it would be hard to prove that she ever wished marriage, as distinct from love and the sense of being chosen. Her few fantasies of this sort appear in "Forever at His side to walk—" (P 246) and "Although I put away his life—" (P 366), the latter spoken from the perspective of a woman who has already renounced the lover but fantasizes the comforts she might have brought him: gardening for him, nursing him, clearing "the pebble from his path," playing for him on her lute, doing his errands, eagerly performing his "weariest Commandment," and carrying sticks to light the fire in his cottage. Inspected closely, this love-in-a-cottage picture seems to scream slavery! Why would Emily Dickinson have chosen marriage, anyway? For loving companionship of the sort she could depend upon at home? For the economic support and community status that her father provided, even posthumously? For motherhood, one of the few female roles she never played in her poetic fantasies?[9] For romantic love, which seems never adequately to have been offered her—her standards being high and Robert Browning unique? For social engagements, when she increasingly craved solitude? Her brother's unhappy marriage and the troubles she sensed in other families (including Mary Bowles's jealous dependence on her husband) demonstrated the fragility of marital peace even among persons she idealized. To imagine that Emily Dickinson would ever have chosen the public responsibilities and private obligations of a minister's, lawyer's, or editor's wife in small-town New England is to capitulate entirely to the conventions of sentimental domestic fiction.

Directly or indirectly, Dickinson chose spinsterhood, which her neighbors regarded as a slightly unnatural condition unless the unclaimed jewel attracted sympathy with a sad story of disappointed love, like the Gould and Wadsworth legends the town fabricated on her behalf. The spinster's role in society was one of charitable service, an option that irritated the poet, prompting this youthful explosion to Jane Humphrey: "work makes one strong, and cheerful—and as for society what neighborhood so full as my own? The halt—the lame—and the blind—the old—the infirm—the bed-ridden—and superannuated—the ugly, and disagreeable—the perfectly hateful to me—all *these* to see—and be seen by—an opportunity rare for cultivating meekness—and patience—and submission—and for turning my back to this very sinful, and wicked world. Somehow or other I incline to other things—and Satan covers them up with flowers, and I reach out to pick them" (L 30). In her maturity, the flowers Satan scattered were few; she seemed to renounce temptation with other things. And her letters show her as a kindly, comforting neighbor—so long as she neither had to see the objects of her charity nor, still worse, be seen by them. Her solution, characteristically, was to choose the most constricted option available to a woman of her class—turning her back more fully to the sinful and wicked world than the teachers she mimicked in this letter ever imagined and settling for the inviolate privacy of an aristocratic New England recluse, responsible only to herself and God.

Not even to her family did she ever fully communicate her vocation as a poet or the achievement represented by the drawerful of manuscript that Lavinia discovered on her death. Yet hiding her light beneath the proverbial bushel barrel, Dickinson made sure the smoldering flame would eventually ignite its container. She used her apparently unproductive seclusion for astonishing artistic ends and drew lifelong artistic benefits from the isolation that afforded her privacy for artistic craftsmanship while shielding her hypersensitive emotional nature from sensory overload.

As the Gould and Wadsworth legends demonstrate, Dickinson's neighbors instinctively attributed the young woman's withdrawal to her supposedly broken heart rather than to her judgment "of the hollowness & awfulness of the *world*," which Austin noticed forming as early as 1851 when his sisters visited him in Boston.[10] By 1863, Samuel Bowles was referring to his friend as "the Queen Recluse," inquiring with amusement in a letter to Austin about the musical entertainments his sister enjoyed in heaven and expressing sympathy for her achievement in overcoming the world.[11] She replied with a squib, "I could'nt let Austin's note go—without a word—,"[12] and a poem reminding him that experiences are discovered by their opposites: fire from ice, red from white, paralysis from vitality, and (presumably) society from solitude and the universe from her chamber (P 689).

Dickinson probably liked Bowles's queen image—one of a constellation of royal terms she tended to employ in interchanges with him. Often she combined it with shrinking, humble metaphors that also reflected aspects of her expanding and contracting self-image. One poem, "A Mien to move a Queen" (P 283), alternates her characteristic images of limitation (references to the wren, a tear, tiny hands, and a soft voice) with those of empowerment (queen, duke, realm, diadem). The strength comes from chosen patterns of behavior, such as adopting a haughty mien or speaking in a commanding voice. The smallness prevents men from fearing this aristocratic mite, and distance, while cutting short opportunities for affection, precludes contempt. "And so Men Compromise—/ And just—revere—." They honor what they might otherwise disdain because distance makes the regal performance more convincing.

The regal aspect of Dickinson's withdrawal came from her habit of exclusion. "The Soul," she said in one of her most famous poems, "selects her own Society—/ Then—shuts the Door—" (P 303). Lavinia tried to defend her sister from charges of snobbishness by arguing that "she was not withdrawn or exclusive really. She was always watching for the rewarding person to come, but she was a very busy person herself. She had to think—she was the only one of us who had that to do."[13] Evidently, Dickinson found most persons unrewarding and easily expelled them from her self-selected society. Her comments to Higginson on the persons without thoughts whom she noticed parading by her window demonstrate that she would look for no help in her thinking from most of her neighbors (L 342a).

There can be no question that her isolation intensified neurotic tendencies in Emily Dickinson and allowed for the flowering of eccentric behavior that contributed nothing to her happiness or anyone else's. Yet the Reverend E. Winchester Donald, Austin's friend and a frequent summer visitor to Amherst, was one of the first to recognize the benefit she may have drawn as an artist from the penalties she paid as a woman when he asked Mrs. Todd on receipt of the 1890 *Poems*, "One other thing: was the inexorable cost of all this illumination her seclusion renunciation & ache?

Would John Baptist be forerunner without the years in the desert, the locusts and all that? Is the nun's self-effacement, her veil and her virginity, the explanation of her unquestioned power? We cannot wear lace and pearls—go often to town & the play, be experts in salads beers and truffles, know what to do with our hands—and expect either to see heaven or to have anyone believe we have seen it."[14] So much for Bowles's taunting questions to his "Queen Recluse": "Is it really true that they ring 'Old Hundred' & 'Aleluia' perpetually, in heaven—ask her; and are dandelions, asphodels, & Maiden's [*vows?*] the standard flowers of the ethereal?"[15] Yet even in her fantasies of celestial bliss, Dickinson retained her habit of limitation in writing: "I went to Heaven / 'Twas a small Town—" where she could be "Almost—/ contented—" (P 374).

Emily Dickinson's reclusive situation resulted from her own choice. Even if her father had wanted to keep his daughters home (an assertion apparently based on Lavinia's late-life tales but not otherwise substantiated), he never confined Emily to the house and, in fact, counteracted her tendencies toward seclusion by sending her away to school, inviting her to Washington, contriving opportunities for her to go to Boston, and finally requiring her to participate in his commencement receptions. It was her own choice not to "cross my Father's ground to any House or town" (L 330). And there were odd behavior choices she made within his house that carried to an eccentric extreme her habit of limitation. It must be borne in mind that these quirks developed only gradually and that the legendary spinster of the 1880s is a later and somewhat distorted development of the poet of the 1860s. When she wrote most of her poems in that brilliantly productive Civil War period, Dickinson was still making periodic medical jaunts to Cambridge, still visiting at her brother's house, and still receiving visitors even though the very pressure of composing and recording so much poetry (apparently about a poem a day in 1862) must itself have restricted her social involvement. Nor is there any evidence that withdrawal or any other eccentricity proved a recoil from disappointed love. It seems more probable that the romantic renunciations emerged from the same deep-seated need to explore and exploit limitations as did the domestic behavior patterns. So did the poetry.

Perhaps the strangest of her eccentricities was her secretive artistic life. Granted, family members, friends, and neighbors all knew that Emily Dickinson wrote, but apparently none of them suspected either the quantity or quality of her poems; and her habit of attaching bits of verse to letters or gifts actually helped to promote the notion of her versifying as a decorative feminine accomplishment. So, perhaps, did her refusal to let Helen Hunt Jackson (another Amherst native, by then a nationally famous author) publish any of her poems despite the other's decisive moral argument that "You are a great poet—and it is a wrong to the day you live in, that you will not sing aloud. When you are what men call dead, you will be sorry you were so stingy" (L 444a).

Other behavior patterns seem decidedly eccentric. Innate shyness, for example, which always made her ill at ease with crowds or strangers, developed with time into almost total seclusion except for her dizzyingly extensive correspondence. Clearly, Dickinson took an intense interest in people she cared about, and her heart ranged widely—happily opening itself to friends of friends and survivors of acquaintances. Yet she refused almost all visitors, including some she had directly invited to call upon her. To soften the blow of her refusals, she developed charming habits like that of sending to a friend kept waiting in the garden a servant with a silver tray bearing a flower or glass of wine and a cryptic note or verse.[16] She gave herself the benefit of visitation without exposing herself to discovery by having a family friend like Mrs. Todd play the piano and sing for her while she enjoyed the performance from a distant part of the house, signifying her pleasure by faint applause and little gifts.[17] The exclusion was selective, however. She was more open to persons she regarded as unthreatening: children, servants, an Indian squaw selling baskets. Her brother's children and their little friends enjoyed her secretive play with them—the mysteries she contrived and surprises she planned.[18] Even these involvements could be strangely distant, as when she lowered baskets of gingerbread from her bedroom window to her nephew's friends below. Dickinson even planned the details of her own funeral in a way that excluded the town, leaving orders that her body (enclosed in a white casket) be carried by family servants out the backdoor, across the garden, through the barn, and over the fields to the grave—wholly evading the usual public procession along Amherst streets.[19]

The white casket, like the white dress in which Dickinson chose to be buried, calls to mind that other idiosyncrasy her neighbors attributed to romantic disaster: her habit of dressing in white. Just when this pattern developed is hard to tell. Sewall traces the tendency to the mid–1860s but doubts that the habit became fixed before her father's death in 1874.[20] When Higginson met the poet in 1870, he found her costumed in a white dress and blue shawl (L 342a). Interpretations of her action vary almost as dramatically as the symbolism spun from Moby Dick's pallor. White is the bride's color, hence Dickinson's choice to signify the mystic marriage with her lover to be revealed in heaven. And it is the color of the shroud and of ghosts, representative of death. It can be found in gothic novels as well as Revelation. This "colorless all-color" of Ishmael's meditation leads Dickinson's critics, like Melville's, to the heart of ambiguity.[21]

If we turn to "Mine—by the Right of the White Election!" (P 528) to resolve this puzzle, we can recognize the tone of triumphant entitlement ringing through one of Dickinson's most joyful lyrics, but we are at a loss to identify the occasion that evoked it, whether mystical marriage, spiritual election, or discovery of herself as a great poet. Some of the poems she grouped with it in fascicle 20 suggest her association of whiteness with frigidity or death. Her juxtaposition of "I think the Hemlock likes to stand" (P 525) with "Dare you see a Soul *at the White Heat?*" (P 365) offers a sharp contrast. The hemlock—black, massive, nobly drooping tree that she identifies with northern climates and races (such as her own)—finds the complement of its dark power in the snow because, she says, it satisfies "An instinct for the Hoar, the Bald." In some moods, anyway, Dickinson too shared this craving that satisfied her awe with its austerity; and she may have complemented the blackness of her tragic moods with Lapland's chill pallor. Yet "Dare you see a Soul *at the White Heat?*" immediately counters the iciness of snow with the contradictory colorless light of "unannointed Blaze"—far more searing than the red flame of ordinary passion. The soul, which has "vanquished Flame's conditions," threatens destruction to the body ("Forge") that still tries to contain it. "Some say the world will end in fire," wrote Robert Frost, "some say in ice"; Dickinson could signify either one by her ambiguous whiteness, which could include the desire and hatred of his quatrain as well as her "White Sustenance—/ Despair—" (P 640).[22]

Another poem, "A solemn thing—it was—I said—" (P 271),

links the white costume more directly to the themes of smallness and renunciation that characterized her personal mythology of growth. Here Dickinson directly associates the choice of white costume with a God-given vocation that involved dropping her life into the mystic (or "purple") well of disappearance from the world until new revelation in eternity. She meditates the "bliss" that might accompany such apparently total self-abnegation and proudly recognizes the growth, the disproval of smallness, the push toward circumference, that would be the paradoxical reward of elected self-denial. That Mrs. Todd entitled the poem "Wedded" in the 1896 *Poems* demonstrates the possibility of reading it as a marriage poem and using it as evidence to support the bridal theory of Dickinson's white costume. The imagery makes more sense, however, in terms of the poet's distinctive metaphor of growth through pressing upon limits—especially when she concludes "And I sneered—softly—'small'!"

In the poem immediately following, the speaker makes no reference to clothes but may already be vested in a shroud. She has died but retained the appearance of breathing so that touch rather than vision confirms the numb coolness of the corpse (P 272). Associations between whiteness and both death and emotional extremes emerge more strongly in this sequence than the bridal motif and sustain the impression that the poet's distinctive costume represented the loss of one kind of life and the assumption of a new one. The "mute Pomp" and "pleading Pageantry—" (P 582) of this private symbol suggest that the glorious entitlement of her "White Election" came at considerable cost, involving renunciation and vicarious experience of that incommunicable "White Exploit" (P 922) of dying.

This lexicon-loving writer occasionally characterized profound change in other people's lives with the word *translation*, which offers further insight into the kind of change her costume signified. In 1852 she reported to Austin on *Dream Life* by Ik Marvel, pleasant reading but inferior to the sketches that had earlier enchanted her, with the comment, "I cant help wishing all the time, that he had been *translated* like Enoch of old, after his Bachelors Reverie, and the 'chariot of fire, and the horses thereof,' were all that was seen of him, after that exquisite writing" (L 75). A little over a year later, she reflected to Emily Fowler on her impressions of this friend's marriage to Gordon Lester Ford: "when it came, and hidden by your veil you stood before us all and made those promises, and when we kissed you, all, and went back to our homes, it seemed to me translation, not any earthly thing, and if a little after you'd ridden on the wind, it would not have surprised me" (L 146). Both Mrs. Ford and Mr. Marvel, of course, remained disappointingly earthbound—neither of them was "translated" or carried across the circumference between this life and a better by the power of either love or artistic creation. But a decade later Dickinson may herself have felt afloat on the wind by virtue of her own poetry (more soaring art than Marvel's essays) and may have considered herself to have transcended her original identity and attained a kind of heaven by God's lifting her in imagination over the barrier of death without her directly experiencing it.[23] In a poem of 1862, at any rate, she used this distinctive word to claim a supernaturally exhilarating aesthetic experience such as the saints might enjoy: "Better—than Music! For I—who heard it—/ I was used—to the Birds—before—/ This—was different—'Twas Translation—/ Of all tunes I knew—and more—" (P 503). This sound carried the poet retrospectively to legends of "a better—/ Melody—" in Eden and projected her, humming in "faint Rehearsal," toward the celestial singers "around the Throne—." Only religion provided imagery adequate to the experience.

Translation was a biblical concept, as Dickinson's epistolary examples demonstrate with their easy mingling of scriptural texts that fuse the stories of Enoch and Elijah, each drawn miraculously to heaven without experiencing death. The word *translation* itself would have been familiar to the poet from Paul's Epistle to the Hebrews, where she read: "By faith Enoch was translated that he should not see death; and was not found, because God had translated him: for before his translation he had this testimony, that he pleased God" (Hebrews 11:5). In this passage Paul worked out the theology of translation, identifying this experience as one initiated by God and accomplished through the power of faith as a reward to the prophet for pleasing God. But the colorful aspects of Dickinson's version come not from Hebrews or even from the comparatively flat narrative of Enoch's translation in Genesis (5:24).[24] They came from the story in 2 Kings of Elijah's comparable translation: "And it came to pass, as they [Elijah and Elisha] still went on, and talked, that, behold, there appeared a chariot of fire, and horses of fire, and parted them both asunder; and Elijah went up by a whirlwind into heaven" (2 Kings 2:11). This was a story that fascinated Dickinson and that she celebrated in several poems, most notably "Elijah's Wagon knew no thill" (P 1254). God alone could portray the details of this miraculous journey, but its destination was clearly heaven—reached by dramatic ascension rather than through the routine tunneling of the grave.

Without dying, Elijah rose—to be seen again at Christ's Transfiguration, when he and Moses appeared to the Apostles as walking and talking with Jesus, who was himself dazzling like a translated saint: "his face did shine as the sun, and his raiment was white as the light" (Matthew 17:2–3). The Transfiguration itself anticipated the most wonderful example of translation, Christ's rising from the dead and ascension into heaven; and the behavior of the risen Christ exemplified the qualities of the person so favored by God. Like Enoch, Elijah, and Jesus, the translated saint would disappear from the ordinary world, leaving worshipers in wonder. He or she would resemble the risen Christ—visible to close friends, fleshless but powerful, already living in the glory that Christian iconography traditionally represents by shining garments. This, I believe, is the state Emily Dickinson signified by her white clothing. As her epistolary examples of Marvel and Mrs. Ford indicate, it was a state she thought possible for persons of her time, though a rare reward for pleasing God—an exceptional heightening of election. It was a particularly appropriate glory for her, whose poetry probed the awesome circumference of death and tried to penetrate its barrier by imaginative strategies if not by faith. Like Jesus, she dressed in white; like Elijah, she saw herself as the center of a superb adventure; like Enoch, she was not found by those who looked for her.

Yet again, renunciation for Dickinson proved the secret of power, and withdrawal from the world—virtual denial of her continuing identity—became the symbol that she had penetrated (at least through imagination) the circumference of ordinary human limitation. If her neighbors chose to think of her as a Miss Havisham rather than an Enoch, she left them to their speculation—discovering that her austere wardrobe and reticent habits evoked pity, which she never wanted, while securing a privacy that liberated her for the artistic work to which she felt called.[25] Her eccentric habits even provided an untroublesome sort of notoriety, itself a small-scale assault on personal annihilation. As a child, Emily was quoted as saying, "I have a horror of death; the dead are so soon forgotten. But when I die, they'll have to remember me."[26] By dying to Amherst for at least the last decade of her life, she cultivated a reputation for exclusion that left people eager for any glimpse into her private mystery and provided herself with an initial audience for the poems that justified her translation.

Reinforcing these rather stylized renunciations that Emily Dickinson herself directly chose to build her metaphorical life action, there were other, less picturesque, limitations that also circumscribed her opportunities. Some derived from her small-town Connecticut Valley environment, some from the Victorian era, some from her femaleness. Yet the consistent pattern that emerges from comparing Dickinson's personal experience with those culturally imposed limitations is one of supplemental personal choice. Her background almost never exemplified these limiting factors to an extreme degree; indeed, she had noticeable advantages over many women of her culture even though sexual and social constraints were always present. What happened, however, is that Dickinson herself tightened the screws on each restriction. By her own choices, she immured herself within the magic prison that paradoxically liberated her art.

The first limitation, one that Dickinson shared with most American contemporaries, was that of small-town provincialism. Amherst's population was small and, except for Irish and black workers, heterogeneously Yankee. Its citizens all knew each other and each other's business. Although Jay Leyda has chronicled how Amherst acquainted even its most retiring daughter with the dread realities of "the violent deaths, suicides, lynch mobs, abortions, dishonesties that are the normal portion of village life," even *The Years and Hours of Emily Dickinson* shows the town to have been a quiet place on the whole and respectable in the Victorian manner.[27] Always more concerned with beauty than morality, Dickinson seems to have taken less interest than many others in her neighbors' sins but must still have felt the lack of cultural resources in a town that, like most others across the United States, offered its citizens few opportunities to appreciate artistic excellence. Yet Amherst was not a backwater. It had a college, literary societies, and a lecture series. The combination of cultural appetite with artistic privation forced this community toward language for expression and enjoyment. Lecturers could be hired and books sent for. For Dickinson in Amherst, as for Hawthorne in Salem and Thoreau in Concord, literature was the only art form familiar enough to be understood, imitated, and eventually created.

That Dickinson turned inward toward books and eventually substituted written correspondence for almost every other kind of communication was, then, only her intensification of a general cultural pattern. If books opened to her a world more exciting than Amherst, she was prepared to renounce the town. Luckily, when she withdrew from lectures, concerts, and tableaux, she had adequate literary resources to make up the loss: a steady supply of reading matter, including popular novels and magazines; correspondents who appreciated her allusive habits; and the good taste to winnow ordinary writing from great literature. She told Higginson that "After long disuse of her eyes she read Shakespeare & thought why is any other book needed" (L 342b). When her preceptor invited her to join his Boston salon of artistic ladies, she chose to stay in Amherst.

Throughout the Connecticut Valley, in South Hadley even more insistently than in Amherst, Dickinson encountered yet another reminder of her finitude in the omnipresent atmosphere of Calvinist piety. But even in religion she was spared the extremes of evangelical fire-and-brimstone terror on the one hand and broad-minded intellectual vapidity on the other. At home, in church, and at school, young Emily confronted the awesome contrast between human weakness and divine omnipotence; she knew her radical insufficiency—her presumably depraved natural condition. She felt great pressure from those who loved her to accept Jesus as her savior, although she knew she must wait for conversion and cipher at its signs. Dickinson's friends Abiah Root and Abby Wood found themselves converted in adolescence, as did Lavinia, who—with Edward Dickinson—formally joined the church during the revival of 1850. Austin joined just before his marriage, leaving Emily the sole outsider within the family. At least in adolescence, her letters showed a somewhat envious awareness of the peace these Christians claimed to enjoy (L 10; 39), but she never formally recognized herself as converted and referred to herself in later years as "but a Pagan—" (L 976).

When Edward Dickinson summoned his minister to examine his daughter spiritually, Mr. Jenkins declared her "sound," but the religion she substituted for her family's Congregationalism imposed radical limitations on normal religious practice.[28] Susan Dickinson's obituary for her independent sister-in-law established a parallel between her literary and spiritual selectivity. Just as "she sifted libraries to Shakespeare and Browning," she stripped devotion of all excess: "To her life was rich, and all aglow with God and immortality. With no creed, no formulated faith, hardly knowing the names of dogmas, she walked this life with the gentleness and reverence of old saints, with the firm step of martyrs who sing while they suffer."[29] Keeping her Sabbath by staying home in her garden, professing disregard for doctrine, refusing to judge behavior in moralistic terms, she responded with her "wildest word" to most of what her neighbors valued as religion.

Nonetheless, it is futile to treat Dickinson as other than a religious poet. She divorced herself from the visible signs of religion in her community to distill its essence, focusing intense spiritual passion on the intimate encounter between herself and God—an interchange in which she hoped to smash circumference and snatch the prize of immortality. The encounter was not always a loving one—often painful and terrible—but it was the central action of her life, to which she applied all the resources she had learned for exploiting her finitude. "God was penurious with me," she asserted, "which makes me shrewd with Him" (L 207). The strategies she developed were poetic ones to bridge the chasm between the finite and the infinite, the mortal and the immortal—a process that is simultaneously the essence of religion and the definition of her quest.

A third overwhelming cultural limitation on Dickinson's growth was the sexual stereotyping of the Victorian era that accorded a decorative and subordinate role to her presumably fragile sex and especially to its genteel representatives within her social class. Physiology joined with social convention to confine women within the home.[30] Discrimination took its intellectual toll as well as an emotional one. Partly as a consequence of adolescent illness and even more because of restrictive notions about feminine needs, most girls of Emily Dickinson's generation were educated less rigorously than their brothers. Even people who thought girls might have adequate intelligence for formal education worried about the physical strain of schooling and questioned the usefulness of a masculine curriculum for young ladies. (Higginson himself, champion of Radcliffe College, failed to complete his daughter's education.) Few girls attended school beyond the primary grades, undertook higher education, or studied the classical languages and mathematics that would equip them for the learned professions they were unwelcome to enter in any event. Domestic skills, the social graces, religious principles, and superficial artistic accomplishments prepared a lady to ornament her husband's home. "How invaluable to be ignorant," Dickinson responded, "for by that means one has all in reserve and it is such an Economical Ecstasy."[31]

Yet she was hardly ignorant, being provided with an education far superior to the norm. At Amherst Academy and Mount Holyoke she studied science, philosophy, Euclid, and Latin—much the same curriculum Austin faced—and endured similar rigors of public examinations. Under the governance of Mary Lyon, the female seminary set high academic standards in order to prepare its graduates for lives of competence and service—preferably in the missions. But Dickinson spent only one year at South Hadley, and even that period (like her previous Academy experiences) was interrupted by parentally mandated intervals at home for rest and domestic training. The contrast between Austin's Amherst College and Harvard Law privileges with his role as paternal delegate in snatching his tearful sister home from Mount Holyoke is a painful one, illustrative of that greater respect for his only son's mind that Mr. Dickinson increasingly displayed (L 23).[32] Still, the elder daughter pursued her education independently. First with Benjamin Newton as tutor, then with Higginson as preceptor, she concentrated her extraordinary intellectual and volitional force on her poetic growth.

Both at school and at home, a young woman of Dickinson's class could exercise her mind in comparative safety by reading imaginative literature, and Dickinson's letters reveal the eagerness with which she seized upon fiction and poetry to counteract educational deprivation. She seems to have read almost anything recommended by her like-minded friends: Shakespeare, of course, and Emerson, Thoreau, Hawthorne, the Brontës, and the Brownings—but also Longfellow, Ik Marvel, and a host of popular writers.[33] It was the current sentimentalism that dominated her early letters, probably because society approved such reading for young ladies—if indulged in moderately so as not to round the shoulders or erode good sense. The popular fiction reinforced values to which the society conditioned its girls.[34] It accorded kind attention to women, both as characters and authors, even as it narrowed their aspirations.

By fixing attention on domestic life and locating heroism in meek acceptance of suffering, sentimental literature exalted women in their capacities as dutiful daughters, sacrificing mothers, and model Christians. It presented life as sadly beautiful without examining the economic or political bases for the sorrow—preferring to justify all crises as moral tests. As I shall demonstrate in a subsequent chapter on Dickinson's role playing, some of the stock situations of this literature are discoverable even in her poetry, as are the compassionate, benevolent feelings that sentimental literature evokes. Yet lyric poetry distills images and feelings at the expense of narrative, and the only way to impose outright sentimental fictions on her work is to spin a narrative that binds the lyrics somewhat arbitrarily, as I have done in reorganizing her love poems to suggest a story—a distinctly sentimental tale like most of those that readers generate in the hope of restoring plot, character, and situation to these imaginatively compelling lyrics. Dickinson exploited even the conventions of sentimental literature to create her poems and call forth her audience.

Sentimental writing, which implicitly honored the restrictions of genteel Christian womanhood, promoted the reputations of writers as diverse as Harriet Beecher Stowe, Lydia Sigourney, Lucy Larcom, and Frances Osgood.[35] Women demonstrated in Dickinson's day that they could turn a profit out of their ostensibly timid calls upon public attention, and they established their own magazines to publish the edifying fiction for which the public appetite appeared insatiable. But Dickinson—always an elitist—refused to superimpose ordinary, culturally acceptable meanings on the amazing sense of her poetry, and she never availed herself of the feminine literary marketplace to which both male and female literati willingly consigned all the sweet singers with whom they would have classified her.

Denial of publication to this astonishingly gifted poet is the limitation within her life that rankles most sharply today. Dickinson, who described her verse as "my letter to the World" (P 441), must have wished an audience. The few poems that reached print anonymously and in corrupted texts reveal an initial willingness to publish, although her reaction against editorial blunders shows an aversion to compromise not possible for more professional-minded poets (L 316). Perhaps she hoped for a while that Bowles, Holland, and Higginson would help her to publish in well-read, respectable journals. When they failed her, she characteristically refrained from offering her verses to the plethora of literary magazines that might have printed some. It was hardly impossible for women poets to publish in nineteenth-century America (though difficult to make a living), but those who succeeded often did so, like their male counterparts, by pandering to conventional tastes and commercial pressures. Too proud to join Hawthorne's "d——d mob of scribbling women," Dickinson stitched her own little "volumes" (Lavinia's word) and tucked them in drawers to await their resurrection.

In "Publication—is the Auction / Of the Mind of Man—" (P 709), Dickinson expressed her contempt for commercial composition. To read this poem only as an ironic attempt at disguising authorial pain is to miss the genteel Yankee pride that spits out the key word, "Auction." Recall Thoreau's sneers at auctions in *Walden*, the associations he draws between bodily death and material accumulation; and remember Frost's New England reversal of consumerist values: "The having anything to sell is what / Is the disgrace in man or state or nation." Edward Taylor had suspected that his Connecticut Valley neighbors would reject salvation itself if allowed to haggle over its cost.[36] Dickinson, a lady comfortably provided for, had nothing to sell in the garage sale of imagination. She substituted the concept of stewardship for that of property in the statement "Thought belong to Him who gave it—/ Then—to Him Who bear / It's Corporeal illustration—" and refused to reduce her proud spirit "To Disgrace of Price—." If her talent belonged to God, he would somehow get the value of it and she perhaps the fame. References to whiteness here link her translated self to her Creator, by whom her "Snow," artistically fashioned, would be validly appraised.

It is amusing that Emily Dickinson's very reserve about publication, coupled with her incremental release of sample verses in multitudinous messages of friendship or consolation, eventually resulted in a local reputation for literary performance. The *Springfield Daily Republican* (which itself had printed several of her poems anonymously), the *Record*, and the *Union* all fostered conjecture that an Amherst lady named Dickinson was the author of Helen

Hunt Jackson's unacknowledged Saxe Holm stories. As early as 1878, then, Dickinson could have read ascriptions of her author-ship in the newspaper with reviewers finding the same character-istics in another woman's prose that their successors would find in her poetry come 1890.[37] Dickinson made no money from her writing and probably never wanted to. She seldom saw her name in print (never with a poem) and most likely gave thanks for the privacy. She did, nevertheless, find a few appreciative readers. Her correspondence with Susan Gilbert Dickinson on "Safe in their Alabaster Chambers—" (P 216) reveals a more sensitive editor next door than in the offices of the *Springfield Daily Republican* or *Atlantic Monthly* (L 238). The eventual editing history of Dickin-son's poems, especially the contributions of Mabel Loomis Todd, demonstrates that the poet had access to responsive, critical read-ers—most of them women. The enthusiasm for literature of all sorts among middle-class American ladies resulted in the emer-gence of a reading audience capable of artistic discrimination be-yond the level the commercial marketplace assumed, capable of welcoming Emily Dickinson's poems as soon as they appeared.[38] Not only Dickinson, then, but others as well managed to tran-scend the stultifying limits of Victorian feminine culture, although her admirers quickly capitulated to that culture by fashioning a sentimental myth around "Emily" herself.

Genteel nineteenth-century American society limited women in their power to make significant choices, encouraging men to think of active decisions and women of passive ones. A woman should wait for a man to choose her in marriage, should learn to subor-dinate her will to her father's or husband's. She should look for signs of God's approval. Yet to emphasize such constraints on fe-male choices is to exaggerate the problem. Women did have im-portant areas of freedom, particularly with regard to religion.[39] Within the home, also, a woman could exercise a great many choices about furniture, clothing, and medical treatment. Al-though some women used their privileges to acquire fashionable property, defining themselves by possessions, the Yankee women of Dickinson's time were more likely to use freedom in making negative choices. They demonstrated thrift and prudence by showing what they could do without; taste defined itself by dis-criminations. Mocking this tendency in her youth, Dickinson amused herself in several letters with references to a neighbor's potentially fatal fastidiousness: "'Mrs. Skeeter' is very feeble, 'cant bear Allopathic treatment, cant have Homeopathic'—dont want Hydropathic—Oh what a pickle she is in —should'nt think she would deign to *live*—it is so decidedly vulgar!" (L 82). Yet this woman, who would eventually require her own doctor to diagnose her from a distance as she paced back and forth in an adjoining room, lived to carry to extremes this habit of selecting, discriminating, excluding.[40]

In subject matter, Dickinson's poems stress both sides of a woman's situation. She could express delight at being chosen—the passive beneficiary of a more powerful being's option, but she also communicated the painful power of making exclusions. At her most ebullient, describing herself as self-sufficient, self-defined, she claimed the right even to positive choice: characteristically a grand one. "With Will to choose, or to reject," she chose, "just a Crown—" (P 508). Yet even this coronation came by a process of negative choices, rejection of the name and roles her family had assigned her.

> I'm ceded—I've stopped being Their's—
> The Name They dropped upon my face
> With water, in the country church
> Is finished using, now,
> And They can put it with my Dolls,
> My childhood, and the string of spools,
> I've finished threading—too—

She asserted her right to do without most of the satisfactions she had been taught she needed.

In her life, as in her poems, Dickinson exploited the opportunity to make negative choices, recognizing that her tendency to deny opportunities marked her off as eccentric and exclusive while exposing her to pain. "Odd, that I, who say 'no' so much, cannot bear it from others," she wrote to Louise Norcross, "Odd, that I, who run from so many, cannot brook that one turn from me" (L 245). Wanting to be chosen by important others, she habitually abstained from positive choices herself: "With one long 'Nay'—/ Bliss' early shape / Deforming—Dwindling—/ Gulphing up—/ Time's possibility" (P 349). Emily Dickinson shaped her life, by a startlingly consistent pattern of negative choices, in a way that intensified every limitation upon her, exaggerated every barrier.

And she did so consciously, not in order to punish herself or court discomfort, but to promote reflexive inward growth. If "No" was "the wildest word we consign to Language," it could somehow liberate other words—including those she would select to formulate the literature of limitation and rejection that initiated her metaphysical quest for circumference.

3

"An Enlarged Ability for Missing"

Artistic Exploitation of Limits

IT WAS through the process of writing letters that Dickinson first explored her literary resources and identified the themes, tone, self-image, and artistic strategies that would characterize her poetry. With only five poems from the years before she started gathering finished copies into fascicles in 1858, we must look to her letters as her stylistic workshop to observe the way she honed her writing by a process of stripping away extraneous details to reveal the essential elements of her life metaphor—the pilgrimage from limitation to circumference.[1] The letters, fluent and stylistically experimental from the start, gradually refined her experience into distilled units of associative imagery anticipating both her poems and her later, cryptic correspondence.

Even Dickinson's earliest schoolgirl prose shows a pleasure in the act of writing itself that would never leave her—a delighted recognition of her ability to express (or hide) herself and manipulate others through her facility with language (L 5; 7). An initial impulse to take pride in the very length of her letters soon evolved into satisfaction with their frequency, their cleverness, their distinctiveness. One of their distinctive traits—the tendency to elaborate on sensations rather than facts—actually encouraged regular production, as young Emily Dickinson never waited for news to justify communication. She obviously prided herself on the flights of fancy and bursts of rhetoric she could generate from minimal materials and liked recognition for her cleverness. She complained to Austin once of his inadequate appreciation—evidently in response to a request from him for clearer writing, a problem she would face with later readers like Higginson, to whom she commented wryly, "All men say 'What' to me, but I thought it a fashion—" (L 271): "I strove to be exalted thinking I might reach *you* and while I pant and struggle and climb the nearest cloud, you walk out very leisurely in your slippers from Empyrean, and without the *slightest* notice request me to get down!" (L 45). Even here, of course, she plays on figurative language to make her point, evading the *"Plain english you know* such as Father likes" that her sister preferred.[2]

The letters of the early 1850s show several of Dickinson's stylistic qualities already in place. Puns and wordplay emerged in her first letter to her brother in Boston, perhaps a device to display her intellectual superiority to her prosaic, cliché-dependent mother: "Mother is warming her feet, which she assures me confidently are 'just as cold as ice.['] I tell her I fear there is danger of icification, or ossification—I dont know certainly which!" (L 42). She coined phrases and enjoyed repeating them, like the image of a box of phantoms mentioned earlier or the "consolation upside down" phrase she quoted to Abiah Root to express her philosophy in disappointments "that had I been gratified, it had been sadder still" (L 69). And she continued to compose humorous set pieces like her Amherst Academy compositions and her valentines. One of these, a letter from a pseudonymous "Judah" to Susan Gilbert, develops into an extravagant play of imagery that carries to a comic extreme her theme of limitation and attempts to draw orthodox religious "consolation upside down" out of pretended disaster:

Dear Friend.
I regret to inform you that at 3. oclock yesterday, my mind came to a stand, and has since then been stationary. Ere this intelligence reaches you, I shall probably be a snail. By this untoward providence a mental and moral being has been swept ruthlessly from her sphere. Yet we should not repine— "God moves in a mysterious way, his wonders to perform, he plants his foot upon the sea, and rides upon the storm," and if it be his will that I become a *bear* and bite my fellow men, it will be for the highest good of this fallen and perishing world. . . . (L 97)

The very closing, "Yours till death," anticipates her most fruitful theme and shows the characteristic drive of Dickinson's imagination, even in its most playful moods.

The main function of Emily Dickinson's early letters seems to have been to grasp attention in intensively personal encounters, something she did by ignoring the news—which would only demonstrate the changes since the last communication—and placing nostalgic emphasis on past associations, especially those she was in a better position to recall than her correspondents. Letters to Austin, for instance, refer frequently to "the empty nails, and the empty chairs in the kitchen," to the spot where his slippers used to rest, to "the rustic seat" where they shared confidences before and would again (L 109; 118). Devices such as apostrophe, exhortation, interpolated set pieces, systematic repetitions, and rhetorical questions deliberately heightened this affective control.

Often Dickinson awakened her readers with startling imagery that directly anticipated poems, such as her wish that "I was a grass, or a toddling daisy, whom all these problems of the dust might not terrify—" (L 182). Figurative language that would grow into one of the familiar symbols of her mature poetry appears as early as 1850 when she wrote, "The shore is safer, Abiah, but I love to buffet the sea—I can count the bitter wrecks here in these pleasant waters, and hear the murmuring winds, but oh, I love the danger!" (L 39). Here the sea represents spiritual turbulence, later the unknown in general and the elemental embodiment of death.

A stylistic trait of the letters that Dickinson carefully nurtured in preparation for her poetry was play on literary and scriptural allusions—yet another device for establishing a privileged relationship with the particular reader who would appreciate their personal resonance and also a means of enlarging trivial circumstances to adumbrate her haunting themes of fragility, loss, death, and immortality. Her play on the biblical warning against invading thieves and despoiling moths served such a purpose in a comic but morally reassuring 1851 meditation to the pious Abiah Root (L 50), just as contemporary literary references linked her to Susan Gilbert.

Yet more anticipatory of the poetry was the technique Dickinson developed in 1852, practicing often then and only irregularly for the next few years, of interpolating brief or extended fantasies into her letters. One was romantic, with her sister rather than herself as its beneficiary; she commented to Susan Gilbert that "Vinnie is sewing away like a *fictitious* seamstress, and I half expect some knight will arrive at the door, confess himself a *nothing* in presence of her loveliness, and present his heart and hand as the only vestige of him worthy to be refused" (L 73). Even in this fairy tale, rejection of love seems likely. Another time she figured herself in person as paddling down the Susquehanna in search of an absent friend (L 69). The rejecting maiden; the quester; what else? It can hardly surprise Dickinson's readers to find her experimenting with yet another role that would dominate her poetry: that of a corpse. She confided to Jane Humphrey how she had tried to anticipate her death: "The other day I tried to think how I should look with my eyes shut, and a little white gown on, and a snowdrop on my breast; and I fancied I heard the neighbors stealing in so softly to look down in my face—so fast asleep—so still—Oh Jennie, will you and I really become like this?" (L 86). Anticipation of one's own death is, of course, a traditional Christian meditative exercise that might have been familiar to Emily Dickinson and her correspondents, but this picture seems to have captured her imagination with exceptional force to become the seed of those great poems in which she would try to penetrate death's awesome circumference. In a more cheerful mood, she evoked a fantasy of heaven as an enchanted garden for the amusement of Dr. and Mrs. Holland (L 175). Whenever Dickinson gave her imagination free play, it gravitated instinctively to thoughts of death and immortality—the Flood subjects to which she was drawn through her intense early awareness of personal limitation and deprivation and of the evanescence of friendship that not even the most artful correspondence could overcome (L 319).

More essential than fact in these letters as in the poems is tone—the sense of a personal voice confiding and communicating emotion. And tone, in turn, depended on the inherent drive of her imagination from any given situation through feelings, toward the abiding themes of death and immortality. Little wonder that Lavinia, even while claiming news for her own letters to their brother, sometimes left the deaths to Emily. Not that the elder sister needed such grave subject matter to inspire her. At one point she claimed to disavow all further epistolary grandeur, preferring to dwell instead on "all the *little* things, and the things called *trifles*, and the crickets upon the hearth, you will be sure to hear" (L 114).

The impulse of her writing was, indeed, to make sure that others heard what she heard, felt what she felt, shared her sensitivity, which she knew to be especially acute.

Feelings were what Dickinson's letters communicated best—often to the exclusion of situation, just as her poems would do. The following confidence to Jane Humphrey, for instance, anticipates "Mine—by the Right of the White Election!" (P 528) in its triumphant tone and shares with it a similar detachment from explanatory circumstance: "I have dared to do strange things—bold things, and have asked no advice from any—I have heeded beautiful tempters, yet do not think I am wrong . . . Oh Jennie, it would relieve me to tell you all, to sit down at your feet, and look in your eyes, and confess what *you only* shall know, an experience bitter, and sweet, but the sweet did so beguile me—and life has had an aim, and the world has been too precious for your poor—and striving sister! The winter was all one dream, and the spring has not yet waked me, I would *always* sleep, and dream, and it never should turn to morning, so long as night is so blessed" (L 35).

At times the tone even conflicted with the apparent message, creating a tension that encourages us to divide a letter into separate parts for analysis, as if unity were undiscoverable. The famous "Brother Pegasus" letter of 27 March 1853, for example, begins with mock solemn reflections on her brother's spiritual state—apparently triggered by a devotional poem he had composed and sent home with his last letter (L 110). From this she moves to allusion, citing a favorite hymn reference to a world "where congregations ne'er break up," a particularly appealing image for her at this point of family division. Then, thinking of family, she adverts to sibling rivalry and belittles her brother's literary achievement even in imitating her father's exaggerated delight in his son's talent: "And Austin is a Poet, Austin writes a psalm. Out of the way, Pegasus, Olympus enough 'to him,' and just say to those 'nine muses' that we have done with them! / Raised a living muse ourselves, worth the whole nine of them. . . ." Well, yes, but what "living muse" did Squire Dickinson's family raise? Surely not "Brother Pegasus," and the scolding she gives him for ignoring her literary pretensions lays bare her own sense of violation as an artist. The letter continues in jolly spirits, however, not to betray strong jealousy, if indeed so modest a poetic effort by her brother aroused such a feeling. She seems much more gleeful over his secret engagement to Susan, itself the sort of event that might inspire amateur versifying and even religious rhymes in a suitor trying to persuade his intended of his piety. She concluded with recognition that he would probably laugh at her letter and with assurances of mutual affection, "I guess we are very good friends tho', and I guess we both love Sue just as well as we can." Then comes the postscript, more famous than the letter: "Love from us all. Monday noon. Oh Austin, Newton is dead. The first of my own friends. Pace." If this exclamation reveals profound grief at Benjamin Newton's death, as Johnson and other biographers believe, it comes at an odd point in a singularly improbable letter whose feisty, mirthful tone wholly violates this single item of news.[3] Tension between form and content exists here to an extreme degree, with Dickinson allowing her family jester role to displace her usual somber reflectiveness on deprivation and death.

Before she learned to balance her own divided feelings, she found out how to control those of her readers; and Dickinson's early letters show remarkable skill in arrogating her correspondents' sentiments to herself—making them reveal their feelings and respond to hers. At times she recognized the voracity of her appetite for love and reassurance to the point of commenting to Susan on their never satisfied hearts: "Have you ever thought of it Susie, and yet I know you have, how much these hearts claim; why I dont believe in the whole, wide world, are such hard little creditors—such real little *misers*, as you and I carry with us, in our bosoms every day. I cant help thinking sometimes, when I hear about the ungenerous, Heart, keep very still—or someone will find you out!" (L 85). Someone could easily find Dickinson out by reading her letters, which wield the authority of hypersensitive feelings to manipulate her readers' responses, deliberately evoking sensations of guilt and meanness in persons so unlucky as not to satisfy her insatiable demands for appreciation. Limitless appetites resulted in constant deprivations. A prime case in point is her 13 July 1851 letter to Austin on the subject of a visit she and Lavinia had hoped to pay him only to have it canceled or postponed in deference to his other plans (L 47). It seems that Austin had received a sharp reprimand from Edward Dickinson for disappointing his sisters. When Emily wrote, ostensibly to calm her brother's dismay, she immediately plunged him into guilt by revealing the omitted center of previous communication about the trip and playing upon his anxiety: "You must'nt *care* Dear Austin, Vinnie and I cant come—it is'nt any matter, I hope you a'nt troubled about it. We *were* disappointed at first, because not very well, and thinking while at Boston we would see Aunt Lavinia's physician; we did'nt want to tell *you why* we were bent on coming, thinking now you were *gone* you might feel anxious about us—." She reports on alternative plans for medical treatment and takes all blame for the upset on herself and her ailing sister. It is a martyr-like exercise in drawing emotional ammunition from her supposed disabilities. The only clear communication from the letter is that everyone involved—the sisters, the father, and especially the brother—felt miserable.

Although Emily Dickinson's early letters report a variety of activities, record a range of friendships, and express many tones from rapture through despondency, their more stylized aspects—those developed in literary terms—present a distinctively vulnerable self-image. The writer shows herself as a woman of intensely affectionate feelings, one who depends to an exceptional degree on the never quite adequate emotional responsiveness of those she loves. She looks back nostalgically to childhood or to other points of unbroken family and of easy intimacy with friends. She looks forward to heavenly reunion, yet is alarmed by the intervening prospect of death that threatens prolonged isolation. Time emerges as her enemy because it brings little but loss, despite occasional blissful reunions with inevitable deprivation in their wake. Dickinson presents herself as one maintaining the norm of home for others who may no longer need or want it. A typical self-portrait shows her running to the door or window, searching for some fleeting sign of recognition from a departing loved one (L 62); and she presents this image in a way that makes her seem a terrified figure in a gothic romance—stranded not in a mysterious mansion but in the Pleasant Street home, which has been made alien through loss. She describes herself as straining to see the white blur of Austin's face, as putting on her bonnet and desperately opening the gate in agonized suspense over whether to pursue him, grateful at last to have returned to the house "without having done any harm" (L 42). When Susan Gilbert leaves for a few weeks' visit in New Hampshire, her Amherst friend details a touching and nerve-racking farewell: "I ran to the door, dear Susie—I ran out in the rain, with nothing but my slippers on, I called 'Susie, Susie,' but you did'nt look at me; then I ran to the dining room window and rapped with all my might upon the pane, but you rode right on and never heeded me" (L 102). Sometimes she fantasizes herself as a wandering waif in search of friend or brother (L 114; 161). A sense of desperation reveals itself in these pictures she draws of herself as well as a powerful sentimental imagination. The figure we see in the most stylized sections of Dickinson's letters strongly resembles the fragile, timid, and victimized speaker of the early poems.

After her brother and Susan returned from their various prolonged absences to settle in Amherst, Dickinson's letters as a whole became even more stylized—more clearly anticipatory of the poems she would soon write if she had not begun experimenting seriously already. An 1856 missive to her cousin, John Graves, exemplifies the control of tone that would characterize the poems, their rhetorical habits, and their characteristic associations of ideas (L 184). Neither reporting news nor showing much interest in Graves's job or romantic prospects, the letter serves mainly to reinforce past affection while showing the familiar play of its author's mind. Dickinson begins by establishing a situation: "It is Sunday—now—John—and all have gone to church—the wagons have done passing, and I have come out in the new grass to listen to the anthems." It is a tranquil scene, then, suitable for nostalgic reflections, and she uses explicit rhetorical devices to draw Graves into her world: "You remember the crumbling wall that divides us from Mr Sweetser—and the crumbling elms and evergreens— and *other* crumbling things—that spring, and fade, and cast their bloom within a simple twelvemonth—well—*they* are *here*, and skies on me fairer far than Italy, in blue eye look down—up— see!—away—a league from here, on the way to Heaven!" The incremental repetition of "crumbling" sets the tone for this spring pastoral, which quickly pivots toward the poet's customary musing on transition toward death. "*Wings* half gone to dust, that fluttered so, last year—a mouldering plume, an empty house, in which a bird resided"—these and other details of nature's crumbling, all reported in staccato bursts of conventional imagery accentuated with frequent pauses and heavy italicization—remind her that "We, too, are flying—fading, John—and the song 'here lies,' soon upon lips that love us now—will have hummed and ended." From this melancholy reflection, typical of the drift of her thinking from natural transitions to death, Dickinson launches upon the theme of immortality that she so easily associates with death in this Sabbath reverie: "To live, and die, and mount again in triumphant body, and *next* time, try the upper air—is no schoolboy's theme!" Nor is this letter a schoolgirl's exercise, though still an apprentice piece; it bears the marks of a polished writer who would soon be distilling such associations of imagery and allusion into her poems. The references to closeness in an earlier April and the affectionate reference to her cousin's happy prospects lead toward a finely worked alliterative conclusion. From such a letter, it is a short step to the early nature poems with their somewhat intellectualized meditations on transience, death, and rebirth.

In an 1854 letter to Susan Gilbert, Dickinson explicitly anticipated the topic and tone of her early poetry, recognizing that her art would necessarily build on limitation, loneliness, longing. "I would paint a portrait," she said, "which would bring the tears, had I canvass for it, and the scene should be—*solitude*, and the figures—solitude—and the lights and shades, each a solitude. I could fill a chamber with landscapes so lone, men should pause and weep there; then haste grateful home, for a loved one left" (L 176). Chiseling away the details of ordinary life from her letters, she concentrated instead on establishing intense rapport with a reader, manipulating that reader's feelings and drawing her or him to share in the sensations of loneliness and loss that Dickinson increasingly recognized as her primary resource for poetic distillation into a literature of solitude.

The portrait that Emily Dickinson outlined to Susan—with its subject, its characters, and its stylistic choices all representing solitude—appeared eventually in "I tried to think a lonelier Thing" by which she sought "An Omen in the Bone / Of Death's tremendous nearness—" (P 532). This is a revealing poem, demonstrating how intensively Dickinson meditated on the isolation she regarded both as her troubling distinction from the rest of humanity and as an artistic resource. She recognized the tie linking solitude with death and found in her capacity for imagining ultimate loneliness a means of testing extinction itself. She pushed her portrait of loneliness to its limit, where it generated a fantasy of a mirror image of herself, equally alien, equally imprisoned in isolating otherness, equally forgotten by an indifferent God, but somehow capable of connecting with the speaker in mutual recognition identified as pity rather than love.

Fascicle 25 in which Dickinson placed this poem includes several related works, including "The Soul unto itself" (P 683), which recognizes the awesome possibility of the soul's becoming "the most agonizing Spy" against itself in a condition that would make solitude a condition of perpetual terror. Presumably there should be no such solitude in a theistic universe, especially in a Christian one that posited a fatherly God; yet this fascicle also includes "Of Course—I prayed—" (P 376) in which God's deafness to the speaker's plea leads to the conclusion "'Twere better Charity / To leave me in the Atom's Tomb—/ Merry, and Nought, and gay, and numb—/ Than this smart Misery." Merriment and gaiety, then, subsist with numbness and nothingness to prove incompatible with the sensations that were her access to consciousness. She found herself imprisoned within her own soul, reaching in desperate empathy toward any other being so outcast—even an imagined being.

It is a paradoxical situation in the history of this most paradoxical poet that her own inadequacy should have been the starting point of her most brilliant poems. She felt herself small, inadequate to challenges, vulnerable to trivial and cosmic threats; and she found herself essentially alone in an alien cosmos. She explored this devastating situation in poems that examined her helplessness from a startling variety of perspectives.

The most obvious of the ways in which Dickinson expressed her sense of smallness and impotence—and the hardest for those of us to admire who like to see this poet as the capable woman she so obviously was—was the child role she habitually adopted, confronting the world through the wide eyes and scared voice of a timid, lonely little girl.[4] It was a mask that apparently struck the poet as a safe refuge from responsibility and as representing a status that allowed free articulation of fears. The child image began early in her poems, recognizable in the 1859 "'Arcturus' is his other name—" (P 70) and soon after in "What is—'Paradise'—" (P 215), in both of which she turned to heaven as a potential refuge for a lonely child oddly displaced on earth. There would be no point in enumerating all Dickinson's childish self-references; no reader can miss their frequency or fail to note the sentimental self-pity with which the child image confronts limiting factors and authority. A few, however, deserve particular attention as revelations of the poet's self-concept.

One of the most distinctive of these poems is "We dont cry— Tim and I," (P 196) from fascicle 9, grouped there with "What is— 'Paradise'—." Here the speaker anticipates the doubling of herself in "I tried to think a lonelier Thing" (P 532) by creating an imaginary companion—the classic comfort of the imaginative child. The little-boy companion, however, proves at least as timid, apprehensive, and vulnerable as the speaker. He is equally incapable of living up to their "brave" and "grand" ideals and even less ready to encounter the dread adventure of death. It is interesting that other poems in this grouping introduce additional companions on whom Dickinson relied for reassurance: Carlo, her dog, serves as her intermediary in "What shall I do—it whimpers so—" (P 186); "Dollie" (her pet name for Susan) provides essential security in "You love me—you are sure—" (P 156); and Christ functions as a kindly schoolmaster explaining away life's sorrows in "I shall know why—when Time is over—" (P 193).

Occasionally, Dickinson ascribed strength to her child self, especially when presented as a rebel. "They shut me up in Prose—" (P 613) recalls childhood punishment by isolation—the confinement of the naughty girl to a closet where she could reflect on her sins. But the imaginative child, so closeted, enjoyed the freedom of her dreaming, and Dickinson takes that situation as a paradigm for adult poetic freedom in an apparently confining world of prose like that she ascribed to her parent in her famous comparison of "Fathers real life and *mine*" (L 65). This poem also anticipates her characteristic comment to her young niece when similarly punished: "Matty, child, no one could ever punish a Dickinson by shutting her up alone."[5] The poet's tendency to exploit limitations could reveal itself in the child role when the childishness is remembered as outlived—much less so in poems representing it as a lifelong condition.

Some of the fears lived out in other poems draw upon the nightmares of childhood, such as the fear of abandonment in "You love me—you are sure—" (P 156) and the fear of rejection in "Good Morning—Midnight—" (P 425). Fear of homelessness appears as well, the horror of being exposed like little Gretel or the orphans of Victorian children's fiction to the wide world's cruelty. In "Up

Life's Hill with my little Bundle" (P 1010) she presents herself as the traditional pilgrim on life's journey, one who accepts homelessness in quest of a permanent home. But more often she struggled to reclaim that temporal home she so extravagantly eulogized in her letters and attempted to regain the security of a protected child, as in "I Years had been from Home" (P 609) where she presents a nightmare in which the returning child discovers, not the "Homelessness for Home—" of the pilgrim but the homelessness *at* home of the helpless alien. In this case, imagination may *cause* horrors rather than assuage them; at least the reader, like the speaker, never knows with certainty whether the dreaded stranger lurks behind the door.

Another poem Dickinson grouped with this one and "They shut me up in Prose—" (P 613) in fascicle 21 explores yet another nightmare of the abandoned child: the fear of starvation. "It would have starved a Gnat—" (P 612), like "I had been hungry, all the Years—" (P 579), presents the speaker as a hungry child who has developed strategies for survival in a world where neither man nor God offers her adequate sustenance. The poem builds upon Dickinson's characteristic themes of hunger, privation, confinement, and death. The gnat, her frequent representative of trifling and bothersome insect life, here emerges as the speaker's superior, if only through its power to destroy itself absolutely while the human sufferer must eschew suicide for fear of damnation. Yet she is being murdered by slow degrees through deprivation of food. In a slightly later poem, "God gave a Loaf to every Bird—" (P 791), she contrasts herself with other inferior beings in point of sustenance and finds that, though starving, she treasures the crumb and preserves it as a "poignant luxury—" representing to her all possibilities of wealth. Other satisfactions for this primal hunger suggest themselves elsewhere, as "Let Us play Yesterday—" (P 728) in which she remembers "Easing my famine / At my Lexicon" and settling for "Logarithm . . . for Drink—/ 'Twas a dry Wine—." As the mathematical beverage reveals, thirst joined hunger as evidence of inadequacy for life and, like hunger, opened appetites for lasting satisfaction, as in "We thirst at first—'tis Nature's Act—" (P 726), which traces temporal need to thirst for "that Great Water in the West—/ Termed Immortality—."[6]

One of the reasons for frustration experienced by Dickinson's speaker is the tendency to covet forbidden fruits, like the strawberries in "Over the fence—" (P 251), or to crave unreachable rewards.

> "Heaven"—is what I cannot reach!
> The Apple on the Tree—
> Provided it do hopeless—hang—
> That—"Heaven" is—to Me!
>
> The Color, on the Cruising Cloud—
> The interdicted Land—
> Behind the Hill—the House behind—
> There—Paradise—is found!
>
> Her teazing Purples—Afternoons—
> The credulous—decoy—
> Enamored—of the Conjuror—
> That spurned us—Yesterday!
> (P 239)

Like "The nearest Dream recedes—unrealized—" (P 319) and "Your Riches—taught me—Poverty." (P 299), which she stitched with it in fascicle 14, this poem acknowledges a romantic yearning for evanescent or alien values, all of which leave the speaker discontented with a condition previously found acceptable or even pleasant. As Dickinson would write to Higginson in 1870, "Enough is so vast a sweetness I suppose it never occurs—only pathetic counterfeits—Fabulous to me as the men of the Revelations who 'shall not hunger any more'" (L 352). And the poems exposed the inadequacy of those counterfeits to quiet inherent longings.

One of the strategies Dickinson devised for appeasing her rich reserve of appetite was a stoical determination to tailor her wants to possibilities, to cultivate minimal hopes. Given the grandeur of her aspirations, it comes as no surprise to find her strategy itself inadequate. The poems expressive of this purposeful self-discipline employ a self-pitying tone and often a child persona. "A little Bread—a crust—a crumb—" (P 159) argues the adequacy of minimal sustenance for anyone this side of immortality—for Napoleon as well as the speaker, since finitude is a condition of this life. Yet with even minimal wants often unsatisfied, it became necessary at times to live on dread (P 770) or to settle for the numb, despairing, purposeless motion that seems to counterfeit life itself in "From Blank to Blank—" (P 761).

Another strategy for coping was to accept suffering rather than flee from it; and here again Dickinson tended to fall back on the child persona whose very helplessness leaves no other recourse. The speaker of "I cried at Pity—not at Pain—" (P 588) tolerates poverty, starvation, insignificance, and early death—rebelling only at the sentimentalism of a spectator who voices idle pity. And the speaker of "'Tis true—They shut me in the Cold—" (P 538) prays heavenly forgiveness paralleling that which she has already granted to the comfortable and ignorantly innocent power figures who have injured her—perhaps even killed her through exposure, since "The Harm They did—was short." In "Precious to Me— She still shall be—" (P 727) the Dickinsonian sufferer continues to value a supposedly superior person who scarcely recalls her existence, "Though She forget the name I bear—/ The fashion of the Gown I wear—/ The very Color of My Hair."

She might well be forgotten, for she frequently presented herself in early poems as an inconspicuous being, the "little figure" who might slip "quiet from it's chair" into the grave "On such a night, or such a night," (P 146) or as "the slightest in the House—" who "took the smallest Room" and could die notelessly if not afraid to face the ultimate pilgrimage alone (P 486). Later, though, she would remember Christ's promise that "The Least / Is esteemed in Heaven the Chiefest—" (P 964), an orthodox reversal of worldly evaluations.

Given her sense of insignificance, inadequacy, and vulnerability, it seems natural that Dickinson should have identified herself with minimal creatures: the "Mouse / O'erpowered by the Cat!" (P 61), "The Drop, that wrestles in the Sea—" (P 284), and "a Phebe— nothing more—" (P 1009). Yet if one examines the poems in which she identifies with such beings, one finds a parallel with the wren images discussed in the first chapter. Dickinson tended to offer promise of growth and release when expressing her sympathy for beings below her in the natural order, as in her commentary on a silent, starving bird—a "Winged Beggar" who, satisfied by a crumb, soars aloft while singing praises to her "Benefactor" (perhaps the speaker but more probably God, source of all blessings including that of a sympathetic heart). The mouse, too, claims a heavenly mansion.

In exploring this theme of primal insufficiency, Dickinson was confronting the existential dilemma of any conscious being in an alien and seemingly hostile world. And her creative imagination, itself shaped by the privations we may discern in her sociopolitical environment or her psychobiography, anticipates in its sensitivity to human isolation when nature is essentially estranged from man, as man from God, the challenges of modern poetry and philosophy. Dickinson plumbed her own limitations because she sensed the centrality of such knowledge to consciousness and recognized confrontation with her own nothingness as a necessary prelude to her quest for circumference. It is perilous to smash through limits without testing them first—measuring barriers and learning to feel comfortable within them.

One of Emily Dickinson's most famous poems both explores and exploits the insignificance that was a central theme of her early work.

> I'm Nobody! Who are you?
> Are you—Nobody—too?
> Then there's a pair of us!
> Dont tell! they'd advertise —you know!
>
> How dreary—to be—Somebody!
> How public—like a Frog—
> To tell one's name—the livelong June—
> To an admiring Bog!
> (P 288)[7]

On the surface, this reads like a statement of extreme insignificance, of denial of identity. As such, it evokes pity for this extreme example of inadequacy. Yet the confiding voice of the poem, so reminiscent of Dickinson's intimate and often secretive early letters, and its conspiratorial tone alert us to something more—to a paradoxical sense of achievement in maintaining this inconspicuous pose and to a surprising fear of discovery. And there is an amusing contempt here for froglike dignitaries who mistake publicity for identity or importance. Even on the most literal level, then, the poem seems to savor the "Nobody" role, a tendency likely to make more sense to us when we recall Western mythology's most memorable exploiter of submerged identity: Ulysses proclaiming himself Noman to evade Polyphemus.[8] Yet Ulysses, by his boasting once apparently safe at sea, brought down upon himself the Cyclops' curse, the wrath of Poseidon, the loss of his men, and ten years of exile. Not Dickinson's "Nobody"! She maintains her paradoxical advantage. Limitation and personal insufficiency, then, may be seen as crucial to her poems but as points of departure and not as statements of a fixed and irremediable condition or, for that matter, as an actual statement of fact. To assert one's nothingness and feel at home with it might give one room to maneuver among superior beings less sensitive to their insignificance in the universe, unconscious of their need for growth.

Dickinson's poems on radical insufficiency were concentrated during the years from 1860 to 1863, beginning later and ending decidedly earlier than another group on a closely related theme, that of deprivation. Not only does the poet introduce herself, then, as a profoundly limited being at her existential core, but she presents her situation as one most characteristically modified by loss. There is a clearer development in these poems of deprivation than in those of limitation and loneliness, one that parallels the overall movement of her poetry from particular situations to more general or abstract statements.[9]

Nothing in Dickinson's universe protected her from loss. Even nature, to which she often turned for pleasure or reassurance, deprived her of its fleeting beauties. The many poems of natural process record the inevitability of change—tending often to renewal, admittedly, but regularly withdrawing satisfactions also. Nature's greatest beauties—sunrises and sunsets, flowers, butterflies, light patterns on the Pelham Hills—proved most evanescent. And nature served as an inevitable emblem of more crucial human losses. An early poem like "It did not surprise me—" (p 39) draws a typically Dickinsonian analogy between the flight of a bird and the departure of a loved one, each forgetting the speaker and thereby intensifying her insignificance. Facing this poem on the fascicle page is "When I count the seeds" (p 40), with its natural emblem of discovery and rebirth. "To venerate the simple days" (p 57) in the same fascicle draws from evanescence a lesson of appreciation. These were themes to which Dickinson would return over and over, treating them in intricately interwoven ways in a great poem like "Further in Summer than the Birds" (P 1068).

Less tolerable than losses to natural processes were those to God, who when presented in anthropomorphic metaphors appears as a burglar in "I never lost as much but twice," (P 49), a contentious landlord in "I had some things that I called mine—" (P 116), a warden in "God permits industrious Angels—" (P 231), and a bouncer in "Why—do they shut Me out of Heaven?" (P 248). The greatest pain came with the withholding of divine love, the withdrawal of apparent favor. "If I'm lost—now—" (P 256) presents the misery of one welcomed within heaven's gates by affectionate angels only to be banished when the "Savior's face" turns away from her—leaving her a bewildered, despairing exile. Particularly when she adopted her childlike stance, such losses proved devastating in their revelation of a hostile universe governed by a God capable of love but choosing to reject.

Among Dickinson's earliest poems was "I had a guinea golden—" (P 23), thought by Mrs. Todd to be a reprimand for a correspondent's letter-writing delinquencies, which recites in balladlike formulaic patterns the speaker's loss of valuable objects: a guinea fallen in the sand (an improbably exotic loss in an American economy); a favorite robin who migrated southward; a star with a pet name; and a missing friend—increasingly personal and painful losses. The famous "I held a Jewel in my fingers—" (P 245) also offers a general symbol for deprivation—with "an Amethyst remembrance" compensating imperfectly for possession. Even a humorous late poem like "Alone and in a Circumstance" (P 1167) whimsically explores deprivation by a spider symbolizing childish fear or wasted time. Dickinson readily found emblems for loss, few so poignant as "It would never be Common—more—I said —" (P 430), her elegy for that self-assurance and entitlement which had offered her the strong identity she felt the need for in the poems of limitation. Here elatedness for apparent fulfillment after long privation gives way to devastating loss.

> When—suddenly—my Riches shrank—
> A Goblin—drank my Dew—
> My Palaces—dropped tenantless—
> Myself—was beggared—too—

All the strategies she had taught herself to use in the alleviation of suffering caused by her radical insufficiency break down, destroyed by the ultimate temptation of dissembling grace. The beggary and helplessness to which she is reduced hurt more than her earlier pain, precisely because she now has a standard (however modest) by which to measure joy: her "moment of Brocade" measured against a lifetime and perhaps more than that of "Sackcloth," her "drop—of India" compared with buckets of slop.

In this poem, as in many others like "Whether my bark went down at sea—" (p 52), "I lost a World—the other day!" (p 181), and "A great Hope fell" (p 1123), Dickinson confronted the loss of dreams—deprivation of those imagined compensations that serve fanciful people as substitutes for the status, jewels, and property discovered to be elusive. This is the topic of one of the first poems she sent to Higginson, a charmingly vivid emblem of fleeting hopes, in which a boy representing the human race pursues a June bee explicitly identified with man's "nearest Dream" that seems easily attainable yet always evades his snatching hand (p 319). The boy, frustrated at the escape of the playful bee he had thought so catchable, gapes like grown men and women "Staring—bewildered—at the mocking sky—" when they turn to God above for the "steadfast Honey" of permanent sweetness that nature hints at but cannot provide and that God may not supply—particularly if he is actually so engaged in his own business, so indifferent to trivial human sports, as the bee who represents his promise here. It was the homesickness Dickinson knew for sure, not the likelihood of fulfilling dreams.

Deprivation could be experienced directly through robbery or failure or indirectly by comparison with someone else's fulfillment—sometimes a more painful experience because of its tendency to erode those minor satisfactions by which Dickinson's speaker tries to secure her self-image. "Your Riches—taught me—Poverty." (p 299) tells how the speaker moves from esteeming herself a "Millionaire" to recognizing herself as a beggar by observing her friend's "Dominions—/ A Different Peru—" that altered her scale of values. Her only comfort at the end is that of having been awakened to the possibility of wealth—in this case a "Treasure" she could have gained but learned too late to want, a "Pearl—/ That slipped my simple fingers through—/ While just a Girl at School."

Another way of examining such comparisons would be to acknowledge the sensitivity of Dickinson's persona in recognizing herself as bereft. Deprivation is, after all, a universal human experience though one easily forgotten when one fingers gems or sits at dinner. Dickinson, however, presented herself as a lifelong quester searching for a treasure already experienced but lost long ago—at infancy perhaps or even at birth.

> A loss of something ever felt I—
> The first that I could recollect
> Bereft I was—of what I knew not
> Too young that any should suspect
>
> A mourner lurked among the children
> I notwithstanding stole about
> As one bemoaning a Dominion
> Itself the only Prince cast out—
>
> Elder, Today, a session wiser
> And fainter, too, as Wiseness is—
> I find myself still softly searching
> For my Delinquent Palaces—
>
> And a Suspicion, like a Finger
> Touches my Forehead now and then
> That I am looking oppositely
> For the site of the Kingdom of Heaven—
> (P 959)[10]

The child persona, from this perspective, may actually represent strength in that it associates the speaker more closely with that romantic dream of original union with the cosmos whose loss is felt as primal deprivation expressing itself in the inability to attain satisfaction through any earthly resource. Even in exile she remains royal, enjoying status accorded by the magnitude of a loss that other people either have not experienced or have expunged from memory.

Such forgetfulness would be unlikely for Emily Dickinson. Her poems on loss, like those on limitation, show the evolution of an habitual stance for coping with such assaults—behavior premised on the assumption of further deprivations. "Where I have lost, I softer tread—" (P 104) reveals such an elegiac habit, while "A

Cloud withdrew from the Sky" (P 895) proposes development of a "Hermetic Memory" to preserve fleeting values. "The Missing All, prevented Me" (P 985) presents the habit of loss as a defense even against such disasters as "a World's / Departure from a Hinge / Or Sun's extinction." The hunger and homelessness themes, now associated with loss, link "Deprived of other Banquet," (P 773) and "Bereaved of all, I went abroad—" (P 784), which Dickinson combined in fascicle 39 to present her persona as adopting a strategy for survival—even for a sort of victory when the starving speaker manages to draw enough nutrition out of herself to rescue a berry for charity. Yet such strategies based on habitual loss offer no protection against anything but exaggerated hopes, as she found in "I cautious, scanned my little life—" (P 178) where the farmer-speaker winnows transient blessings from those considered permanent and stores the lasting goods in seeming security only to find the "priceless Hay" vanished from its barn. Confidence gives way to cynicism here and to anxiety about preservation of related values by the friends to whom she addresses this parable.

Yet loss became for Dickinson an instigator of appreciation. She noted how mourners love to sit beside their dead (P 88), how starving men attach "Undue Significance" to food and anticipate more pleasure from it than it can give (P 439), how even revenge loses its thrill when attainable (P 1509). Longing itself engenders aspiration and noble if futile strife for those "Eastern Exiles" with whom she identified in their quest for a forsaken heaven (P 262).

Sometimes Dickinson adopted a cynical stance, as when she related the myth of Jason and the Golden Fleece in a way that reveals the mythical quester as well as his prize to prove a "sham" (P 870). Yet this disavowal of the mythical dream seems less indicative of her settled views than the position she adopted in "The Things that never can come back, are several—" (P 1515) in which she itemizes "Childhood—some forms of Hope—the Dead—" among permanent losses. But she thinks of those who will come back—explorers or sailors who embark on expeditions from which they return to enrich those left behind with their discoveries. When thinking of these venturers returning "here," however, Dickinson changes the nature of her discourse, not by questioning their coming "here" but by reflecting on the subjectivity of here-ness and identifying "Heres" known to us as types of some arche-typal location equally accessible to any spirit—presumably most so to the dead, who now experience this archetype. Sent to Mrs. Holland a few months after her husband's death, the poem offers comfort beyond that suggested in its introductory lines and opens a typological reading of the quest that suggests the illusory quality of loss rather than of gain. This vestige of Puritan language hints at Christian consolation.

Deprivation, then, could and often did turn Dickinson's mind toward heaven and its wished-for lasting values. But it also alerted her to the danger caused by frustrated yearnings, and the poems frequently suggest violent reactions to pent-up hope. In "Talk with prudence to a Beggar" (P 119), she warned that "Anecdotes of air in Dungeons / Have sometimes proved deadly sweet!" "I cannot buy it—'tis not sold—" (P 840) and "Art thou the thing I wanted?" (P 1282) express revulsion against the very good for which the speaker has searched and suffered. She presents herself as "Like God" in her capacity to reject even "The mystery of Food." The anger and vindictiveness evident in these poems strike the reader most memorably in "As the Starved Maelstrom laps the Navies" (P 872), where she catalogs examples of destructive ap-petite: the maelstrom demolishing whole navies; the vulture rip-ping the sheep; and the comically epicurean tiger awakened to the bliss of carnivorous dining and henceforth satisfied only when banqueting on man. A human being, superior in memory and capable of prolonged anticipation, harbors a "finer Famine" yet.

Like the tiger, the vulture, and the bird reserving its crumb, the Dickinsonian persona fights for survival, demands nutriment for growth—especially since the speaker conceives of herself as a small person obviously in need of expansion into power. By con-centrating on her radical insufficiency, then, and mulling over the deprivations that diminished even that inadequate identity, Dick-inson nurtured in herself a tigerlike appetite for something more—something that would satisfy the most discerning palate. Paradoxically, however, she found the deprivation itself a stimulus to growth, remarking in a letter near the end of her life that "An enlarged ability for missing is perhaps a part of our better growth, as the strange Membranes of the Tree broaden out of sight" (L 951). It is interesting that she chose a visually circumferential simile here to illustrate the processes of spiritual size. If anyone ever concentrated on enlarging the ability for missing, surely it was Emily Dickinson.

The limitations and losses that Dickinson discovered in her human condition, carefully stylized in the choices she made in her life, and explored so hauntingly in her writing of both prose and poetry, intensified her longing for replenishment and growth. Hunger engendered a craving for satisfaction and helplessness a rage for power. Few writers have confronted these needs so steadily; yet Dickinson's compulsion to deal with them should not be regarded in purely personal terms as an example of one woman's adjustment to a stifling familial, cultural, economic, or even cosmic order. As is evident from the naturalness with which she approached these topics in letters to the full spectrum of her friends and as is discoverable, too, from the almost universally sympathetic response of readers to the poems that express her sense of limitation and privation, Emily Dickinson spoke to the human condition. If other people manage to subordinate their fears to businesses other than circumference, she could not escape so easily—nor chose to.

The terms in which Dickinson expressed this dilemma of human limitation were religious ones—with powerlessness paired with omnipotence, finitude with infinity, mortality with immortality, deprivation with plenitude, misery with blessedness, man with God. Trapped within the deliberately narrowed circuit of her mortal life, the poet first sensed and then deliberately exacerbated cravings for the alternatives supposed to be beyond circumference, in God's domain. Her quest for fulfillment was a religious one, in the sense of enacting man's search for union with the infinite. But it was not an orthodox quest. Most of the people Emily Dickinson knew in her Calvinist circle of acquaintance were able to address the mystery of the universe as a sort of puzzle to be solved by fitting together pieces of doctrine, morality, and pious behavior to produce an apparently neat joining of the human with the divine. Many experienced conversion by which they felt that Christ had broken the boundaries of Dickinson's circumference in their behalf, offering promise of immortality through divine acceptance. Lacking these formulaic resources of fulfillment represented in her community by the Congregational Church, the poet ignored alternative theological, philosophical, scientific, or psychological systems for overcoming the mortal privations that dominated her consciousness. Nor does it seem likely that she would ever have perceived her situation in other than religious terms. Deprived of routine religious consolation, however, she worked out her own strategies for growth.

The strategies Emily Dickinson adopted were literary ones. Rather than substituting literature *for* religion, she used its resources as instruments *of* her own religious development. Despite her many deprivations, she had received gifts as well—chief among them being the verbal fluency and the imagination that had been her delights from childhood. These turned her to literature as a means of enlarging her circuit. In the next several chapters, I shall analyze some of the ways in which the poet exploited the capacities of literature to foster growth. Her first strategy was to find companionship through her reading, to explore other responses to problems of limitation and loss and to see how she might adapt these responses. The second was to cultivate the dramatic imagination developed by her reading to play vicariously a number of alternative roles, testing the possibilities of human power. Yet a third strategy was to exploit the potential of language to break through the circumference of intellectual boundaries dividing human sensation from divine awareness; characteristically even that experiment worked by compressing the usual formal and stylistic aspects of poetry to distill that surprising essence of sense experience which is the domain of the lyric. In turning to poetry in the late 1850s, then, Dickinson was not evading the problems articulated in her early letters but confronting them in a distinctively artful way.

PART TWO

Literary Strategies for Growth

4

"The Precious Words"

Literary Sources of Support

ONE OF Emily Dickinson's habitual responses to problems she confronted was to draw literary support for threatened self-esteem, as did the figure in one of her poems whose experience offers insight into the way she used other people's writing as a source of ego strength: "He ate and drank the precious Words—/ His Spirit grew robust—/ He knew no more that he was poor, / Nor that his frame was Dust—" (P 1587). This character suffers from typical Dickinsonian constraints: poverty, sterile routine, awareness of mortality. His release from his oppressive condition comes through a book that loosens his spirit, thereby liberating faculties hitherto repressed within a constrictive environment. Literature endows him with "Wings," a customary Dickinson symbol for release and empowerment. In some fashion, then, a book fortifies this character to pierce circumference by transcending limitations that may still be real (the language never denies the poverty or corruptibility) but are no longer recognized as coercive. Appropriately, given the miraculous power here ascribed to literature, Dickinson writes the poem in sacramental language with an opening line that presents reading as a eucharistic action and associates literary diction with the incarnate Word. Although written in the third person, this poem represents Dickinson's own experience of liberation through reading.

Given her dedication to reading, it comes as no surprise that Dickinson's literary experiences continue to receive intensive scrutiny. With Capps's inventory of books available to her or that she is known to have read and reviews from Whicher to Sewall of her response to literary sources, we have considerable information about the poet's taste and appreciable revelation of literary influences upon her writing.[1] Anderson's warning, however, about the limitations of influence searching on "such a burry original" remains pertinent and has been echoed by Sewall in his sensitive analysis of her competitive reading habits.[2] The trend in criticism lately has therefore moved away from source studies to differently focused examinations of Dickinson's relationships with literary precursors and contemporaries.[3] My interest here, however, is not in source or influence study as such, or in examination of the poet's uneasiness with literary forebears, or even in analogies between her work and that of others, but rather in the uses to which Dickinson put literature in helping her to cope with problems identified in earlier chapters. I intend to explore ways in which Dickinson turned to literature for companionship in her largely self-imposed isolation and to examine her identifications with characters and authors with whom she shared vicarious experiences both of entrapment and liberation.

What impresses me about Dickinson's use of reading as a tool for growth is her exceptional resourcefulness in putting everything available to use: Calvinism as well as romanticism, minor sentimental writers as well as Shakespeare. A book, for her, need not have been a particularly great one to exert reinforcing power for someone intent on pushing against circumference. She applied her reading as a strategic resource for opening perspectives on problems of limitation and deprivation that might otherwise have proven disabling. And she discovered in authors models of an artistic life not otherwise exemplified in her environment. For a private writer, the anxiety of influence that might have beset the more public poet assumed subordinate importance in contrast to the dazzlingly exciting truth that other people actually wrote and that their achievements (personal as well as literary) made a difference for her.

The most obvious use of literature for almost any sympathetic reader is for vicarious experience, for identification with other lives—perhaps more glamorous ones. Fictional characters can confront familiar problems in a great variety of ways. They can test possibilities of reaction without lessening the reader through their defeats; they can serve as models of heroism. Dickinson found this resource a helpful one in dealing with her self-image as small, insignificant, vulnerable. She told in "Unto like Story—

Trouble has enticed me—" (P 295) how she summoned courage from the storied martyrs who taught her that "Feet, small as mine—have marched in Revolution / Firm to the Drum—/ Hands—not so stout—hoisted them—in witness—/ When Speech went numb—." Like other poems she grouped with this one in fascicle 12, "I've heard an Organ talk, sometimes—" (P 183) and "Alone, I cannot be—" (P 298), this celebrates the power of imagination liberated through art to overcome impotence and loneliness. Stories, both romantic and historic, suggest the heroism of renunciation, the drama of martyrdom, the honor that succeeds disgrace, and in general the valor of courage. They also teach readers to view their own lives in imaginative terms as more fascinating than any novels in the bookstores, because more subjectively compelling and more amazing in their possibilities than any work of fiction limited to plausibility: "*Our* Novel—when 'tis small enough / To Credit—'Tis'nt true!" (P 669).

Another delight of reading was companionship with fellow writers, and Dickinson's letters supported her poems in expressing gratitude for their very existence. She took a vast interest in authorial lives, turning to memoirs and biographies with the same fervor she brought to novels or volumes of poetry. The first such experience of sorority with Elizabeth Barrett Browning overwhelmed her like a conversion experience.

> I could not have defined the change—
> Conversion of the Mind
> Like Sanctifying in the Soul—
> Is witnessed—not explained—
>
> 'Twas a Divine Insanity—
> The Danger to be Sane
> Should I again experience—
> 'Tis Antidote to turn—
>
> To Tomes of solid Witchcraft—
> Magicians be asleep—
> But Magic—hath an Element
> Like Deity—to keep—
> (P 593)

Poetry transformed her world and released her from restrictions of the dark, the ordinary, the sane, and the prosaic. That this release had been accomplished by a woman (herself an invalid) seemed especially glorious. Yet other authors penned "Tomes of solid Witchcraft" to renew this excitement, and Dickinson learned to drink "Strong Draughts of Their Refreshing Minds" (P 711).

Despite her ability to identify with fictional characters, Dickinson's comments on her reading show surprisingly little interest in plot or characterization. Such responses as "'What do I think of *Middlemarch*?' What do I think of glory—except that in a few instances this 'mortal has already put on immortality'" (L 389) demonstrate a drastically different reaction to literature than one that focuses on content. She read for tone and for the emotional response the writing released in her. The definition of poetry by which she startled Higginson reveals an affective theory of literature fully as radical as Poe's: "If I read a book [and] it makes my whole body so cold no fire ever can warm me I know *that* is poetry. If I feel physically as if the top of my head were taken off, I know *that* is poetry. These are the only way I know it. Is there any other way?" (L 342a). Dickinson shared in the liberation her reading represented and attempted to follow imagination to its source. Themes, plots, ideas, and opinions aroused curiosity—as she indicated in "A precious—mouldering pleasure—'tis—/ To meet an Antique Book—" (P 371), but the "Enchantment" came from the thrilling presence of a stranger bringing wonderful news: "He traverses—familiar—/ As One should come to Town—/ And tell you all your Dreams—were true—/ He lived—where Dreams were born—." Susan Dickinson, similarly susceptible to the elation of an ennobling presence, borrowed from this poem her salute to Emerson: "when I found he was to eat and sleep beneath our roof, there was a suggestion of meeting God face to face, or one of the Patriarchs of Hebrew setting, or, as 'Aunt Emily' says, 'As if he had come from where dreams are born'."[4] Whether the poet herself responded that way to Emerson remains unknown but is certainly probable. She read for elation and for release. In examining her reading, then, we should look for sources of such elation in the literature she knew and search less for influences on her thinking than for triggers to her emotions—and especially for those literary resources that offered her the supreme elatedness of escape from limitation by awakening the tune within herself.

To judge from its opening line, one would think that "He ate and drank the precious Words—" (P 1587) pertained to the Bible and that the book endowing its reader with freedom ought to be *the* Book, the Good News. Yet Dickinson critics tend to view literature as her defense against religious constriction and see "Tomes of solid Witchcraft" (P 593) as correctives to the one great tome of godliness. The Bible, however, was this poet's favorite book, and I argue that it—along with the largely Calvinist reading matter that accompanied it in the Dickinson household—served as the first and formative literary resource in her quest for growth. Granted, Calvinism reinforced her sense of limitation, but it also directed her imagination toward freedom and empowerment by extending hope of transformation through grace. In any event, Calvinist Christianity dominated the milieu from which Dickinson sprang. The very tension Dickinson felt between herself and her more securely churched neighbors sharpened alertness to that biblical heritage they all shared through this tradition—especially biblical language, narratives, and myth structure.

Dickinson's early letters often served as literary reviews of each week's sermons, with particular attention to tone and style and including specific reference to her emotive response, like the observation that "We had such precious sermons from Mr Dwight. One about unbelief, and another Esau. Sermons on unbelief ever did attract me" (L 176). Sermons on deprivation—one on lack of faith in the abstract and one on a biblical figure who sold his birthright—cut straight to the heart of her problems and exerted a natural fascination. That was one of the merits of Calvinism for Emily Dickinson. It established a cultural base that allowed her to communicate about her central problems. Like Hawthorne's Dimmesdale, who preached eloquently about his vileness only to have his congregation find his remarks precious and uplifting, Dickinson could confront her sense of abysmal limitation in letters as well as poems without alarming her readers or having any but the Higginsons' Unitarian-Transcendentalist coterie imagine her insane.[5]

The Bible and Calvinism gave Dickinson a vocabulary fraught with spiritual adventure. From childhood, she had thrilled to the words even when misconstruing them as comically as in the clergyman's prayer she remembered as "Oh thou who sittest upon the Apex of the Cherubim, look down upon this, thine unworthy Terrapin" (L 806). How pleasant that diction so grandiloquent could chime in a near rhyme, thus locking forever the opposite notions of God presiding among the angels while man subsided among the turtles. Other words thrilled her also and found their way into her writing: words like immortality, redemption, election, grace, and glory. Detachment from the church did not in Dickinson's case mean a break with the spiritual drama biblical language expressed. She reveled in the oppositions of Puritan language structure: the exalted and the humble, the elect and the reprobate, the light and the dark, Jesus and Satan, God and man. One of the great delights of her religion was its expansion of a person's view in time and space, making a cosmic joke of the worldly person's circumscription.

> How much the present moment means
> To those who've nothing more—
> The Fop—the Carp—the Atheist—
> Stake an entire store
> Upon a Moment's shallow Rim
> While their commuted Feet
> The Torrents of Eternity
> Do all but inundate—
> (P 1380)

For someone so enthralled with language, biblical diction proved a superbly flexible and ennobling expressive resource.

The Bible itself, of course, was even more remarkable in its capacity to stimulate imagination, especially when read in light of current historical studies by Strauss and Renan that pointed out the mythical element of biblical literature and allowed the reader to approach its narratives as fictions rather than literal truth. Such an approach reached New England through Theodore Parker, the radical Transcendentalist minister of whom Dickinson commented: "I heard that he was 'poison.' Then I like poison very well" (L 213). Considering the rigid orthodoxy normally ascribed to her parents, it comes as a shock to learn that Edward Dickinson's last gifts to his daughter were Frothingham's sympathetic book on Parker and George Eliot's poems—both mind-joggling sources of theological contamination had he worried about it (L 449). Dickinson's views on scriptural inspiration appeared later in a lighthearted remark to Mrs. Holland: "The Fiction of 'Santa Claus' always reminds me of the reply to my early question of 'Who made the Bible'—'Holy Men moved by the Holy Ghost,' and though I have now ceased my investigations, the Solution is insufficient—/ Santa Claus, though *illustrates*—Revelation" (L 794). She and Austin scandalized their pious mother with philosophical and theological speculations—Emily matching Austin's suggestion that "there was no such person as Elijah" (L 650) with such remarks in her poems as "But Ararat's a Legend—now—/ And no one credits Noah—" (P 403) or "And tho' in soberer moments—/ No Moses there can be" (P 597). The fictionalizing tendency gave the poet freedom to rework literary material in ways that would cast new light on her most pressing concerns.

Although the Bible might be fictional for Dickinson, it was nonetheless an enthralling romance that only needed fresher telling to revive its fascination. Her "Diagnosis of the Bible, by a Boy—" (P 1545), especially in its earliest version, confronts the problem of staleness with its deadening effect on tone. The biblical story would impress readers more dramatically, she suggested, if retold to clarify the linkage of Old and New Testaments, thereby stressing the typological connection between Eden and Bethlehem. It would benefit also if the speaker ascribed glamour to the thrillingly reprobate villains, Satan and Judas, and romantic charm to the poet-hero, David, while involving the reader in the drama by confronting the modern boy with the choice of salvation at heavy worldly cost or apparently enticing defeat. The poem calls for a freshening of tone in Bible stories at the expense of moralizing; it prefers captivation of the reader to condemnation.

Dickinson found the Bible a great story in itself, the sublime rendering of salvation history from the Fall in Genesis to the restoration of Revelation, a mythical pattern admirably attuned to her private myth of growth from limitation to circumference. Within this overall design were many parallel stories showing God's repeated rescue of his fallen people—a heartening theme to one obsessed with her inadequacy and need for support. The story reached its climax with the crucifixion, apparent defeat and paradoxical victory, and would arrive at its happy ending with the gathering of the saints beside God's throne. Characteristically, however, Dickinson's imagination drew her to the Bible's frustrated saints, who resembled her imagined self in their experience of unmerited privation. She asserted that "It always felt to me—a wrong / To that Old Moses—done / To let him see—the Canaan—/ Without the entering—" (P 597) and complained "Moses was'nt fairly used—/ Ananias was'nt—" (P 1201). From the story of Abraham and Isaac, she drew a bitter lesson: "Moral—with a Mastiff / Manners may prevail" (P 1317). Other Old Testament stories offered encouragement to the small and seemingly disadvantaged reader, particularly that of Jacob who "worsted God" in a sense by demanding the Angel's blessing (P 59). Her effort to emulate David led to her felling herself with her own pebble (P 540); still the biblical narrative challenged the weak to display courage. Freedom to read these narratives as fiction meant an opportunity to suggest revision.

Dickinson's fictional conjectures seem to have stopped with the Old Testament; she spoke of Christ in more orthodox terms and sympathized with him as the most attractive of the frustrated saints. Writing in 1873 to her cousin, she recalled a sermon of twenty years before by the Reverend Edwards Amasa Park as "the loveliest sermon I ever heard," which rendered "the disappointment of Jesus in Judas" compellingly as "a mortal story of intimate young men" (L 385). "'They have not chosen me,' he said," (P 85) presents Jesus' disappointment in his disciples, and "He forgot— and I—remembered—" (P 203) illustrates the speaker's experience of betrayal by likening it to Christ's sorrow at Peter's denial. Twice she recalled the story of the thief who drew victory from death by imploring the "Paragon of Chivalry" (P 1305) for remembrance in his kingdom (P 1180). She identified with the thief here and with the still more mysteriously liberated Paul and Silas, whose escape from prison she celebrated in another poem grouped with this one in the same set of manuscripts (P 1166). The Gospels offered further encouragement to one beset with feelings of insignificance in that Jesus characteristically exalted the humble—especially in choosing his disciples, whom he elevated with his "Fisherman's Degree" of Christian election (P 401). The Epistles of Paul, to which Dickinson alluded in "'And with what body do they come?'—" (P 1492) and "'Sown in dishonor'!" (P 62), also anticipated reversal of earthly defeat. The Bible, then, provided ample evidence that loss might not be permanent, that limitation could yield to expansion, and that God's design in history affirmed hope.

The Calvinist tradition so dominant in Dickinson's background intensified this biblical sense of spiritual drama and centered it in each person's soul. Hers was a conversion religion, one that stressed the radical transition from man's naturally depraved condition to a grace-filled state. Calvinist theology fostered attentiveness to limitations as an almost indispensable prelude to salvation. Those whom God predestined for salvation were likely to identify themselves as sinful, weak, and unworthy. The psychology that emanated from these beliefs vivified ordinary life, making every event a dramatic test of salvation and investing even the most routine incident with symbolic portent. At its best, the Calvinism of Dickinson's era still retained the original Puritan capacity to admire the world and find it good, stare into the soul and find it flawed, look up to heaven and find acceptance.

Despite her professed indifference to doctrine, the poet's dual concern with both limit and liberation drew her closer to the Puritan spirit than her church-going Congregationalist neighbors generally came. Given her historical period, of course, Emily Dickinson never set eyes on an authentic Puritan—nor had anyone else a century after the Great Awakening when Jonathan Edwards tried to reignite Calvinist dogma with its original pious zeal in the new light of Newtonian physics and Lockean psychology. Since his time, much had happened to New England Calvinism, and the version Dickinson experienced was attenuated though still conservatively evangelical.[6] Original Sin itself, that foundation of total depravity, had been downgraded by New Divinity theologians following in Edwards's wake. According to Samuel Hopkins and Nathanael Emmons, "Sin is in the sinning" rather than in the person. Having modified Edwards's doctrine of Original Sin, his successors undermined as well his argument against free will and identified both sin and holiness as volitional behavior. Conversion, too, they redefined as the free choice of the regenerate person to turn toward God and live by the gospel. Successive waves of awakening had focused attention on the role of specific evangelical leaders as agents of conversion, thereby subordinating the prior necessity for regeneration through grace.

By the 1840s, conversion had come to seem almost a duty, and authority figures such as Mary Lyon had mastered ways of instigating the desired result. The pressure for conversion Dickinson experienced at Mount Holyoke could never have happened in Edward Taylor's time, when he waited eight years to gather his church until he could find the requisite saving remnant of visible saints. Nor would Edwards have trusted the blurring of true and false awakenings. But if conversion were a voluntary act, then it was one that could be coerced by such community pressure as Dickinson felt. Her sense of herself as a rebel has meaning it never could have had when saving grace was recognized as a rare and exclusive divine gift. Rather than rebelling against the New England way, she became more conservative than her neighbors in sifting the evidence for election and waiting for God to show himself.

The odd lacunae in the poet's moral sense—her startling indifference to the adulterous intent suggested by the "Master" letters in contrast to her abashed apologies for minor faults like misaddressing envelopes and misspelling words—suggest that she never quite accepted the notions of personal sinfulness that permeated her social milieu and found voice in her youthful rhetoric. Nor did she pick up the neo-Pelagian notion popular in more liberal-minded parts of New England that posited so perfect a degree of human innocence as to preclude the need for saving grace except for those voluntarily fallen into sin, thus prompting Hawthorne's Hilda (so ironically self-defined as "a daughter of the Puritans") to imagine that she could maintain her snowy innocence by avoiding Miriam's contamination. Dickinson seems never to have convicted herself seriously of the sin that lay in the sinning but stressed instead her share in the universal human state of limitation that others have expressed in the idea of Original Sin. Two late poems, "'Heavenly Father'—take to thee" (P 1461) and "Of God we ask one favor," (P 1601), blame God rather than man for the natural finitude that prevents man from satisfying his creator: "We apologize to thee / For thine own Duplicity—." Guilt-wracked Dickinson was not.

Instead of settling for religious routine, Dickinson restored those qualities of passion, drama, and suspenseful attentiveness that had been lost in a more prosaic righteousness of piety, respectability, and (often institutionalized) good works. She embarked on the private pilgrimage of an isolated soul and represented her condition in a revealing poem that demonstrates the continuity of Puritan personality traits and a Puritan myth structure in the struggle for immortality:

> This Consciousness that is aware
> Of Neighbors and the Sun

Will be the one aware of Death
And that itself alone

Is traversing the interval
Experience between
And most profound experiment
Appointed unto Men—

How adequate unto itself
It's properties shall be
Itself unto itself and none
Shall make discovery.

Adventure most unto itself
The Soul condemned to be—
Attended by a single Hound
It's own identity.
(p 822)

For Dickinson, consciousness rather than intellect or will was the defining property of the soul, and this consciousness accompanied identity but subsisted outside it, being the immortal partner. Like the original Puritans, she had come to value a sort of worldliness. Persons engaged in their callings would be aware of neighbors, even though her Puritan ancestors would probably have joined Hawthorne's putative ones in scoffing at belles-lettres as "a business in life" or "mode of glorifying God, or being serviceable to mankind."[7] And the godly person must be attentive to natural revelations of divinity, as Anne Bradstreet could have told her and Edward Hitchcock did.[8] But the fundamental awareness must be of death, the terminus of known life and entry into the mysterious. Dickinson's fascination with death, then, and her probing at circumference are Puritan traits, inherited from people who interpreted life symbolically in terms of God's secrets. The language of this poem expresses a noble and courageous view of this "Adventure" of pilgrimage that must be performed alone. With their congregational experiment, the New England churches had tended to soften the isolation of Bunyan's journey, but Dickinson restored it and with it the drama of suspenseful spiritual life.

Her Calvinist heritage, then, helped to instill in Emily Dickinson her sense of herself as a small, vulnerable quester—deprived of external aids to salvation and even of lasting assurance of grace; but it also provided her with a belief system that recognized limitation and deprivation as entry points to growth. The very rigidity of her environment served naturally, if ironically, as a stimulus to spiritual exploration:

> Contained in this short Life
> Are magical extents
> The soul returning soft at night
> To steal securer thence
> As Children strictest kept
> Turn soonest to the sea
> Whose nameless Fathoms slink away
> Beside infinity
>
> (P 1165)

The sea to which Dickinson turned, her symbol for the unknown and awesome beyond the sheltering circumferential shore, would entice her to other vantage points to supplement or qualify the Calvinist dogmatism she could never wholly accept. These perspectives would come—not from philosophy or theology—but from literature, especially that of nineteenth-century England and America.

Aside from Shakespeare, who, along with the Bible, served as Dickinson's primary literary resource, her reading concentrated on contemporary authors, those actively writing while she was. Despite the themes and concerns she shared with the major British romantic poets, then, there is little evidence that she read them intently, although she must have known their works at least by reputation. Given Dickinson's fascination with fleeting time and the reconstitution of experience in consciousness, her alertness to nature as a potential (although rapidly rejected) source of psychic healing, her awareness of process, her yearning for the infinite, and her haunting attentiveness to death, one would expect her to have turned to her century's poetic masters: Wordsworth, Coleridge, Keats, and Shelley. Yet the evidence is slim for her having done so—relatively few references in the letters to Wordsworth and Keats, none to Coleridge and Shelley, many to lesser writers like Ik Marvel and Harriet Prescott Spofford. Evidently it was important to Dickinson to recognize a supportive society of contemporary authors to whom she turned as personal resources even

more than as literary inspirations. Nationality made little difference in her choices; she responded ardently to Emerson, appreciatively to Longfellow, in an awe-struck way to Hawthorne even as
she thrilled to the accomplishments of the Brownings, Tennyson,
the Brontës, and "*my* George Eliot" (L 710). Like Mrs. Browning's
Aurora Leigh and Marian Erle, Dickinson "read for hope."[9] And
she moved like Aurora from expository, informative prose (heavily theological) to poetry in which she found enlarged possibilities.

> thus, my soul,
> At poetry's divine first finger-touch,
> Let go conventions and sprang up surprised,
> Convicted of the great eternities
> Before two worlds.[10]

Nor did she fear the pressure of literary influence on her artistic
independence, having Emerson's word for the invulnerability of
individual genius in the presence of powerful precursors: "Take
thankfully and heartily all they can give. Exhaust them, wrestle
with them, let them not go until their blessing be won, and after
a short season the dismay will be overpast, the excess of influence
withdrawn, and they will be no longer an alarming meteor, but
one more bright star shining serenely in your heaven and blending
its light with all your day."[11] The allusion here to Jacob and the
angel, one of her favorite biblical stories, would have reinforced
this advice on Dickinson's mind. She did indeed wrestle with
other writers even as she blessed them and sought their blessings.
She identified with authors and their characters in much the same
way as she identified with Jacob, Esau, Moses, the thief on Calvary, and the suffering Jesus. Like the Bible, the fiction of her own
era (including narrative poetry) both confronted her with the realities of limitation and loss and held out hope for liberation. Over
and over, she alluded to fictions dealing with captivity and release.

The explicit connections young Emily Dickinson drew in her
letters between herself and literary figures demonstrate the uses to
which she put her reading for communication of private anxieties.
A November 1851 missive to Austin spun out an elaborate association between the Amherst siblings and Hawthorne's Salem re-
cluses in *The House of the Seven Gables*: "How lonely it was last
night when the chilly wind went down, and the clear, cold moon

was shining—it seemed to me I could pack this little earthly bundle, and bidding the world Goodbye, fly away and away, and never come back again to be so lonely here, and then I thought of 'Hepzibah' how sorrowful *she* was, and how she longed to sleep, because the grave was peaceful, yet for affection's sake, and for the sake of 'Clifford' she wearied on, and bye and bye, kind angels took both of them home, and it seemed almost a lesson, given us to learn. I dont mean that you are *him*, or that Hepzibah's *me* except in a relative sense, only I was reminded" (L 62). Dickinson's own readers have likened her more often to Hester Prynne, with her speculative imagination freed by solitude and her will strengthened by restrictions, but it was typical of her to identify instead (even at age twenty) with Hawthorne's comically pathetic spinster in her self-chosen confinement to the Pyncheon homestead. Flight out into the world may have seemed like liberation at first to Clifford, but Hepzibah recognized it from the start as a manic, desperate, perilous action; return home—even to a long-experienced prison—seemed a blessing at the time even though ultimate liberation for the Pyncheons required entry into a larger world. It is revealing that Dickinson likened Austin to Clifford, victim of double confinement, both at home and in prison (her judgment on Boston's Endicott School where he was then teaching?), and Hawthorne's exemplar of the suppressed poet with his love of beauty and sensitivity to impressions that exposed him principally to mockery and pain. Their father may have resembled a more moral Judge Pyncheon with his public enterprise, but Emily and Austin (as a young man, anyway) felt themselves imprisoned aesthetes dependent on each other for spiritual support.

Prison imagery recurs, far more pronouncedly, in Dickinson's many references in the early 1860s to Byron's dramatic monologue "The Prisoner of Chillon." This poem tells the story of Bonnivard in his own voice, presenting him as a religious more than a political rebel and thereby qualifying him to be recognized in New England as a Calvinist hero—a surprising bridge between Dickinson's religious heritage and romantic poetry. Byron essentially ignored the historical context of Bonnivard's ordeal, focusing attention instead on his lengthy captivity in the castle of Chillon on an island in Lake Geneva—a kind of double imprisonment, since the lake reinforced the castle in denying him freedom. The personal aspects of the hero's suffering dominate the poem: the execution of his father, the death first of the middle brother chained with him to dungeon pillars, and then (with lingering sentimental detail) of the younger brother, followed by glimpses of his isolated ordeal afterward in which a bird's brief song could be mistaken for angelic visitation and a glimpse of the Alps taken for evidence of a continuing outside world, while the prisoner paced the circuit of his dungeon and measured the depths of his consciousness. Given her attentiveness to limitation and deprivation, Dickinson could hardly have failed to identify with Byron's Bonnivard; and her allusions to the poem in four letters to different recipients, starting in 1861 with one to her unknown "Master" and ending just before her death with one to Higginson, demonstrate the force of this identification, especially from 1861 to 1864 (L 233; 249; 293; 1042). "The Prisoner of Chillon" presented her with powerful imagery of despair and inner numbness, such as she was developing herself in poems like "It was not Death, for I stood up," (P 510) and "After great pain, a formal feeling comes—" (P 341). Byron presented Bonnivard's "Hour of Lead" in section IX.

> I had no thought, no feeling—none—
> Among the stones I stood a stone,
> And was, scarce conscious what I wist,
> As shrubless crags within the mist;
> For all was blank, and bleak, and grey,
> It was not night—it was not day,
> It was not even the dungeon-light
> So hateful to my heavy sight,
> But vacancy absorbing space,
> And fixedness—without a place;
> There were no stars, no earth, no time,
> No check, no change, no good, no crime—
> But silence, and a stirless breath
> Which neither was of life nor death;
> A sea of stagnant idleness,
> Blind, boundless, mute, and motionless.[12]

Yet the prisoner regained his awareness at enormous cost in agony, perhaps prompting Dickinson's conclusion in "No Rack can torture me—" (P 384) that "Captivity is Consciousness—/ So's Liberty."

What fascinated the New England poet most about Byron's hero was his attitude when liberated, his hesitation to leave the prison that had become so familiar as to preclude the outer world while driving him mentally inward. When confined in Cambridge for eye treatments, Dickinson wrote to her sister: "You remember the Prisoner of Chillon did not know Liberty when it came, and asked to go back to Jail" (L 293). This appetite for restriction, so characteristic of her, found expression in "A Prison gets to be a friend—" (P 652), a poem strikingly similar to Byron's in its imagery of the beam (pillar), prison fare, and circuit of habitual pacing. It includes these revealing stanzas:

> We learn to know the Planks—
> That answer to Our feet—
> So miserable a sound—at first—
> Nor even now—so sweet—
>
> As plashing in the Pools—
> When Memory was a Boy—
> But a Demurer Circuit—
> A Geometric Joy—

Still, she recognized the unnaturalness, even cruelty, of confining an otherwise free spirit. When exiled herself for medical care, she explained her dog's remaining in Amherst (a relatively Alpine setting) rather than Cambridge (Chillon): "Carlo did not come, because that he would die, in Jail, and the Mountains, I could not hold now, so I brought but the Gods—" (L 290). Many years later, when Helen Hunt Jackson died, Dickinson alluded yet again to her favorite Byron poem with the comment that "I think she would rather have stayed with us, but perhaps she will learn the Customs of Heaven, as the Prisoner of Chillon of Captivity" (L 1042).

The body and the emotions might accede to imprisonment— not so the imagination. That, best represented for Dickinson by poetry, remained instinctively at liberty. An 1851 letter to Sue calls attention to a humorous allegory of poetic freedom: Longfellow's "Pegasus in Pound."[13] Longfellow whimsically introduced the mythical winged steed into a New England village (not unlike Amherst), attracted there by a mellow autumn morning. Although the landscape accords with this spirit of poetry, its Yankee inhabitants prove unreceptive. Industriousness crowds out imagination. Pegasus, snuffling the seasonal fragrances and alert to the piping quails, is startled by the factory whistle that summons the townspeople to their grim enterprises. After schoolboys discover him on the village common, town officers thrust him into confinement: "And the wise men, in their wisdom, / Put him straightway into pound." They advertise him as a stray. Patient for a while, then fretful at neglect, Pegasus waits until midnight for his escape, then snaps his chains and soars off among the stars— leaving a magical fountain by his hoof prints.

The satiric implications of this tale as a commentary on art and public values must have struck young Emily forcefully. She extended its application to Longfellow himself and to his latest volume of poetry when she remarked: "Longfellow's 'golden Legend' has come to town I hear—and may be seen *in state* on Mr. Adams' bookshelves. It always makes me think of 'Pegasus in the pound'—when I find a gracious author sitting side by side with 'Murray' and 'Wells' and 'Walker' in that renowned store—and like *him* I half expect to hear that they have '*flown*' some morning and in their native ether revel all the day; but for our sakes dear Susie, who please ourselves with the fancy that we are the only poets, and everyone else is *prose*, let us hope they will yet be willing to share our humble world and feed upon such aliment as *we* consent to do!" (L 56). It was writers, not books, she envisaged on the shelf, an occasional poet among the grammarians and textbook authors, and Longfellow was one of the few whose popularity in small-town New England entitled him to shelf space normally reserved for more practical works.

Although Longfellow's direct influence on Dickinson was only an early one and chiefly had the effect of nurturing a tendency toward melancholy reflectiveness, he continued to excite in her dreams of liberation. As late as 1882 she was writing—again to Sue—about a news item reporting the capture of an Egyptian rebel. "Had 'Arabi' only read Longfellow, he'd have never been caught—" (L 768), she wrote, before signing herself "Khedive" and adding as a postscript the familiar lines from "The Day is Done": "Shall fold their Tents like the Arabs, and as silently steal away." She was probably thinking also of Longfellow's "The Leap of Roushan Beg," in which an Arab bandit chief eludes his pursuers by inspiring his steed to leap a thirty-foot chasm to safety.[14]

This stirring "vision of life and death" would have stimulated Dickinson's own circumference-vaulting imagination.

She responded in a more intensely personal way to Elizabeth Barrett Browning's *Aurora Leigh*, disregarding the moral and aesthetic concerns of that blank-verse novel to plunge into the central issue of Aurora's painful escape from the confinement of a woman's socially mandated role as helpmate to the comparative freedom of a self-defined artistic identity.[15] Dickinson identified Aurora with Elizabeth Barrett and herself with both and took great pride in their transcendence of limits: "That Mrs. Browning fainted, we need not read *Aurora Leigh* to know, when she lived with her English aunt; and George Sand 'must make no noise in her grandmother's bedroom.' Poor children! Women, now, queens, now! And one in the Eden of God" (L 234).

Aurora Leigh connected brilliantly with Dickinson's themes of limitation (best represented by the impoverished and debased Marian Erle) and deprivation (represented by Aurora herself). It was Aurora's youth that most drew Dickinson's attention with the "mother-want about the world" the girl felt after the early death of her Florentine mother, followed a few years later by the death of her loving father and the loss of her Italian homeland with its freedom and its sensuous beauty.[16] Confined to her spinster aunt's rigidly ordered English home, she was subjected to the miseducation and training in useless accomplishments that Dickinson noted in her second copy of the poem as late as 1880.[17] Poetry, as noted earlier, liberated Aurora from such stultification and encouraged aspirations that led to literary celebrity. Dickinson must have admired Aurora's fidelity to her inner life as stimulated by nature and art.

> I had relations in the Unseen, and drew
> The elemental nutriment and heat
> From nature, as earth feels the sun at nights,
> Or as a babe sucks surely in the dark.
> I kept the life thrust on me, on the outside
> Of the inner life with all its ample room
> For heart and lungs, for will and intellect,
> Inviolable by conventions. God,
> I thank thee for that grace of thine![18]

And she may have noticed with equal respect Aurora's later self-discipline in keeping the life thrust on her as a literary celebrity removed from the inner life that drove her to increasingly honest and demanding poetic expression.

Aurora released herself, through a literary career, from her aunt's constrictions and Romney's limited perspective. Elizabeth Barrett's poetic recognition, however, left her still confined on Wimpole Street until Robert Browning rescued her as his bride, thereby impressing himself as liberator in the hearts of Victorian women around the world. While Mrs. Browning lived, Dickinson paid little attention to her husband. But when "Her—'last Poems'—/ Poets—ended—" (P 312), she found herself singing along with the widower "off charnel steps" (L 298). Once she recognized Browning as a sufferer who transcended deprivation as had his wife, she was able to appreciate the many poems in *Men and Women*—that "broad Book" she praised to Higginson (L 368) and obviously her favorite of his volumes—dealing with limitations and losses like those she herself encountered: frustrated love, religious doubt, and unsatisfied artistic ambition. Among these fifty poems it was those on love that she remembered and most often quoted.

What "the consummate Browning" (L 966) offered Dickinson in his handling of relatively conventional subject matter was a fresh and exuberant tone as a corrective to the sentimental sweetness or moralistic didacticism she encountered elsewhere. The characters of Browning's monologues contend strenuously with their fears and doubts; they rebound from failure with intensified hope; and they live in and through epiphanies like the "moment, one and infinite!" that transformed existence for the speaker of "By the Fire-side," allowing him to look backward with still breathless gratitude and forward with a confidence invulnerable to age.[19] Browning fortified her even in her challenges to God, taking exuberant delight in the intellectual, emotional, and volitional stimuli of religious uncertainty. He would have agreed with her that "It is true that the unknown is the largest need of the intellect, though for it, no one thinks to thank God" (L 471).

By the time Dickinson turned to Robert Browning, she had grown comfortable with physical confinement—a spatial restriction that led, for her, to imaginative release so long as she could maintain control of time. It seems to have been Browning's temporal sense itself that meant the most to her, judging by her niece's recollections of the uses to which Dickinson put his poetry in everyday life as a validation for those choices that bewildered more prosaic persons.[20] Reacting to a neighbor's pity for her presumed burden of idleness, the poet flashed back Browning's exclamation, "Time, why, Time was all I wanted!" from "Any Wife to Any Husband." Mrs. Bianchi remembered also how her aunt loved to quote another favorite line with "her pet gesture of bravado" during domestic squabbles: "Who knows but the world may end tonight?" Both citations express the thrill of living and loving in the immediate expectancy of loss and draw a kind of desperate optimism from inevitable defeat.

The speaker of "The Last Ride Together" might well be downcast. His mistress has rejected him, thus spelling the end of his life's ambition. Instead, he responds with pride, thankfulness, and benediction. He accepts the past without giving way to might-have-beens and lives now for the present while she rides with him in one final night of closeness:

> My mistress bent that brow of hers,
> Those deep dark eyes where pride demurs
> When pity would be softening through,
> Fixed me a breathing-while or two
>   With life or death in the balance—Right!
> The blood replenished me again:
> My last thought was at least not vain.
> I and my mistress, side by side
> Shall be together, breathe and ride,
> So one day more am I deified.
> Who knows but the world may end to-night?[21]

The poem freezes time to perpetuate this single moment of blissful expectancy. The process of riding together subsumes all else but the flitting dream of heaven. Should the world end tonight, it would not be disaster but fulfillment to lovers thus freed from mundane and temporal constraints. For Dickinson, too, the sense of balancing on the boundary of time—just where it meets immortality—proved exhilarating.

In a youthful mood of mock solemnity (perhaps of jealousy as well), Emily Dickinson wrote from Mount Holyoke to Austin and Lavinia about their amusement with the *Arabian Nights*: "Cultivate your other powers in proportion as you allow Imagination to captivate you!" (L 19). Her own experience ultimately opposed her advice. Those "other powers" of industriousness, practical good sense, and service that everyone taught her to value became, for her, constraining forces; they habituated her to those "Customs . . . of Captivity" (L 1042) from which reading freed her. Books heightened her sense of possibility, however, so that—in company with the character whose story introduces this chapter—Emily Dickinson herself "danced along the dingy Days / And this Bequest of Wings / Was but a Book—What Liberty / A loosened spirit brings—" (P 1587).

5

"I Play at Riches"

Acting Alternative Roles

DURING editorial preparation for the 1891 *Poems*, Higginson alerted Mrs. Todd to his reservations on including a seeming exception: "One poem only I dread a little to print—that wonderful 'Wild Nights,'—lest the malignant read into it more than that virgin recluse ever dreamed of putting there."[1] He wondered whether Lavinia had shown signs of shrinking from potential gossip but decided finally to go with his aesthetic judgment: "Indeed it is not to be omitted." Time has justified his scruples somewhat as is evident from the sexually charged interpretations many readers have imposed on this poem, although good will toward the poet rather than malevolence probably underlies most assumptions of her erotic license. Emily Dickinson's twentieth-century reputation hardly rests on the chivalry of a Victorian gentleman. That Higginson's main worry concerned the "virgin recluse's" sexual honor is evident from his quite different response the previous year to a poem equally suspect in moral terms but involving a different sphere of behavior. "We *must* have that burglary," he had written then to Mrs. Todd, "—the most nearly objective thing she wrote."[2] Although "I know some lonely Houses off the Road" (P 289) presented his retiring gentlewoman as a plotting housebreaker, its fantasy could be excused as something like imaginative objectivity. Even so, his comments on both poems reveal Higginson's unwillingness to accept the poet's statement that the "I" who represented her verse was to be recognized as "a supposed person," not herself (L 268).

Even in our post-New Critical age, with the objectivity of art strongly emblazoned in the minds of literary judges, Dickinson's readers persist in interpreting her poems subjectively—detaching them sharply from the impersonal mode common to the Victorian poetry that influenced them. Yet it becomes clear, when one reads Dickinson's poetry in the light of Victorian literary conventions, that she took advantage of the author's privilege to adopt the voices of imagined characters and to enter vicariously into situations remote from her own life. Nor did she need to wait for twentieth-century validation. She could recall Ik Marvel's apology for his *Reveries of a Bachelor* in which he justified his play of fancy in situating a persona conspicuously like himself, but not really himself, in domestic circumstances he had never adopted for the specific purpose of experiencing sensations otherwise closed to him. She must have sympathized with Marvel's rejoinder to matter-of-fact critics like her father: "What matters it, pray, if literally there was no wife, and no dead child, and no coffin, in the house? Is not feeling, feeling; and heart, heart? Are not these fancies thronging on my brain, bringing their own sorrows, and their own joys, as living as anything human can be living? What if they have no material type—no objective form? All *that* is crude—a mere reduction of ideality to sense,—a transformation of the spiritual to the earthy,—a leveling of soul to matter."[3] And what did it matter if Edward Dickinson's respectable daughter never broke into a house at midnight or indulged in steamy reunions with a lover? Poetry, even lyric poetry, has an element of fiction. Many of Dickinson's favorite writers—Shakespeare and the Brownings, for instance—chose dramatic forms, and there is reason to believe that she incorporated a substantial measure of dramatic objectivity into her apparently subjective verse.

Live theater was one of those artistic experiences Dickinson sacrificed by remaining in Amherst, but she found small-scale experiences of dramatic art by participating in a Shakespeare reading club as a young lady and attending occasional dramatic readings. Most of these must have disappointed her to judge by her remarks to Louise Norcross: "Do you still attend Fanny Kemble? 'Aaron Burr' and father think her an 'animal,' but I fear zoology has few such instances. I have heard many notedly *bad* readers, and a fine one would be almost a fairy surprise" (L 199). Perhaps because of her Norcross cousins' enthusiasm for theater, Dickinson indulged in dramatic fantasies for them, thanking Loo once for a new cape with the query, "Do you think I am going 'upon the boards' that

I wish so smart attire? Such are my designs, though. I beg you not to disclose them! May I not secure Loo for drama, and Fanny for comedy?" (L 225). To judge from later family memoirs she need not have looked so far from home for comic accompaniment, as her sister, Lavinia, cultivated a reputation for her lively takeoffs on Amherst neighbors.[4] The poet herself enjoyed celebrity for her mock sermons. Drama, on a small scale, was a feature of Dickinson life; and acting was one of Dickinson's many kinds of serious play, especially when it helped her to work out the drama of her own heart, "Only Theatre recorded / Owner cannot shut—" (P 741).

One of the things distinguishing young Emily Dickinson from her schoolmates was her enduring commitment to play. Even in her early twenties she wrote to her brother (then in law school), "I wish we were children now. I wish we were *always* children, how to grow up I dont know" (L 115). Adulthood threatened her with a share in her father's "*real life*," so different from what she called "*mine*" (L 65). In her own way, she clung to that glory and gleam of infancy that Wordsworth premised in his immortality ode. Childhood, for him, represents a transitional point between that unity with the world (undifferentiated merging of the infant's identity with the mother and through her with the universe) that gives comfort to infancy and the somber reflectiveness of adult life with its philosophical rather than sensate relationship to the not-me. In sections VII and VIII of the ode, Wordsworth introduces his "six years' Darling of a pigmy size!" as the "best Philosopher," still delightedly discovering life.[5] No longer simply seeing, hearing, feeling like the infant, however, this preschool child devotes his energies to mimetic action, enacting adult situations ("A wedding or a festival, / A mourning or a funeral") and presenting "all the Persons, down to palsied Age, / That Life brings with her in her equipage." Play serves as prelude to adult responsibility, and the poet wishes he could spare the child this entrance into care-burdened maturity.

Dickinson, clinging to play even after maturing her "philosophic mind," used mimesis to reverse this thrust toward adulthood in an attempt to retain the abundant options discovered by the sporting boy. She played with alternative roles that fate or custom had closed to her, exploring the potential of other lives apparently richer or more powerful; "I play at Riches—to appease /

The Clamoring for Gold——" (P 801), she wrote in a poem dealing
with private drama as an alternative to want. Living vicariously
through other lives relieved the pressure of her own limitation and
deprivation; it allowed her to imagine power, even perhaps prepare for it. She claimed that this outlet—essentially derived from
her empathic experience in reading—had saved her from such
burglary in reaction to deprivation as she had startled Higginson
by envisaging in "I know some lonely Houses off the Road" (P
289). Dickinson used her imagination to borrow other lives,
choosing roles that compensated for the powerless self-image she
so habitually constructed for herself. Her mimetic experimentation began early in her poetic career and continued throughout,
reaching its climax in the early 1860s—a period when it seems
especially risky to assume subjective self-revelation in her poems.

In view of Wordsworth's observations about the function of
play and Dickinson's own explicit longing for delayed maturity,
evident in her observation that a young friend "is more of a
woman than I am, for I love so to be a child" (L 39), it can hardly
prove surprising that the child role was the one she adopted most
regularly. On first thought, it seems an intensification of her self-
image as small and vulnerable. Yet a child has paradoxical powers
derived from its very lack of development—including the advantage of seemingly limitless potential. The child of either sex is free
to play any adult role: mother, father, fireman, cowboy, nurse,
president, circus star. Nothing has been defined, excluded. And
the child, still ignorant of social conventions, remains free to raise
disturbing questions and to make outrageous statements—free
even to address God as "Burglar! Banker—Father!" (P 49). Christian tradition called attention to the child's acceptability before
God in a way that prompted Dickinson's scathing comment on
her respectable neighbors: "I meet some octogenarians—but men
and women seldomer, and at *longer* intervals—'little children,' of
whom is the 'Kingdom of Heaven.' How tiny some will have to
grow, to gain admission there!" (L 190). It took death to stimulate
such reverse growth in her father to the point that, as a corpse, he
could accept Santa Claus's ornament for his grave (L 425). His
daughter, by contrast, resisted growing up (as the world saw it)
or rather down (from the perspective she claimed to share with
Jesus). Power and dominion belong to the small. Given this topsy-
turvy theory of growth (theoretically shared with her society's

sentimentalists but in practice disregarded in contemporary child-rearing), Dickinson delighted in reversing adult-child authority roles. She enjoyed dubbing the toddler Ned "My little Uncle" or "Little Brother" and signing herself as "His Niece," terming herself at one time his "most little Aunt" and soon after his "boundless Aunt," even violating yet another logical category by calling herself "Uncle Emily" (L 291; 398; 526; 315). To a child, *her* child anyway, all things are potential. Identifying her childhood with her nephew's, she claimed to share his total perspective by reporting to the lad—in disgrace for stealing a pie—that "Mother told me when I was a Boy, that I must 'turn over a new Leaf'—I call that the Foliage Admonition—" (L 571). And turn over new leaves she did, many of which might more properly have been expected to grow on entirely different trees.

Dickinson's child role, particularly its boyish variant, has attracted considerable critical and psychological interest, especially with reference to social constrictions on a middle-class, nineteenth-century girl.[6] Yet the boy personae she adopted experienced comparable problems to those of the girl restrained from climbing a fence toward strawberries by fear of staining her apron (P 251). In many ways all children were similar, and Dickinson shared Mark Twain's preference for the naughty and venturesome members of either sex—those who pull off their stockings to wade in a stream forbidden to "Boy that lived for 'Ought to'" (P 1545). Still, don't Dickinson's boys enjoy power and privilege denied to her girls? Yes, but one wonders why readers assume that girls would welcome the consequences of such liberty. The barefoot boy in "A narrow Fellow in the Grass" (P 986) tells of his summer adventures beyond the fence of the family farm. Unlike Whittier's idyllic representative of rural boyish freedom, however, this one stoops to pick up a whiplash for sport only to discover it a writhing snake that freezes him in terror. Remembering his horror, he still finds himself as an adult experiencing "Zero at the Bone—" in the presence of such reptiles. A similar misadventure befalls the children of "Sweet is the swamp with its secrets," (P 1740), who betake themselves from a snake ("summer's treason") "At that enthralling gallop / That only childhood knows." Free to stroll around the neighborhood, another boy-speaker gets to alarm himself with a view of the undertaker and the sight of a discarded mattress that arouses his fear of corpses (P 389). When she gathered "A narrow Fellow in the Grass" into set 6 of her poems, Dickinson placed it immediately after "When I have seen the Sun emerge" (P 888), which concludes its comparison of solar and terrestrial glory with the comment that "The Earth has seemed to me a Drum, / Pursued of little Boys." Boys may have better opportunities than girls, then; but in the cosmic sense the differences hardly matter.

Commentary on Dickinson's boy role tends to focus on the discrepancy between young Emily's position in the family and Austin's, with less attention given to the literary images of boyish life that extended her immediate observation beyond her home. Hence, little attention is paid to the many poems in which she introduces pitiful urchin-waifs, reminiscent of Fagin's boys or the miserable pupils in Dotheboys Hall. "Trudging to Eden, looking backward," (P 1020), however, makes overt reference to one of Dickens's appealing orphans, David Copperfield, whose childhood (as all admirers of Victorian fiction well know) was a troubled one—characterized by the isolation, hunger, and homelessness Dickinson arrogated to herself in the poems of limitation and deprivation. His story had a happy ending ultimately, but the happiness followed upon desperation. The poet generalizes from David's experiences in the poem immediately following, in which she presents "the Heavenly Father" leading "the Little One predestined / To the Native Land" through briars and brambles, yanked onward "Oftener by the Claw of Dragon / Than the Hand of Friend" (P 1021). Childhood, from this perspective, appears grueling even for the elect. Other poems introduce similarly Dickensian urchins (always boys) whose freedom to move about in the world is simply the consequence of their abandonment to it. Such waifs appear in "The Hollows round His eager Eyes" (P 955), "I cried at Pity—not at Pain—" (P 588), "He told a homely tale" (P 763), and "The Beggar Lad—dies early—" (P 717). Many of Dickinson's boy figures appear as outcasts in need of the domestic protection and nurture from which her girl figures were less likely to be exiled. In playing boyish roles or fantasizing reveries about their excursions into the world, Dickinson demonstrated to herself that the power boys seemed to enjoy was a sadly mixed blessing. If she were to play seriously at riches, she would have to experiment with other roles—adult ones.

Perhaps status rather than gender or youth would offer escape

from limitation, deprivation, and powerlessness. One of the striking features of Dickinson's poetry is its regal diction—borrowed
in part from the Bible but more obviously from British literature
and even fairy tales. Kings, queens, dukes, and earls populate her
poems; crowns and gems ornament their dominions. The language resonates with imperial splendor.[7] Noticeably absent are
any of those American terms of distinction to which a patriot
might aspire—to which her father *did* aspire. Although her letters
introduce us to presidents, governors, lieutenant governors, pro-
fessors, and judges, Dickinson's poems offer a more traditional
and aristocratic hierarchy, and she is as likely to present herself to
us in a queen's role as in any lesser one. The distinction, she dem-
ocratically assures us in "I met a King this afternoon!" (P 166), is a
matter of appearances, a question of receptivity to royal vision.
There is a typically confident American ring to this humorous
poem with its delightful elevation of the common lad but a more
profound democratic impulse to "Wait till the Majesty of Death"
(P 171), also in fascicle 8, which stresses the equalizing aspect of
death—not for Dickinson the great leveler so much as the common ennobler. In "The Court is far away—" (P 235), written at
about the same time, Dickinson presents herself as the frightened
subject who has offended her earthly monarch and implores his
mercy just as he will "one day—a Child—" implore a larger boon
from God, in whose empire czars will find themselves as helpless
as she does now. Dickinson remains conscious of the arbitrariness
of rank as she explores the interchange between her powerful and
powerless characters, and she recognizes also the subjective self-
esteem that underlies power and can tolerate its wide diffusion:
"Who Court obtain within Himself / Sees every Man a King—"
(P 803).

What about her tendency to see herself as a queen or an earl, her
two favorite titles? Whenever we know anything of the titled persona's background, we find that she has recently been elevated to
dignity. The notion of coronation delighted Dickinson, even in
the American context in which she identified it with ordination,
as in this comment on Abby Wood Bliss's missionary husband:
"Mr Bliss' *Coronation* takes place tomorrow, at the College church.
Charge to the Heathen, by the Pastor! Front seats reserved for
Foreign Lands!" (L 180). This statement captures the drama of the
change even while shadowing forth the typology of earthly and

heavenly crowns. Both served her as visible evidence of election. "He put the Belt around my life—" (P 273), a poem in which she fantasizes herself a newly invested earl, builds upon this religious parallel to associate coronation with conversion. The ritual of installation seems to have been a secret one in this case, unknown to the rest of the community; still it requires the gracious behavior she envisages herself displaying in "Smiling back from Coronation" (P 385). In "The Day that I was crowned" (P 356), the suddenly royal persona takes less pleasure in her change of state than in "The Grace that I—was chose—," the election that made change possible. And it is a real conversion, authentic as the centuries-long transformation of "Carbon in the Coal" to "Carbon in the Gem." The latter better suits her sudden majesty.

The idea of surprising elevation to noble rank fascinated Dickinson, who liked to imagine herself transformed into the most unlikely aristocrats: "No matter—now—Sweet—/ But when I'm Earl—/ Wont you wish you'd spoken / To that dull Girl?" (P 704). Anticipating crests, eagles, ermine, and attention, she savors the joke of her current inconspicuous status—even her feminine gender that would seem to disqualify her for this particular election. Not for a grander one, however. As Rebecca Patterson has noted, Dickinson went back to the British legend of the lord of Burleigh to provide the context for her poems on sudden coronation.[8] The heroine of that tale was a humble village maiden married to a seemingly ordinary man who escorted her after their simple wedding to his presumably modest home some distance from her village. Approaching Burleigh House after long travel, she asked who owned it—only to hear from her husband, now revealed as the tenth earl, "It is all yours, and you are the countess of Exeter." Dickinson, fantasizing herself in the role of the miller's daughter, stopped short of imagining the completion of such happiness but decided to prepare herself for yet greater splendor in case she "should be a Queen, tomorrow" and be "Summoned—unexpectedly—/ To Exeter—" (P 373). She may have derived this situation from "The Lord of Burleigh" (though not in all its particulars); in any event, she merged it with another Tennyson poem on the same theme, "The Beggar Maid," in which King Cophetua swears a royal oath to make the beautiful beggar maid his bride.[9]

Tennyson's poem takes the noble couple beyond the point of happy discovery, however, to a life led not entirely happily thereafter. Surrounded by wealth and service, blessed with an attentive husband and three children, the countess grows faint within her unaccustomed sphere and wishes her husband still the landscape painter with whom she fell in love. Upon her early death, her sympathetic consort commands that she be buried "In the dress that she was wed in, / That her spirit might have rest." No wonder that Dickinson once exclaimed of a flower: "I had rather dwell like her / Than be 'Duke of Exeter'—/ Royalty enough for me / To subdue the Bumblebee" (P 138). Aristocracy brought no promise of happiness, though evidence of change. At times she imagined herself in her suffering as "The Queen of Calvary—" (P 348), even its "Empress" (P 1072).

A striking feature of the aristocrats with whom Dickinson identified was their paradoxical powerlessness. None of them could be said to make a difference in the way a kingdom functioned; none reigned like Queen Victoria. In the one poem where such a figure faces a test, the search for a pearl, he fails (P 452). The earl, delayed in his effort by excessive forethought and doubts of his worthiness, loses the treasure to a Malay diver who springs into instant action and retrieves the treasure without ever suspecting its value. Aristocracy, whether designated by masculine or feminine titles of rank, provided Dickinson no actual, immediate power even though it typified that endowment of grace which even beggars and lawyers' daughters could anticipate in heaven.

There was another status to which Dickinson could have aspired within the normal progression of a woman's life—that of a bride who reigns in the popular understanding as a sort of queen-for-a-day. This would have been the goal toward which her culture directed her and one she could observe in practice through her friends as well as read about in books. The group of bridal poems clustered in the period from 1860 to 1862 testifies to her curiosity about this role and her willingness to test vicariously to learn whether marriage could assuage her feelings of loneliness and inadequacy. Several poems suggested that it could, indeed, provide that "State—Endowal—Focus—" (P 489) she elsewhere associated with heaven. In "The World—stands—solemner—to me—" (P 493), her most serene report on bridal elevation, she established a close imagistic connection between marriage and regal accession. In both cases, the wonder of the change was the fact of being chosen—the sense of election.

Dickinson's first bridal poem, "I'm 'wife'—I've finished that—"
(P 199), directly identifies marriage as the point of severance between childhood ("the Girl's life") and aristocratic power. She
claims a new identity, oddly described: "I'm Czar—I'm 'Woman'
now—." Observe the quotation marks around "Woman"—a more
unbelievable status than the masculine imperial role she links with
it. The speaker feels a strangeness in her new role, supposes that
her girlhood meant pain if this condition is comfort—just as
earthly life will feel deficient by contrast with heaven. A sense of
satisfaction dominates, impressing the reader with the apparent
sufficiency of marital bliss to correct earlier limitation; but the ter-
minal line "I'm 'Wife'! Stop there!" abruptly cuts off speculation
about later happiness. Later, in "I am ashamed—I hide—" (P 473),
Dickinson presents us with a timorous bride persona, apprehensive of coping adequately with her new privileges. "So late a
Dowerless Girl—," she has no idea how to behave in her new
station: how to adorn herself in cashmere fabrics, how to style her
hair for regal ornamentation, how to deport herself with aristocratic grace. She wishes for a complete transformation of character
to suit her new state and prays for an attitude "too proud—for
Pride—." Like Tennyson's countess of Burleigh, this speaker feels
out of place with her new glory even though marriage itself hardly
strikes one as equivalent to coronation. For Dickinson, it *was*
. equivalent in that it represented a radical transition from one state,
one identity, to another. As with any interchange of values, marriage entailed great risk, as she noted in the mercantile, contractual
language of "I gave myself to Him—" (P 580) in which marriage
figures as an investment in which either partner might be hurt.
Relatively late among her bridal poems, this one expresses doubt
about the bride-speaker's own value (her ability to satisfy her
"Purchaser's" expectations). Given the element of "Mutual—
Risk—" entailed in this transaction, she also suggests doubts
about the bridegroom's value.

A truism about Dickinson's bridal poems is that the groom is
missing. He figures only as the one who has chosen the bride-
queen and accorded her status. This makes sense if one thinks of
these poems as experiments in role playing rather than as fantasies
of a particular relationship with a specific lover. The poet could
get the feel of bridal status without fleshing out the wedding party
in her fantasies. A bride reigns more or less alone—briefly. To

envisage marital life, however, calls for a sense of routine inter-change, and that in turn requires a more fully developed husband figure. It is the lack of such a fictive person that makes Dickinson's few projections of married life so shadowy. Like the novelists who end their volumes with a wedding, she offered only sketchy pic-tures of the bride's ongoing involvement with the man who chose her, crowned her, severed her from girlhood in a manner that al-lowed for no return. Do Dickinson's marriage projections prove the bridal moment worth the sacrifice? Perhaps, but they offer a mixed picture. In "Doubt Me! My Dim Companion!" (P 275), the wife reminds her husband of "the Life—/ Poured thee, without a stint—/ The whole of me—forever—" and wonders what else she can offer him to satisfy his desires. Calling him "Caviler" in the last line, she evinces a loss of respect for this husband in reaction against his questioning of her. The mutual risk here seems more obvious than in the bridal poems.

Two troubling poems suggest an illusory quality to marriage and report variously on disappointment. The speaker of the first is a male persona, a bridegroom who has lost his ghostly bride after "Her sweet Weight on my Heart a Night / Had scarcely deigned to lie—" (P 518). She has vanished like a dream, in a way that makes him wonder whether he has simply imagined her or whether (so uncertain has he become of his senses and conscious-ness) she has created him in her dream. Had the wedding night ever occurred? Had the bride been translated, like Dickinson's fan-tasy of young Mrs. Ford? Had the groom encountered a celestial visitant, as Keats's Endymion did, or been betrayed by another *belle dame sans merci*? Had there been a bride at all?

The opposite question—Had there been a groom?—comes to mind in reading "Ourselves were wed one summer—dear—" (P 631), another strange reflection on marriage. The reader, expect-ing the "dear" to refer to a spouse, learns with surprise that a woman addresses these lines to another woman, another "queen." She compares their marital experiences, stressing her sister's ad-vantages in two references to the other woman's June wedding, presumably a timely one—a fittingly festive celebration. The June bride has withdrawn to a typical honeymoon abode, surrounded by flowers. Here we have the sentimental quintessence of idyllic marriage. But what of the speaker? When did she marry? That same summer, we learn, but at the end and apparently hastily.

Why did she marry? Evidently to imitate the June bride. When her companion's "little Lifetime," presumably her girlhood, "failed" or ended (a startlingly negative way to represent matrimony), the speaker "wearied" of her own and allowed herself to be "overtaken" by "Some one" in the darkness—imagery more suggestive of rape than courtship. Receiving the "Sign" she wanted as her equivalent of the more fortunate bride's, she entered into a new life, but her cottage apparently stood on an icy island, so that her garden—sown in frosts—could only remain sterile. Despite the affectionate introductory address, then, and the seeming pleasure in the other's good fortune, the speaker of this poem is frustrated. She blames her hardship—her abrupt transition from queen to shivering drudge—on the other woman, who had acted out the presumably normative wifely role and thereby enticed her into it. A bitter poem, it expresses Dickinson's resistance to the implications of bridal.

On the other hand, the poet's presentations of marriage tended for the most part to be more attractive in a sentimental vein—to fantasize the June bride's idyll rather than her September sister's misery. "I learned—at least—what Home could be—" (P 944) tells of the speaker's discovery through some sort of experience (reading *Aurora Leigh*, perhaps, and fantasizing the heroine's afterlife with Romney?) of the satisfactions to be gained in a quiet domestic routine. She envisages the couple, herself and spouse, by their fireside and in their garden. She thinks of them balancing a little work with their recreation, though of a sort that makes the usual hierarchical sexual distinctions between the husband's "Problem [or "labor"]—of the Brain" and the wife's "Ruffle ["Thimble"]— or a Tune—," denigrated as "some foolisher effect." Nor will they confine their happiness selfishly but will venture forth in the evening to minister to less fortunate neighbors, returning home at night for more intimate seclusion. Yet Dickinson concludes the poem by identifying it as purely a reverie.

> This seems a Home—
> And Home is not—
> But what that Place could be—
> Afflicts me—as a Setting Sun—
> Where Dawn—knows how to be—

A slightly earlier poem, "She rose to His Requirement—dropt /

The Playthings of Her Life" (P 732), examines another woman's experience for vicarious review of a conventionally successful marriage. What did it mean for a wife to rise to her husband's requirements—presumably the sexual ones Susan Gilbert evidently felt inadequate to during her engagement to Austin Dickinson as well as the steady domestic routine of housework?[10] To judge from the imagery of this poem and its elegiac tone, it meant loss: of girlhood, play, possibility, and wonder. The wife, however, accepts the result of her marital investment as quietly as the woman in "No Notice gave She, but a Change" (P 804) accepted death in a poem Dickinson included in the same fascicle.

Bridal, then, might mean glory; marriage—even at its sentimental best—assuredly did not. What, then, if one were to substitute a special kind of alliance, one that need not entail actually living with the groom within this life? Given Dickinson's sense of contrast between the bride and the wife, it seems reasonable to have speculated on optional possibilities such as secret union with the beloved (endowal and focus without the state) and celestial marriage (taking advantage of eternity's perpetual now of bliss in distinction to earth's diurnal monotony). This is the condition she celebrated in "Title divine—is mine!" (P 1072), a poem she sent to Samuel Bowles and later to Susan—evidently an imaginative working-out of a situation she thought she could sustain. Within the relationship she describes—perhaps purely a matter of fantasy—she can act out the bride role in private, imitating the self-conscious behavior of the new wife and savoring her bridal status. With neither the "Sign" that represents public acknowledgment of her union nor the "swoon" of sexual consummation, she relishes her secret title. She, too, has been chosen; and that is the primary joy of marriage. She, too, is regal, although presiding over sacrifice. She still has the childish advantages of play and possibility even when playing at marriage.

Obviously the playing-out of secret marriage in her poetic fantasies could hardly be so detailed as her pictures of more ordinary wedlock. There would be no domesticity, scarcely any continuing contact with the groom. Nor would such contact be predictably serene. A poem undated by Johnson but assigned by Franklin to an 1861 grouping reflects her early awareness of the tension that could develop between secretly plighted lovers. The man might question her fidelity, raise doubts about the continuing validity of their imagined marriage.

> Rearrange a "Wife's" affection!
> When they dislocate my Brain!
> Amputate my freckled Bosom!
> Make me bearded like a man!
>
> Blush, my spirit, in thy Fastness—
> Blush, my unacknowledged clay—
> Seven years of troth have taught thee
> More than Wifehood ever may!
>
> Love that never leaped its socket—
> Trust entrenched in narrow pain—
> Constancy thro' fire—awarded—
> Anguish—bare of anodyne!
>
> Burden—borne so far triumphant—
> None suspect me of the crown,
> For I wear the "Thorns" till *Sunset*—
> Then—my Diadem put on.
>
> Big my Secret but it's *bandaged*—
> It will never get away
> Till the Day its Weary Keeper
> Leads it through the Grave to thee.
> (P 1737)

Although this poem has been read as an allegory of Dickinson's hidden poetic identity that would be revealed after her death to the wonderment of readers who would feel compelled to "rearrange" her sexuality by recognizing her presumably masculine creative powers,[11] I read it as a dramatic monologue addressed by a secretly pledged "wife" to her skeptical "husband" who may even be trying to escape from their tie by questioning her continued love. Denying the possibility of change in her feelings, she exclaims that he would have to transform her utterly—unsex her, in fact—to alter her commitment. Far from expressing a desire for male traits, she sketches the metamorphosis in grotesque detail. Only if hacked to pieces and recombined as a manikin corpse would she betray her lover. She asserts that she has sustained seven years (biblically, any very long time) of betrothal, learning through all her being (flesh and spirit) the meaning of marriage. No wife could know so much nor suffer so profoundly for her loyalty. The anger that spits out the first stanza of this poem softens into pride thereafter in her achievement and modulates in the end into confidence in her celestial triumph when the marriage will be recognized in heaven and the lovers eternally joined.

Complex feelings reveal themselves here in a poem that demonstrates Dickinson's awareness of the pain that comes from secret marriage in which the wife lacks the settled security of "Forever at His side to walk—" (P 246) or the ecstatic sense of safety after peril in "Wild Nights—Wild Nights!" (P 249), both collected in this fascicle. Acknowledged marriage might offer such protection in life's storms; secret marriage could not. Neither of the conjugal situations she fantasized offered assured release from her vulnerability, although her imagination obviously emphasized the appeal of having a stronger, complementary figure to exalt the timid Dickinsonian persona by choosing her and according her a status that typified election.

If Dickinson assigned herself roles to test the possibilities of apparently fuller lives and spun out stories involving other figures in situations she somehow found attractive to her imagination, we may reasonably expect to discover her compensating through fantasy for the inadequacies she sensed in herself. When frustrated by restrictions on girls, she played at being a boy. When mortified by her apparent nonentity, she crowned herself a queen. When consigned to probable spinsterhood, she acclaimed herself a bride. Yet the limitations of Higginson's "virgin recluse" seem to have involved her sexual deprivation much less than her withdrawal from the nonfamilial world. When one reflects upon her isolated life and her peculiarly shrinking habits in midlife and later, one recognizes how tightly Emily Dickinson circumscribed her options in every sphere but imagination. Hence one would expect to find her using her imagination to open a path beyond the Homestead, and she did so most emphatically. Far more numerous than her boy or bridal poems are those fantasies in which the persona figures as a traveler—sometimes on a quest, sometimes simply wandering. As the place names in her poems demonstrate, Dickinson loved geography and found the world fascinating—particularly its exotic reaches. As her letters and some of her poems show, she followed with interest the various voyages of exploration by which nineteenth-century Americans and Europeans were mapping and apparently subduing the globe (even here, however, she paid more attention to the 1847 disappearance of Sir John Franklin on his Arctic expedition and on his wife's consequent search for him than she did to successful explorations).

The poet seemed curiously unmoved by the great westward migration of her countrymen, perhaps feeling threatened by Austin's occasional impulses to seek his fortune in Illinois or Michigan. There is no evidence that Dickinson envied the pioneers; one gets quite the contrary impression from her comment on the family's move from Pleasant Street back to the Homestead: "It is a kind of *gone—to—Kansas* feeling, and if I sat in a long wagon, with my family tied behind, I should suppose without doubt I was a party of emigrants!" (L 182). Not to Kansas but to more exotic places did she venture in her imagination—up Alps, across deserts, through jungles, and most often, in the time-honored tradition of restless New England youth, off to sea. She captured the thrill of adventure in "Exultation is the going / Of an inland soul to sea, / Past the houses—past the headlands—/ Into deep Eternity—" (P 76). Mountain-born, she had always been sheltered by the maternal swells of land in which Amherst was cradled. The sea represented boundlessness compared to envelopment, danger as distinct from safety, and eternity as distinguished from time. For her the ocean represented the unknown and always suggested death. Yet there could be a heady thrill in meeting the challenge—a thrill whose complex nature is suggested by two poems she attached to this one: "I never hear the word 'escape' / Without a quicker blood," (P 77) and "Going to Heaven!" (P 79). If she could venture beyond the shore, she could overcome all other boundaries.

Still, there were constrictions other than the mountains to wall her in and curb whatever venturesome spirit the Dickinson persona could muster. One was the habit of obedience that included fidelity to parental cautions against anything that might injure the sheltered daughter or even cause her discomfort. In "Is Bliss then, such Abyss," (P 340) the child-speaker yearns to set forth into the world but finds that the happiness she seeks requires fording a barrier—either swamp or stream. Will she risk her shoe to accomplish a goal? Clearly she knows her concern is trivial; freedom outvalues clothing. But when brain and foot collide, the foot determines the issue: "Verdict for Boot!" As a venturer after pleasure and self-satisfaction, then, Dickinson presents herself as a failure.

When travel was interpreted as quest, however, Dickinson's fantasy projected more earnest effort—sometimes successful, sometimes not. Her quest poems show the speaker encountering prodigious obstacles to reach unspecified goals. Occasionally she identifies the objects of her travel: to meet Mrs. Browning (P 363); to find her way home (P 207); to get to heaven (P 279). She plays explicitly with the conventional pilgrim metaphor for human life and confesses mixed feelings about the purported journey, not really believing herself bound for heaven but grateful that the loved ones she buried *did* believe it and have presumably reached their desired haven (P 79). As one examines Dickinson's travel poems as a whole, it develops that travel is always a metaphor for pilgrimage and that the goal is forever beyond mortal circumference.

Given the awesome implications of journeying for Emily Dickinson, she naturally stressed the attendant dangers and raised questions whether the goal justified the risks. One poem draws an implicit analogy between a little Arctic flower oddly transplanted to an alien climate blessed with "continents of summer" and "firmaments of sun" and herself venturing into Eden (P 180). Habituated to an austere environment, the flower may perish in the biologically hostile tropic atmosphere. And what about herself? Will she be comfortable in Paradise? She leaves the question open: "What then? Why nothing, / Only, your inference therefrom!" The flower, described only as "wandering down the Latitudes," undertook a complex journey. Its fragile human analogue found dangers along her way: burdocks clawing at her gown, bogs defiling her shoes (P 229), all the horrors of an animistic, threatening nature (P 9).[12] Even when she distanced herself from the misery by narrating the adventures of other—presumably stronger— characters, as in "Two Travellers perishing in Snow" (P 933), Dickinson evaded full-scale tragedy in her account only by offering heavenly recompense for mortal agony. Her travel narratives offer little incentive for wayfaring.

Most disturbing of all are the ocean voyages that allegorize man's entry into cosmic mystery. Fascinating but fatal, the ocean beckons her characters. One, a little girl, ventures hopefully to-

ward the sea—accompanied by her dog, who offers protection
only against terrene enemies (P 520). The sea that they visit as
friends proves both malevolent and animistic. Mermaids cajole the
little venturer; frigates reach out hands to drag her in. Worst of
all, the sea pursues her so that she no longer controls the visit but
is herself attacked and forced to seek refuge in the town. Helpless
against natural force (figured here even as sexually abusive), the
venturesome child discovers her finitude. Another Dickinson persona, this one a merchant-speculator, stands safely on the shore,
wondering what fate befalls the ship to which she has entrusted
her hopes (P 52). More often we discover the speaker aboard the
vessel. One finds herself swept up in a tumultuously uncontrolled
journey and trusts to a divine helmsman for safe passage just as
she notes other navigators doing in life's pilgrimage (P 10). Another, like Noah, keeps releasing her dove to seek out land on a
globe awash with mortality (P 48). Reference to the bird by its
Latin name, "Columba," reinforces biblical hope with historical
evidence for safe travel.

But a startling number of Dickinsonian vessels end in shipwreck. Four sailors survive in "Glee—The great storm is over—"
(P 619); forty drown. Raised in New England—even though inland, Dickinson would have heard shipwreck tales like Longfellow's "The Wreck of the Hesperus," about a famous catastrophe
off the Cape Ann coast—near where Lavinia went to school in
Ipswich and close to Judge Lord's Salem home. Hawthorne, also
a Salem man and the descendant of generations of sea captains,
summoned to her mind images of weird ocean happenings (L 542).
Even Ik Marvel described an ocean storm with vivid drama, emphasizing a sailor's drowning and the narrator's desperate efforts
to save him.[13] Typically, Dickinson's boats resemble her speakers
in their smallness and fragility. One is "A little boat adrift!" (P 30),
another a toddling "little—little boat," (P 107), another but "A
little Brig I knew—" (P 723). All are lost, sunk into an ocean un-
disturbed by grief. In human perspective, she tells us, the ship-
wrecks are tragic; not so from an angelic point of view by which
the same craft that to sailors' eyes "gurgled down and down" may
be seen to have "Retrimmed it's masts—redecked it's sails—/ And
shot—exultant on!" (P 30). No such exultation attends the victim
of this grim tale of nature's destructiveness and man's mortal insignificance:

> The waters chased him as he fled,
> Not daring look behind;
> A billow whispered in his Ear,
> "Come home with me, my friend;
> My parlor is of shriven glass,
> My pantry has a fish
> For every palate in the Year,"—
> To this revolting bliss
> The object floating at his side
> Made no distinct reply.
>
> (P 1749)

Less fortunate than the little girl and her dog who manage to reach the town in safety, this poor soul is offered a merman's paradise instead of the heaven Dickinson generally suggested for her voyager-victims, and he winds up himself an object and probable food for fishes. Better to have stayed at home.

Except for the emblematic and unavoidable journey of the soul toward God, Dickinson's fantasies of travel gave her no more incentive than did her biographically documented excursions to seek fulfillment through motion (L 54). As with the other experiments in role playing she tried concurrently, this one reinforced her tendency to accept and welcome limitations—to prefer the problems she identified in her life to those she might encounter in pushing toward growth and power. By extending her life imaginatively into the swamp, the court, the bridal chamber, and even the depths of the sea, she repeatedly justified her innate tendency toward constriction. There were more congenial roles for her to play, though not on the surface such appealing ones.

As is already obvious, the stories Emily Dickinson fabricated for herself in testing alternative ways of satisfying desires for growth and fulfillment were overwhelmingly unhappy ones—not necessarily tragic, often melodramatic. If she had elaborated them into full-scale narratives, even Marvelian reveries or Hawthornesque sketches, we would quickly recognize them as examples of sentimental and gothic fiction. When Clark Griffith called attention to the "eminently public literary convention" in which Dickinson wrote, even in articulating her seemingly personal griefs, he pointed to her cultural context.[14] More recent studies, especially those focused on the reading and writing habits of Victorian women, encourage examination of her poetry in terms of the conventions seized upon by others of her era to give voice to their hidden conflicts by creating characters who would act out their fantasies and help them to create new, stronger selves. Whether in sentimental fiction, which idealized sufferers and offered the comfort of compassion, or in gothic fiction, which both evoked and expressed fears while providing an outlet for psychological conflict, writers could distance themselves from troubling aspects of their psyches by impelling fantasized characters into imagined crises.[15] Although distinctly more overt in prose fiction than in lyric poetry, this strategy can be recognized in Dickinson's work.

In considering the poet's relationship to her literary context, we must consider the ways in which several of her poems reenact situations she would have remembered from her reading, such as the passages from *Aurora Leigh* and *Jane Eyre*, from which Dickinson is said to have borrowed.[16] The poet probably did dwell on the plights of fictive characters and fantasize how it would feel to face such crises, wonder how she might herself react. Active readers do so, and some of the more imaginative of them create new literature out of their originally derivative fantasies. One of the remarkable features of Victorian novels—verse ones like *Aurora Leigh* as well as prose ones—was their capacity to stay with characters through a succession of traumatic incidents, watching the growth or decay of personality through a succession of tests. The most memorable incidents tended to be sad ones: deaths, betrayals, renunciations, unhappy discoveries. With or without happy endings, the narratives struck the imagination most strongly with the possibilities of sorrow—possibilities to which Dickinson was already well attuned. In her poems she seems to have tried out some of the literary miseries life had denied her, as when she fantasized blindness in "Before I got my eye put out" (P 327) and again in "Had we our senses" (P 1284) in apparent attempts to experience vicariously the sufferings of both Rochester and Romney.

Dickinson derived narrative contexts for her fantasies from lyric poems also. Anderson's citation of the Tennyson poem "Love and Duty" as a probable source for "There came a Day at Summer's full," (P 322) alerts us to be vigilant for fictive aspects of even those poems most often interpreted autobiographically.[17] We know that Dickinson remembered "Love and Duty"; she quoted its opening line in one of her letters (L 801). And she would have found Tennyson's approach to the story of lovers meeting only to renounce each other both moving and imitable. She too wondered "What sequel?" might follow "love that never found his earthly close" in speculating on lovers forced to hope for heavenly recompense.[18] The religious sense is stronger than the moral in Dickinson's poem, unlike Tennyson's; the forms vary, but the concentration on one climactic interview is shared, as is the awareness of change in each person's future life—preferably the growth in character that comes of transcended sorrow and strengthened will. Perhaps Dickinson did, indeed, have such a dramatic meeting with a lover, as various biographers have tried to argue on the basis of slim evidence beyond this poem; if not, she had no need of direct experience to supplement what she read. The feelings in her poems could be authentic and the tensions real even within a borrowed context.

Given her profound concern with smallness, limitation, and deprivation, it was only natural for Dickinson to make early and ardent use of the sentimental literary conventions then dominating literature for and by women. Characters such as her vulnerable personae populated sentimental narratives that focused attention on weak, innocent figures. The assumptions underlying this literature were that such persons required protection from life's assaults. They were best off in sheltered environments leading tranquil lives of quiet contentment. Home was presumed to be the bastion of security for those not strong enough to battle the callousness and even the sin of the outside world. Dickinson's writings, especially her early letters, reflect an acceptance of these unaspiring values. Contemptuous of big cities, she prefers country life and urges her brother home to the simple joys of brown bread and the orchard (L 45; 53; 60). She celebrates home: "Home is a holy thing—nothing of doubt or distrust can enter it's blessed portals. I feel it more and more as the great world goes on and one and another forsake, in whom you place your trust—here seems indeed to be a bit of Eden which not the sin of *any* can utterly destroy" (L 59). And in her poems she often holds up a domestic ideal of human peace. The housewife in "The Night was wide, and furnished scant" (P 589) sits in snug indoor comfort through a tumultuous winter storm, shivering vicariously for the poor outside but commenting contentedly to her husband (represented only as "the Sofa opposite—") how much she prefers even winter in his company to May without him. "It's thoughts—and just One Heart—" (P 495) reinforces this sense of the adequacy of modest domestic pleasures, just as the speaker of "Although I put away his life—" (P 366) fantasizes a love-in-a-cottage idyll although she has renounced the man who might have offered her so cozy a haven.

Disasters in sentimental fiction are those that disrupt such simple bliss by detaching vulnerable characters from the security of home somehow (orphanhood, rejection, loss of home to debt or drink), by depriving the family of those who represent its heart (chiefly mothers, small children, and maiden daughters), or by destroying the basis of domestic harmony (through romantic betrayals and abandonments). The plots of such stories are pathetic; the emotions they seek to arouse tender ones: pity, compassion, benevolence, indignation against cruelty. Dickinson's poems—especially the earliest—made overt use of these conventions, familiar to her from the sentimental literature she admired and attractive to her security-seeking temperament. The worry about being forsaken that she mentioned in the paean to home just cited caused her, in private life, to cling desperately to her family—living as a protected child until her death. Both in letters and in "I should not dare to leave my friend," (P 205) she expressed fear of leaving home lest someone sicken or die there without her attendance (L 86; 166). She liked to imagine herself as a nurse or an angel of mercy. And the mercy would be extended most readily to the weak persons so dear to sentimental writers—to aged parents, to children, and to forsaken souls like the one she comforts in "Poor little Heart!" (P 192). Her obsession with smallness and dependence led her to project family life in intensely sentimental terms.

Having reviewed Dickinson's poems on limitation and deprivation so extensively in chapter 3, I need hardly demonstrate here her fascination with the suffering caused when life's simple blessings of home, food, and family love are denied to a vulnerable persona—especially a child. Although occasional Dickinson characters pine for lost crowns or jewels, most of them yearn for more basic sources of security, even of survival. And she identified with characters cut off from the customary domestic comforts, such as her beggar lad and wandering waifs. Even in a poem so generally read autobiographically as "I was the slightest in the House—" (P

486), the poet may have been impersonating a sentimental victim familiar to readers of nineteenth-century fiction: the lonesome governess. At times the poet empathized with even more drastically alienated characters, like the suicide of "He scanned it—staggered—" (P 1062). Whatever this man had lost, he could not face life without it.

Characters in sentimental literature tended to die less dramatically than the suicide, going into declines instead or fading into picturesque deaths. Emphasis on weak and vulnerable characters meant that many would lose their pathetic struggles against life's harshness. In nothing was Emily Dickinson so sentimental as in the obsession with death characterizing her early poems. Some of them pay roundabout homage to the ideal of domestic bliss by citing the commonplace comforts the dead miss out on: harvests, Thanksgiving celebrations, Christmas stockings, and the ordinary comforts of farm and family. These are the values she eulogizes in "I'm sorry for the Dead—Today—" (P 529) and in "'Twas just this time, last year, I died," (P 445)—the latter spoken in the voice of a young child, thereby compounding the reader's pity by intimating the family's grief on those first holidays after their loss. "Her Sweet turn to leave the Homestead" (P 649) draws upon similar images of normal domestic happiness by comparing the young woman's funeral to a wedding celebration and gently revealing the maiden's grisly fate.

To judge by the concentration of elegies in Emily Dickinson's collected poems, one would think she had endured many losses to death. Indeed, the critic who has looked most systematically at her poems on this topic assumed that she attended at many deathbeds and watched with tender attentiveness the passing of her friends.[19] Except for Emily's 1844 visits to her dying schoolmate Sophia Holland, however, biographical evidence for such supposition is lacking.[20] The narrative in "We talked as Girls do—" (P 586) about two young friends sharing their intimate feelings and their hopes for the future only to have death suddenly interrupt their plans seems to be another of her fantasies and quite a characteristic one. Fascinated with death as that circumferential barrier between time and eternity, Dickinson read literary death scenes with avidity and sought out details to complete (or stimulate) her imaginings of deaths within her general circle of acquaintance. Her early elegies played out conventional sentimental tales. In

"Delayed till she had ceased to know—" (P 58), for instance, potentially saving news arrives too late to rescue the dying woman;
like the fragile maiden of Irving's "The Pride of the Village" who
receives her soldier-lover's apology for his betrayal too late to save
her from the churchyard, this figure slips into endless sleep. Most
of Dickinson's early elegies salute humble, frail people: the child
of "She lay as if at play" (P 369), the wife of "How many times
these low feet staggered—" (P 187), and various meek, self-effacing victims like those of "She died—*this* was the way she died." (P
150) and "Her final Summer was it—" (P 795). Their passage is
noted only in their homes or along the village street; no suggestion emerges that such lives might have an impact beyond the domestic sphere—just that cobwebs proliferate when a housewife
joins the daisies.

Death in these poems looms as inimical to the family unit that
it disrupts, but may prove a blessing to its apparent victim by
rescuing the weary, wounded, and helpless from life's challenges.
The character of "A poor—torn heart—a tattered heart—" (P 78)
is carried by angels to God after giving up an overwhelming
earthly struggle. The grave serves as protector and comforter for
"Some, too fragile for winter winds" (P 141) as for "This heart
that broke so long—" (P 145). Nor need death eliminate the family
circle. These tender hearts, sheltered now in heaven, continue to
yearn over their survivors, so that a Civil War bullet may be recognized as the happy agent of reunion for a soldier with his
mother (P 596) or the mother be presented as an immortal care-
taker of her orphan brood, as in "Mama never forgets her birds,"
(P 164), the distinctly sentimental elegy Dickinson sent to Louise
and Frances Norcross when their mother succumbed after a long
sickness. The conventionalism of these early elegies in which
Dickinson identified herself with the fragile victims or adopted the
persona of a mourner appears most starkly in the contrast between
her early elegies and those she wrote late in life, when death
robbed her directly. "Though the great Waters sleep," (P 1599),
her elegy for Judge Lord, expresses faith rather than feeling. Its
power lies in its restraint, as is true also for the great elegy she
wrote for her father three years after his death: "Lay this Laurel on
the One / Too intrinsic for Renown—/ Laurel—vail your deathless tree—/ Him you chasten, that is He!" (P 1393). No Papa bird
cooing down from heaven here! No simpering over the sufferings

of the man God chastened to make him strong. But Edward Dickinson would have been an improbable figure for sentimental elaboration.[21]

His daughter, on the other hand, recognized a vulnerability in herself that allowed her to play sentimental roles. One that appealed to her imagination was that of the declining maiden, and the reader can discover among her poems of 1858 to 1860 a cluster dealing with projections of early death. In "I hav'nt told my garden yet—" (P 50), the speaker anticipates sudden death yet feels too shrinking and meek to acknowledge her interesting status to the community—not even to the hills, garden, and bees on which in her shyness she has evidently depended for comfort. In the very next poem (written on the back of the same sheet), the speaker addresses her closest friend from within the grave (P 51). Housed now within the tiny dwelling in the burial village that she used to pass while walking home from school, she pictures her new home as a comfortable abode—one that is peaceful and attractive with its modest garden. Should "Dollie" grow weary, she offers loving welcome. Similar premonition of early death appears in a later poem in which the speaker asks someone to feed a little bird for her "If I should'nt be alive / When the Robins come," (P 182).

More enthralling than the dying maiden role, because more various in its possibilities for development and in its capacity for releasing emotion, was that of the unhappy lover. Fortunate love, as we know from novels, has comparatively little dramatic interest—perhaps the sweet thrill of mutual discovery as in "The Rose did caper on her cheek—" (P 208), the joyful tension of the wedding day as revealed in the bridal poems, and then the serene domestic idyll of Dickinson's more positive marriage poems. Unhappy love, however, entails conflicting emotions, episodes of crisis, opportunities for anticipation and regret. As I mentioned in chapter 2 when reviewing the implied narrative of Dickinson's love poems, the story they spell out is a sentimental one. Since the poet chose to write almost all poems on this theme in the first person and from the perspective of the woman, biographers try to read the poems as fairly explicit records of her own experience—thereby getting into quandaries over whether the poet and her lover had one decisive meeting, as in "There came a Day at Summer's full," (P 322), or more, as in "Again—his voice is at the door—" (P 663), and worrying about when the events described may have occurred in terms of the oblique correspondence between the author's biography and the apparent chronology of the poems.

It should be obvious by now that Dickinson was capable of playing roles outside her own experience. Two poems may conflict in narrative detail because they convey episodes in two different though closely related stories. Fortunately, no one has yet attempted to demonstrate that Dickinson ever actually drowned herself for love like the valiant speaker of "Me prove it now— Whoever doubt" (P 537), although the voice of that poem is fully as personal as that of "I got so I could hear his name—" (P 293), which has left scholars studying the Homestead floorboards in hopes of intuiting that notable angle "Where he turned so, and I turned —how—/ And all our Sinew tore—." Whether the fantasies she developed in these love poems originated directly in relationships with any man or men, they obviously grew out of a psychological need that drew the poet to literature emphasizing romantic sorrows and that inclined her to adopt the role of a suffering maiden lover.

It was a role, as I have demonstrated earlier in this study, that accommodated itself superbly to Dickinson's small and vulnerable self-image. But what sentimental literature demonstrated to her was that suffering stimulated growth, as Tennyson concluded in "Love and Duty," where the characters gradually achieve a nobleness and maturity as a result of their experience of pain. They are *not* left just with "streaming eyes and breaking hearts," though they must have undergone such grief in passing. Literature showed that frustrated love could lend glamour to an otherwise colorless life and could elevate the woman's status in particular. It was she who would be exalted by grief—and who, in most sentimental writing, would be drably contented without it. By the odd expedient of freeing the sorrowful woman from the constrictions of sentimental domesticity without requiring her rebellion against home and its values, sentimental literature allowed Dickinson to present herself as a romantic heroine. Whereas playing apparently empowering roles like boy or bride had failed to enlarge her sense of self, intensifying her own problems fictively by playing the part of a tragic lover extended her range of sensation. Stronger feelings could be distilled in that way than by pretending to happiness, and feelings were the essence of her poetry.

The soft, gentle emotions fostered by sentimental literature, nevertheless, failed to satisfy the craving for sensational experience that sent young Emily running home to "Awe" as a child rather than to maternal comforting (L 405). Although Dickinson empathized with sentimental victims of early death and romantic loss, she responded more intensely to the gothic figures she encountered in her reading. As scholars interested in Dickinson's relationship to the women's culture of her Victorian era have recently been demonstrating, this poet joined her contemporaries in assuming fictive roles that allowed her to assert suppressed aspects of her personality and that fostered expression of hidden conflicts—particularly those springing from the feminine submission to a more powerful male other that was considered normative in sentimental portrayals of family life.[22] The poet's claim about appointing "awe" her foster mother demonstrates her tendency to characterize her own domestic experience in metaphorical terms. In doing so, Dickinson often endowed her timid mother with sentimental characteristics (especially in the years of her long final sickness) and her father with the awesome gothic qualities of the mysteriously compelling stranger: "His Heart was pure and terrible and I think no other like it exists" (L 418). Her own self-image partook of both sets of conventions, though she achieved greater emotional range and stronger poetry through playing the role of gothic victim than the sentimental heroine. As a gothic figure, she could allow herself to be exceptional—not typically feminine like a meek sentimental maiden but remarkable, eccentric, perhaps menacing, or even insane. She could exploit her chosen isolation to delve into psychological depths. She could confront her fears and cry out in terror.

Like most American writers, Dickinson stressed the interior, psychological aspect of gothicism rather than its exterior trappings of haunted abbeys, spectral apparitions, and mad monks. In "One need not be a Chamber—to be Haunted—" (P 670), she directly discounted external terrors by comparison with one's own deepest capacities for self-destruction. Far more threatening than outside enemies was "Ourself behind ourself, concealed—," the sense of her own vulnerability to personal inner depths. Her fear, she said, was of "The Loneliness One dare not sound—" (P 777) that left her imprisoned in herself and vulnerable to maddening impulses almost impossible to control: "The Horror not to be sur-

veyed—/ But skirted in the Dark—/ With Consciousness sus-
pended—/ And Being under Lock—." The struggle she faced,
then, was one of self-control—trying to govern an explosive consciousness.

Sometimes it helped Dickinson to identify vicariously with
other gothic victims like the man buried alive and smothered just
at the point of rescue whom she presented in "In falling Timbers
buried—" (P 614). Even more than her sentimental narratives, the
poet's gothic tales were overwhelmingly presented in first-person
voice, thereby intensifying the drama even when she placed herself metaphorically in situations she surely never directly experienced such as this familiar example of gothic terror now enriched
by Franklin's correction of the manuscript to include Dickinson's
intended conclusion.[23]

> A Pit—but Heaven over it—
> And Heaven beside, and Heaven abroad;
> And yet a Pit—
> With Heaven over it.
>
> To stir would be to slip—
> To look would be to drop—
> To dream—to sap the Prop
> That holds my chances up.
> Ah! Pit!   With Heaven over it!
>
> The depth is all my thought—
> I dare not ask my feet—
> 'Twould start us where we sit
> So straight you'd scarce suspect
> It was a Pit—with fathoms under it
> Its Circuit just the same
> Seed—summer—tomb—
> Whose Doom to whom
>
> 'Twould start them—
> We—could tremble—
> But since we got a Bomb—
> And held it in our Bosom—
> Nay—Hold it—it is calm—
> (P 1712 / P 443)

In so precarious a situation, the speaker struggles for control, for the behavioral equivalent of calmness. In the midst of crisis, feelings must be suppressed—only to well up, of course, in the nightmarish replay of terror she describes in "That after Horror—that 'twas *us*—" (P 286) in which the soul confronts its near encounter with death, its narrow escape from the plunge "Into Conjecture's presence—." Her reference here to holding a bomb with gingerly care anticipates a later, cheerier play on the same image when she remarks with comic courage that "A Bomb upon the Ceiling / Is an improving thing—/ It keeps the nerves progressive / Conjecture flourishing—" (P 1128). Playing gothic roles offered the same advantages to one intent upon testing the limits of her nerves and intensifying all her powers of speculation.

Sometimes Emily Dickinson had to coax out her gothic imagination artificially, as in this passage from an 1859 letter to Mrs. Holland on the specters she conjured up to scare herself when her father and sister went away: "I am somewhat afraid at night, but the Ghosts have been very attentive, and I have no cause to complain. Of course one cant expect one's furniture to sit still all night, and if the Chairs do prance—and the Lounge polka a little, and the shovel give it's arm to the tongs, one dont mind such things! From fearing them at first, I've grown to quite admire them, and now we understand each other, it is most enlivening!" (L 204). More often the reader encounters Dickinson's gothic victim persona in a less picturesque situation but in a condition of essential terror—frightened by the universe because terrified of herself. "To my quick ear the Leaves—conferred—" (P 891) presents her as cowering under an overwhelming fear of nature's conspiracy against her attempts to hide: "Creation seemed a mighty Crack—/ To make me visible—." But why should she dread exposure (as her life style as well as her poems abundantly confirms that she did)? Perhaps from a sense of guilty horror—not at anything she had done but what she knew enough from her hidden rage to recognize that she might do. A lady who could feel "a Bliss like Murder—/ Omnipotent—Acute—" (P 379) had tensions to control that Ik Marvel never imagined in his innocent little Bella. But the fear of eruption itself protected her from related dangers, and she noted in "I lived on Dread—" (P 770) that her hideous gothic diet at least provided a stimulus to keep alert in dangerous situations; it prevented despair, which would have let her stumble into the pit—bomb and all.

Despite her comments on the adequacy of internal terrors, Dickinson occasionally introduced the conventional environmental horrors of gothic fiction. Her poetry abounds in stormy nights, in journeys into darkness, in sudden awakenings to alien circumstances. She mentions witchcraft and even claims to have seen a ghost (P 274). "A House upon the Hight—" (P 399) may be haunted—or may prefigure a heavenly mansion, itself haunted by an awesome spirit. In "What Inn is this" (P 115), she presents herself as a stranger venturing into an apparently comfortable hostel only to find that her weird journey has led her to the grave. Death, in these poems, looms as a perpetually disturbing presence personified as a courteous but conquering stranger who breaks down all defenses (P 390). Like the beguiling suitor of "Because I could not stop for Death—" (P 712) who bears off the Dickinson persona on a carriage ride to the grave, this "postponeless Creature" deprives its victim of that control over herself for which she has been battling in all the gothic poems.

Introducing her lover as Death, Dickinson alerts the reader to an aspect of the love poetry not explicable in sentimental terms. The male presence in the gothic poems disturbs rather than protects. Dickinson's father-master-lover figure elicits awe, terror, even rage.[24] She finds him fascinating but cruel and knows that she must somehow evade his dominance that reduces her to a condition of feminine victimization even as she gathers to herself his power. Not surprisingly, then, the "love" poems that play out her gothic romantic scenario confront us with a destructive passion like that of Heathcliff and Catherine.

The roles Dickinson enacts in playing out this passion show her as a more forceful figure than those she fantasized in her sentimental drama of renunciation. Rather than weeping farewell to her lover, she pursues him—tunneling through walls if need be (P 398). Together they defy society and the barriers it places to their love. In "They put Us far apart—" (P 474), she recounts how she and her lover have kept faith with one another through torture, dismemberment, and execution. Aware only of each other, they ignore such horrors as would normally unnerve them. Such all-consuming passion persists beyond death—not in heavenly reunion like that she had projected in "There came a Day at Summer's full," (P 322), but rather in the necrophiliac encounter of "If I may have it, when it's dead," (P 577). Like Heathcliff seizing upon Catherine's body, Madeline Usher bearing down Roderick in her deathly embrace, or Annabel Lee's lover lying down by her side in a tomb by the side of the sea, Dickinson's gothic lover plunges into death-loving madness.

Just as readers find autobiographical persuasiveness in Dickinson's sentimental love poems (not, however, in her gothic ones), they find the madness of her gothic poems convincing and persist in looking for biographical evidence to explain how she could have experienced the sensations detailed in so many poems and yet have escaped to tell about them.[25] The question she raised at the end of "The first Day's Night had come—" (P 410) with its narrative of psychological rebellion against the conscious self seems pertinent: "Could it be Madness—this?" Not if we assume, as I do, that she was enacting yet another role in this group of poems—one that allowed her to express inner turmoil and confront very real fears of internal disintegration without giving way to them. She could hold onto the bomb while working her precarious way across the pit. Those knowledgeable in gothic fiction may notice a normative aspect even to Dickinson's attempts to express and experience madness by playing the madwoman role. It was, after all, one of the conventional female parts, as witness the first Mrs. Rochester. Like the child (but even more safely), the madwoman could speak the unspeakable. Like a man, she could act violently—could burn a house down or attempt a murder. Quite probably Dickinson speculated on the uses of such freedom and its costs—acting out this role among many others to measure its capacity to empower her.

Gothic literature confronts the imaginative person with divided and conflicting selves—with masculine and feminine elements of the psyche warring against each other and with the conscious mind's compulsion for control in conflict with violent and destructive unconscious forces. Not surprisingly, madness often results from this psychological disruption. A fairly straightforward example of gothic role playing with divided personality appears in "I read my sentence—steadily—" (P 412) in which Dickinson presents herself as a condemned convict attempting to maintain psychological control in a situation of extreme terror by introducing her soul to death—maintaining civilities and thereby exercising the only power remaining to the ego. Even in assuming a distinction between self and soul, however, the speaker betrays psychological division. The chasm becomes yet more evident when the soul (in this case presumably the id) acknowledges herself already a friend of death and wanders off with this unsettling ally, abandoning the ego to annihilation—expressed in the concluding grim pun, "And there, the Matter ends—." Death triumphs here, with the unconscious mind that is its partner in a conspiracy against rational control.

Madness, in exposing the consciousness to intense, unmediated sensation, opened a world of emotional experience in Dickinson's poems that let her explore the full range of ungoverned feelings. As is evident from her presentation of manic-depressive interchanges in "The Soul has Bandaged moments—" (P 512), insanity sometimes offered welcome freedom and with it the ecstasy of escape when the soul "dances like a Bomb, abroad, / And swings upon the Hours." The rational mind warns us, of course, that a dancing bomb will explode and destroy its environment along with itself; still the tone of these stanzas on manic release overpowers even the reader's judgment to the point that one regrets the psychological bomb's forced return to captivity and horror. The "ghastly Fright" terrifying the soul in its dungeon, however, may well be a glimpse into herself and her necessarily repressed violence. In a related poem, "'Twas like a Maelstrom, with a notch," (P 414), Dickinson deftly substituted roles to leave the reader experiencing the gothic terrors of incipient psychic explosion. Escape from horror in this case proves simply a reprieve for later destruction, and the speaker of the poem questions its solace. Caught up in such terrors, she suggests, one welcomes the explosion and consequent release from feeling. Even "you," the reader, can experience such need.

Submission to terror may actually bring rewards, as Dickinson proclaims in "'Tis so appalling—it exhilirates—" (P 281), which concludes:

> Others, Can wrestle—
> Your's, is done—
> And so of Wo, bleak dreaded—come,
> It sets the Fright at liberty—

> And Terror's free—
> Gay, Ghastly, Holiday!

Exhilaration can come of madness, then—even a psychic holiday, but Dickinson's gothic poems never suggest madness as actual release from terror; they recognize it instead as an intensifier of fright by demonstrating the persona's inability to protect herself from self-destruction. Except in stages of mental numbness, madness increases pain. To that extent it expands the self's awareness of its powers but also its recognition of the need for limits upon those powers. What gothic fantasizing accomplished for Emily Dickinson was to demonstrate the explosive energy she could release by pressing in upon her limitations and exploiting her fears. The roles she played in these poems liberated her imagination far more intensely than any of her more positive dramatic experiments, but they alerted her both to the necessity of control and to the challenge of achieving it.

Choosing a life "too simple and stern to embarrass any"—a point she may have hastened to enjoin upon Higginson lest he confuse her with the often discreditable representatives of her poems (L 330)—Dickinson explained once in a poem how her curiosity about more venturesome lives led her to vicarious experimentation with the options for power and growth she conjectured as the fate of happier persons: "I think To Live—may be a Bliss / To those who dare to try—/ Beyond my limit to conceive—/ My lip—to testify—" (P 646). As is evident from her playing at riches, there proved to be few limits to her powers of either conception or articulation. She entered into fictive characters and tested their varieties of bliss—also their varieties of pain. Had she had to settle within any of these imagined lives (boy, queen, bride, sailor, languishing sentimental maiden, or hysterical gothic victim), she discovered that she would have found each as constraining as her own, but the power to move among them offered the delightful freedom that counts among the chief blessings of literary imagination.

> The Vision—pondered long—
> So plausible becomes
> That I esteem the fiction—real—
> The Real—fictitious seems—

How bountiful the Dream—
What Plenty—it would be—
Had all my Life but been Mistake
Just rectified—in Thee
(P 646)

Bounty, plenty, escape from limitation—these were the rewards Dickinson gained from vicarious participation in a remarkable range of human roles. Even though her imagination consistently emphasized the dark side of such adventures, she felt freedom and with it a confirmation of her own comparative strength. If all people were as limited as she so clearly felt herself to be and as her fantasies now proved to her that they were, there was no further need to try for growth in any of the conventional ways. Rather than pushing *beyond* herself into the world outside, she would do better to push in *upon* herself to distill her amazing psychological, imaginative, and expressive force. She would let her energy explode into poems that held tight within them both her own tensions and those she derived from borrowed lives. The challenge facing her was that of formal control

6

"My Little Force Explodes"

The Poetics of Distillation

SHORTLY AFTER appointing Higginson her "Preceptor" and supposedly vesting him with teaching authority, Emily Dickinson
confided a technical problem: "I had no Monarch in my life, and
cannot rule myself, and when I try to organize—my little Force
explodes—and leaves me bare and charred" (L 271). She may have
been reacting to some of his earlier "surgery," having already indicated that he had apparently criticized her for paying too much
attention to minor defects such as the spelling errors she readily
acknowledged while ignoring larger faults (L 261). Although Higginson could never afterward remember his specific advice, and
although his half of their correspondence mostly perished when
Lavinia burned her sister's personal papers after the poet's death,
it seems probable that the larger faults he identified were structural
problems—the same defects of organization and control some
modern readers have recognized.[1] The poems she was writing in
1862 exhibited her astonishing creative energy but sometimes betrayed problems of craftsmanship. If she recognized structure as a
problem, she may have turned to Higginson for guidance, remembering his warning in the "Letter to a Young Contributor":
"Such being the Majesty of the Art you presume to practice, you
can at least take time before dishonoring it."[2] On the other hand,
she often addressed Higginson ironically and self-defensively in
those first months of their acquaintance, and the possibility remains strong that she anticipated no such editorial help. She had
already, many times over, demonstrated her ability to organize a
poem. The problem, if she really felt one existed, was one of energy untamed—betrayed by strong beginnings that occasionally

seemed to go nowhere and by explicit organizational designs that sometimes broke down.

The most painful example of such organizational collapse may well be "I got so I could hear his name—" (p 293, quoted in full on page 25). In this case, the tight parallel construction of the opening three stanzas reinforces the sense of hard-won self-control empowering the speaker to increasingly active behavioral changes: "I got so I could hear his name—"; "I got so I could walk across / That Angle in the floor"; "I got so I could stir the Box—/ In which his letters grew." She reports a series of triumphs here, each backed by details that show how totally the speaker had involved herself—physically, emotionally, and imaginatively—in reliving the few and painful experiences of intimacy with her lover. The parallelism breaks down in the remaining three stanzas when she tries to turn to God as a substitute for the absent man. Powerful memories of the lover have obliterated images of God— introduced here as "a Grace" rather than a person. The speaker claims that she could "dimly recollect" this specter and "shape my Hands—" as though to address the unknown person in an habitual but empty action, with no language accompanying the gesture. Lack of language here reflects lack of anything to say—lack of any clear conception even of desire. And it reflects uncertainty of audience. Whereas the box of letters represented a presumably two-way communication of intimates, this pantomime of prayer represents neither speaking nor listening between beings. The total breakdown—possibly of the speaker, surely of the poem—comes in the final stanza with its unresolved pileup of phrases that fail to constitute a sentence or articulate an idea. A dangling "if" clause raises doubts about the existence of an author behind the cloud and prevents the speaker from announcing her "Business." If this speaker's "Business is Circumference," she has gone bankrupt. Here, too, Dickinson's textual variants do nothing to cope with organizational collapse but concentrate on issues of diction. Had she sent a copy of the famous poem to Higginson, his response to it might have been instructive.

But the poet did not ask such counsel. With the single exception of "Safe in their Alabaster Chambers—" (p 216), to be discussed below as an example of Susan Dickinson's editorial advice, the poems she mailed off to Worcester in the summer of 1862 were not the ones with which she is known to have struggled, nor did they exemplify structural flaws. "I'll tell you how the Sun rose—" (P 318) combines narrative and descriptive elements in clear arrangements. "We play at Paste—" (P 320) builds on comparison of familiar materials. "The nearest Dream recedes—unrealized—" (P 319) strikes the reader as well ordered, witty, and lively. If Dickinson were looking for structural help, she would have sent her mentor different poems or at least shared her poetic workshop with him as she did with Sue, to whom she showed alternative versions of "Safe in their Alabaster Chambers—" while she sent only one (the strongest) to Higginson. Johnson's variorum edition of Dickinson's poems shows a heavy concentration of alternatives and revisions in her work at the time she started writing to her preceptor, although it may only be that sending out more poems resulted in a greater variety of forms being retained by recipients and thus made available to later editors.

We can only guess Higginson's comments at the time on the basis of Dickinson's replies and his later recollections. It seems that he found her rhythms "spasmodic" and that he commented on her unconventional rhymes, perhaps even suggesting experimentation with free verse—to judge from her retort that she "could not drop the Bells whose jingling cooled my Tramp—" (L 265). Like her, he seems to have concentrated at first on technical details. But he also thought her "uncontrolled," a judgment that brought her pleas for surgery and request for rule. Yet one of the poems she sent with this letter complaining of explosive force that supposedly worried her was "I cannot dance upon my Toes—" (P 326), a delightfully ironic work in which she deftly demonstrated her insight into the unfamiliar arts of ballet and opera and represented herself as deploying exuberant energy with graceful ease. The poem gives clear evidence of technical control, skill, and playfulness from its ostensibly humble beginning to its expansive conclusion. After this initial burst of correspondence, however, Higginson's Civil War service as officer of a black regiment precluded his working with his Amherst "gnome," and their communication after the war was more a friendly interchange than a tutorial involvement (L 280). On one of the few occasions when he responded to a particular poem, he wrote in 1874, "Your poem about the storm is fine—it gives the sudden transitions" (L 405a). But Higginson found the woman herself baffling and complained before their first meeting about the "fiery mist" in which she surrounded herself so that he could neither know nor help her (L 330a). After the poet's death, Higginson had the opportunity to edit the poems in collaboration with Mabel Loomis Todd but took little advantage of the chance to modify structure. In revising "Of all the Sounds despatched abroad," (P 321) for publication in the *Christian Union* just before the 1890 *Poems* appeared, Higginson omitted the sixteen-line middle stanza, probably to avoid the unorthodox imagery of buried dust cavorting in the grave that might have shocked pious readers in their first introduction to Miss Dickinson. Not form but content seems to have prompted his editorial decision.

Many more poems went next door to the Evergreens than found their way to Higginson's various addresses, and Susan Dickinson proved her sister-in-law's most responsive reader. Susan valued the poems, shared them with friends, and is credited with getting several of them published in the *Springfield Daily Republican*.[3] Only one exchange of correspondence between the friends with respect to a particular poem survives, but fortunately it concerns one of the greatest—represented below as Emily sent it to Sue in 1861.

> Safe in their Alabaster Chambers—
> Untouched by Morning—
> And untouched by Noon—
> Lie the meek members of the Resurrection—
> Rafter of Satin—and Roof of Stone—
>
> Grand go the Years—in the Crescent—above them—
> Worlds scoop their Arcs—
> And Firmaments—row—
> Diadems—drop—and Doges—surrender—
> Soundless as dots—on a Disc of Snow—
> (P 216)

Dickinson had been working on this poem for several years, trying to express the condition of the "elect" dead within the grave as they await the general resurrection. It was a topic that attracted her, given her fascination with death and the mysteries thereafter including the always uncertain possibility of immortal life, and it was a theme that she would be likely to have thought about differently from her converted and therefore confident sister-in-law.

She presents these Christians who have been saved as "Safe" in imagery suggestive more of a bank deposit vault than of anything holy. How their condition varies from that of the "unsafe" remains in doubt while the earth continues; not until the Day of Judgment will the sleepers rise from their satin-lined caskets (if then). But the world remains, placing their untouchable isolation in spatial and temporal perspective.

In the 1859 version of this poem, a cheerful sentimental scene of natural exuberance registers the world's indifference to human absence while demonstrating the preferability of the simplest forms of life to the richest trappings of death.

> Light laughs the breeze
> In her Castle above them—
> Babbles the Bee in a stolid Ear,
> Pipe the Sweet Birds in ignorant cadence—
> Ah, what sagacity perished here!

Evidently, this second stanza had displeased both Emily and Susan, prompting the poet to develop the sublime imagery of the substitute second stanza above with its astronomical perspective that places the casketed, entombed corpses within a planet that itself spins among the myriad stars of the Milky Way in a universe that makes even the solar system look trifling and the most decisive turns of world history (such as Napoleon's triumph over the doge of Venice and his empire, eleven centuries old) sink into silence. If there is a God in this universe, he is not smiling above the sky of the "Light laughs the breeze" stanza but exists in a way unimaginable to those limited in their conceptions by time and space. It was this appalling version that Dickinson sent to Higginson with her first inquiry about whether her poems were alive. So far as we know, he made no direct comment on it, although he later chose the 1859 fascicle version for his *Christian Union* article rather than the one she sent him.

We do have Susan's response, however: "I am not suited dear Emily with the second verse—It is remarkable as the chain lightening that blinds us hot nights in the Southern sky but it does not go with the ghostly shimmer of the first verse as well as the other one—It just occurs to me that the first verse is complete in itself it needs no other, and can't be coupled—Strange things always go alone—as there is only one Gabriel and one Sun—You never made a peer for that verse, and I *guess* you[r] kingdom does'nt hold one—I always go to the fire and get warm after thinking of it, but I never *can* again—."[4] Going by her own affective theory of poetry as articulated to Higginson eight years later, obviously a paraphrase of Sue's judgment ("If . . . it makes my whole body so cold no fire ever can warm me I know *that* is poetry"), Dickinson had the satisfaction of knowing from Sue what Higginson was never able to assure her: that she wrote living poems (L 342a). But she rejected Sue's counsel to let the first stanza rest alone and continued her attempts to vary perspective, writing two alternative closing stanzas and sending one next door with the query "Is *this* frostier?"

> Springs—shake the Sills—
> But—the Echoes—stiffen—
> Hoar—is the Window—and numb—the Door—
> Tribes of Eclipse—in Tents of Marble—
> Staples of Ages—have buckled there—[5]

Holding closer to the tomb imagery of the first stanza, this tries to elaborate on the qualities Sue had admired while extending the sense of time. The reply to her question, if any, is lost to us. The poet apparently made her own judgment in favor of the cosmically chilling stanzas she sent to Higginson. Yet Sue's analysis reveals a profoundly sensitive response to the opening section of the poem—one that caused her to undervalue any attempt at completion.

Apparently, the sister-in-law could peer comfortably through the "fiery mist" that obscured Higginson's vision—could fling it around herself as well when she wanted to. Both the explosive energy and the need for control were familiar to her. As Sewall has demonstrated, the Dickinsons of the poet's generation (and the next) evolved a distinctively heightened rhetoric.[6] They talked in figurative language and loved to tease and startle with their wit. And they aimed their linguistic bombshells at the most exalted topics, often religious ones. The language worked expansively, as one sees even in Lavinia's remark that "I, you must know, am the family inflater. One by one the members of my household go down, and I must inflate them."[7] Emily Dickinson, equally fond of balloon images, soared most freely of all—much to the delight of her family, who loved to recall how she had astonished a Washington worthy on her 1855 expedition by inquiring, when the plum pudding reached the table all aflame, "Oh, Sir, may one eat of hell fire with impunity here?"[8] Her letters and prose fragments show her playing with heaven's glow as well as indulging in questions and aphorisms that habitually linked her own small self with cosmic possibilities. "To be remembered is next to being loved, and to be loved is Heaven, and is this quite Earth? I have never found it so," she exclaimed once to a neighbor (L 361). To Mrs. Holland she remarked, "Had we known the Doctor was falling, we had been much alarmed, though Grace—perhaps—is the only hight from which falling is fatal" (L 678). For Mrs. Higginson, who thought her mad, she raised an encouraging question: "I fear we have all sorrow, though of different forms—but with Life so very sweet at the Crisp, what must it be unfrozen!" (L 472). And she endowed Mrs. Holland with her unfailing capacity for surprise in the remark, "Each expiring Secret leaves an Heir, distracting still" (L 359). Surprise, expectancy, curiosity, and insouciance leap from her letters and from recollections of those who knew Emily Dickinson. Hers was a boundless imagination, a force of mind only ironically characterized as "little."

What *were* little, actually minimal, were the forms to which Emily Dickinson confined this imaginative exuberance. In prose she favored aphorisms and darting witticisms, in poetry a few stanzas of hymn meter. Here we recognize the severe New England parsimony readers have noticed in her poems: the frugality, economy, conciseness, reticence, and simplicity that Donald Thackrey identifies as prevailing traits of her poetry.[9] Habituated to making do with little or doing without entirely, she proved amazingly resourceful in suggesting a cosmos within a quatrain. Consider, for example, how she creates a prairie in the startlingly reductive literary form of a recipe.

> To make a prairie it takes a clover and one bee,
> One clover, and a bee,
> And revery.
> The revery alone will do,
> If bees are few.
> (P 1755)

Here we have a sublime presentation of American landscape—and not only that landscape but a formula for producing any other.

Take a small number of basic elements and apply reverie. Or use "revery alone." Even Dickinson's recipes varied only by deletion, wasting no words on details of assemblage (L 369a). When Susan recommended doing without a second stanza, then, she must have hit a responsive chord in advising a poet who customarily revised a poem by contracting it.

The ultimate refinement of such frugality would be a portentous silence: "There is no Silence in the Earth—so silent / As that endured / Which uttered, would discourage Nature / And haunt the World" (P 1004). Especially when dealing with the most profound issues, Dickinson preferred to pare down her exposition, and the choices she made in constructing and ordering her poems reflected an extreme ideal of verbal economy. Although rejecting Sue's advice on that one poem, she habitually eliminated everything from her poems but their energetic reach.

In nothing was Dickinson's frugality so evident as in her manner of recording her poems. Even the fascicles, which represent her most ceremonious copying-over of finished or nearly finished poems, demonstrate her tendency to confine these fragments of infinity within the most circumscribed area. Readers accustomed to the broad white spaces we associate with Dickinson's printed poems may look for them in vain within the fascicles. Especially with the earliest ones that she began assembling in 1858, she crowded poems together—as many as possible to a page, in fine handwriting that filled up all the space. Later, as her penmanship grew more sprawling, additional space appeared; but the poems continued to crowd the page—joined by work sheet jottings at the foot of the sheet or beside or beneath a line. Very rarely did she leave as much as half a page free on the back of a sheet; and when analyzing the ordering principle of the fascicles, one can never neglect the probability that she jammed some of the shorter poems onto pages more to plug in gaps on the paper than to carry out thematic or imagistic patterns: "You cannot solder an Abyss / With Air" (P 546). Sometimes she enlarged her writing to make a poem swell to fit its space; more often she tightened penmanship toward the foot of the page. When she needed extra paper in the unbound sets, she preferred to pin small scraps to a sheet rather than wasting an additional one. According to R. W. Franklin, editor of Dickinson's *Manuscript Books*, the poet's basic organizational unit was always the single sheet—overwhelmingly so after she stopped sewing fascicles around 1864.[10] The scraps of paper that constitute a great part of our record of her composition in the last decade or so of her life demonstrate her economy yet more astonishingly—introducing us to a poet who crowded her verses onto the linings of envelopes, the backs of old correspondence such as an invitation to a taffy pull almost half a century gone, and even the inside of a cooking-chocolate wrapper.[11] She wasted nothing, and it is no wonder that she cultivated the briefest poetic forms.

Given the interest Dickinson expressed in organization during the period she was arranging most of the fascicles and given her subsequent editors' difficulties in finding any arrangement that makes sense of these scattershot lyrics that consistently intersect the thematic clusters her early editors imposed on them and that look so starkly disarranged in Johnson's chronological order, it would be satisfying to discover that the poet herself worked out a coherent arrangement in the fascicles.[12] Several scholars assert that she did; others find no such design.[13] Franklin explains the fascicles as a private reference system for the poet that allowed her to locate poems for later use when she wanted to rework one of them, send a copy somewhere, or adapt a stanza to a specific use.[14] To do so, he acknowledges, she would have had to know the booklets remarkably well in order to find poems without any sort of titling system, table of contents, topical organizing system, or now indispensable index of opening lines. Her reversion to unbound sets of work sheets suggests to him that the fascicles outgrew their function.

Even without accepting the theories of scholars who see a coherent narrative design in the fascicles, I do regard Dickinson's ordering of the poems as instructive to the reader and, throughout this study, have been calling attention to poems she placed in close proximity—especially those widely separated in Johnson's three-volume edition, which allows a three-hundred-page interval between poems ascribed to 1862, not including any of the nine poems at the back of his collection that Franklin has now dated tentatively on the basis of fascicle evidence.[15] By using the fascicle as context for study of a poem, one can observe intersecting image patterns, note concentrations of particular types of poems, conjecture her use of one poem as a complement or answer to another.

Fascicle 37, for example, holds twenty-one poems from about 1863. It includes three definition poems—those on publication, remorse, and renunciation. It emphasizes, by strategic initial and conclusive positioning, poems on solitary confrontation with the self, from "Conscious am I in my Chamber," (P 679) and "You taught me Waiting with Myself—" (P 740) at the opening to "My Soul—accused me—And I quailed—" (P 753) at the end. And it places similar emphasis on recognition by someone important— either a special person or God.

The fascicle provides revealing linkages between poems. "Suspense—is Hostiler than Death—" (P 705) appears on the reverse side of "You taught me Waiting with Myself—" (P 740), perhaps because both present uncertain expectancy. Next come two poems that share a page, both associating tragedy with silence: "Drama's Vitallest Expression is the Common Day" (P 741) and "Life, and Death, and Giants—" (P 706). Then come, again sharing a page, two poems on nature; the first, "Four Trees—upon a solitary Acre—" (P 742), presents the mystery of trees set by God in solitude to fill out his design while the second, "The Grace—Myself—might not obtain—" (P 707), is obviously a brief notation to accompany her gift of a flower—a plant positioned by her to accomplish her own design. "Remorse—is Memory—awake—" (P 744) and "Renunciation—is a piercing Virtue—" (P 745) appear together here as they do in Johnson, thus strengthening speculation that she was driven to define these two baleful sensations by seeing a connection between them (perhaps a narrative context like the Ninth Book of *Aurora Leigh*, in which Aurora and Romney renounce each other because of his remorse for the harm his good intentions did Marian Erle). Two poems, "I sometimes drop it, for a Quick—" (P 708) and "It dropped so low—in my Regard—" (P 747), appear to have been juxtaposed on a page as a consequence of a shared initial verb. By placing "All but Death, can be Adjusted—" (P 749) on the reverse side of "Publication— is the Auction" (P 709), Dickinson may have been opening a hope for fame that readers of the more familiar poem feel she had foreclosed. Questions of self-esteem as contrasted with the regard of others link the three final poems on overlapping pages: "My Worthiness is all my Doubt—" (P 751), "So the Eyes accost—and sunder" (P 752), and "My Soul—accused me—And I quailed—" (P 753). Patterns exist, therefore, to a sufficient extent to illumine individual poems though not enough to support coherent interpretation of the fascicle as a whole. And, of course, Dickinson left many poems out of the fascicles as early as 1862 and increasingly thereafter. The booklets were private documents for her own use, not arrangements she saw fit to share with others when she showed them copies of her work.

In "Essential Oils—are wrung—" (P 675), written about the time her interest in fascicles was tapering off, Dickinson drew an implicit analogy between the forcible expression of rose-attar to provide fragrance in a lady's drawer and the distilled imaginative life she had pressed out of her own mind in poetic form to suffuse the drawer in which Lavinia would eventually find her dead sister's treasure. One thinks of all the "Summer" of life she forfeited for the stern discipline of her art that pressed lasting, beautiful essence out of emotional pain. And one thinks as well of the formal elements she crushed within the vise of her tight poetic mold to distill her poems. For Dickinson, distillation—despite its inevitable association with distortion and suffering—was the essence of poetry. "This was a Poet—It is That" (P 448), strangely impersonal with its distancing, dehumanizing pronouns, best articulates Dickinson's distinctive purpose to press down hard enough upon the ordinary givens of her experience to distill a sweet fragrance or heady liquor of imaginative energy. Unlike the popular poets of her day who concentrated on "ordinary Meanings" (narrative and moral), she would release the "amazing sense" of physical-psychological sensation (a feeling like Sue's shivering before the fire). And she would do so by disclosing or uncovering resources available to anyone but appreciated by few. Her poetry, she recognized, was one of concentrated passion—no less energetic for not being expansive, actually more explosive. In analyzing Dickinson's manner of writing, the reader must be alert to everything she left out, only suggested, or pressed down upon with such violence as to leave nearly unrecognizable. Both in content and form, she perfected a poetics of distillation.

A case in point is her compression of narrative, a surprising characteristic in view of her delight as a reader in narrative verse. Her poems distilled plot, character, and setting to release a radiance of suggestion—just enough to justify her in occasional narrative experiments. Sometimes she borrowed biblical or historical stories to spare herself the trouble of introducing characters and developing situations. In "A little East of Jordan," (P 59), for example, she moved rapidly over the encounter of the gymnast and the angel to rush toward the exclamatory conclusion in which she claimed that Jacob had "worsted God!", thereby raising wonderful speculations about the prospects of other antagonists who might think themselves outmatched. So, too, with several of her poems about disasters at sea that emphasize anguish for the dead rather than details of what happened.

If we compare Dickinson's "Glee—The great storm is over—" (P 619) with Longfellow's "The Wreck of the Hesperus," which shares with it a balladlike brevity and objectivity, we note how much more populous the Longfellow poem seems with only its few crew members (the skipper, his little daughter, and a Spanish sailor representing the rest) than hers with its forty-four sailors.[16] By quoting the skipper's encouraging words to the child and detailing his actions in lashing her for safety to the mast, Longfellow arouses our interest in these people and evokes pity for the frozen bodies discovered in the wreck. Emphasizing action, he guides feeling. Dickinson, on the other hand, begins and ends with feelings: "Glee" at first for the survival of four sailors, wondering sorrow at the end for the other forty. Strictly speaking, hers is not actually a poem about a wreck but about the problem of telling about one adequately afterward; and the implication is that narration must yield to silence: "And the Children—no further question—/ And only the Sea—reply—."

More often this poet omitted narrative detail entirely to leave the reader with the intense emotional and imagistic sensation of an event but without any situational context. Here in one of her most famous poems, for example, we know the triumphant sense of entitlement that she so exuberantly proclaims but have no information about its cause.

> Mine—by the Right of the White Election!
> Mine—by the Royal Seal!
> Mine—by the Sign in the Scarlet prison—
> Bars—cannot conceal!
>
> Mine—here—in Vision—and in Veto!
> Mine—by the Grave's Repeal—
> Titled—Confirmed—
> Delirious Charter!
> Mine—long as Ages steal!
> (P 528)

Is this a celebration of reciprocated love, of salvation, of discovering poetic identity? As she presented all these circumferential experiences in the language of election, the reader has no textual mandate to prefer one of these explanations to another. If we want to attach this exclamation to a story, we must fabricate the narrative ourselves.

Even more distillation occurred when Dickinson approached that other staple of nineteenth-century popular poetry: moral message. Despite her often illuminating insights into human behavior and her brilliance at coining aphorisms, she took no interest in telling readers how to live their lives or in studying through verse how she should make her own choices. "What shall I do," she asks (P 186), not what *should* I do; and she mocks "Boy that lived for 'Ought to'" (P 1201). In this she differed from the typical lady contributors to the *Springfield Daily Republican*, one of whom—a Miss Matilda Burton—enjoined "Kindness" upon her readers in lines that included "Sorrows on ev'ry side / Frowning we find; / Sad hearts need sympathy—/ Let us be kind."[17] But it was not only the amateur versifiers who thought poetry should be didactic. Throughout *Aurora Leigh*, Barrett Browning articulated a dialectical study of the purposeful life—with Aurora debating within herself and with Romney about the function of art and Romney arguing the priority of Christian service—a dialectic they apparently resolved in a marriage of mutual compromise. Quite possibly, Mrs. Browning's defense of poetry as a useful vocation helped to fortify her Amherst reader, but there is no evidence of such moral argumentation—such weighing of values—in Dickinson's poems. She ignored the ethical high seriousness of the major Victorian poets.

She could, of course, write cloyingly didactic poems in imitation of popular verse—such as "If I can stop one Heart from breaking" (P 919), which concludes that if I can "help one fainting Robin / Unto his Nest again / I shall not live in Vain." Luckily Dickinson tended to perch ironically upon the edge of bathos without tumbling. Even a poem like "Trust in the Unexpected—" (P 555) draws a playful lesson from the stories of Captain Kidd, the philosopher searching for his "Talismanic Stone," and Doubting Thomas. Elsewhere the poet turned conventional moral consolation upside down as in "They say that 'Time assuages'—/ Time never did assuage—/ An actual suffering strengthens / As

Sinews do, with age—," an expression of persistently maintained grief that she sent to Higginson when her dog died (P 686). Most memorable among her capsizings of traditional morality is "Tell all the Truth but tell it slant—" (P 1129), a striking example of her delightfully skewed generalizations about human nature.

Not only the concerns she disparaged but even the experiences most central to Dickinson's poetry were likely to be distilled or compressed beyond ready recognition. If one were to identify her supreme achievement, it would be the communication of inner states of consciousness—the revelation of mental processes. Within that hidden realm, Dickinson's most characteristic mental condition is one of numbing anguish most adequately expressed by silence as in "There is a pain—so utter—" (P 599) or in the strikingly displaced metaphors of "After great pain, a formal feeling comes—" (P 341), a brilliant poem about the mind's self-protective abandonment of consciousness. Like most of her poems on extreme mental states, this one provides no narrative context. Pain has overwhelmed consciousness of anything but itself and skews even its own sensations. The nerves, which should be all aflutter carrying messages to the brain, sit like granite monuments—thus foreclosing the possibility of either knowledge or sensation. Not the mind but the heart does the questioning, with little prospect of finding answers. The feet, moving like mechanical toys on possible or impossible surfaces (even the punning possibility of "Ought," which includes duty, anything, and nothing) carry the body nowhere, for it has no sense of direction; the person settles into the nothingness Jonathan Edwards defined as "the same that the sleeping Rocks Dream of" and "a state wherein every Proposition in Euclid is not true, nor any of those self evident maxims by which they are Demonstrated & all other Eternal truths are neither true nor false."[18] Yet this total emotional paralysis may remit; one may outlive it—and must—in order, like Melville's Ishmael, to return to tell about it. While it lasts, though, it is like dying; and Dickinson often transferred the characteristics of death and dying to conditions of emotional arrest—most notably in "It was not Death, for I stood up," (P 510) and "I felt a Funeral, in my Brain," (P 280). The poet left out much in these poems that her readers want to know: things like what condition the speaker actually describes, how she got there, and how she emerged. But she concentrates her expressive gifts on the sensations of mental extremity themselves, thereby distilling the anguish, the numbness, and the horror.

Even in her presentations of natural scenery—often her most accessible poems—Dickinson eliminated most of the descriptive elements that would have recorded her precise observations and concentrated instead on her own perceiving consciousness. Definitional detail evades us even in this famous related poem demonstrating the psychologically minded indirection by which this poet regarded nature:

> There's a certain Slant of light,
> Winter Afternoons—
> That oppresses, like the Heft
> Of Cathedral Tunes—
>
> Heavenly Hurt, it gives us—
> We can find no scar,
> But internal difference,
> Where the Meanings, are—
>
> None may teach it—Any—
> 'Tis the Seal Despair—
> An imperial affliction
> Sent us of the Air—
>
> When it comes, the Landscape listens—
> Shadows—hold their breath—
> When it goes, 'tis like the Distance
> On the look of Death—
> (P 258)

What slant of light is this? How low must the sun sink on the horizon to project its pink, or gold, or silver ray across the snowy fields? The poet makes no attempt to describe the sense impressions but only to register their emotional resonance. This is done by the oxymoronic phrases "Heavenly Hurt" and "imperial affliction" that link exultation with anguish. And the speaker, generalizing from her reaction to that of a universal "we," personifies nature itself as attentive to these promptings from beyond circumference.

Here, too, definition comes by negation. There is "no scar,"

"None may teach it." When the speaker strains for an analogy to clarify her experience, she characteristically hits upon one outside Emily Dickinson's experience. Those "Cathedral Tunes" stimulate the imagination with their "Heft," presumably that "*weight* of glory" Dickinson cited once from 2 Corinthians 4:17 when telling a friend about a morning landscape that awakened painful awareness of her mother's recent death (L 815). Never having been in a cathedral, except imaginatively in "I've heard an Organ talk, sometimes—" (P 183), Dickinson probably relied on the memoirs of American Protestant travelers in Europe to discover how it would feel to hear grandly complex vocal and instrumental music in a Gothic or Romanesque setting from whose spell the visitor would constantly struggle to free himself. Perhaps she recalled Ik Marvel's report of Holy Week services in the Sistine Chapel when "the sweet, mournful flow of the *Miserere* begins again, growing in force and depth till the whole chapel rings, and the balcony of the choir trembles; then it subsides again into the low, soft wail of a single voice, so prolonged, so tremulous, and so real, that the heart aches—for Christ is dead!"[19] The death of God, the death of a loved one, her own death: All these things registered on Dickinson through this visual emblem of the dying day. And it was fitting that she should reveal these awarenesses only gradually and by indirection—foregoing natural exactitude for depth of psychological response to intuited absence.

In form as well as content, Dickinson cultivated a poetics of distillation, as one immediately observes in leafing through any collection of her poems. There are no long poems, few wide ones, many quatrains, and even fragments. Knowing the sublime reach of her poems, we are astonished at the minute limits within which she confined them: ode aspirations in nursery rhyme shapes. Not cathedral tunes, symphonies, or even natural sounds guided her verse forms but the familiar, simple melodies of American Protestant hymns—though even in borrowing these hymn measures she adapted them mainly by compression. She probably agreed with Aurora Leigh, who replied to the question "What form is best for poems?" with "Let me think / Of forms less, and the external. Trust the spirit, / As sovran nature does, to make the form. . . ."[20] Or else to give the form—the one Dickinson had picked up in church and therefore associated with human aspira-

tion to express the ineffable, to reach out to God beyond circumference.

In structuring her poems within constricted boundaries, Dickinson began with conventional rhetorical systems of organization:
the parallelism, contrast, opposition, and negation so well documented by Lindberg-Seyersted in her invaluable study of this
poet's voice.[21] Most interesting among her organizational expedi-
ents, and most useful as a device for thematic inclusiveness with
formal concision, is the technique of slantness by which Dickinson intersected rhetorical categories within a poem and merged
thematic and metaphorical patterns. It is this technique that supports the poet's characteristic irony and allows her paradoxes to
collide with each other. The reader is forced to participate in dis-
sociating and reuniting the parts of a poem, thereby experiencing
its tightly held energy. But as anyone who has ever tried to sum-
marize a Dickinson poem can testify, there is no way to explain
one of them without expanding upon it and introducing a logic
that one often only intuits in the text.

A tension exists in Dickinson's poems between the sharp sensory images and the single abstract words she so obviously loved.
She often built a poem toward one of them, sometimes only to
condense the meaning in one striking polysyllabic word like the
"Provincially" that resolves "The Robin's my Criterion for
Tune—" (P 285), but more often to highlight a central thematic
concern. "The gleam of an heroic Act" (P 1687) works toward
"Imagination"; "The Soul's Superior instants" (P 306), "We thirst
at first—'tis Nature's Act—" (P 726), and "Such are the inlets of
the mind—" (P 1421) toward "Immortality." All three concluding
lines of "A Spider sewed at Night" (P 1138) end in polysyllabic
abstractions—surprisingly arranged in inverse order of importance to the poet: "Immortality," "Strategy," "Physiognomy."

One of the few poems to which Dickinson returned after a long
interval (1862 to 1878) and drastically restructured demonstrates
the importance of this technique. In the earlier version, "Two Butterflies went out at Noon—" (P 533) moved from the speaker's
description of the butterflies' brief excursion into the firmament
to her own ignorance of their fate—ending with "No notice—
was—to me—." The revision (drastically incomplete on a work
sheet riddled with variants) stays with the butterflies themselves,

offering much livelier images of their antic behavior in stanza two and a harrowing description of their wreck in stanza three; this version ends with a mock moral riddled with portentous polysyllabic words.

> To all surviving Butterflies
> Be this Fatuity
> Example—and monition
> To entomology—

Earlier in the revision she had replaced "Firmament" with "Circumference" as the object of their quest, so the defeat of the butterflies offers more warning to human readers than to lepidopterous. For Dickinson, engaged in a quest beyond circumference toward immortality through force of imagination, these abstract endings provided satisfying resolutions to the metaphorical coils of her poems. If one were to offer a formula for a Dickinson poem (or for her poetic intention), it would be a progression from her most common opening word, "I," to her most distinctive conclusion, "Immortality" or "Circumference." And as we have come to expect from this distilling poet, she connected "I" with infinity by a process of exclusions, ruthlessly eliminating whatever incident, imagery, or syntax might push them apart and carefully selecting the few words that fused them.

A similar momentum from vigorous beginning to brief, abstract conclusion can be traced in the stages of Dickinson's writing from the time when she complained to Higginson of her ungoverned energy to later periods when she managed to impose her own rule upon many poems. The problem of explosiveness, if one could call it a problem, hit her most strongly between 1861 and 1863. Even on the printed page, one can feel the force in all those breathless dashes, those italicized words, those exclamations. Textual analysis reveals the emergence of her interpenetrating metaphorical clusters in those years. Seldom uncontrolled (as in earlier sentimental poems that veered into excess or later fragments that drifted into space), these poems express energy and demand it of the reader. Later, when the turmoil that generated this awesome power abated, Dickinson imposed her own sort of discipline, often by adopting intellectual rather than emotional forms of expression—even in the presentation of feelings.

The year 1863 brought a great rush of definition poems in an apparent attempt to impose order on experience and arrive at communicable generalizations. Often these poems began, like "Presentiment—is that long Shadow—on the Lawn—" (P 764), with polysyllabic abstractions and went on to explain and exemplify them. The same year brought the cluster of poems defining publication, renunciation, and remorse. It also brought attempts that resulted in failures to define as in "'Nature' is what we see—" (P 668), in which the speaker, who begins by classifying and exemplifying natural phenomena on the basis of sense impressions and then advances to the generalization that nature's defining characteristic is harmony, discovers that "Nature is what we know—/ Yet have no art to say—." In the same way, her attempts to classify and define the pine tree in her daily line of vision result in confession of ignorance in "By my Window have I for Scenery" (P 797): "Of it's Voice—to affirm—when the Wind is within—/ Can the Dumb—define the Divine? / The Definition of Melody—is—/ That Definition is none—." The dumb cannot *define* the divine, of course, but can at least *suggest* it, as Dickinson did in her metaphorical definition of faith as "the Pierless Bridge" (P 915). Using an elaborated metaphor as an equivalent to logical definition, the poet found a way to articulate mystery.

Approximately ten years after this concentration of definition poems, Dickinson focused her creative energy on a group that attempted to distill the essence of familiar beings in the natural world. It is possible that this grouping represents yet another stage in her struggle for control, emerging as it did right after her father's death in April 1874. "Existence has overpowered Books," she told Higginson a month later, "Today, I slew a Mushroom—" (L 413). The same letter included part of "The Mushroom is the Elf of Plants—" (P 1298), a poem she sent in complete form to her Norcross cousins at the same time. Although written in the aftermath of her first major family tragedy, the poem is surprisingly humorous and playful—not struggling so obviously to control tension as the earlier definition poems. Getting away from herself and her passions (except perhaps her identification with small, slighted existences), she distilled the essence of "Vegetation's Juggler," Nature's "Apostate." Other such poems followed on the arbutus (P 1332), the bat (P 1575), the rat (P 1356), and bees (P 1405), although the greatest concentration of these natural-essence poems characterizes various birds.

A sense of delight and release pervades the late bird poems, as though Emily Dickinson had found a way to distance herself from her obsessive concerns while polishing her poetic artistry in these gems of description that had the additional merit of being readily shared with readers bewildered by the mysteries she continued to probe in other writings of the same period. In attempting to fix or define the joy-giving minor figures in the natural world, the poet released much of the exuberance that never left her and did so in ways that brought rewards in the form of praise from readers and requests for more—as did, "Before you thought of Spring" (P 1465), the cheerful portrait of the bluebird that Dickinson sent to an Amherst neighbor and to Helen Hunt Jackson in Colorado. Thanking Dickinson, Jackson asked "What should you think of trying your hand on the oriole?" (L 601a). Her friend responded with "One of the ones that Midas touched" (P 1466), "A Route of Evanescence" (P 1463), and a note, "To the Oriole you suggested I add a Humming Bird and hope they are not untrue—" (L 602).

Their truth was to sensation, process, and affect, rather than to ornithological detail—to the feelings engendered by these birds, as in the famous hummingbird identified by its synesthetic whir of color and its impression of miraculous speed. Like the earlier definitions, some of these essence poems assume an intellectual manner, though mainly for the fun of breaking through to a sense of nature's playfulness—as in another bluebird poem with the portentously scholarly opening line "After all Birds have been investigated and laid aside—" (P 1395). Robins and bobolinks shared honors with hummingbirds and orioles; and the last poem Dickinson ever sent to Higginson, "No Brigadier throughout the Year" (P 1561), celebrated the contentious blue jay that directed her thoughts toward the almost inevitable cosmic question: "Unfair an Immortality / That leaves this Neighbor out—."

Another phenomenon of Dickinson's late writing that demonstrates her attempt to control and define her cosmic force was her tendency to write poems on the subject of words themselves and, through them, about poetry as if trying to explain to herself and a few family members to what she had committed her life. "A Word is dead" (P 1212) went to the Norcross cousins in a letter, as did "A Word dropped careless on a Page" (p 1261), while "A little overflowing word" (p 1467) went to Susan. In 1878, Dickinson applied eucharistic diction in a short poem on language.

> Your thoughts dont have words every day
> They come a single time
> Like signal esoteric sips
> Of the communion Wine
> Which while you taste so native seems
> So easy so to be
> You cannot comprehend its price
> Nor it's infrequency
>
> (p 1452)

Lest there be any doubt of her thesis statement, her draft of this poem offers nine different variants on the surprising word "easy."[22] In itself this draft indicates the problem she had in completing her last poems. Despite the beautifully controlled and delightfully expressed natural-essence poems, the classically disciplined late elegies, and the concise wisdom poems on words, Dickinson experienced increasing difficulty in bringing her poetry to completion. (No punctuation, not even the customary dash, lent finality, for example, to the poem cited above.) Yet the collations of fragments still reflected her original energy and her distinctive angle of vision, evident even in the disorderly work sheet draft of "The Bobolink is gone—the Rowdy of the Meadow—" (p 1591) in which the poet clearly delights in this character who "swung upon the Decalogue / And shouted Let us pray—" before leaving "The Presbyterian Birds" to conduct their grim burial services for the fallen year while the speaker "swaggers" in jubilant remembrance. It was never vitality that Emily Dickinson distilled from her poems.

Although Dickinson's principal commentaries on words came late in life, her passion for language held steady from her earliest letters and enlivened all the poems. Not surprisingly, then, her habit of distillation to release sense and essence exhibited itself most markedly in the smaller units of her writing from the sentence to the individual word. Omitting all words but the key ones (and often highlighting those by capitalization, italicization, or positioning on the line), she described her style once by explaining

"I only said the Syntax—/ And left the Verb and the pronoun out—" (P 494). No wonder "the sentence toiled—" under the pressure of intense feeling that had to be carried without the usual supports. What syntax remains to a sentence without a predicate, without an identifiable subject, without articles, prepositions, and conjunctions? Dickinson's readers have had to figure out such toiling sentences for themselves much as the paleozoologist she once described pieces together fossil evidence to conjecture an enormous organism.

> A science—so the Savans say,
> "Comparative Anatomy"—
> By which a single bone—
> Is made a secret to unfold
> Of some rare tenant of the mold,
> Else perished in the stone—
> (P 100)

Ellipsis, carried to an extreme, is Dickinson's most characteristic stylistic trait. Although she claimed to leave out only "the Verb and the pronoun," she more often omitted the noun—even the subject noun—thereby confronting her readers with riddling verses, some of which probably made more sense to the original recipients than they do to us when we encounter them on the printed page in that they seem to have been composed to accompany gifts of flowers or fruit that would introduce themselves, like the flower of which Dickinson wrote "Be Mine the Doom—/ Sufficient Fame—/ To perish in Her Hand!" (P 845) or the cocoon she sent to her little nephew with the query "Drab Habitation of Whom?" (P 893).

She adopted other kinds of syntactic tightening also, sometimes concentrating several in one poem like "Did you ever stand in a Cavern's Mouth—" (P 590) with its verbal contraction "as 'twere," its logical contraction "The Question of 'To die'—," and its laconic Yankee colloquialism "It's liker so."[23] More interesting is her transposition of lexical categories, substituting a noun for an adjective to intensify horror and sharpen imagery in a line otherwise dominated by an intransitive conditional verb: "How Goblin it would be—" (P 590). Other verbal usages assume particular interest in the line "As cool as Satyr's Drums—" (P 590) with its startling attribution of temperature to diabolical instruments that the reader can barely imagine let alone understand sufficiently to use as the basis for an explanatory analogy.

Fundamentally, Emily Dickinson distilled her poems to individual words and word clusters, thereby forcing the smallest units of language to release their explosive power. The most memorable parts of her poems tend to be phrases, many of which wrench lexical or logical categories: "ablative estate" (P 1741), "miles of Stare" (P 243), "Duties Diamond" (P 700), "a Panther in the Glove" (P 244), "Muslin souls" (P 278), "Etherial Blow" (P 315), "Syllables of Velvet—/ Sentences of Plush" (P 334), "Audience of Idleness" (P 354), "Litanies of Lead" (P 364), "a Gnat's Horizon" (P 372), "Peat life" (P 422). Obviously Dickinson delighted in words—their plenitude and their particularity. "What a beautiful Word 'Waters' is!" she exclaimed to Mrs. Holland with her characteristic zest for the glorious within the ordinary (L 833). It may well be this reverence for words and pleasure in them as personal acquaintances that accounts for her haphazard capitalization of any part of speech she wanted to emphasize. The reverence involved respect for the power of words to drill their way into consciousness and cause enduring if unpredictable changes. Words live, she asserts in "A word is dead / When it is said, / Some say." (P 1212), and can injure with their limitless force, breeding "Infection" of despair centuries from the author's lifetime (P 1261). She presented language in sacramental terms on various occasions, most notably in "A Word made Flesh is seldom / And tremblingly partook" (P 1651), a reflection linking the poet's diction with Christ's incarnation. Each of us may have tasted this power; few would dare to exercise it if they recognized what it could do. Dickinson welcomed words with delight, employed them with reverence, and excused them when they failed her summons.

Her habits of compression led this poet to highlight individual words and memorable phrases, but it also led her to distinctive uses of particular words to stress their particularity and assert her private engagement with them. Consider, for instance, her singular use of collective nouns to detach individual, insignificant members from the mass. Counterpointing "a Plush" (one tiny thread of a chair cover, one hair of a stuffed toy) with "a Star" (a seemingly microscopic but actually vast image), she startles the reader of "What Soft—Cherubic Creatures—" (P 401) by freshening the perspective on values. So too with her "I wish I were a Hay—" statement (P 333) that Higginson rejected in deference to public protectiveness of grammar despite Mrs. Todd's enjoyment of its odd appeal. This poet who thought of herself as so very small managed to set her readers looking closely at minimal things—and smiling with her as they did so.

Dickinson's definition poems and her general concern with naming as an index of power also demonstrate her attentiveness to language and her concern that its force be respected. Yet diction often failed to encompass the inexpressible, as she signaled in an early definition poem, "'Hope' is the thing with feathers—" (P 254), that deliberately violates the lexicographer's cardinal rule about precision. What kind of "thing"? A birdlike thing as the feathers and song suggest: But the tenor overwhelms the vehicle, and the analogy breaks down in the puzzling conclusion with its absurd assumption that hope might ever go begging for help. Maybe hope is another kind of thing as well, infinitely suggestible but never defined. As Dickinson observed elsewhere, "By intuition, Mightiest Things / Assert themselves—and not by terms—" (P 420). Not that such realization discouraged her from experimenting with terms or from laughing at the hackneyed language by which her less sensitive neighbors attempted to express the mysterious in ways that simply enmeshed them in mixed metaphors:

> We pray—to Heaven—
> We prate—of Heaven—
> Relate—when Neighbors die—
> At what o'clock to Heaven—they fled—
> Who saw them—Wherefore fly?
> (P 489)

She used such sentimental clichés herself, of course, in the Mama bird elegy and in various letters, but she preferred fresh metaphorical ventures.

Sometimes Dickinson's verbal distillation condensed poems so tightly as to render them inexplicable or nearly so unless the reader has an external referential context to adumbrate the shadows of her words. When she stripped away excess, she left the key words naked, as in this brief analogy: "When Bells stop ringing— Church—begins—/ The Positive—of Bells—/ When Cogs—

stop—that's Circumference—/ The Ultimate—of Wheels" (P 633). It is the second half that confuses us. What cogs? What do they stop doing that proclaims circumference with the same assurance that cessation of church bells announces worship? Presumably she had in mind the cogs of a mechanical wheel whose turning maintains motion and, in the case of the clock wheel that she probably intended, marks off time. When time stops, we have reached circumference—the barrier between it and eternity. In the context of other circumference poems, this one makes sense. It makes even fuller sense in the context of another cog poem, "Did life's penurious length" (P 1717) in which she mentions "the cogs / Of that revolving reason / Whose esoteric belt / Protects our sanity." So the cogs may represent a cerebral mechanism whose smooth operation guards against intellectual circumference as well as against death. Into the white spaces that surround the isolated words on the printed page, the reader must fill an interpretive context built out of other associations from Dickinson's writing. It is a complex journey from "I" to circumference despite the visual spareness and apparent simplicity of the brief verses that guide us insistently toward the poet's goal.

But how much rule did this poet want as she smashed against the barriers of mortal limitation with this awesome armature of isolated, death-defying words? Not much, one gathers from Dickinson's indifference to editorial advice—even to Sue's suggestion about that one particular poem although Sue's urging toward brevity and sharp impact coincided with the poet's own well-established penchant for distillation. Nor does it seem probable that she worried much about the explosions that came of merciless pressure upon such volatile material, though perhaps about the charring effect on herself of such experiments in poetic sorcery. Perhaps she simply wanted to caution Higginson about the mines he was trudging upon so flat-footedly with his comments on spelling and rhyme.

The explosive energy of Dickinson's poetry asserted itself from the first valentine and lasted almost to her death. It clutched at the reader from vigorous opening lines like "Blazing in Gold and quenching in Purple / Leaping like Leopards to the Sky" (P 228) and "The Trees like Tassels—hit—and swung—" (P 606). At times she felt drunk with spiritual energy: "Inebriate of Air—am I—/ And Debauchee of Dew—" (P 214) but drunk in a way that sent her reeling into the heavens, unlike the drunkard of one of her latest poems who sinks gratefully into the protective ditch (P 1645). Higginson, with his calming guidance, somehow escaped this force until confronted with the poems almost *en masse* in Mrs. Todd's copies.

Explosive imagery reinforces this sense of vibrant energy and startles us by declaring Dickinson's identification with eruptive forces like bombs, guns, volcanoes, and electricity. Emotions either jubilant or angry could ignite her fire, as she reminded Judge Lord by cautioning that "The withdrawal of the Fuel of Rapture does not withdraw the Rapture itself. / Like Powder in a Drawer, we pass it with a Prayer, it's Thunders only dormant" (L 842). Knowing the poems she had stashed away by the time she wrote this in 1883, she must have suspected the impact of the "Powder in a Drawer" she would leave to amaze her survivors.

Even more fascinating to Dickinson than the gun or bomb was the volcano—presumably because of its greater capacity for surprise. A gun, after all, is designed to kill and is instantly recognizable as an agent of death. But a volcano looks like an ordinary mountain. People can pick wildflowers on its meadows, graze sheep on its slopes, build houses at its base, and perhaps even live out their lives in peace upon it—unless it erupts. This combination of tranquil appearance and sudden explosive force excited her; it seemed a perfect analogy for herself when boiling rage and stirring passion threatened to erupt and injure. A number of poems explore this symbol, but the clearest application of the analogy to herself comes in "On my volcano grows the Grass" (P 1677) with its troubled warning. The contrast here between the idyllic meadow landscape and the subterranean energy that must eventually explode is a powerful one, given the probability that such eruption would ravage the mind. Luckily the lava fell as poems.

Even when she held to New England natural imagery rather than flitting imaginatively to Sicily, Dickinson revealed her "Vesuvius at Home" (P 1705) by emphasizing violent forces, especially in her many storm poems—most of which flash with lightning. She imposed a certain domestic control at the start of "The Wind begun to knead the Grass—" (P 824) by employing a household verb but then let the storm erupt like an hysterical housewife with wilder actions like flinging, scooping, throwing, wrecking, and quartering. The bread-baking simile certainly suggests a similar storminess in Higginson's genteel lady poet who might herself break out in a carnival of destruction.

It was lightning, which she once named "The Doom's electric Moccasin" (P 1593), that seized Dickinson's imagination most powerfully with its combination of light and danger. It afforded sudden revelations in "The Soul's distinct connection" (P 974), in which she likened the soul's awareness of danger in sudden crisis to a storm's effect on the eye: "As Lightning on a Landscape / Exhibits Sheets of Place—/ Not yet suspected—but for Flash—/ And Click—and Suddenness." Unleashed and therefore menacing electricity, lightning resembled the beneficent force that, when tamed, was illumining and otherwise empowering America in the age of Edison. And it suggested the flash of personal inspiration that the poet celebrated in "The farthest Thunder that I heard" (P 1581). Basically positive in her poems (however alarming), lightning represented illumination, power, even the radiance of fame— and its evanescence. In "Fame is the one that does not stay—" (P 1475), Dickinson told how renown flees unless its possessor does so first by dying, disappearing, or becoming "that most insolvent thing / A Lightning in the Germ—/ Electrical the embryo / But bindless is the Flame."[24] Did she see herself as such an electrical embryo, to flash into flame and fame at death?

If so, she had reason—based on responses of readers during her lifetime. Higginson commented on those "luminous flashes" that came to his scholar, isolating her from uninspired mortals (L 330a). Sue, we remember, likened the "Grand go the Years" stanza of the "Alabaster Chambers" poem to "the chain lightening that blinds us hot nights in the Southern sky." When the poet died, Sue employed lightning imagery again in her memorial tribute, describing her sister-in-law as "quick as the electric spark in her intuitions and analyses."[25] Years later Martha Dickinson Bianchi turned to electricity for a descriptive metaphor, observing that her aunt "put so much of her own supernatural imagination into a person or event or just the ordinary weather, that few if any other minds could have conceived the voltage of her impressions or reactions."[26] Even now this "waylaying Light" (P 1581) continues to startle, illumine, and alarm her readers.

Poetry, as Dickinson knew better than her mentors, could and should explode. Therefore, she would treat it with respect, "rule" it in the sense of ordering for appropriate purposes. Just as a gun must be aimed accurately and with caution, so must a writing implement that launches bulletins from immortality instead of bullets and plants them in the brains of unborn readers. Writing to Louise Norcross, the poet reflected in 1880 upon the force even of epistolary art: "What is it that instructs a hand lightly created, to impel shapes to eyes at a distance, which for them have the whole area of life or of death? Yet not a pencil in the street but has this awful power, though nobody arrests it. An earnest letter is or should be life-warrant or death-warrant, for what is each instant but a gun, harmless because 'unloaded,' but that touched 'goes off'?" (L 656). If prose had such destructive potential, how much more must poetry with its tensely compacted force?

Dickinson's poetics of distillation eliminated as much dross as possible from the verses, leaving a residue that was alive, potent, explosive. The strategy resolved through practical experiment her problems of smallness and loss and confirmed the reassuring insights she had gained from reading and role playing: For this artist, at least, compression rather than expansion proved the secret of growth, purposeful self-deprivation the key to empowerment. In a poem that brilliantly described her fragmented, condensed art, Dickinson applied a chemical analogy of water's distillation into steam to exemplify her distinctive aesthetic process in both its stylistic and thematic dimensions.

> Banish Air from Air—
> Divide Light if you dare—
> They'll meet
> While Cubes in a Drop
> Or Pellets of Shape
> Fit.
> Films cannot annul
> Odors return whole
> Force Flame
> And with a Blonde push
> Over your impotence
> Flits Steam.
> (P 854)

Just as air molecules fuse despite attempts to separate them and light waves eventually merge, so will discrete parts of a poem—if kindred elements. And just as steam results from compression of water subjected to intense heat, so poems result from pressure on language in the cauldron of imagination. This is a new form of power—not the remnants of original matter (none of which, she knew from her science classes, could ever possibly be lost). "What a beautiful Word 'Waters' is!" How much more forceful a word is "Steam"! By her poetics of distillation, then, Dickinson harnessed the erratic energy that both frightened and exhilarated her. She let her "little Force" erupt and dazzle. Just as steam powered the ships and factories of her America, even the locomotives her father sent charging through Amherst, Emily Dickinson directed its artistic equivalent to thrust her imagination toward circumference.

PART THREE

Pushing against Circumference

7
"Out upon Circumference"
Testing Barriers

LAVINIA DICKINSON liked to tell about her sister's first-semester examinations in mathematics at Mount Holyoke Female Seminary.[1] Emily, unprepared to recite on the first four books of Euclid, is said to have brazened out the situation by advancing to the chalkboard, drawing some sort of diagram, and casting such a bewildering spell of language that "the dazed teacher" awarded her top honors. Although Emily's report after this trial expressed relief at survival without reference to outwitting one of the "real ogres" on the college faculty, her admirers may hope that Lavinia's account was accurate (L 19). We may hope, still further, that the diagram represented a circle and that the verbal spell included such Euclidean terms as circumference and circuit, which she later rendered both magical and riddling in her poems. Any professor of literature who has ever stood at a chalkboard attempting to illustrate one of Dickinson's more complex circle images would give much for a transcript of the future poet's 1847 minilecture.

There is no escaping the circle imagery. Dickinson wrote constantly about circles, spheres, discs, circuits, diameters, and circumferences—reinforcing these abstract geometric terms with more concrete images such as crowns, diadems, balls, balloons, and drops of dew. Yet what she meant by these image clusters and what she intended in asserting to Higginson that "My Business is Circumference" remain among the most baffling puzzles to Dickinson scholars—most of whom have felt obligated to comment on this terminology without always agreeing on interpretation. Confronted with a private symbol system, we would do best to explicate it as systematically as possible—preferably beginning with the commonplace meanings of key terms and then anchoring those meanings to the poet's distinctive usage. Before flying off into elaborate symbolic theories, we should draw a few circles and name their parts.

Fortunately we all know what a circle looks like: a 360-degree round plane, bounded by a line known as the circumference and sometimes intersected by diameters that divide the circumference into arcs. Every circle has a center, whether visually marked or not. The word *circumference*, Webster's *Dictionary* told Dickinson, has three meanings: "the line that goes round or encompasses a . . . circle"; "the space included in a circle"; and "an orb; a circle; any thing circular or orbicular."[2] Given the inevitable confusion of these meanings, scholars often disagree on whether *circumference* designates the full content of the circle or only its edge.[3]

Several questions arise in elucidating Dickinson's circle symbolism. What does her circle actually represent? Is it any round space—a geometric abstraction? Is it the poet's sense of self, the sphere of consciousness welling out from her personal center? Is it life—hers particularly or life in general? Can the term apply to any bounded, protected inner space? And does the word *circumference* apply to that inner space as a whole or only to its perimeter? Does this circumference move in any way; if so, does it expand in an Emersonian process of growth? What fascination did this terminology hold for Emily Dickinson, and how far does explication of it help us in understanding her poems? There are those who suspect her of bamboozling us like the poor Mount Holyoke professor with a verbal smoke screen and others who believe that she was trying to unriddle the universe with her distinctive use of this familiar mathematical vocabulary. Counting myself in the latter group, I surmise that a serious attempt to answer the questions above will provide insight into this poet's beliefs about her perilous private situation in a cosmos of swirling, magnetically interactive, but mutually repellant spheres.

It seems clear upon reading Dickinson's poems that the circle is always inner space, separated by some boundary from external space or substance. Sometimes it is simply an orb of absence, as when she writes that "Place was where the Presence was / Circumference between" (P 1084). More often there was something to be guarded within the circle. I think it safe to judge that the poet's primary use of the image related to the private space of personal consciousness—to her own identity—and that other circles connoted, by metaphorical extension, either consciousness or the range of knowledge accessible to consciousness. This identity exists within the circumferential margin that represents its limit. When speaking of this inner space, I shall use the term *circuit*, also defined by Webster as "the space inclosed in a circle, or within certain limits"; and I shall refer to the realm accessible to consciousness (the world as we normally know it) as the circuit world. Circumference, then, represents the boundary itself between the circuit of personal space and whatever might be outside. It is margin, never center.

The circuit world, for Dickinson, comprehended consciousness, identity, the senses, and matter. It encompassed mortality, finitude, and limitation. Most of what the soul recognizes as itself, both positive and negative human properties, is subsumed within the circuit. There are as many circuits as beings—each bounded by its own circumference and external space. Other circuits represent the not-me of alien personal identities. Swirling outside the circumferences of private circuits is a vast sea of general space representing infinity, immortality, and that empowerment beyond human limitation to which the self aspires. The response of consciousness to this force beyond circumference can only be awe. But awe is a sublime emotion, involving fear as well as wonder and attraction. The private self, unable to conceive in sensate terms of its ability to exist beyond its circuit as "Costumeless Consciousness" (P 1454), dreads being merged into the universe and cowers self-protectively behind the same wall that must be penetrated somehow for the soul to escape finitude and limitation. Emily Dickinson's simultaneous impulse toward withdrawal and self-protection and her appetite for empowerment made her concentrate on circumference, that dreaded yet enticing barrier.

The range of barrier images in Dickinson's poems may be suggested by "I had not minded—Walls—" (P 398), in which rock walls, even the geological mass of the planet, establish limits. The poem also presents obstacles that seem more easily overcome: the hair, filament, law, cobweb, straw fortress, and finally the veil of a lady's bonnet. Oddly, the barriers become more formidable to the speaker as their gossamer qualities increase. For Dickinson, the flimsiest boundaries seemed the most threatening—perhaps because most pliable to pressure, least capable of protecting her from immersion in the not-me outside her circuit, most likely to tantalize with partial visions. Her fecund imagination generated barriers, if only to make her paradoxically more conscious of her limitations and more desperate for escape.

The poet necessarily observed boundaries most intently from the inside—from within her private circuit. That was her area of private control: the dimension of her senses, consciousness, and sense of selfhood. Therefore, she looked to boundaries for protection of these values that seemed to secure her identity. On the other hand, she tended to scorn other circuits and to identify the circuit world in general with a numbing mundane routine likely to obliterate aspirations. Her obligation was to do the best she could within her own circle, wary always of a tendency to close out external space or force excessively. She remembered from the prisoner of Chillon story how contented one could become in a prison.

The inevitable tension between Dickinson's tendency toward withdrawal and self-protectiveness and her longing for infinity, immortality, and power expressed itself in attentiveness to limits—each one a sort of circumference. In a satirical poem on growth, she hinted at the advantages she derived from the very narrowness of her circuit—a calculated narrowness, as we have already seen. "Size circumscribes—it has no room" (P 641) presents us with the paradoxical story of a giant so enormous in his bulk as to occupy his circuit completely, thereby shutting off awareness of other realities (admittedly disturbing little nuisances like gnats, flies, and calumnies) in his insistence on "Ease of Gianture." By contrast, the tiny person (like the poet's self-image) occupies a smaller compass but perhaps a less cramped one, less exclusively self-obsessed. If "Size circumscribes," perhaps minuteness liberates to some extent.

Yet the poet recognized her own tendency to assert "Gianture" within her narrow circuit and worried that "this Circumference" of mortal life, so instinctively guarded and conserved, might "Engross my Finity—" to the extent of excluding God, immortality, and awe—all of them beyond her circuit (P 802). Fortunately, God intervened in this poem by slashing circumference with his diameters, thus merging time into eternity. More often, in keeping with Dickinson's "sumptuous Destitution" motif, the very narrowness of her circuit incited desires for the infinite realm beyond in a way that the giant's ampler compass would discourage: "'Tis Beggars—Banquets best define—/ 'Tis Thirsting—vitalizes Wine—/ Faith bleats to understand—" (P 313). Knowing life's round to be "penurious" and her circuit pitifully small, she yet recognized that an ampler enclosure within private circumference would only make her more comfortable within her prison. It was better to pull the walls in more tightly, to let the pressure hurt.

Here we arrive at Dickinson's unique approach to the goal of expansion beyond personal limits—now easily visualized through the geometric circle image. The literary sources that have been cited for her symbol fail to help us here, since both the Shelley passage cited by Diehl ("Possessing and possessed by all that is / Within that calm circumference of bliss") and the Barrett Browning lines quoted by Walsh ("bats, that seem to follow in the air / Some grand circumference of a shadowy dome") present static images, while anyone who reads Dickinson's poems clearly discerns an impulse toward motion.[4] But is it the outward-thrusting circular motion we associate with Emerson's circle, his "flying Perfect"?[5] Distinctly not: rather the reverse. Where Emerson echoed Sir Thomas Browne and others in asserting the expansiveness of this universal symbol, declaring that "around every circle another can be drawn," Dickinson countered with the implied rejoinder that within every circle another can be inscribed. Just as she deliberately restricted her life, intensifying every limitation, and elided her poems, expunging every extra word or mark of punctuation, she drew circumference in upon herself to tighten her private circuit—quite deliberately risking explosion of her consciousness into the outlying realm of awe. As Emerson envisaged the circle, it promised infinite expansion of the personal circuit world; as Dickinson envisaged it, the circumference contracted its circuit with a pressure that forced the enclosed consciousness to struggle against finitude, to push toward immortality, to prefer awe to complacency, to grope toward God even at the risk of self-destruction.

Dickinson captured the force and fascination of this external energy in a well-known poem.

> Behind Me—dips Eternity—
> Before Me—Immortality—
> Myself—the Term between—

> Death but the Drift of Eastern Gray,
> Dissolving into Dawn away,
> Before the West begin—
>
> 'Tis Kingdoms—afterward—they say—
> In perfect—pauseless Monarchy—
> Whose Prince—is Son of None—
> Himself—His Dateless Dynasty—
> Himself—Himself diversify—
> In Duplicate divine—
>
> 'Tis Miracle before Me—then—
> 'Tis Miracle behind—between—
> A Crescent in the Sea—
> With Midnight to the North of Her—
> And Midnight to the South of Her—
> And Maelstrom—in the Sky—
>
> (P 721)

The "Term between," the self, is her circuit—edged by circumference. Swirling outside circumference are eternity and immortality, God, miracle, and boundless power. She, so enclosed, pictures herself here as a ball tossed by those "Billows of Circumference" she mentioned elsewhere (P 1343). Why not burst beyond circumference and escape into this marvelous sea?

Because, in part, the self has no means of envisaging itself once the circuit leaks or shatters into infinity. Even when the poet anticipated the general resurrection, when time would be over and mortal finitude abolished, she felt how "each separate Consciousness" would still concentrate on its own fate, still be locked in its private circuit. To know man—especially in his introspective neo-Puritan variety—is to suspect his tendency toward confinement even on that final day when "Circumference be full—" (P 515). And until the resurrection, there will remain the instinctive human resistance to death, even when it can be presented so gently as "but the Drift of Eastern Gray, / Dissolving into Dawn away, / Before the West begin—" (P 721). Few explorers feel enough ardor for that symbolic west to take the risk—a very real risk, since Dickinson recognized that immortality might yet prove a myth—that the break through circumference could bring annihilation. Circumference, for Emily Dickinson, is death—the transitional point between the familiar circuit world and either immortality or nothingness. She never knew which, though she hoped for fulfillment of Christian promises and generally imagined such fulfillment when she tried to peer beyond circumference.

The fascination of circumference in Dickinson's poems, then, goes far beyond obsession with death itself. *That* interested her only as a barrier that must be penetrated to see to the other side. The quest of her poetry was to press beyond mortal limits while remaining safe, to gain a perspective on the mysteries beyond circumference without passing through death. These barriers, however, yielded few momentary glimpses. The poet must be alert for such "Bulletins . . . from Immortality" (P 827). She must make circumference her business and attend to that business with puritanical zeal for her distinctive earthly calling; and as we can guess from her parallel statements that "*My* business is to love" and "*My* business is to *sing*," she thought of circumference in energetic terms—as a noun readily activated into a verb (L 269).

This poet, consequently, had to reckon with death—to probe at it and push against it in hopes of seeing through it. That is why so many of her poems dealt with death; it *was* circumference (at least whenever the circuit represented consciousness); it loomed as a barrier obscuring awesome mysteries; it also distracted the self-protective consciousness from studying those mysteries. The story Dickinson told in "A single Clover Plank" (P 1343) demonstrated the distorted perspective of the circuit world when confronted with the prospect of escape beyond its immediate margin. The speaker, naively expressing circuit values, reports on the adventure of a bee "saved" from "sinking" into the firmament (what a topsy-turvy world that "sinking" betrays!) by a clover, which—in its idle swaying—struck the bee and retained him at grass level where "The Billows of Circumference" could no longer sweep him skyward. That the bee had been injured in this purported rescue—stunned, perhaps killed—seems not to matter. He had been withheld from circumference even though that firmament was his native air, his proper area of motion. Like other flying creatures, the bee symbolized for Dickinson the possibility of soaring *to* circumference without passing *through* it.

Emily Dickinson had many other related symbols, all straining for revelation beyond life's mortal margin. Writing once to Mrs. Holland, she observed, "I suppose there are depths in every Consciousness, from which we cannot rescue ourselves—to which none can go with us—which represent to us Mortally—the Adventure of Death—" (L 555). Locked in the circuit of her own consciousness, she strained to comprehend this adventure and pursue her quest beyond it. She did so symbolically (there being no other way for one not visited by mystic visions—all of which have to be expressed symbolically, anyway, within the constraints of human language). Dickinson's most important symbols were circumferential ones, those dealing with any barrier or transition point within the range of human experience: natural circumferences like sunrises and sunsets, horizons, transitional seasons, bulbs, cocoons, and flying creatures; circumferential points in the human life cycle and in states of consciousness; even divinely mediated circumferences such as conversion and sacrament. In dealing with these topics, she treated each as an analogy with death, as an end to what can be comprehended by reason and the senses and as a possible point of entry to whatever might be imagined beyond.

Beginnings or endings of any sort could function as circumferential symbols, and Dickinson exhibited a typical poetic responsiveness to the analogical possibilities of natural transitions. Especially in her early years as a writer, she concentrated on the resemblances between nature's changes and the human life cycle of birth, maturation, death, and (perhaps) resurrection. Many of her nature poems—circumferential in themselves because of their focus on conditions at the end of one state of being and the start of another—employed circle imagery to reinforce the private symbol, sometimes (as with flowers, horizons, and the sun) because of inherently curving forms, occasionally because the eye (itself spherical, as Emerson reminded her) rounded the outlines. Even the grass, a basically linear image, appears in a Dickinson poem as "A Sphere of simple Green—," enhanced with "Dews . . . like Pearls—" (P 333). Looking at such "Dews" from outside their circumferences or at horizons from within their circuits, Dickinson could explore the varied potential of her circular symbols.

The earth itself is spherical, after all, and so is its horizon. Also circular are the sun and moon, which daily draw the eye toward eastern and western boundaries of sight while raising conjecture about the realms beyond physical vision: "the land—the Sunset washes—" in the domain of "Western Mystery" (P 266). Dickinson's attentiveness to nature's daily cycles, however, only intensified her awareness that each person remains locked within a private circuit, apart from cosmic progressions, even while obviously enclosed within the earth's ampler sphere and its circumferential curtain of sky. Astronomical spectacles like sunsets "Blazing in Gold and quenching in Purple / Leaping like Leopards to the Sky" (P 228) and even the aurora borealis elevate human aspiration for flitting moments but inevitably depart without penetrating the private circuit and thus altering human perspective. Yet the creatures of nature felt no such exclusion. "It would please you to see how intimate the Meadows are with the Sun," she told a friend as evidence for the potential recovery of Eden, and continued with the observation that "While the Clergyman tells Father and Vinnie that 'this Corruptible shall put on Incorruption'—it has already done so and they go defrauded" (L 391). The minister, of course, referred to human corruption, and the poet's efforts to recover Eden or "put on Incorruption" by penetrating through circumference to the glory radiated by the sun at its rising and setting generally resulted in frustration.

So did artistic attempts to capture these dazzling displays of natural glory. Neither Dickinson as poet nor any other artist could capture the transitional splendor, show "How the old Mountains drip with Sunset / How the Hemlocks burn—" (P 291). The heavenly fire and the images that it projects, obscures, shifts, then withdraws had defeated even the Renaissance landscape painters: "These are the Visions flitted Guido—/ Titian—never told—/ Domenichino dropped his pencil—/ Paralyzed, with Gold—." In its defiance of artistic arrest as in its tantalizing distance from man, sunset offered daily rebuke to human finitude.

Dickinson turned her eyes toward the horizon in search of still other circumferences, lifting her eyes to the hills around Amherst and traveling in imagination toward the even more compellingly circular margin of the sea. Her speakers look outward upon the ocean toward the final circumferential barrier of the horizon that outlines so distinctly the curve of the planet. "And you have felt the horizon hav'nt you—," she asked in her second "Master" letter, "and did the sea—never come so close as to make you dance?" (L 233). Ocean journeying served this poet analogically as a quest upon circumference to reach the hoped-for immortality beyond

its horizon. Referring to her habitual questing condition, she acknowledged its identity with living in the constant presence of
death when she wrote, "You must let me go first, Sue, because I
live in the Sea always and know the Road" (L 306), and again "I
am pleasantly located in the deep sea, but love will row you out if
her hands are strong, and don't wait till I land, for I'm going
ashore on the other side" (L 209). The "other side": That was the
focus of her attention, the goal of her quest, but geographical
symbolism reinforced her awareness that the other side of circumference could be reached only through death. Worrying about her
dying aunt, who had spent "her last inland Christmas," Dickinson
wondered "Does God take care of those at sea? My aunt is such a
timid woman!" (L 207). Often timid herself and characteristically
protective of her little circuit, the poet nonetheless accepted the
risk.

She focused attention on temporal as well as spatial circumferences, paying particular heed to transitional seasons. Summer and
winter themselves did not excite her interest so much as the subtle
passages between them. Dickinson was mistress of the subtle hint
of change, the dawning intuition of loss and recovery. As with her
sunset poems, distinctly more memorable than the sunrise group,
she emphasized the flight away from her of natural beauty. Most
frequent among her reflections on seasonal barriers are those la-
menting the loss of summer, always represented in relation to the
other stages of the annual cycle as in this 1859 meditation: "The
gentian is a greedy flower, and overtakes us all. Indeed, this world
is short, and I wish, until I tremble, to touch the ones I love before
the hills are red—are gray—are white—are 'born again'! If we
knew how deep the crocus lay, we never should let her go. Still,
crocuses stud many mounds whose gardeners till in anguish some
tiny, vanished bulb" (L 207). Less funereal but still somberly re-
flective is "These are the days when Birds come back—" (P 130),
commemorating a gentle transition—one the speaker would willingly deny, though she knows she is taking only "a backward
look" at summer, itself already lost beyond circumference.

Various spring poems explore the renewal analogy more fully,
proclaiming nature's resurging vitality as its answer to "Nicode-
mus' Mystery" of new birth with the jubilant welcome the poet
offers spring in "An altered look about the hills—" (P 140) and in
"The Dandelion's pallid tube" (P 1519), where she hails a linear

break in winter's circumference to be followed by the familiar
spheric and seed-scattering flowers that announce "The Proclamation of the Suns / That sepulture is o'er." But for what or
whom is it over? For the plants anticipated in "When I count the
seeds" (P 40) but not so surely for the dead friends the speaker has
also buried. At times, Dickinson expressed uncertainty even about
nature's renewal, as in "When they come back—if Blossoms
do—" (P 1080) and "Summer begins to have the look" (P 1682),
which concludes with an acknowledgment of general finitude:
"Conclusion is the course of All / At *most* to be perennial / And
then elude stability / Recalls to immortality—." No wonder she
wished she could hold the year permanent just at the circumference of the vernal equinox "Between the March and April line—/
That magical frontier" (P 1764). Referring once to nature as the
"Typic Mother," Dickinson expanded upon analogies between the
seasons, human life, and the broader course of God's providential
design for history (P 1115). Autumn she interpreted as "The Revelations of the Book / Whose Genesis was June," pointing ahead
to spring's renewal after passage through winter's bleak circumference.

Among Dickinson's many images for smashing through that
icy barrier, the most frequent early ones involved seeds and bulbs:
desiccated remnants of dead plants, improbable but faithful
sources of new flowers. Most of these poems can be dismissed as
sentimental effusions belaboring a routine analogy, especially
those that liken the bulbs to children. Far more effective as emblems for protective circuit breached by shattering circumference,
however, were her cocoon and butterfly poems, most of them
more humorous than sentimental. Both in "A fuzzy fellow, without feet," (P 173) and in "Cocoon above! Cocoon below!" (P 129),
she reveled in the cocoon's spectacular "secret" of its seasonal unfolding. Beginning in the summer as a foolish-looking and startling caterpillar, the larva winds itself into a cocoon for protection
in the icy months, only to emerge as a butterfly in the spring—
soaring now rather than dropping. Part of the fun she derived
from this evidence of broken circumference came from its seeming reversal of industrious Yankee values. Caught in their own
circuit world of workaday routine, her neighbors would prefer the
cocoon to its liberated tenant, oblivious to the implications of this
symbol for their own heavenly release when they hoped them-

selves to be invested with the saints' equivalent of "The Butterfly's Assumption Gown" (P 1244). Attentive only to appearances and preferring drab ones, New Englanders ignored this emblem of the immortality for which they were supposedly toiling (P 1685). Meanwhile, the butterfly flitted playfully above "In purposeless Circumference—" (P 354), a most remarkable notion for Dickinson to have conceived and ample evidence of the chasm between natural processes and her human quest.

Having broken through one circumference, the butterfly showed no impulse to push beyond the encompassing firmament—unlike the poet, who represented her sense of pressure within her circuit in "My Cocoon tightens—Colors teaze—" (P 1099), a poem indicating the painfulness of growth even as it offers promise of liberation. The speaker hesitates, even fears, to push through the protective margin of her outgrown circuit to assume her "Power of Butterfly" but has no choice about pressing outward into new identity and a freedom inconceivable within the homelike prison.

Birds, bees, butterflies—all the soaring creatures who populate Dickinson's poems exemplify freedom to move about within firmamental circumference. Though small, fragile, and apparently timid, they all have the power displayed by the bird of "She staked her Feathers—Gained an Arc—" (P 798), who sails "among Circumference," "At home—among the Billows—As / The Bough where she was born—." So would the bumblebee have soared, had he not been "saved" by the firmly rooted clover that grounded him (P 1343). Yet bird flight, too, proved an inadequate analogy for Dickinson's aspirations as suggested here:

> Some things that fly there be—
> Birds—Hours—the Bumblebee—
> Of these no Elegy.
>
> Some things that stay there be—
> Grief—Hills—Eternity—
> Nor this behooveth me.
>
> There are that resting, rise.
> Can I expound the skies?
> How still the Riddle lies!
> (P 89)

One kind of flight, represented by fluttering creatures and even by sunsets and seasons, differs from another. Dickinson craved permanence of a sort denied to ephemeral beings, and she wanted flight to smash through circumference, not just drift "among" it. How can one rise while resting except through death's reversal of worlds by which the buried may be lifted into eternal life? It was this transition that absorbed her attention—this and the hope of catching glimpses beyond circumference even before death motivated other approaches to the riddle when natural analogies failed her. Easy to develop, sunset and seasonal metaphors and a host of plant and animal emblems represented predictable cyclic patterns within earth's massive circuit. Even when they seemed to penetrate one circumference (like the bulbs and cocoons), they immediately encountered other firmamental barriers. Her problem was a distinctively human one or one involving interaction between the human and the divine. Natural circumferences hinted at solutions without providing them, and the poet found human experience a richer source of meditation on her most absorbing theme.

Much more satisfactory than natural transitions as representations of the poet's push against circumference were the major transitions in the human life cycle, each of them a movement from one identity to another. The most important such change was, of course, death: the ultimate circumference. All the rest proved essentially interchangeable within Dickinson's symbol system, and each life passage adumbrated death. When she identified the general situation of women as "Born—Bridalled—Shrouded—/ In a Day—" (P 1072), she combined life's major transitions to suggest their essential unity as encounters with circumference. All these transitions involved changes in personal consciousness and sense of identity and allowed the poet to confront human fears at any violation of protected circuits even when movement beyond one or another boundary offered seeming improvements in status and power.

True to her pattern of taking less interest in entrances upon the circuit than in breaks out of it (evident in her sunrise and sunset poems and early spring and late summer ones), Dickinson paid less attention to birth than to death, the latter so overwhelmingly dominant a circumferential theme as to justify a full chapter's analysis. Her lack of concern with entry into life and her tendency to develop this theme almost exclusively through flower and animal metaphors surprises the reader, although avoidance of the topic of human birth fits with her refusal to play maternal roles in her poems. Still, her few references to birth are decidedly circumferential ones involving breaks through barriers.

Note, for example, Dickinson's two references to fledgling birds emerging from their shells—behavior analogous to the butterfly's escape from the cocoon. One would expect a sense of triumphant release but finds instead an impulse toward withdrawal back into the original circuit. The speaker of "Let Us play Yesterday—" (P 728) urges her friend to return imaginatively to childhood, to a point before adult freedom, and she uses an egg analogy to indicate how the friend had precipitated birth into a new identity: "Still at the Egg-life—/ Chafing the Shell—/ When you troubled the Ellipse—/ And the Bird fell—." Strange verbs these: "troubled" and "fell." It was not empowerment and ability to fly that greeted the fledgling but helplessness in an alien environment ("You—and Eternity—the / Untold Tale—"). Falling into the unknown, the tiny creature might yearn for restoration to the familiar protective circuit of the egg, cramped and dark as it must have been; but the rhetorical question, "Can the Lark resume the Shell—," answers itself. Recognizing the egg circuit as a prison symbol, however, the speaker dreads return to its confinement and concludes with a prayer for continued freedom. The break out of a circuit involves risk, then, but to return within it would prove disastrous. That human birth involves entry into a new circuit that must itself be shattered to fulfill aspirations for power and permanence is not yet apparent in this poem, though suggested. At any rate, Dickinson found the egg analogy a useful one for other cases of liberated force and wrote once to her cousins about the power of language with the observation that "We must be careful what we say. No bird resumes its egg" (L 379).

But what about those romantic intimations of immortality from recollections of early childhood? What about Dickinson's sense of herself as a stranger, an outcast prince, a Wordsworthian infant? She presents such persons in strikingly circumferential imagery.

> The lonesome for they know not What—
> The Eastern Exiles—be—

Who strayed beyond the Amber line
Some madder Holiday—

And ever since—the purple Moat
They strive to climb—in vain—
As Birds—that tumble from the clouds
Do fumble at the strain—

The Blessed Ether—taught them—
Some Transatlantic Morn—
When Heaven—was too common—to miss—
Too sure—to dote upon!
(P 262)

Borrowing directional and color images from the sunrise and sunset poems, she tells of strangers who have ventured by mistake upon earth's circuit and into human life. Having entered from the east like the sun, they are now pushing against the western circumference: that moat to be crossed or stile to be climbed (this time without the dominie's assistance). Recollections of "Heaven" before entrapment in life's circuit make them impatient for release back into that spacious environment, that "Western Mystery" or "land—the Sunset washes—" (P 266) beyond circumference. In a striking reversal of the bird-egg analogy for birth, she presents the concept here as entry into a circuit rather than release from one, so that in context the egg analogy becomes more suggestive of death's liberation than of entry into life, at least when the analogy is applied to immortality-craving beings.

After birth comes bridal as the next circumferential point in life—one implied in "Let Us play Yesterday—" (P 728) in the speaker's impulse to recover childhood rather than move ahead into a new stage of maturity. Still a bit homesick for the protection she associates with the "egg," even though possessive of her new freedom, she tries to evade movement through the next transition: that to adult status as a wife. Dickinson's bridal poems explore circumferential possibilities, using a typical life passage as a metaphor. The poet strips away the social and ritual aspects of weddings (unlike funerals, which she occasionally details). Taking away attendants, family, the clergyman, and even the groom, she reduces the population of these narratives to one person: the bride herself at the point of transition to wedded life. Nothing matters but the change, both welcomed and dreaded. The transition is that from a girl's life to a woman's, from a probationary status to a settled one.

We remember the speaker of "I'm 'wife'—I've finished that—" (P 199), who proclaims herself both "Czar" and "Woman" and exclaims "How odd the Girl's life looks." She has passed through the circumference of her earlier life and undergone a "soft Eclipse"; now she recognizes the analogy between her achievement and that of the saints, who have crossed death's circumference into heaven. The speaker of "Ourselves were wed one summer—dear—" (P 631) accepted the transition almost by necessity, not because she pushed out of the girl's life, but because it "failed" her friend and her; the fragile circumference that had protected her circuit just collapsed. Brides in these poems continue as children until the point of absolute rupture with their past. One "dropt / The Playthings of Her Life" to assume new duties (P 732); another played a sort of hide-and-seek game with her bridegroom (P 473). On the other side of marital circumference came that new status and power recorded in "The World—stands—solemner—to me—" (P 493): that new identity won through practicing death and achieving gain that David Porter identifies as the essence of Dickinson's bridal group.[6] No wonder her imagined brides hesitate to smash through the marital circumference, given the obvious analogy with death as the passageway to expanded life.

It is not the public wedding ceremony that represents this circumferential event in a woman's life. Dickinson ignores that. It is the sexual consummation, the tearing of the hymen, that confirms the transition and makes return to the girlish circuit impossible. And we always meet Dickinson's speakers just before or just after that rupture. Perhaps her greatest bridal poem introduces the girl-woman at the point just on the verge of circumference that the poet found most fascinating as an emblem of the human condition at the ultimate extreme of the circuit but not quite "upon Circumference," surely not beyond it.

> A Wife—at Daybreak I shall be—
> Sunrise—Hast thou a Flag for me?
> At Midnight, I am but a Maid,
> How short it takes to make it Bride—

Then—Midnight, I have passed from thee
Unto the East, and Victory—

Midnight—Good Night! I hear them call,
The Angels bustle in the Hall—
Softly my Future climbs the Stair,
I fumble at my Childhood's prayer
So soon to be a Child no more—
Eternity, I'm coming—Sir,
Savior—I've seen the face—before!
(P 461)

Still a virgin, the speaker is about to become a bride, a wife. We find her on the immediate verge of transition, understandably expectant and eager—yet tense, too. The analogous circumferential metaphors cry out for recognition here, starting with the night and sunrise references in the first stanza. She has arrived at "Midnight," circumference of a new calendar day—a point of darkness. She anticipates sunrise, new light and life breaking through her circuit and releasing her into the "East" of new life and "Victory." The natural analogies here serve to reinforce the bridal theme by summoning routine if spectacular natural initiations to clarify this emotionally complex human transition.

The second stanza, by contrast, jolts the reader with its rush of unexpected references that extend the process of analogy still further, confronting us with the relationships between bridal and death, matrimony and conversion, wifely life and salvation. Who is "my Future"? Initially we expect the bridegroom but ultimately discover the "Savior" or Christ. No longer does her "Childhood's prayer" suffice, craving protection as it probably does for her outgrown circuit world—and addressed, presumably, to a power hitherto safely removed in heaven but now approaching her with plans for intimate encounter. Bridal attendants give way to "Angels" as the speaker recognizes that she must cross several circumferences at once: that her sexual initiation means death, that her wifely status implies salvation. In its fusion of birth, bridal, and burial images, this poem brilliantly unites all the customary circumferential points of the human life cycle, representing all such points of simultaneous beginning and ending as foreshadowings of death.

As I have explained earlier, I classify Dickinson's bridal poems as examples of role playing and believe that the poet played these roles because she thought them extremely important: because life had denied her the one major circumferential passage most women can anticipate, experience, remember, and record—birth being hidden from us and death unreportable. Birth began in mystery; death would end in it; but marriage moved from the known into the knowable. As such it was an inevitable Dickinsonian theme and one that served simultaneously to elaborate upon the two related circumferential experiences of birth and death. That marriage blurred into dying, therefore, and the bridegroom into Christ was only the natural working out of her metaphorical pattern in which death was the antitype of all human circumferences and Christ the antitype of all lovers, masters, and saviors.

In "I live with Him—I see His face—" (P 463), the speaker's union with her lover suggests that of marriage but is deliberately distinguished from it. His acceptance of her anticipates her passage across circumference. The poem strongly implies this woman's status as bride of Christ, and the compact between the lovers suggests election. Thus reassured about her eventual status, the speaker sees "Death's single privacy" only as "forestalling" her rights, not annulling them. She expresses confidence in "Immortality." Circumference has been broached, it seems, without destruction of the circuit in its continuing temporal context, but the initiating action came from the other side—from the lover rather than the speaker, and the speaker is content to wait for eventual union. This poem, too, may be an example of role playing. If Tennyson could impersonate a bride of Christ in one of his poems, so could Dickinson, and she did so all the more convincingly as the salvation theme proved the necessary unfolding of her bridal metaphor.

In addition to the relatively formulaic points of passage in human life, there are critical personal junctures of similar interest to Dickinson as circumferential analogies. Such was the private "solstice" of "There came a Day at Summer's full," (P 322) that anticipated "Resurrections" beyond the barrier immediately confronted by the lovers. Such also was "That first Day, when you praised Me, Sweet," (P 659), which "Glows Central—like a Jewel / Between Diverging Golds—." There were sudden events, then, capable of fracturing a life—of smashing a circuit and forcing entry into a new dimension. It is this startling sort of transition that Dickinson attempted to define in "Crisis is a Hair" (P 889), where she warned,

> Let an instant push
> Or an Atom press
> Or a Circle hesitate
> In Circumference
>
> It—may jolt the Hand
> That adjusts the Hair
> That secures Eternity
> From presenting—Here—

By representing the crisis as a hair, the poet emphasizes the fragility of the barriers protecting the circuit world, which can defend itself only by preternatural stillness; any motion, turbulence, or even growth will cut through the flimsy fortification protecting the person from "Eternity." Given the impossibility of arresting time or atoms, change becomes inevitable despite its threat to the personal circuit that instinctively resists change of any sort, even salvation.

The cramped, narrow circuit walling itself defensively against external influences often represented psychological truths to Dickinson, who presented the brain as a self-enclosed circle unable to protect itself against threatened ruptures. She was fascinated by circumferential states of consciousness, by those points at which the brain explodes or seeps beyond barriers as one mental condition gives way to another. Despite the brain's jealous protection of its internal space, she recognized the greatest danger when it succeeded in isolating itself as a circuit of emptiness, numbness, and resistance to change. "'Tis a dangerous moment for any one when the meaning goes out of things and Life stands straight—and punctual—and yet no signal comes," she wrote late in life, "Yet such moments are. If we survive them they expand us, if we do not, but that is Death, whose if is everlasting."[7] Yet she knew the mind's tendency to isolate itself in just such a self-contained circuit of misery, especially when prompted by pain with its "Element of Blank" (P 650). The mind already emblematizes the most alienating aspects of personal extinction in its very refusal to open itself to prospects of infinity and power. If one refuses to move through death, Dickinson implies, one will be stuck within it; death remains the inescapable reality.

Dickinson's poems offer little evidence that the psychological circuit can be protected from rupture. Over and over, we find it opening up in her poems—with varying results most dramatically represented in the radical alternations between confinement and dangerous liberty of "The Soul has Bandaged moments—" (P 512), in which the soul occasionally escapes beyond the circumference of despair without ever achieving actual freedom. Each subsequent confinement, however, hurts more intensely; the prisoner may hesitate to leave his cell but will die to resist being pushed back into it, and the bird released from its egg can never again find shelter within the shattered ellipse. Although one would hope to find breaks in the brain's confining circuit serving as entryways to restorative influences outside, Dickinson offered no guarantees. Circumference, once broken, could never be refused, and there was danger that the consciousness might just trickle out into nothingness or unravel like the ball of yarn that represents the mind's random disassembly in "I felt a Cleaving in my Mind—" (P 937). More comforting were the transitional states of "It ceased to hurt me, though so slow" (P 584), in which the speaker recognizes that she has already crossed a circumference out of pain without quite knowing it, or of "My first well Day— since many ill—" (P 574), in which the speaker uses natural progressions as yardsticks to measure her own advancement beyond a circuit of sickness. Discovery of substantial change outside her consciousness encourages hope for other kinds of growth: "My loss, by sickness—Was it Loss? / Or that Etherial Gain / One earns by measuring the Grave—/ Then—measuring the Sun—." Outside the circuit in which she has been confined, she achieves perspective.

The circuit world isolates and protects itself in Dickinson's poems—especially those dealing with psychological states and the brain's defensiveness. Yet openings in its circumferential frame are inevitable, necessary, desirable. Violations of the soul's defenses hint at rewards waiting beyond the equally guarded circumference of individual human life.

> One Joy of so much anguish
> Sweet nature has for me

> I shun it as I do Despair
> Or dear iniquity—
> Why Birds, a Summer morning
> Before the Quick of Day
> Should stab my ravished spirit
> With Dirks of Melody
> Is part of an inquiry
> That will receive reply
> When Flesh and Spirit sunder
> In Death's Immediately—
> (P 1420)

The "Dirks of Melody" penetrate the mind's carapace to introduce a joy in nature's ebullience that unsettles the circuit's stasis. Joy, as threatening to the self-imprisoned consciousness as despair, provides intimations of possibilities outside the self, and the final lines suggest comfort beyond the painful mortal circumference even though the circuit world desperately protects itself against penetration by infinity.

A more routine circumferential experience of the mind is the daily transition between sleep and waking, between dreams and rational applications of consciousness. Seldom did Dickinson represent the process of sinking into sleep, although "Dont put up my Thread & Needle—" (P 617) confronts us with a weakened invalid sleeper who trusts that dreams will connect her tenuously to the normal routines of life's circuit. Unable to continue her chores until she revives from sleep and sickness, she promises to dream she is sewing. Explicit presentations of dream visions are also infrequent in the poems, with the strangely phallic narrative of "In Winter in my Room" (P 1670) the most memorable example. Most often Dickinson employs dreams to reverse habitual assumptions about reality, to shift outside life's circuit for a fresh perspective. An early poem addressed to her father "to whose untiring efforts in my behalf, I am indebted for my *morning-hours—*viz—3. A M. to 12. P M. these grateful lines are inscribed" rebukes commonplace notions about the relative values of sleep and waking with the assertion that "Sleep is the station grand / Down wh', on either hand / The hosts of witness stand!" (P 13). As such, sleep fulfilled those religious goals her family emphasized, much as the playful butterfly's flittings represented an assumption unsuspected by cocoon-preferring Yankee proponents of industriousness and early rising. Morning, she reminded her father, symbolized Resurrection—not daily stumbling out of bed. As imaginative processes, dreams bridged a mental circumference analogous to the division between circuit life and resurrected being.

"Awakening" was already, in Amherst vocabulary, a metaphor applied to an early stage of Calvinist conversion, itself the most significant circumferential point in spiritual life. In this case Christ would initiate the change; he would draw the elected saint across the circumference of mortality into immortality, out of sinfulness into salvation. A person born into the Dickinson or Norcross families, attending Congregational Church services from childhood, educated at home and school in Calvinist values, and surrounded by an evangelical community could look forward to conversion as an almost guaranteed step toward spiritual maturity, nearly as predictable as marriage (or as painfully and invidiously withheld). The morphology of conversion developed by the New England Puritans for their congregations of visible saints had been modified by Dickinson's era but not essentially changed; it had only become more routine and semiautomatic. There were likely stages of awakening, sanctification, and conversion in the development of the individual saint of which Emily Dickinson was well aware. And there were occasional periods when grace seemed to pour out upon the whole community and promise salvation even to members hitherto apparently dormant. In 1873, the poet could laugh at such an outburst, remarking to Frances and Louise Norcross that "There is that which is called an 'awakening' in the church, and I know of no choicer ecstasy than to see Mrs. [Sweetser] roll out in crape every morning, I suppose to intimidate antichrist; at least it would have that effect on me. It reminds me of Don Quixote demanding the surrender of the wind-mill, and of Sir Stephen Toplift, and of Sir Alexander Cockburn" (L 389).[8] In other words, this so-called awakening struck her as a mad adventure though based on noble dreams.

But, then, perhaps Dickinson herself was still sleeping; she had never been awakened, although she had reported many years earlier to the pious Abiah Root about a season of false awakening such as Jonathan Edwards reported in his "Personal Narrative" and against which he warned ministers eager to harvest conversions (L 11). Adolescent Emily—like young Jonathan—had wept for her sins, delighted in prayer, imagined herself pious, and then drifted back into her habitual routine without ever actually pushing beyond her spiritual circuit. She apparently regarded pushing as her duty and blamed herself for not trying hard enough; the more orthodox Edwards would have detected signs of human effort without divine grace and recognized her saintly role playing as an empty delusion.[9] Rather than seeking out awakenings thereafter, however, Dickinson seems to have sealed her circuit more tightly against incursions from beyond circumference.

But conversion fascinated this young woman, and she observed the processes of her friends' transitions, begging for details of what they felt. Her letters to Abiah Root from 1846 to 1852 adopt the hackneyed vocabulary of Calvinist piety and present their author as an aspiring though somewhat cautious prospective Christian. One detects more candor, though no less curiosity about the topic, when she writes in 1850 to Jane Humphrey during the awakening that drew her father and sister into communion with the church and reports to her about the resolutions Vinnie, Abby Wood, and other friends had found to their religious quests. Both doubt and wonder are evident in her comments: "I cant tell you *what* they have found, but *they* think it is something precious. I wonder if it *is*? How strange is this sanctification, that works such a marvellous change, that sows in such corruption, and rises in golden glory, that brings Christ down, and shews him, and lets him select his friends!" (L 35). These are circumferential metaphors given her by her Calvinist culture, which had already vitiated their imagistic vitality through overuse by people incapable of envisaging the metaphors. But Dickinson could imagine, in lively ways, what her friends were talking about. Evidently she wondered whether *they* did.

The essence of conversion was change. The presumed saints should have crossed the barrier between finitude and infinity, mortality and immortality, the human and the divine. But *had* they? Dickinson observed attentively "those on whom *change* has passed" and noted the behavioral evidence. "They seem so very tranquil," she told Jane, "and their voices are kind, and gentle, and the tears fill their eyes so often, I really think I envy them." Almost. The changes here give little sense of acquired power or new vitality. The behavior of these young ladies sounds like her own a few years earlier. Nor did the final Calvinist test of perseverance especially confirm their claims. Among those who pressed young Emily to accept such change were Susan Gilbert and Lavinia, neither of whom matured into any model of serenity and tearful meekness. Had the poet convinced herself of their escape beyond the circumference of sin and spiritual death, she might have been more responsive to conversion pressures. Instead she claimed her inability "to give up the world" (even while being the only Mount Holyoke collegian to stay behind while all the saved and searching students went off to a menagerie) and withdrew increasingly from communal religious rituals—not because she ceased questing for God and all he offered her beyond circumference but because she was probably the only person she knew who felt impelled to continue the quest (L 23; 16). Meanwhile the only obvious circumference some of her converted friends moved across was the barrier that separated the presumably elect from the apparently unsaved, and the poet found the division painful. Piety, so far as she could see, locked believers into their own narrow circuit—isolating them from others and perhaps even from grace.[10] Meanwhile, the poet pursued her solitary spiritual quest for insight beyond circumference and access to the "Western Mystery" (P 266) to which Christ and the Bible beckoned her, but she never felt that assurance of salvation for which she yearned even as it evaded her intensely inquiring ironic mind.

The imagery by which Dickinson expressed her shifting relationships with God deviated often from traditional Calvinist language. "Given in Marriage unto Thee" (P 817), for instance, with its identification of the speaker as "Bride of the Father and the Son / Bride of the Holy Ghost," sounds more Catholic than Congregational and buttresses slightly the improbable claims of readers who hope to find Amherst's "Wayward Nun" (P 722) a hidden papist. Yet even a version of this bridal imagery corresponded at points to Calvinist conversion patterns, and one can read "Fitter to see Him, I may be" (P 968) as a report on the speaker's experience of sanctifying changes in herself since Christ's grace first assured her of election, so that her only remaining fear is that the Savior may not recognize the gradually developed beauty of his bride when he comes to claim her. Several poems about mysterious guests suggest divine visitation: "Conscious am I in my Chamber," (P 679), "I cannot see my soul but know 'tis there" (P

1262), and "He was my host—he was my guest," (P 1721), among others. And at least one poem, "It was a quiet way—" (P 1053), provides a happy report on the soul's journey with Christ to heaven. In it we have a love poem in which the suitor carries off the speaker beyond circumference in an episode that reminds us of "Because I could not stop for Death—" (P 712) but involves reciprocated devotion rather than betrayal, a completed quest rather than a stalemated one.

In reading Dickinson's poems for evidence of conversion, we must be alert as always to the probability of role playing. One who habitually acted out the parts of seemingly more fortunate persons and of all whom she imagined to have escaped from limitation would certainly try out the role of the elected saint: the one part in life's drama she had been taught to think essential. And we must anticipate her playing the opposite role as well, to savor this most radical possible experience of deprivation. Juxtapositions of fascicle poems present no clear line of saving action—or of spiritual defeat, for that matter, only of restless search.

Fascicle 33, for example, gives us an absorbing cluster of poems. "The Child's faith is new—" (P 637) generalizes on the loss of innocence to experience and on that loss's result in cynicism about God's promises; the disaffected child "gains the skill / Sorrowful—as certain—/ Men—to anticipate / Instead of Kings—." The next poem ratifies the disappointment with a first-person account of loss. "Except the Heaven had come so near—" (P 472), she writes, she would feel less frustrated by its current distance: "But just to hear the Grace depart—/ I never thought to see—/ Afflicts me with a Double loss—/ 'Tis lost—And lost to me—." These are not the celebrations of an elected saint. But the poem immediately following them, "To my small Hearth His fire came—" (P 638), reads like a jubilant song. It offers sunrise imagery betokening another sort of circumference overcome, representing a dazzling and changeless enlightenment. It salutes eternal summer and all that it implies. The speaker addresses nature personally, calling attention to the reality and permanence of this change by comparison with nature's shifting show. She is reporting her conversion, it seems, not just awakening. If we take these three poems as a narrative sequence, then, we have evidence for the poet's having crossed circumference with God's help. But the skepticism dwells in our memories, and it would be risky to draw conclusions from such evidence, which leaves open the possibility of a triple loss as well as of victory.

The danger seems yet graver when we turn to the next fascicle and encounter "One Blessing had I than the rest" (P 756), in which the first four stanzas (all in the past tense) read like an experience of grace. The speaker tells of happiness, plenitude, fulfillment of dreams and prayers. The circuit of her mortal capacity for joy has been strangely filled with a "perfect—paralyzing Bliss—/ Contented as Despair—." Perhaps this oxymoronic language in itself, harking back as it does to poems representing the mind's self-entrapment, should lead us to suspect that the speaker has never crossed circumference. But she certainly thought she had, and the experience released her from her sense of limitation until the glorious awakening was withdrawn to leave her with a tragic sense of deprivation and betrayal. She has been granted a glimpse beyond circumference but has been denied access to the promised joy. Her appetite for fulfillment outside her circuit world now rages within her. It may yet be fulfilled. Paradise has been deferred rather than denied. She is still held back from bliss, though, and feels more bitterly alienated. "Victory comes late—" (P 690), placed just before this poem in fascicle 34, similarly laments God's frugality with joy, asking "Was God so economical? / His Table's spread too high for Us—/ Unless We dine on tiptoe—." Perhaps such straining to push beyond barriers was God's purpose in being so parsimonious. Perhaps he enticed men to outgrow or smash their protected circuits by raising hopes for plenitude beyond. One can be sure of spiritual aspiration in Dickinson's poems but not of religious assurance.

There were also natural epiphanies experienced by this poet, accustomed as she was to interpreting nature's signs in terms of emotional and spiritual circumferences. In 1880, Dickinson wrote to Mrs. Holland that "The Snow is so white and sudden it seems almost like a Change of Heart—though I dont mean a 'Conversion'—I mean a Revolution" (L 678). Either one would be a circumferential event: revolution being more proper to nature or to man within the natural sphere and conversion proper to God or to man within the spiritual sphere. Glistening snow manifested one kind of change and implied the other. But nature failed to accomplish conversion in man, much as it might hint at it. Sometimes, as in "Oh Shadow on the Grass," (P 1187), natural epiphanies raised false hopes in questers straining toward conversion. Like the premonitory shadow "Indicative that Suns go down—" (P 764), this one presages change. But whereas the sun enters the "Western Mystery" (P 266) and then returns, the speaker interprets the end of daylight in her own case as a permanent loss of opportunity. Just as Emerson once reproved himself for settling for "a few herbs and apples" from all the wealth and power the day offered, Dickinson's speaker finds she has been too enthralled by the natural spectacle itself to interpret or apply the message it might have brought her from beyond circumference, and she identifies the failure here as evidence against her election.[11] A happier natural epiphany is reported, however, in "Somewhere upon the general Earth" (P 1231), where the speaker tells of herself as having been "consecrated" by a "Magic" that still exists somewhere but that has left her behind, not frustrated in this case but more than ever expectant. Having experienced brief release from her confining circuit, she delights in God's expansiveness as represented to her by nature and concludes the poem with a prayer: "Oh God of Width, do not for us / Curtail Eternity!" Not liberated beyond circumference but not satisfied either within her mortal circuit, Dickinson pursued an essentially religious quest throughout her life and used her poems to probe the barriers between her natural vision and the glories of which she craved assurance.

However eager she proved herself for communication with the infinite, Emily Dickinson early discovered her separation from the organized church that supposedly included Amherst's converted saints. Two vignettes from her childhood, both recounted late in life, reveal the sequence of her youthful alienation. An 1884 letter to a cousin, Clara Newman Turner, recalls the innocence and enthusiasm she displayed when her own "Child's faith" was new (P 637): "The cordiality of the Sacrament extremely interested me when a Child, and when the Clergyman invited 'all who loved the Lord Jesus Christ, to remain,' I could scarcely refrain from rising and thanking him for the to me unexpected courtesy, though I now think had it been to all who loved Santa Claus, my transports would have been even more untimely" (L 926). This anecdote gives charming insight into Emily at that naively affectionate stage of childhood when a little girl feels herself the object of everyone's love and offers her own bountifully in return: to Jesus, whom she

had been taught to love; to Santa Claus, who had earned her gratitude with his Christmas remembrances; and even to the minister,
whom she perceived as offering her a special present. Yet a story
she had told Mrs. Holland ten years before recalls a diametrically
opposite response to the same situation: "When a Child and
fleeing from Sacrament I could hear the Clergyman saying 'All
who loved the Lord Jesus Christ—were asked to remain—' / My
flight kept time to the Words" (L 412).

What had happened to send the eager little participant into desperate flight? Had she stopped loving Jesus, as the stories would
suggest? No: We have poems and letters enough to prove the opposite. But she had discovered the narrowness by which the minister and congregation defined "all who loved the Lord Jesus
Christ"—had learned that "all" included only those whose claims
of conversion entitled them to participate in the communion service that was about to begin. Everyone else, including children
manifesting ardent but undiscriminating affection, must leave. She
had learned that the church was a limited circle that excluded her,
and she seems never to have made an earnest effort to push into its
circuit—probably suspecting that those who loved Jesus and those
whom he loved could not be so accurately identified and should
not be so intent on walling themselves *in* when the whole purpose
of religion was to open human circuits *out* into that awesome space
beyond circumference as revealed by Scripture and intuited by
faith. She grew into a detached and ironic spectator of this church
as it went about its processes of encirclement, and her 1851 comments to Austin that "I have just come in from Church very hot,
and faded, having witnessed a couple of Baptisms, three admis-
sions to church, a Supper of the Lord, and some other minor
transactions time fails me to record" betray none of that awe or
even jealousy one would expect her to have felt had she really
sensed that these persons had penetrated mortal circumference (L
46). Despite the minister's urgent calls for conversion *now today*
and despite reports of a new awakening in Amherst so that "Our
church grows interesting, Zion lifts her head—I overhear remarks
signifying Jerusalem," she regarded herself as a permanent and
willful outcast from the church and from the eucharistic sacrament
that bound its members in insufficiently cordial fellowship.

Yet the idea of sacrament became important to Dickinson, and
the word itself remained central to her vocabulary throughout life.

Whether or not she had learned Calvin's definition of a sacrament as "a testimony of divine grace toward us, confirmed by an outward sign, with mutual attestation of our piety," she recognized its essential attributes as a manifestation of the spirit in matter, a visitation of infinity in finite form, a cooperation between God and man, and an expression of mutual love.[12] Sacraments, established by God but practiced by men, proved the permeability of the circumference bounding the mortal circuit, thus opening access to eternity and to awe. They proved God's continuing participation within man's circuit. She took them as signs of hope for ultimate victory: for the possibility that death might be breached and immortality experienced without absolute forfeit of consciousness or identity. Not only *had* Christ involved himself in humanity; he still *did* so, symbolically. Sacraments consecrated men. And since they used as their material signs a natural element (water) and products of human labor employed upon familiar agricultural crops (bread and wine), they included nature and work also within the domain of the sacred. It is this sense of the holy within the ordinary and of the immortal within the temporal that underlies Dickinson's private use of sacrament as a symbol of circumference penetrated and opened out. Her poems removed the concept from the church and applied it to man and nature in circumstances inspiring reverence.

Excluded herself from the formal communion service in her church, Dickinson nonetheless valued and tried to attain the sense of consecrated community that she identified as essential to the idea of sacrament. Thus we find her speakers seeking alternative natural liturgies—including that of "These are the days when Birds come back—" (P 130), in which she asks, as a child, to join in nature's equivalent to the Christian liturgy from which, also as a child, she has been excluded. Here, too, the celebrating community is an alien one—more obviously so than the Amherst congregation, and she craves permission to participate without assurance of acceptance. At other times she claimed to know the feeling of unity and communion that sacramental action effected, referring once to a small but sufficient grouping of friends as "Crowded—as Sacrament—" (P 495) and in another poem to intimates who "lap one Air / Dwell in one Blood / Under one Sacrament" (P 491). She reports on a private experience in "It might be lonelier" (P 405), which asserts that "The Sacrament—of

Him—" enters within the tight circuit of the speaker's lonely life. Were her circuit already crowded by human friends, she implies, this divine visitor might have been kept out or pressed back. In her solitude, then, she enjoys private communion with the divinity who transfuses circumference to enhance and consecrate life within her circuit. Appearing in fascicle 28 just before "Some— Work for Immortality—/ The Chiefer part, for Time—" (P 406), this poem suggests the speaker's sense of the penetration of infinity into the finite and her recognition of time as a human fallacy in trying to regulate eternity.

Several poems represented Dickinson's sense of reverence toward the concept of sacrament and its dignifying effect on the gifted person. In "My Worthiness is all my Doubt—" (P 751), for example, the speaker reports her humble conformity of herself to grace (perhaps God's gift, perhaps a lover's) by saying "So I—the undivine abode / Of His Elect Content—/ Conform my Soul— as twere a Church, / Unto Her Sacrament—." And she responds to natural epiphanies with the same reverence for the sacredness that transforms matter all too briefly, leaving the responsive spirit to feel a sense of violation in "A quality of loss / Affecting our Content / As Trade had suddenly encroached / Upon a Sacrament" (P 812). However they came—through natural epiphanies, experiences of love, or special moments of personal beatitude— those occasions when the material seemed imbued by the spiritual, when the routine was invested by the sacred, and when mortality suddenly put on immortality were expressed in Dickinson's writing in sacramental terms.

There were only two sacraments in Amherst's Congregational Church, rooted as it was in the Reformed Protestant tradition, but both of them, baptism and the eucharist, appeared in her poetry. In keeping with her comparative lack of interest in birth, Dickinson more or less ignored the christening ritual, presenting baptism instead as any symbolic representation of new life, as we have seen in the case of the young woman who described herself as "Baptized—this Day—A Bride—" (P 473). A more interesting perspective on this sacrament comes in "I'm ceded—I've stopped being Their's—" (P 508) when the speaker disavows her infant baptism and the identity conferred with it and then asserts another baptism enacted by and for herself. Baptism in New England Puritan churches and their successors served as a child's introduction to the community and as the seal of God's covenant with the saints. Although not conferring full church membership (dependent upon conversion and certified by eucharistic participation), it indicated the community's expectation that God intended the child's salvation. The baptized child and young adult could pursue salvation hopefully. Yet full grace was wanting. This speaker has experienced a narrow "Crescent" or empty "Arc" rather than a complete circle of faith. Now, as an adult, she rejects the identity imposed on her by other people's choices. Perhaps she senses the frustration of those earlier covenantal hopes and thinks of the sacramental ritual as simply another empty game by which as a child she experimented with roles she never got to play as an adult. The dolls that she mentions were given, after all, in anticipation of eventual mothering responsibility; yet Dickinson never raised a child. And the string of spools prepared little hands either for manual labor like that performed by women in New England factories (and that Dickinson never for a moment considered) or for the fancy needlework she apparently despised. She has simply not matured into the stereotyped woman she assumes her family had anticipated, and she rejects her baptismal identity as a sign of those false expectations. But ritual confirmation of the sacredness of new identity still captures her imagination, so she conducts her own adult baptism to seal a different sort of election—her own choice of self-image and its symbol. Not surprisingly, the symbol she chooses is a circular one indicative of status and plenitude. Instead of the skimpy arc or crescent, she will have a diadem—a crown. No longer a potential part of someone else's circle, she draws her own circumference.

Still more absorbing to Dickinson's imagination was the sacrament of the Lord's Supper, which commemorated Christ's Passover observance, death, and Resurrection (his triumphant though agonizing passage through circumference) and brought him back symbolically in material signs to be consumed by the faithful communicants. No ritual she knew of went further than this in demonstrating the permeability in both directions of those barriers between limitation and aspiration; and the eucharist became her all-encompassing symbol for transitions across circumference.[13] In commemorating Christ's Passion, after all, the church remembered the most humbling deprivation in human history but one that ultimately reversed the primal deprivation of the Fall.

"Do those at Sacrament / Commemorate Dishonor," Dickinson inquired rhetorically, "Or love annealed of love / Until it bend as low as Death / Redignified, above?" (P 833). Christ's action, then, transformed humiliation into glory and death into life, and the sacrament symbolically repeated that circumference-piercing action.

One of Emily Dickinson's greatest poems employs eucharistic imagery to commemorate a different action: the death and hoped-for rebirth of the natural year as represented by her intuited loss of summer. As usual an outsider in sacramental ritual, the speaker senses rather than observes the crickets' liturgy as the insects manifest to her the sacredness of natural life.

> Further in Summer than the Birds
> Pathetic from the Grass
> A minor Nation celebrates
> It's unobtrusive Mass.
>
> No Ordinance be seen
> So gradual the Grace
> A pensive Custom it becomes
> Enlarging Loneliness.
>
> Antiquest felt at Noon
> When August burning low
> Arise this spectral Canticle
> Repose to typify
>
> Remit as yet no Grace
> No Furrow on the Glow
> Yet a Druidic Difference
> Enhances Nature now
> (P 1068)

What a masterstroke of humbling wit to replace the visible saints of her local congregation with these pitiful crickets! Yet Dickinson's hidden insects carry out a more complex and comprehensive liturgy than any known in Amherst, forcing her to combine elements of Druidic solstice celebrations with Calvinist ordinances and the Catholic mass in an attempt to represent its awesome suggestiveness. It is the high-church Catholic ritual that seems to dominate here, with the cricket songs welling up from some dark natural cathedral and the August light deepening and glowing like sanctuary candles; and the Catholic doctrine of Christ's real presence in the eucharist comes to mind with its extrasymbolic witness to transcended barriers. A sense of holiness dominates this poem, a depth of reverence and faith. "Grace" seems the key word (gracefully linked with "Grass" as a sign of natural consecration). The ritual itself remains invisible to the speaker, most obviously so in a longer version she sent to her cousins with a stanza emphasizing her isolation: "Nor know I when it cease, / At candle it is here; / When sunrise is, that is it not. / Than this, I know no more." In the hush of the ritual she describes, in the quiet reverence of the speaker's response, and in the fundamental theme of summer's subtle slippage into fall, this poem communicates invisible processes of change all of which testify to the salvific effects of sacred action. The circuit worlds of the planet and of the speaker's mind have been visited from beyond circumference by a natural manifestation of grace that enables the poet to accept the coming death of the year in expectancy of renewal.

Christianity recognizes two principal revelations from God to man: natural and scriptural. Paralleling scriptural revelation for Calvinists was sacramental action, not considered superior to Scripture and its preached interpretation but rather supplemental. Reformed doctrine characterized the sacraments as "visible Words" because their actions represented the Bible's saving truths.[14] Given Dickinson's feelings for and about language, it is no wonder that she turned around the terms of the traditional definition to introduce words themselves as sacraments—at least those few that adequately expressed the poet's vision. Once, she likened such words to "signal esoteric sips / Of the communion Wine" (P 1452). "A Word made Flesh is seldom" (P 1651) linked St. John's identification of Christ as Logos, the incarnate Word, with communal eucharistic action to represent the magical force of language. Awe and dread accompany such power. Just as the unelected communicant eats and drinks to his damnation, so does the poet wield power beyond his conscious control—force from beyond circumference that enters and transforms the circuit. Language here plays Christ's role, consenting to share its strength with those who love it and condescending as a compound of humanity and divinity to fulfill man's needs. The Word made visible, visions transformed into words: Both bridged circumference.

If words had quasi-sacramental power, then poetry as the most selective and forceful deployment of language also offered a prospect of penetrating circumference—this time from the mortal side. Where sacraments irradiated natural matter with the nimbus of eternity, art could occasionally project the human consciousness into more-than-mortal spheres. That was what Dickinson meant in citing George Eliot as an example of a mortal who had already put on immortality, demonstrating her power, not by reporting visions of another world, but by revealing the glory already shining in this one (L 389). Though fascinated by the possibilities beyond circumference, after all, Dickinson retained her allegiance to the circuit of consciousness and her love for everything beautiful and pleasing here at hand. "The mysteries of human nature surpass the 'mysteries of redemption'," she explained to her Norcross cousins while commenting on Eliot, "for the infinite we only suppose, while we see the finite." Artists who could suggest infinity while presenting the finite struck her as humanity's most encouraging examples of questers on the brink of circumference. By pressing against its barriers with all the force of art, they achieved transformations—the sort of transformations that challenged Dickinson herself. When she described Elizabeth Barrett Browning's awakening and enriching influence on her, therefore, she employed the language of conversion as the only imagery adequate to expression of enhanced spiritual life achieved through poetry: "I could not have defined the change—/ Conversion of the Mind / Like Sanctifying in the Soul—/ Is witnessed—not explained—" (P 593).

Responding to art almost as an influx of grace, Dickinson emphasized the potential of painting, music, and poetry to liberate the responsive person from circuit routine and to communicate creative joy. Sometimes, as in "I would not paint—a picture—" (P 505), it was enough simply to experience art and respond. Painting, music, and poetry all overcome barriers of mortal finitude by achieving bright impossibilities and lifting their admirers balloon-like toward a spiritual firmament. By summoning sensations from beyond circumference, they suggest a plenitude that humbles man even while expanding his horizons. They confront his imagination with tantalizing dreams that beckon him upward in a state of "sumptuous—Despair—" at inevitable human limitations. When the speaker of this poem disavows her aspiration to be a poet, it is because she has come to regard poetry in superhuman terms exciting awe and reverence. She would not be a poet who could stun herself "With Bolts of Melody," but then who is or ever has been except the divine Creator? Poetry in its ultimate expression would entail seeing God and living (P 1247), an impossible goal for finite artists.

Dickinson would, however, be a different sort of poet—one who struggles valiantly against human limitations in an attempt to express the ineffable and therefore encounters the sublime frustrations she describes in "The Tint I cannot take—is best—" (P 627), with its review of those states of consciousness and natural revelations that entice with their suggestions of eternal, immutable perfection. Art attempts, however imperfectly, to capture such circumferential epiphanies as "The eager look—on Landscapes—/ As if they just repressed / Some Secret—that was pushing / Like Columns—in the Breast—."[15] An inherently circumferential experience, art stimulated constant dissatisfaction with finitude; it alienated the responsive person from circuit limitations; and it opened perspective on undreamed-of joys. It provided an alternative to religion as a means of advancement into the mysterious and beautiful unknown.

> The fascinating chill that music leaves
> Is Earth's corroboration
> Of Ecstasy's impediment—
> 'Tis Rapture's germination
> In timid and tumultuous soil
> A fine—estranging creature—
> To something upper—wooing us
> But not to our Creator—
> (P 1480)

If not to the Creator, then to whom or what? Probably to "Awe," Dickinson's impersonal name for the force beyond circumference. The paternal idea of God may have seemed too personal to account for the abstract power of music. And a personal Creator can be faulted too directly for the deprivations and limitations with which art makes man impatient. But awe suggests no such involvement with man's troubles or aspirations, generates no narrative fantasies (except perhaps that of little Emily running home to "Awe" as a foster mother). It simply *is* in its perfection and can be defined not by its divine essence but by man's response.

In this context we can interpret Dickinson's most gnomic statement on art and circumference, the poem she sent to Daniel Chester French in April 1884 to honor the unveiling of his statue of John Harvard in front of University Hall in Cambridge: "Circumference thou Bride of Awe / Possessing thou shalt be / Possessed by every hallowed Knight / That dares to covet thee" (P 1620). The artist pressing perpetually at the limits of mortal expression pursues what she called in her accompanying letter "an aim forever touched with dew"—always new, ever fresh, and never fully achieved. He is a knight on a quest for this great boon representing the ultimate reach of human aspiration. "Circumference," the object of the quester's passion, is personified here as already a bride, married to "Awe"—that stronger mysterious force beyond humanly experienced boundaries. (We are in the realm of chivalric romance with knights chasing other men's wives as their mistresses to inspire them to valiant deeds with no hope of consummating their necessarily chaste passions.) "Circumference", of course, is also death: end point of the mortal circuit. Joined now in loving union with "Awe," however, she offers riches to those admirers pure hearted enough to devote themselves to her in the courtly romance envisaged here—one that ought to end in renunciation, one would suppose, but concludes instead with the knight's paradoxical possession of the lady and her husband's wealth. In courting the lady, the suitor wins her lord's favor also, though "Awe" would be unreachable except through "Circumference" as intermediary. And, Dickinson asserts, success in this celestial court of love is possible (in fact, assured) for any quester sufficiently endowed with grace to make the effort.

Most knights, presumably, would pursue a different mistress. Few yearn for death, no matter what glorious alliances it may form. Dickinson tells French here that the artist must seek out the limits of human possibility, knowing that the limiting point is death. He must, in fact, desire death actively and pursue it as a goal, confident that its intimacy with "Awe" (and the infinity, immortality, and ecstasy that word implies for her) would lead him to glory. He must be death's friend, as she represents herself to be in addressing this poem, not to the mortal knight, but to "Circumference" herself.

The context in which the poem first appeared is an illuminating one, though we have no way of knowing that a poem so abstract was actually written for Daniel Chester French or for any specific occasion. Dickinson often reached into her fascicles and work sheets to send remembrances to her friends. But it is suggestive, at any rate, to think of the immediate known circumstance. Was she celebrating French's statue? If so, she overvalued it and may have responded instead to some idealized sculpture in her own imagination. Or was she thinking of John Harvard himself, whose generous and wholly gratuitous dying action has memorialized his name to an extent he never could have imagined? "*Every* hallowed Knight," indeed! And what would she have thought if she could have foreseen that, within a century of her death, Harvard University would number her manuscripts and personal belongings among its treasures (even those mysteriously bridal white dresses now encased in glass)? By coveting circumference, even though it meant death, the Dickinsonian quester could hope for empowerment beyond all privation—for transcendence of every limit to human aspiration.

She could hope—but not know, and an even more abstract poem betrayed its author's fears about venturing toward circumference.

> I saw no Way—The Heavens were stitched—
> I felt the Columns close—
> The Earth reversed her Hemispheres—
> I touched the Universe—
>
> And back it slid—and I alone—
> A Speck upon a Ball—
> Went out upon Circumference—
> Beyond the Dip of Bell—
> (P 378)

Here we have one of those poems that cries out for a chalkboard and a geometry lesson from the poet. To make sense of it, we must visualize the speaker's position along the margin of an exploding circle (itself, perhaps, the finest visual emblem of Dickinson's symbolic system). The narrative, written in past tense, reports a sequence of changes. At first the speaker had been entrapped somehow within a circuit. She sounded desperate for escape but found no release. As the poem progresses, our suspicion is confirmed that she has been buried just within earth's circumference in the outer layer of the circuit. There we would expect her to remain, like the tenants of Dickinson's famous "Alabaster Chambers" (P 216). If dependent on her own power, she would seem helpless; although it is possible that the pressure of her push against the stifling firmament might have been the final force precipitating the crisis that followed when an instant pushed, an atom pressed, and this circle hesitated in circumference (P 889).

Miraculously, the circumference yielded; the circle opened. It split in half apparently, thereby throwing open the circuit within. And the hemispheres, now separated, rolled at her touch along each other's circumference to create parallel arcs with bell-shaped hollows between them. The speaker, having been imprisoned within the circuit, now experienced sudden release into an environment so startlingly unexpected as perhaps to make her wish for renewed confinement, like the prisoner of Chillon or the fledgling emerging from its egg. Venturing out, she found herself alone in a void, walking "upon Circumference" to explore her situation. What did she find? We have no way of knowing, but the tone of the poem offers less hope than we might expect after all those intimations of glory and fulfillment beyond circumference.

The Dickinson character, whom we normally encounter inside circumference and pressing against its barrier, has advanced a stage. Now she stands *upon* it but not yet *beyond* it. Feeling overwhelmed in space, she perceives herself as even tinier and more helpless than ever, not a triumphant quester but a "Speck upon a Ball," and she clings to the unsettled margin of her once familiar circuit. Emerging on the other side of death, then, she has entered the outer margin of circumference and gained the opportunity to investigate it. But we have no sense that she has fallen into the arms of God or awe, that she has fulfilled any aspirations beyond escape from confinement. We leave her in uncertainty and fear— not yet ready to leap into the apparent void that may still prove to be "the land—the Sunset washes—" (P 266). Being "upon Circumference" still means confinement to the domain of death even though looking externally now toward the mysterious space outside the circuit rather than the familiar territory within. Once Dickinson's speaker gets her bearings, then, she may yet use the altered perspective of death to gain otherwise impossible insight beyond circumference even while still clinging to the remnants of her mortal circuit.

8

"Dying in Drama"

Death as Circumference

EXTREME AS IT was in its depiction of human isolation upon a forbidding circumference, "I saw no Way—The Heavens were stitched—" (P 378) presented an image of man's fate that Dickinson applied broadly in her lifelong commentaries on our tenuous hold on the planet. The imminent contingency of death struck her as life's most fascinating feature, as the source of all adventure, and as a perpetual incentive to wonder. No one can read her collected poems and letters without discovering her intense involvement with the fact of death, though readers respond differently to the poet's obsession—interpreting her reflections as either morbid or healthy depending in large measure on their own dispositions to confront death's enigma with evasion, despair, curiosity, or hope.

Certainly there is no evading Dickinson's attentiveness to the topic, from the generalization in her sprightly 1850 valentine that "The *worm* doth woo the *mortal*, death claims a living bride" (P 1) to the personal application of her final letter, "Little Cousins, / Called back. / Emily" (L 1046). From the time she reserved news of Amherst deaths for the content of her letters to Austin, she exhibited a distinctive fascination with death scenes, graveyards, and mourning—not only in those sentimental early poems strongly imbued with the maudlin cult of death that dominated mid-nineteenth-century American popular culture and that found expression in the macabre outpourings of all those sweet singers whom Mark Twain satirized in Emmeline Grangerford but also in her most brilliant creations. As we have seen from examining the circumferential poems about natural transitions, life passages, and changing states of consciousness, all life's vicissitudes pointed this poet's thoughts toward death as the ultimate and inevitable change. No matter how strongly one fortified the circuit of consciousness and mortal existence, the circumference would ultimately give way with whatever lay beyond circumference absorbing the contents of the circuit. All life's deprivations, however routine, foreshadowed the circuit's catastrophe to the point that young Emily could speak of her sister's and Jane Humphrey's departures for their respective boarding schools as evidence that "the grave opened—and swallowed you both—" (L 30). Literally or metaphorically, it had already swallowed many whom she loved and would seize the others; ultimately it would claim her as well. Death as circumference dominated her thoughts.[1]

Given the drive of Dickinson's imagination to identify limits and explode beyond them, she could hardly have evaded death as her most constant theme. Not her "Flood subject," however; that was immortality. Reading the poems and letters on death, we must actively consider the questioning about immortality that prompted her fascination. Death presented itself as a barrier, a closed door; but she insisted on trying the lock in any way she could to discover whether she could trust Christian promises of eternal and intensified life. Would the limitations that pained her in life give way to power, the gift that seemed to her to subsume the glory and dominion (L 292)? Was there a heaven to repay life's deprivations? Might human cravings for fulfillment ever be satisfied? To find out, the poet balanced herself on the perilous edge of circumference—living always in the presence of death with mind and nerves astoundingly alert.

Exhilarated by the very precariousness of her perch, Dickinson responded gleefully as often as with dread. She reveled in the drama of life on the brink—particularly the brink of immortality—and she habitually represented the human condition in circumferential metaphors. When her mother, partially paralyzed by a stroke and further disabled by a broken hip, lamented the disruption of her circuit routine, the elder daughter responded in terms as characteristic as they were startling: "I tell her we all shall fly so soon, not to let it grieve her, and what indeed is Earth but a Nest, from whose rim we are all falling?" (L 619). Falling into what? Dickinson herself never felt sure, but the flight image lends hope of soaring instead—of liberation, empowerment, even of delight. The circuit world clung to its children, however, and clutched at its flying birds with an impulse the poet voiced in a letter to a departing friend shortly after Samuel Bowles's death: "but Mrs Nellie has Wings—/ Hours—have Wings—/ Riches— have Wings—/ Wings are a mournful perquisite—/ A Society for the Suppression of Wings would protect us all" (L 550). It was a droll suggestion, that of forming a typical American benevolent association for the suppression of vice and then treating as vice the metaphorical evidence of salvation, itself presumably the reward of virtue. Desiring such figurative wings herself while fearing the use others might make of them to bereave her circuit world yet further, the poet articulated the conflict she felt on the edge of circumference.

Many poems and letters focus on death as the dividing line between the circuit side of existence as now experienced and the other side of mystery. In "These tested Our Horizon—" (P 886), Dickinson salutes those who probed the barrier and disappeared beyond it into "Anticipation / A Dice—a Doubt—." Only retrospect remains behind within the circuit, from within which the survivors still find the horizon a barrier to vision. As with this horizon image, Dickinson summoned other transitional metaphors discussed in the previous chapter to represent death as circumference. She linked death explicitly with sunset in "Like her the Saints retire," (P 60), while offering a late-summer flower (the aster) and a spring bulb (the daffodil) as counterarguments to loss. Reminded of her recent dead at the conclusion of an 1878 letter to Dr. Holland, she apologized "But I intrude on Sunset, and Father and Mr Bowles" (L 544). They had ventured into the sunset while others remained behind to watch for the sunrise, yearning for replenishment of loss and breakdown of those obstacles to the satisfaction of man's unappeasable appetites that she recorded in "As Watchers hang upon the East," (P 121), but heaven only "beguiles the tired" with hopes of appeasement within the circuit. One must follow the setting sun to achieve the fulfillment typified by this world's sunrises, streams, and feasts.

In addition to the many poems using natural transitions as adumbrations of death, there were others in which Dickinson used human contrivances like gates and doors to represent this most fascinating barrier. A weary flock of sheep seeks admission to death's sheepfold in "Let down the Bars, Oh Death—" (P 1065),

although the poem makes no explicit reference to anything beyond the gate but offers an end to wandering as itself a sufficient
goal. The poem immediately following this one in set 6a, "Ample
make this Bed—" (P 829), extends the implication of rest to a
human corpse finding refuge in a grave, though in this case a future beckons beyond the immediate interment: "Make this Bed
with Awe—/ In it wait till Judgment break / Excellent and Fair."
From within the circuit, on the mortal side of death, all the survivors can do is prepare a comfortable resting place for the
"Country Burial" (Dickinson's title for this poem), pretending
that the dead are only sleeping and that the sheep will flock out of
their fold in the morning. It is the instinct of the circuit world to
restrain wanderers and to hold them as firmly as possible within
circumference. When Samuel Bowles was dying, for example,
Dickinson wrote to Mrs. Holland that "Dear Mr Bowles is hesi-
tating—God help him decide on the Mortal Side!" (I. 525). But he
either fell or climbed across to the other side, that of immortality
or nothingness. To borrow imagery from several of her poems,
he entered a door through circumference and closed it behind
him, like the person who violates the dancing ring of playmates
that symbolizes the vulnerable attractions of the circuit world:
"Of the Heart that goes in, and closes the Door / Shall the Playfellow Heart complain / Though the Ring is unwhole, and the
Company broke / Can never be fitted again?" (P 1098).

Journey imagery served Dickinson most often to represent the
passage out of the circuit into and beyond circumference. The
woman of "She died—*this* was the way she died." (P 150) jour-
neyed through a gate that removed her from "the mortal side."
She seemed a timid venturer, one the speaker liked to think of as
welcomed by angels to a more secure celestial home. On the other
side, then, might come triumph like that suggested in "Upon
Concluded Lives" (P 735), which follows the journey to the point
of disappearance outside the circuit. On "the Dying Side" is "Funeral"; on the other side "Coronal"; they salute on the road at the
point of circumference. What made the journey so terrifying was
its isolation. Despite the friends clutching the traveler back on the
mortal side and the possibilities of angelic welcome on the other,
the pilgrim faced the marginal road entirely alone and engaged in
the adventure Dickinson described in a poem sent to her cousins
shortly after the death of her eight-year-old nephew, Gilbert: "Be-

hind the hill is sorcery / And everything unknown, / But will the secret compensate / For climbing it alone?" (p 1603).

In any event, one had no real choice, as Dickinson showed in "Our journey had advanced—" (p 615), a poem presenting the penultimate episode in a quest narrative. The speaker has arrived at the limit of the circuit and finds retreat impossible despite reluctance to move ahead into the unknown cities. Between the circuit behind and the cities before lies circumference, "The Forest of the Dead—," where the speaker halts before the inevitable forward movement. Yet just as we expect the speaker's surrender to the guardians of the cities, we find eternity hoisting its own white flag of truce or surrender—itself yielding to apparent conquest by the apprehensive pilgrim. God, the omnipresent defender of the mysterious community beyond circumference, seems to offer welcome. Awe, then, subjects itself to possession by the knight who pursues circumference or death (p 1620). Despite fear and apparent defeat, the quest ends happily with promise of the victory that Dickinson anticipated in another poem she placed near this one in fascicle 21, "At last, to be identified!" (p 174), in which she employed sunrise and journey imagery to suggest the glorious new vision on the other side of mortality: "At last, the lamps upon thy side / The rest of Life to *see*!" Moreover, it is knowledge of herself that is to be perfected there, not just understanding of external aspects of God's design. Identity, which one fears to lose with consciousness at death, itself paradoxically depends upon death and emerges gloriously on the other side of circumference.

Those circumferential mental states most nearly analogous to death—despair, catatonia, madness—often aped death's physical qualities of stiffness and numbness; they created an absence within a person comparable to the distance death sets between the corpse and the circuit world. Whether they also foreshadowed mental cessation at death remained a haunting question for Emily Dickinson. What if consciousness stopped? What if awareness ceased just as the quester approached those visionary cities? The irony would be too cruel. Although recognizing the threat of mental annihilation, Dickinson generally asserted a faith in continuing consciousness—the sort of faith she articulated to Mrs. Holland on the death of the poet Bryant: "How unspeakably sweet and solemn—that whatever await us of Doom or Home, we are mentally permanent. / 'It is finished' can never be said of us" (l 555).

Thus fortified with hope of lasting awareness and with trust in the accessibility of awe to those valiant enough to seek circumference, Dickinson presented herself as an obstinate quester seeking glimpses of "the other side" and demanding ultimate entry. One of her most powerful poems throbs with the frustrated expectancy of one making a purposeful assault on death for the sake of gaining a perspective denied within earth's horizon.

> Just lost, when I was saved!
> Just felt the world go by!
> Just girt me for the onset with Eternity,
> When breath blew back,
> And on the other side
> I heard recede the disappointed tide!
>
> Therefore, as One returned, I feel,
> Odd secrets of the line to tell!
> Some Sailor, skirting foreign shores—
> Some pale Reporter, from the awful doors
> Before the Seal!
>
> Next time, to stay!
> Next time, the things to see
> By Ear unheard,
> Unscrutinized by Eye—
>
> Next time, to tarry,
> While the Ages steal—
> Slow tramp the Centuries,
> And the Cycles wheel!
> (P 160)

This time she has ventured unsuccessfully upon the mysterious seas. She has opened herself to mysteries but has, as yet, no vision to report. But reference to "the disappointed tide" suggests an oceanic force beyond circumference that will come for her again, that will batter down the sea walls erected by circuit-loving persons who mistake this life for salvation and death for loss. The speaker, eager for escape from time and the circuit, looks forward enthusiastically to her next exploratory voyage. That this poem voices its author's own eagerness for new vision is suggested by the title Susan Dickinson gave it when submitting it to the *Inde-*

pendent for its March 1891 publication. Entitling it "Called Back," Sue linked the poem to her sister-in-law's deathbed letter to the Norcross cousins with its suggestion of return to a home outside circumference.

Perhaps one had to wait to be called back. Attempts to initiate such journeys often fail in Dickinson's poems, with the circuit world enforcing its own ironically distorted notion of salvation in actions that frustrate attempts of its soaring questers to escape. Represented by the clover that "saved" the bumblebee by braining it (P 1343) and the tree that lowered the gracefully ascending balloon by mangling it, the circuit world mindlessly intrudes upon the quest and remains callously indifferent to the aspirations it lacerates: "And Clerks in Counting Rooms / Observe—''Twas only a Balloon'—" (P 700).

Confined as she was within her mortal circuit though excited personally by the enticement of escape, Dickinson herself resisted the flight of others. Praying for Bowles to choose "the Mortal Side" and threatening her "Society for the Suppression of Wings," she did what she could to tether her friends' balloons. Her many poems on the dying of other people emphasize circuit values, from the graveyard emotionalizing over departed sweetness to the sublime elegiac reflections on loss. When she presents herself in these poems, it is often as a nurse to the dying—as one laboring with futile charity to alleviate suffering and retain life. "I bring an unaccustomed wine" (P 132), for instance, narrates a failed attempt to nurture a dying friend, while "I should not dare to leave my friend," (P 205) expresses a kind of jealous insistence on being the principal minister of comfort and "Promise This—When You be Dying—" (P 648) claims the right to perform the final acts of love. For someone who actually attended at only one deathbed, her mother's in 1882, this concentration of poems suggests a fascination with the physical process of dying—something she resisted with the industriousness characteristic of the circuit world but nonetheless found compellingly attractive to an imagination probing for access to the other side of mortality.

The tension in Dickinson's own mind expresses itself in the confusion readers feel about the "Jealousy for Her" that arose in "The last Night that She lived" (P 1100), a particularly detailed and moving deathbed poem. Told from the perspective of one remaining in the circuit, the narrative emphasizes the impact of this woman's dying on the world she leaves behind. The "smallest things" of household routine are "Italicized" by the alertness of observation the attendants bring to her chamber. What remains after the death is sheer matter: hair to be placed neatly and the head to be positioned, but none of the consciousness that has been either transformed or obliterated. Within the circuit world of matter and time and intellectual awareness, the speaker and her fellow attendants feel a jealousy *for* the dying woman. They resent the continued existence of other people "While She must finish quite."[2] But it seems likely that the speaker also feels a jealousy *of* the departed one. The death scene itself is revealing with the struggle for preservation all on the part of the survivors while the woman for whom they have been laboring has consented to death and allowed her life to float away upon the mystic sea. Now that she has gone beyond circumference, even her circuit-protecting attendants admit curiosity about what it all means. The necessity "Belief to regulate—" with which they are left involves two kinds of belief: that about the change that has been forced upon their household and that about the implications of death for immortality. The "great light" of dying intensifies appreciation of the circuit world even while exposing the need for a different sort of illumination.

Another poem presents the moment of dying in an impersonal but highly dramatic way, concentrating on the exact moment of escape: "The instant holding in it's claw / The privilege to live / Or warrant to report the Soul / The other side the Grave" (P 948). We know nothing about the dying person, not even gender. Instead we learn of "The Muscles" grappling with "the Will" and finally "The Spirit" shaking "the Adamant" that had once been an active body. Time itself enters the lists against immortality as "The Second poised—debated—shot—" even while the soul, undeterred by the struggle to anchor it within the circuit, "Escaped the House unseen—." "Unseen": That was the frustration of such deathbed observations for Dickinson. It was impossible to follow the soul, possible only to watch intently for signals just this side of death in an attempt to discern the dying person's attitude and ultimate prospect. That the dying woman of "The last Night that She lived" (P 1100) mentioned something and then forgot both it and her auditors and that this soul escaped in silence while its would-be watchers found themselves more than ever obsessed with time raised doubts about the possibility of glimpsing immortality in a dying person's eye, but Dickinson continued the effort.

Calvinist tradition had trained the poet to watch for signals of salvation or reprobation at the point of death, to look for evidence that Christ had come for the saint who persevered to the end. The poet's reports and questions about dying attitudes and last words, therefore, conformed to a pattern of curiosity about such things that seemed not only normal but normative to the people she knew. They shared her curiosity about each person's readiness for death. Dickinson's 1854 letter to the Reverend Edward Everett Hale, inquiring if Benjamin Newton "was willing to die, and if you think him at Home," raised predictable questions about her friend's postcircumferential status, and she need hardly have explained "I should love so much to know certainly, that he was today in Heaven" (L 153). Years later, in 1878, she reported bluntly that "Mr Bowles was not willing to die," a comment not based upon despair as to his celestial prospects but expressive of gratitude for his loyalty to the circuit world from which she so reluctantly excused him (L 553). After Bowles's death, she told Higginson that it seemed "there was no World" and no light—just "Darkness."

"To know just how He suffered—would be dear—" (P 622), a poem not recognizably associated with any one death, expresses the intensity of Dickinson's curiosity about dying and her eagerness to discern the passing person's insight at the circumferential moment. The question in this case is not one of election; she believes that the dying person's final gaze would fix on Paradise. Her concern is much more for the emotional implications of leave-taking from the circuit world. She wants to know the strength of its appeal, evidently hoping for continuing evidence of human love right to the point of death. This is a serene poem, however, assuming intensification of all good beyond circumference. Consciousness, for example, would grow more conscious, not be expunged; earthly love would merge into "Love too best to be—"; time blend into eternity. Unable to follow the dying friend immediately into this paradisal new life, the speaker keeps raising questions that have more chance of enlightening her about the person's attachment to the world already known than of opening insight into another.

Death impinges on the circuit world chiefly as an insatiable source of deprivations; and Dickinson, acutely sensitive to loss, resented its maraudings. Whatever advantages the dead might gain from crossing circumference were still denied to those they left behind, so that the poet tended to concentrate in much of her writing on the lessening of the circuit world caused by the grave's "Robberies" of "our pilfered Things" (P 607). Sometimes, as in "Of nearness to her sundered Things," she wondered who were the mourners, who the journeyers, who was left behind. When word came of her father's fatal seizure, she reported that she discerned by the look on Austin's face that "we were all lost, though I didn't know how" (L 414). Edward Dickinson's survivors were lost, then, not he, and his daughter's poems and letters registered greater fear of forfeiting close friends to death than of encountering circumference herself (P 831).

When she represented the effect of death's pilfering, Dickinson relied most heavily on the continued presence of objects no longer valuable and on the cessation of activities that had characterized the dead within the circuit world. With sentimental concentration on the loss of simple pleasures, the poet emphasized the ordinary objects left behind by someone like the person remembered in "'Twas the old—road—through pain—" (P 344) whose journey to another world had forced her to forsake in this one her hat, her shoe, and "Her little Book—/ The leaf—at love—turned back—." Another friend left a thimble, someone else a book marked with favorite passages (P 360). More often the loss made itself felt through an absence of activity. Dickinson's poems indicate that busyness is the circuit world's dominant characteristic, industry its major value. "The Busy Darling's" "tenderer industriousness" in "Her final Summer was it—" (P 795) might have alerted the dying woman's friends to the reason for her zeal in finishing her business but let them deceive themselves instead with confidence in her vitality. Inactivity violates the circuit world even when the material objects that have been the product of earlier industriousness remain behind.

The value of lives taken away seems to increase in proportion to their distance: "In broken mathematics / We estimate our prize / Vast—in it's fading ratio / To our penurious eyes!" (P 88). Nor is the loss entirely one-sided. The circuit world retains enough smugness about its own values to pity the dead for the

privation they suffer in leaving it behind so that the speaker of
"I'm sorry for the Dead—Today—" (P 529) voices sentimental
sadness for those farmers who lose out on the harvest and its attendant festivities. She worries about the homesickness they must
feel when cut off from circuit routine, "Set separate from the
Farming—/ And all the Neighbor's lives—."

For some people, however, flight from the circuit world seemed
to offer relief, and Dickinson recognized that the dead more often
tired of the living than the living of them (P 482). The persons
remembered in "A poor—torn heart—a tattered heart—" (P 78)
and "She bore it till the simple veins" (P 144) find dying a release
as they journey beyond the sunset. And the speaker of "Where
bells no more affright the morn—" (P 112) looks forward with
humorous indolence to a paradise of reprieve from industriousness and its pressures. She dreams of basking forever in a heaven
blessedly immune to "Father's bells" and factory whistles. Routine
activity terminates with death on both sides of circumference.
Even survivors within the circuit turn their energy to searching
for the lost, while the dead advance into a condition of repose only
figuratively suggestible as sleep. Paying greater attention to those
absent than those present, the survivors find themselves drawn in
imagination and affection beyond circumference, as his Amherst
friend reminded Higginson when comforting him after the death
of a baby daughter in 1880 (P 1490). Deprivation can be inspiring
(even "divine"), then, when it prods people to strain beyond the
circuit world and to recognize a superior kind of reality outside it.
Within the circuit, however, people have difficulty estimating
"The distance that the dead have gone" (P 1742) and the impossibility of their return.

But they *have* gone, and Dickinson presents death as an adventure for the dying whether they resort to it only for purposes of
escape or courageously challenge it in their quest for fulfillment.
Death is her "White Exploit" (P 922) and "most profound experiment / Appointed unto Men—" (P 822). Often it seems an occasion of triumph (P 455). So ennobling is this adventure that even
the circuit world accords it honor, however unwelcome its source.
The grand solemnity of funerals testifies to death's exalting transfiguration even of the simplest person, and anyone is capable of
instigating "That short—potential stir / That each can make but
once—/ That Bustle so illustrious / 'Tis almost Consequence—"

(P 1307). *Almost* consequence within the circuit. Dickinson obviously harbored doubts about fanfare and grandeur so reluctantly and passively accepted. The plans she made for her own funeral forced the circuit world to conform to her own less ceremonial but discernibly prouder wishes. Beyond circumference, however, the "Majesty of Death" (P 171) might privilege the suddenly elevated soul with welcome glory—the sort she anticipates in her coronation poems.

As I noted earlier in my discussion of Dickinson's role playing in her travel poems, she regarded journeys as danger-fraught venturings into the unknown and presented every kind of travel as a prefigurement of death. The journey taken by the character recalled in "Could live—*did* live—" (P 43) "from scene familiar / To an untraversed spot—" is quite explicitly the movement from within the circuit through circumference to the other side. The poet once acclaimed Jesus and the martyrs as models for those brave and generous enough "To put this World down, like a Bundle—/ And walk steady, away," (P 527)—a purposeful rejection of the circuit that she found antithetical to human instincts. When her cousin, Perez Cowan, longed for death after losing his sister, Dickinson warned him that "It grieves me that you speak of Death with so much expectation. I know there is no pang like that for those we love, nor any leisure like the one they leave so closed behind them, but Dying is a wild Night and a new Road" (L 332). Fixed to the circuit world by love as well as apprehension, she admired those who undertook such journeys with a willingness to fly that surmounted their continuing affection for the world they had known. "Went up a year this evening!" (P 93) expresses her wondering respect for those who venture in death's metaphorical balloon to soar beyond circumference.

Faced with the necessity of traversing the "new Road" herself eventually, the poet often anticipated the journey and generally steeled herself for the test. She, who left her own home so rarely and reluctantly, proclaimed herself "ready to go!" if safely buckled by Christ in his carriage and escorted by him on the steep downhill journey into the sea of mystery and beyond it (P 279). Once she even hinted at suicide, so eagerly did she anticipate escape when demanding "What if I say I shall not wait! / What if I burst the fleshly Gate—/ And pass escaped—to thee!" (P 277). What if? Perhaps the last line's disparaging reference to those "who died—

yesterday" warns the reader as well as the speaker to keep her eye on the circuit world and recognize that from *its* perspective anyway death represents no triumph, that *its* ends (whatever they may be) can never be attained by dying. It was not the termination of life that excited her but the prospect of its intensification beyond circumference. The exultation she occasionally expressed at the thought of completing life's perilous journey came from anticipation of wonderful surprises beyond the limiting circuit world.

> 'Tis so much joy! 'Tis so much joy!
> If I should fail, what poverty!
> And yet, as poor as I,
> Have ventured all upon a throw!
> Have gained! Yes! Hesitated so—
> This side the Victory!
>
> Life is but Life! And Death, but Death!
> Bliss is but Bliss, and Breath but Breath!
> And if indeed I fail,
> At least, to know the worst, is sweet!
> Defeat means nothing *but* Defeat,
> No drearier, can befall!
>
> And if I gain! Oh Gun at Sea!
> Oh Bells, that in the Steeples be!
> At first, repeat it slow!
> For Heaven is a different thing,
> Conjectured, and waked sudden in—
> And might extinguish me!
> (P 172)

Given the prospect before her, she valiantly risked loss as of minimal account. Even dead loved ones served as inducements to carry on the quest, as she once remarked: "We do not think enough of the Dead as exhilirants—they are not dissuaders but Lures—Keepers of that great Romance still to us foreclosed—while coveting their wisdom we lament their silence. Grace is still a secret. That they have existed none can take away. That they still exist is a trust so daring we thank thee that thou hast hid these things from us and hast revealed them to them. The power and the glory are the post mortuary gifts."[3]

Beyond death's barrier, then, lay that "great Romance" already revealed to the dead but only wonderingly intuited by the living. No wonder the poet coveted those "post mortuary gifts" and tried to glimpse the marvels promised to her but as yet foreclosed. The dead already in possession of such secrets served as lures beyond circumference, especially those departed loved ones who seemed most eager to experience the vision. Chief among these lures for Emily Dickinson was her little nephew, Gilbert, whom she visited the night of his death by typhoid fever and whose dying words lingered in her memory. "'Open the Door, open the Door, they are waiting for me,' was Gilbert's sweet command in delirium. *Who* were waiting for him, all we possess we would give to know," she told Mrs. Holland (L 873). Whatever the child meant by his imploring—whether he fantasized Christ and the angels above or only his playmates outside—he had answered the Calvinist question about his destiny in circumferential language to which his aunt was already sharply attuned. He had begged for a door to be opened, had demanded a chance for escape. Yet those remaining behind in the circuit world saw no break in the barrier; to them Gilbert seemed only to have run "to the little Grave at his Grandparents' feet," thereby burying himself in the mystery that already enveloped the family dead. But it was possible that he had glimpsed immortality while dying, probable that he experienced the power and the dominion thereafter. Already Gilbert enjoyed that "Rendezvous of Light" (P 1564) toward which his aunt was groping in her own longer journey. She described herself as fording the mystery the boy had leaped across.

Left behind in the circuit world, mourners could only conjecture the fate of their dead, and such imaginings tended to concentrate on possible continuities. Since those within the circuit valued busyness, one of Dickinson's inquisitive speakers could wonder "What did They do since I saw Them? / Were They industrious?" (P 900) and could object to their complete withdrawal before giving answers. The activities of the departed, however, were unlikely to be the laborious duties assumed to be God's will in her New England. Rather, Dickinson envisaged "Those fair—fictitious People—" (P 499) who had gone before her as "Inheriting Delight / Beyond our faint Conjecture—/ Our dizzy Estimate—." "Knowing—where We only hope—," they might indulge in endless celebration like the dancers she depicted in "There is a morn by men unseen—" (P 24), enjoying a perpetual May Day revel

on a mystic green where "to light measure, move the feet /
Which walk no more the village street—/ Nor by the wood are
found—."

Such celebrants served as incentives to continued questing for
their mystic green, but the poet felt frustrated by her inability to
glimpse their happiness through any force more objective than her
imagination. Much of the interest she exhibited in people's dying
moments emerged from intense curiosity about what the departing ones, like Gilbert, may have seen at the immediate juncture of
circumference. Yet she wrote in "I've seen a Dying Eye" (P 547)
about inadequate evidence. The eye seems to search before it
closes "Without disclosing what it be / 'Twere blessed to have
seen—." Nor does the dying eye even disclose whether it has fastened upon anything itself. All remains mystery, she concludes,
"Until the Cheated Eye / Shuts arrogantly—in the Grave—/ Another way—to see—" (P 627). A kind of anger smolders in this
poem about the cruel insensitivity of the dead to the questions of
the living whom they are luring toward circumference without
giving adequate insight into the journey's goal.

Unable to follow the dead beyond circumference or to witness
directly their coronations or dancing there, the poet still enclosed
within the circuit world was left to study the effect of their disappearance on the familiar environment in the hope of conjecturing
something about the new life the dead were presumably already
experiencing. But she might as well have directed her questions to
the corpses stretched out in the frosty isolation of her "Alabaster
Chambers" (P 216) as look for answers from the previously com-
municative faces and hands of the newly dead. The impervious-
ness of dead saints to earthly knowledge and everything the world
might want to report of its continuing activity was matched by
their inscrutability with regard to anything they might have discovered in another life. "Had You earlier blundered in," one of
Dickinson's speakers tells a would-be minister to a person already
gone, "Possibly, e'en You had seen / An Eternity—put on—" (P
388), but no chance of communication remains. Instead the mourners confront "The quiet nonchalance of death—" (P 194) and the
"multiplied indifference" (P 519) of those who so recently loved
them.

Dickinson's stylistic choices bespeak her frustration at the arrogant silence of the dead. In "These—saw Visions—" (P 758), for

example, she refers to the eyes, cheeks, lips, face, fingers, and feet of the corpse exclusively by impersonal pronouns. "These" performed actions in the past; now we act upon them to prepare them for burial. They "saw" the same "Visions" we still see. If they now see different ones, we have no way of knowing. In "Under the Light, yet under," (P 949) it is the heavy iteration of prepositions (under, further, over) that drums into the reader's consciousness the fact of separation. Dickinson frequently chooses mechanical imagery to clarify the distinction between vital motion and cold stasis. She presents the dead heart as a still timepiece in "A Clock stopped—" (P 287) to register the "Decades of Arrogance" dividing the circuit and ultracircumferential worlds. In "How many times these low feet staggered—" (P 187), she calls on machine images like "soldered mouth," "awful rivet," and "hasps of steel" to suggest the iron rigidity that once had been a lively woman.

Given the circuit world's respect for action, it is hardly surprising that immobility proves the most devastating evidence of death's withdrawal from life. Where there had once been "laughter and ability and Sighing" (P 813), "merry Arms" and "dancing Eyes" (P 369), there remains only "quiet Dust." An industrious housewife turns indolent, with her defection registered in dust, cobwebs, and smudged windows (P 187). "Was ever idleness like This?" (P 654) the poet asks about a basking corpse. In "Death sets a Thing significant" (P 360), idle fingers demonstrate the loss of one routinely associated with physical tasks like sewing or intellectual habits like reading and annotation. The activities themselves may have been unimportant, but they assume a value as evidence of earlier involvement with the circuit world and its inhabitants. The idleness of the dead, on the other hand, like the coldness of their corpses, testifies to their current indifference. They have stopped sending signals and thus manifest their having ceased to care, like the dying woman who ignored the beseeching of survivors for her return and simply "Removed our invitation by / As Some She never knew—" (P 804). The dead might be keepers of secrets, therefore, but they hardly served Dickinson as sources of revelation. If she wanted a preview of the mysteries beyond circumference, she would have to adopt her own angle of vision rather than rely on messengers literally alienated by death.

Her role-playing habits came to Dickinson's rescue here. She who had performed the parts of earls, brides, and converted saints would instinctively try out two other roles that seemed to offer empowerment beyond mortal limitation: those of the dying person at the very point of circumference and of the person who, having experienced death, now looks back at the circuit from the perspective of eternity. "But we—are dying in Drama—," she wrote once, "And Drama—is never dead—" (P 531). Reality and fantasy blur here in "We dream—it is good we are dreaming—" with the speaker claiming to dream that she is playing a theatrical death role: playing to the hilt the melodramatic part of a murder victim. Yet she dreads discovering that the performance involves actual dying. Sometimes players have truly been killed on the stage; more often not. Even so, every person—even an actor—*is* actually dying by degrees at any moment. For adults, conscious of their mortality, the game can never be so simply a matter of play as the shoot-outs children perform in their cops-and-robbers or space-invaders games. Playing at dying allowed the poet to extend her experience imaginatively even though it confronted her all too directly with the eventual reality of her own extinction from the circuit world.

The layering of unreality in this poem serves ingeniously to overcome human psychological defenses. The Freudian truism that one cannot dream one's own death yields here to the possibility of dreaming oneself on a stage performing any role. If an actor can fantasize himself playing Othello, a dramatically inclined poet could imagine herself as Desdemona. Thus Dickinson extended her imagination to cope with a disability she had confessed in an adolescent letter to Abiah Root. Explaining her inability to conceive of eternity as anything better than dreaded stasis, she confessed, "I dont know why it is but it does not seem to me that I shall ever cease to live on earth—I cannot imagine with the farthest stretch of my imagination my own death scene" (L 10). Six years later, however, she told Jane Humphrey about the sentimental reverie in which she deliberately envisaged herself a picturesque corpse visited by grieving neighbors (L 86). This fantasy, of course, confined itself to the circuit world; she imagined herself one of those arrogant corpses failing to disclose whatever of eternity they might have seen. When Emily Dickinson finally did "become like this," she faced death with the familiarity of one long accustomed to "dying in Drama" (P 531). Speaking on the solemn occasion of her funeral, Higginson read Emily Brontë's poem,

"No coward soul is mine," while explaining to the gathered as-
sembly that their friend "who had put on immortality, but who
really never seemed to have put it off—frequently read this passage to her sister."[4] He may have borrowed the notion of mortality
putting on immortality from Dickinson's tribute to George Eliot.
It was a privilege the poet ascribed to imagination and one that
she herself deliberately cultivated when she positioned a fantasized
self beyond the circuit and played a role she hoped would yield a
perspective unattainable from her own vantage point within. Hers
was a serious, highly purposeful assault on human limitation
though not ultimately a successful one in that the circuit world
and the consciousness attuned to it continued to dominate even
those poems ostensibly spoken from beyond the grave.

The characteristics Dickinson had stressed in her observations
of corpses were those she applied to herself when assuming the
role of a dead person. She spoke of her cessation of breath as a
"Trick" or "Pantomime" in one poem but responded to the supposedly voluntary stillness of her lungs with the alarmed exclamation, "How numb, the Bellows feels!" (P 272). In another
poem, "I've dropped my Brain—My Soul is numb—" (P 1046),
the speaker presents herself as palsied and stonelike. External action ceases while the spirit still strains "To Being, somewhere"
with little sense of where or when new life would be possible.
Physical immobility itself proved not to open insights.

What about the actual process of dying? The speaker of an 1860
poem, "Dying! Dying in the night!" (P 158), expresses terror at
venturing alone into the darkness. She feels betrayed by Jesus,
whom she had expected as her escort, and begs for her friend
"Dollie" to help her embark. Her fears of death's hurting may be
mitigated by attention from within the circuit world until she actually vanishes "Into the everlasting snow." A braver speaker addresses us in an 1863 poem, "The Sun kept setting—setting—
still" (P 692), who announces "'Tis Dying—I am doing—but /
I'm not afraid to know—." She describes her experiences in Dickinson's typical circumferential imagery, each time stressing the
ways in which the dying person's sensations at the point of circumference differ from those on the circuit side. The sun sets, but
at noon. Dusk drops, but the only dew beads the speaker's fore-
head. Progressive verb forms ("setting," "dropping," "drowsing")
bespeak ongoing action but are paralyzed by their omnipresent

past-tense auxiliary "kept." All motion and perception have ended, then; the only continuing activities are the dying the speaker is doing and the knowing that she continues to experience. But is there any special new kind of knowing that supersedes muscular and sensory powers? The poem gives no evidence of such vision.

Instead, these enactments of dying simply tell us in a more personal voice about the absences of life processes that Dickinson's poetic observations of other deaths had emphasized. Her dying speakers recognize their loss of normal powers. One, previously gifted with "A Sense that smote and stirred—/ Instincts for Dance—a caper part—/ An Aptitude for Bird—" (P 1046), now finds herself rigid and insentient. Another, probably not yet at the point of death, promises to continue habitual acts of love and service until physically prevented; "If I should cease to bring a Rose," she warns her friend, the cessation will mean that "*beyond* the Rose / I have been called away—" (P 56). The circuit world, then, maintains its dominance to the end and has trouble visualizing its own conclusion.

Dickinson's most famous poem spoken from beyond the grave confronts precisely this problem: the assertiveness of the circuit world against the claims of complementary vision.

> Because I could not stop for Death—
> He kindly stopped for me—
> The Carriage held but just Ourselves—
> And Immortality.
>
> We slowly drove—He knew no haste
> And I had put away
> My labor and my leisure too,
> For His Civility—
>
> We passed the School, where Children strove
> At Recess—in the Ring—
> We passed the Fields of Gazing Grain—
> We passed the Setting Sun—
>
> Or rather—He passed Us—
> The Dews drew quivering and chill—
> For only Gossamer, my Gown—
> My Tippet—only Tulle—

> We paused before a House that seemed
> A Swelling of the Ground—
> The Roof was scarcely visible—
> The Cornice—in the Ground—
>
> Since then—'tis Centuries—and yet
> Feels shorter than the Day
> I first surmised the Horses Heads
> Were toward Eternity—
> (P 712)

The representative of the verse here is a decidedly imaginary person—not Emily Dickinson's self-projection (which would be of one straining for escape beyond circumference and intensely alert to all details of transition) but a woman contented within the routine of circuit busyness. Her opening words echo some of Dickinson's own habitual usages but present a contradictory value system adapted to worldly achievements. This lady has been industrious—too busy to stop her work, whatever it may have been. Dickinson, too, proclaimed herself too busy in her self-descriptive July 1862 letter to Higginson and in a letter to Mrs. Holland that Johnson and Ward place conjecturally at the same time on the basis of obvious verbal echoes (L 268; 269). To Higginson she wrote: "Perhaps you smile at me. I could not stop for that—My Business is Circumference—." To Mrs. Holland, "Perhaps you laugh at me! Perhaps the whole United States are laughing at me too! *I* can't stop for that! *My* business is to love." Her businesses, then, differed from the routine employments of the circuit citizens who might be mocking her. What the poet could not stop for was circuit judgments. Her businesses, as she reported them that intensely productive summer, were love, song, and circumference—all of them leading her outside the circuit. Circumference, from the perspective of the circuit world, was death and the cessation of industry, although there might be a different life beyond it. The speaker of this poem, however, is too busy with ordinary duties to stop for Death, who naturally stops her instead. She is less like Emily Dickinson than like that whirlwind of domestic industriousness, Lavinia, whom her sister once characterized as a "standard for superhuman effort erroneously applied" (L 254).

Caught up in the circuit world of busyness, the speaker mistakes Death for a human suitor; her imagination suggests no more awesome possibility. Two persons, in fact, have come for her, Death and Immortality, though her limited perception leads her to ignore the higher-ranking chaperon.[5] The relationship between the two figures—analogous to that between circumference and awe (P 1620)—attracts none of her notice. In fact, she pays little attention even to her principal escort, being occupied instead with peering out the carriage window at the familiar circuit world. She sees the schoolchildren playing in their circumferential ring, little realizing that she has now herself become that playfellow who will go in and close the door—thus breaking the circle (P 1098). And she sees the "Gazing Grain" indicative of the late-summer crop Death is already reaping even as she herself gazes back into the circuit, indicative also of some farmer's midlife industriousness— the sort another circuit-minded speaker pitied when death deprived him of harvest (P 529). Rather than attending to mysteries, this speaker focuses only on the familiar until a novel perspective on the sunset jolts her into awareness of her own transitional state. Rather than making friends with Immortality, she concentrates on mortality.

The consequence of her distorted values is that the speaker winds up with eternity as an inadequate substitute for either: the endless static stretch of time that young Emily had repudiated in an 1846 letter to Abiah Root (the same letter in which she confessed her inability to imagine her own death). "Does not Eternity appear dreadful to you," she asked then, "I often get thinking of it and it seems so dark to me that I almost wish there was no Eternity. To think that we must forever live and never cease to be. It seems as if Death which all so dread because it launches us upon an unknown world would be a releif to so endless a state of existense" (L 10). Indeed, Death does not launch the persona of this poem into another world (Immortality would have to be enlisted for that, rather than sitting ignored in the back seat of the carriage in which she and Death will eventually ride off together after abandoning the speaker). Instead Death leaves his date buried within the margin of the circuit, in a "House" that she can maintain like one of those "Alabaster Chambers" (P 216) in which numb corpses lie but which are designed and built of elegant materials still gratifying to the circuit-locked mentality. A quester for circumference would greet Death more enthusiastically, and would both value and cultivate Death's ties to Immortality. For such a quester, the destination of the journey might prove more wondrous.

Yet the circuit world intruded upon consciousness to the end of communicable experience even in "I heard a Fly buzz—when I died—" (P 465), a poem whose speaker eagerly anticipated dying as a prelude to new vision and strained toward promised revelation. Now the speaker, having reached the other side of circumference, looks back upon the transitional adventure. Playing at death in an attempt to glimpse the revelation beyond it, the Dickinsonian persona seems to have achieved the necessary angle of vision. Yet she looks backward into time rather than forward into immortality, back into the circuit world rather than out into the mysteries beyond. The poem narrates a death scene in which both the dying person and her friends watch attentively to witness "the King"—presumably Christ come to welcome his saint. The speaker has cut her ties to the circuit world; she has willed her property, made provision for disposing of her body, and said farewell to friends. She waits expectantly to begin her journey. But just as she and we anticipate her vision, the sense of hearing takes over from sight (an apt perception in terms of sequential sensory deprivations at death). The fly's buzzing possesses her mind, even blurs her vision with the sound she perceives synesthetically as a maddening blue screen that blocks celestial revelation. The fly, representing the trivial but nonetheless firm clutch of the circuit world, obscures the dying person's total consciousness to the point that even when narrating her ironic story from beyond circumference, she still concentrates on the circuit world and its final bitter deprivation. Not even by playing the role of a dead person, then, could Dickinson achieve perspective on the mysteries she wanted to probe. Imagination—although fused in a blending of dream and drama—could never fully place her outside the circuit, however she might pivot on its brink.

The failure of her role-playing strategy in this daring effort to fling consciousness across circumference from a position of safety in the circuit world forced Dickinson to concentrate on a different kind of interpenetration of the barrier—that by which the dead retain an influence upon the circuit from their position outside. Those inside circumference could not grasp beyond it, but those on the outside could still—in some fashion—reach in. Hence her emphasis on memory and fame as modes of circuit continuation after death. She told Judge Lord's executor, Benjamin Kimball, that "I once asked him what I should do for him when he was not here, referring half unconsciously to the great Expanse—In a tone italic of both Worlds 'Remember Me,' he said. I have kept his Commandment" (L 968). When Samuel Bowles died, she confided to his widow, "To remember our own Mr Bowles is all we can do" (L 532). Memory, of course, depended on the actions of the survivors; it was not controlled by the dead even when requested by them. It seemed to Emily Dickinson an almost celestial power, as she intimated in the remark that "I think Heaven will not be as good as earth, unless it bring with it that sweet power to remember, which is the Staple of Heaven—here" (L 623) and in the exclamation to Sue, "Show me Eternity, and I will show you Memory—/ Both in one package lain / And lifted back again—" (L 912). As an almost heavenly power, remembrance seemed to her a force evading deliberate control. "You cannot make Remembrance grow" (P 1508), she cautioned once in likening calculated celebrity to a rootless plant in contrast to the "Iron Buds" of the authentic tree that could never be cut down. She looked ironically at the external substitutes for memory that proliferated in her monument-building, portrait-dedicating, statue-erecting era of supposedly great men and mocked the affectation of "a stupendous Tomb / Proclaiming to the Gloom / How dead we are—" (P 1674).

Dickinson counted fame, like power and dominion, among her "post mortuary gifts." Its aura must radiate from beyond circumference or not at all. She asserted, "The first We knew of Him was Death—/ The second—was—Renown—/ Except the first had justified / The second had not been." (P 1006), and reiterated this idea in a number of related poems such as "I see thee clearer for the Grave" (P 1666), "Fame is the one that does not stay—" (P 1475), and her tribute to "Fame's Boys and Girls, who never die / And are too seldom born—" (P 1066). Given her conviction about fame as an aura from beyond circumference, ungovernable from within the circuit and awarded only to true worth that continues to enrich the circuit, her comment to Higginson on the unimportance of immediate publishing makes perfect sense as an act of faith in the enduring vitality of her poems. "If fame belonged to me," she noted with becoming modesty, "I could not escape her—

if she did not, the longest day would pass me on the chase—and the approbation of my Dog, would forsake me" (L 265). The history of her poetic reputation certainly bears her out. The fame she envisaged, nevertheless, might be impersonal, like that she described in the strikingly circumferential imagery of this quatrain that she grouped in the same set with "The first We knew of Him was Death—" (P 1006): "Fame is the tint that Scholars leave / Upon their Setting Names—/ The Iris not of Occident / That disappears as comes—" (P 866). Remembering Dickinson's designation of herself as Higginson's scholar, we can note the personal application of this sunset metaphor. The name sets with the person who ventures beyond circumference, but a nimbus of light remains to irradiate the circuit world with the continuing influence of the scholar's quest for knowledge. Personal notability may fail, then, but vivifying work remains.

The work that Dickinson judged most likely to confer such fame was art, which seemed to defy death in its ability to unite souls in a "Vital Kinsmanship" beyond circumference. "There be Immortal friends / Whom Death see first—" (P 645), she wrote in a probable tribute to Mrs. Browning; and such friendship worked in two ways: to project the surviving friend imaginatively beyond death and to retain the artistic legacy for the perpetual enrichment of the circuit world. Even when their "mortal name be numb," she claimed elsewhere, the martyr poets and painters could sustain other people through the encouragement of their art (P 544). Most powerful as an expression of Dickinson's faith in art's power to penetrate circumference is "The Poets light but Lamps—" (P 883), which asserts that the art they leave behind them disseminates the circumference of dead poets, transcending time or even using it as an intensifier of immortal artistic power. Few persons would ever exercise such influence from beyond circumference upon the circuit world, and even most of these would do so through their work rather than through the memories of friends equally vulnerable to extinction. "Time's sublimest target / Is a soul 'forgot!'" (P 8), Dickinson wrote in one of her earliest poems, but she had boasted even earlier—with startling prescience—"when I die, they'll have to remember me."[6]

Death somehow clarified the meaning of lives and assisted the survivors in the circuit world in their evaluative efforts. Dickinson's elegy for her mother spoke of the family's "Fashioning what she is, / Fathoming what she was" (P 1573) in an effort to make sense of her transition beyond circumference. On a more generalized level she recognized how "Death's bold Exhibition" demonstrates "Preciser what we are" and enables those remaining to infer "the Eternal function" (P 856). Estimates of lives that had been spent, then, cast at least a flickering light into the other world while sometimes igniting a clarifying blaze in this one. "The Admirations—and Contempts—of time—/ Show justest—through an Open Tomb—" (P 906), Dickinson noted, and her commentaries on the dead exhibited both sets of responses.

The lives Emily Dickinson held in contempt were those that had not been lived intensely, those that failed of growth and force. She looked for "Maturity of Fate" as a measure of value, comparing a "Junior of Fourscore" with "A Hoary Boy" in "Not all die early, dying young—" (P 990). The ancient person's unspent powers rebuked him. They showed him unfit to embark upon the great adventure of death and condemned the aged stripling to a purely natural dying, like that of a toad (P 583). The disappearance of such a person would have little impact even on the circuit world, as the poet intimated in "That odd old man is dead a year—" (P 1130). It is his hat the neighbors miss after the death of this virtual stranger—something he must have left behind and that they could find if they cared enough. The hat, being "stated," however, simply represents his habits. Routine motions had been the only indications of his existence; their cessation offers the sole evidence of his departure, unless by chance he left behind some even more obscure and insignificant "indurated mate." The last stanza, beginning "Oh Life, begun in fluent Blood / And consummated dull!", cries out the poet's anguish at this pitiful abuse of human promise. Even death seemed too great a privilege, too noble an adventure, for unworthy persons who somehow stumbled onto the "new Road," so that Dickinson exclaimed in wonder once:

> That this should feel the need of Death
> The same as those that lived
> Is such a—*Feat*—
> Of Irony
> As never was achieved—

> Not satisfied to ape the Great in his simplicity
> The small must die, the same as he—
> Oh the Audacity—
> (P 1112)

Wasted lives meant wasted dying. The poet made no attempt to follow those she scorned across circumference. But most of Dickinson's comments on the dead were charitable ones; she expressed admiration far more often than contempt. By comparing intensely lived existences with torpid ones, she articulated in "More Life—went out—when He went / Than Ordinary Breath—" (P 422) her standard of human value.

That memorable men and women have lived seemed to Dickinson "Certificate for Immortality" (P 1030), and she even speculated on the differential application of Christ's promise of abrogated death in "Do People moulder equally, / They bury, in the Grave?" (P 432), intimating that contemptible people just die and disappear while admirable persons, by their dying, serve as stimulants to immortality. The very best might somehow merge the circuit world with that of awe without stopping at circumference. For them the biblical pledge was fulfilled: "Death was dead." But who such persons might be or what might be the nature of their seamless living the poet could only guess.

Emily Dickinson kept on speculating all her life about those possibilities "behind the Door—" (P 335) that captured her imagination. She kept inquiring about the destiny of those she loved and about her own prospects. When her mother died in November 1882, she wrote to her Norcross cousins, "We don't know where she is, though so many tell us" but went on to express a hopeful conviction: "I believe we shall in some manner be cherished by our Maker—that the One who gave us this remarkable earth has the power still farther to surprise that which He has caused. Beyond that all is silence" (L 785). "Surprise" is the key word here. We know from family reports that this woman loved surprises and secrets.[7] When she failed to penetrate beyond circumference by her observations and role playing, she came to think of the wished-for next life as God's wonderful secret to be revealed only after death. As she told Perez Cowan in the same letter that defines death as "a wild Night and a new Road," "I suppose we are all thinking of Immortality, at times so stimulatedly that we cannot sleep. Secrets are interesting, but they are also solemn—and speculate with all our might, we cannot ascertain" (L 332). An early poem defines dust as "the only Secret" and death as "the only One / You cannot find out all about / In his 'native town'." (P 153)—this even though death exhibits the familiar Yankee virtues of industriousness, punctuality, sedateness, and laconic speech. The grave held its own secrets, encompassing nothing in its void but "Gravity—and Expectation—and Fear—/ A tremor just, that All's not sure" (P 408), and curiosity about the fate of its tenants drew captives of the circuit world into "That oblique Belief which we call Conjecture" grappling with "a Theme stubborn as Sublime" (P 1221).

Dickinson was stubborn herself in flinging her intellectual and imaginative powers against this obdurate riddle. She seems to have anticipated rather than dreaded the ultimate disclosure of the secret, expecting a happy surprise whenever she might penetrate the barrier of death. Yet death remained the insuperable circumference. No strategy she ever tried succeeded in projecting her beyond it in a way that did anything but trace more clearly the limits of her mortal circuit. But failure served as incentive to speculation. Dickinson wrote once to her sister-in-law that "In a Life that stopped guessing, you and I should not feel at home—" (L 586). Neither of them ever stopped, not even Sue, who had seemed to settle early in life for the formulaic answers of Calvinist dogma. Years after the poet's death, her friend was still guessing, still pushing and probing at circumference; and Sue's conjectures about her dead husband seem to speak even more powerfully for and about his sister. "My hands shake so I cannot write," Sue confided to her sister, Martha, "Austin is beyond recall, but *living energy somewhere.*"[8]

9

"A Prognostic's Push"

Premonitions of Immortality

GUESSING AT the secrets God had hidden beyond circumference constituted the essential work of Emily Dickinson's life, the resolution of riddles the impelling drive of her imagination. Discontented with the routine answers that seemed to satisfy most people and unwilling to rest in the uncertainty that sufficed for others, she concentrated her intellectual and emotional energy on the effort to make connections between "this side" and the other, the finite and the infinite, time and eternity. Her niece summed up the poet's drive for ultracircumferential insight in the observation that "Her essential rebellion was against Life defrauded of the truth about Death. It was her Tyrant need-to-know that shut her in and left her knocking—'knocking everywhere'."[1] This spiritual restlessness never culminated in calm assurance, nor did it settle into tragic despair. It remained a constant incentive to speculation.

One of the striking features of Dickinson's letters from adolescence until her death is the constant associative process by which she linked commonplace images and situations with thoughts of death and suppositions about what lay beyond. The Puritan analogizing habit that had led Samuel Sewall two centuries before to read the fragility of man's life into the shattering of a wineglass and that encouraged Cotton Mather to turn the most trifling circumstance to spiritual profit lived on in this daughter of New England to turn all her thoughts toward immortality, though her haunting doubts about it led to far more troubled meditations than theirs.

The 1856 letter to John Graves, discussed earlier as evidence of the consciously literary structure of Dickinson's letters as she prepared herself to explore her central themes poetically, exemplifies

this tendency to link the circuit world with the mysteries beyond
circumference—acknowledging death as the barrier to knowledge
but darting beyond it in imagination (L 184). The crumbling wall
dividing the Dickinson house from the Sweetsers' precipitated a
prolonged meditation on crumbling things, the evanescence of
natural life, and human mortality. "To live, and die, and mount
again in triumphant body, and *next* time, try the upper air—is no
schoolboy's theme," she exclaimed before moving with strained
bravado to personal application: "It is a jolly thought to think that
we can be Eternal—when air and earth are *full* of lives that are
gone—and done—and a conceited thing indeed, this promised
Resurrection! *Congratulate* me—John—Lad—and 'here's a health
to *you*'—that we have each a *pair* of lives, and need not chary be,
of the one 'that *now* is'—." A "jolly thought," perhaps, but no real
jollity rings through this letter; the thoughts of crumbling prevail
over those of resurrection. The notion of mortality's dissolving
wall dividing a pair of separate lives offered little comfort to one
concerned with maintaining her own consciousness even while
trying that "upper air" on the other side of death. Anxiety dominates this letter, an anxiety about connections across the wall between earth and heaven that would characterize later correspondence also.

Dickinson consistently and characteristically drew all her close
friends into her reflections on this compelling theme, and letters
throughout her life probed the barrier of death. In April 1873, for
instance, distant sounds of robins and wagons precipitated this
reflection to her Norcross cousins: "Remoteness is the founder of
sweetness; could we see all we hope, or hear the whole we fear
told tranquil, like another tale, there would be madness near. Each
of us gives or takes heaven in corporeal person, for each of us has
the skill of life" (L 388). Real confidence speaks in this letter, far
greater cheerfulness than the affected jollity of the parallel spring
reflection to Graves written before she had grown comfortably
familiar with circumferential barriers—barriers she came to recognize as penetrable in some fashion by consciousness from
within the protected circuit. Life was a skill at which Emily Dickinson became increasingly adept. Yet her father's death the following year and the subsequent deaths of Samuel Bowles, Dr. Holland, Charles Wadsworth, her mother, her nephew, and Judge

Lord called forth further anxious questioning about mortality and the possibility of continuing consciousness.

An 1862 poem registers Dickinson's lifelong gnawing fascination with the question of immortality while demonstrating her resistance to formulaic answers.

> This World is not Conclusion.
> A Species stands beyond—
> Invisible, as Music—
> But positive, as Sound—
> It beckons, and it baffles—
> Philosophy—dont know—
> And through a Riddle, at the last—
> Sagacity, must go—
> To guess it, puzzles scholars—
> To gain it, Men have borne
> Contempt of Generations
> And Crucifixion, shown—
> Faith slips—and laughs, and rallies—
> Blushes, if any see—
> Plucks at a twig of Evidence—
> And asks a Vane, the way—
> Much Gesture, from the Pulpit—
> Strong Hallelujahs roll—
> Narcotics cannot still the Tooth
> That nibbles at the soul—
>
> (P 501)

The assurance of the opening statement seems to break down as the poem develops. The hope of immortality finds insufficient supports in human wisdom. Science, philosophy, and theology all prove inadequate to the task with dogmatic pulpit pronouncements the most ludicrously insufficient. Even faith appears allegorically here as a silly young girl meandering blithely toward an uncertain destination. The pulpit orator knows the way in some literal-minded sense. His gesture presumably points onward and upward, though he himself remains immobile in his perch. But the poem offers countervailing evidence for hope from human impulse. It demonstrates over and over the drive of mortal beings toward an existence beyond death. Something outside circumference entices these pilgrims to move toward it, however helpless they may be to establish momentum and direction from the material and intellectual resources of the circuit world. The martyrs offer strong evidence for the force of this appeal from the other side of death. Still stronger is the unappeasable appetite that "nibbles at the soul" and will not be quieted.

Nothing ever deterred the poet herself from her quest for the mysterious "Species" of life beyond the circuit world's capacity to classify. Conscious always of a cosmic power in the universe to which her own faculties responded, she groped and struggled toward whatever illumination she could find, always probing for connection with the fountain of life—whether personified as God or abstracted as awe or immortality. Few writers have concentrated so intensively on the unanswerable question.

> How Human Nature dotes
> On what it cant detect.
> The moment that a Plot is plumbed
> It's meaning is extinct—
>
> Prospective is the friend
> Reserved for us to know
> When Constancy is clarified
> Of Curiosity—
>
> Of subjects that resist
> Redoubtablest is this
> Where go we—
> Go we anywhere
> Creation after this?
> (P 1417)

Nor have many others shared her sense that hints were all around her, still undiscerned. "Not 'Revelation'—'tis—that waits," she told Higginson in 1863, "But our unfurnished eyes—" (P 685), and she concentrated on opening all her senses to insight. An oriole's song, she observed, offered either commonplace or divine experience depending on the sensitivity and openness of the auditor: "So whether it be Rune, / Or whether it be none / Is of within" (P 526). She quickened her senses to recognize runes, though not generally to unriddle them. "The Riddle we can guess / We speedily despise——" (P 1222): a fate she never faced with regard to immortality.

Searching, stumbling, and speculating, Dickinson pursued her relentless quest for assurance—like Melville, unable either to believe or to rest easy in unbelief. Yet a quatrain she sent once to Samuel Bowles expressed doubts about cynicism with regard to immortality and intimated a modest hopefulness: "Ourselves we do inter with sweet derision. / The channel of the dust who once achieves / Invalidates the balm of that religion / That doubts as fervently as it believes" (P 1144). After interring herself imaginatively in poems discussed in the previous chapter, she continued to anticipate validation of other views than skepticism. Her poems and letters suggest that the religion she hoped to validate was that Protestantism in which she had been educated even though her actual experience of Christianity entailed doubts irresolvable from within the mortal circuit. Nor did she suppose that her more orthodox neighbors had attained firm assurance, whatever their claims. "When it becomes necessary for us to stake our all upon the belief of another in as for instance Eternity," she remarked in the draft of a letter, "we find it impossible to make the transfer— Belief is unconsciously to most of us Ourselves—an Untried Experience."[2] Her yearning for assurance prompted inquiries to those people she hoped could provide it. After James Clark died, to whom she had turned for companionship in grief after the death of the Reverend Charles Wadsworth, their mutual friend, she inquired of Clark's brother, "Are you certain there is another life? When overwhelmed to know, I fear that few are sure" (L 827). A similar inquiry elicited the following confession of faith from Washington Gladden after Wadsworth's death and during Judge Lord's grave illness: "'Is immortality true?' I believe that it is true—the only reality—almost; a thousand times truer than mortality, which is but a semblance after all. I believe that virtue is deathless; that God who is the source of virtue, gave to her 'the glory of going on, and not to die'; that the human soul, with which virtue is incorporate, cannot perish. I believe in the life everlasting, because Jesus Christ taught it. Say what you will about him, no one can deny that he knew the human soul, its nature, its laws, its destinies, better than any other being who ever trod this earth; and he testifies, and his testimony is more clear, more definite, more positive on this than on any other subject, that there is life beyond the grave" (L 752a). This credo was what Emily Dickinson wanted to know; in some moods she believed it, in others doubted, in few felt certain.

A grouping of poems from 1883 employs the image of a "Prognostic's Push" to represent Dickinson's drive to thrust by the force of her imaginative conjecture beyond circumference to the mysteries it concealed. She was looking for knowledge in advance of experience: for several kinds of knowledge that awaited clarification beyond the grave, if then. The first of these poems, sent to James Clark near the first anniversary of Wadsworth's death, speculates on the nature of man's transformed life after death. How, she wondered, could the soul manifest itself without the body?

> The Spirit lasts—but in what mode—
> Below, the Body speaks,
> But as the Spirit furnishes—
> Apart, it never talks—
> The Music in the Violin
> Does not emerge alone
> But Arm in Arm with Touch, yet Touch
> Alone—is not a Tune—
> The Spirit lurks within the Flesh
> Like Tides within the Sea
> That makes the Water live, estranged
> What would the Either be?
> Does that know—now—or does it cease—
> That which to this is done,
> Resuming at a mutual date
> With every future one?
> Instinct pursues the Adamant,
> Exacting this Reply—
> Adversity if it may be, or
> Wild Prosperity,
> The Rumor's Gate was shut so tight
> Before my Mind was sown,
> Not even a Prognostic's Push
> Could make a Dent thereon—
> (P 1576)

Within the circuit, body and soul interact to produce identity; matter is essential even to spiritual expression. Sheer abstraction of beauty, truth, or grace eludes the imagination. Forced to pose questions from within the circuit that are unanswerable here, she instinctively directs her speculation outside—only to encounter the impersonal force of "Adamant" rather than a confiding God. The circumferential gate to circuit rumor withstands the energetic thrust of her prognosticating curiosity.

Circumferential imagery appears again in the second poem of this triad, "Expanse cannot be lost—" (p 1584), written shortly after Gilbert's death. Rather than speculating on the child's newly ethereal condition, his aunt pushes her speculation now against God's nature—particularly his infinity, which contrasts so sharply with human limitation and loss. Gilbert, to whom Dickinson addresses the second stanza, has passed beyond death's gate into a new world to which others follow him immediately in their imaginations and ultimately through their own encounters with death. The poem expresses confidence in the heavenly "Tracts of Sheen" into which the child has advanced but frustration at the closing of the door to insight.

The third of these poems, "This Me—that walks and works—must die," (p 1588), directs the inquiry toward the author's personal fate, the destiny of her own soul. She speaks bluntly here of her uncertainty, offering less comfort than in the earlier poems. Death and doubt remain insuperable realities, though she still conjectures a destiny that necessitates questioning even while foreclosing the possibility of answers. From the circuit side, she found the gate impenetrable; but gates, unlike walls, are designed to open somehow. She never stopped her "Prognostic's Push" against the lock.

Beyond "Rumor's Gate" lay immortality, which evoked Dickinson's endless wondering. Much more than death, immortality enchanted her; in fact, death's principal attraction was its perspective on whatever lay beyond. When she identified immortality to Higginson as her "Flood subject" in 1866, she did so in circumferential language of sea and shore: "I was told that the Bank was the safest place for a Finless Mind" (L 319). From the bank of her circuit, she gazed out upon the sea of timelessness and infinity, upon that metaphorical water that promised satiation of all appe-

tency. In "We thirst at first—'tis Nature's Act—," she observed
that the material water for which men and women thirst only "intimates the finer want—/ Whose adequate supply / Is that Great
Water in the West—/ Termed Immortality—" (p 726). Grouped in
fascicle 36 with "Behind Me—dips Eternity—/ Before Me—Immortality—" (p 721), this poem articulates her sense of herself as
temporarily estranged from the fulfillment out of which she has
come and to which she is destined. She faced a problem, however,
of disproportion between circuit and postcircumferential worlds.
How, from within the circuit, can one conjecture the force that
encloses us? How can one compare a glass of water with an ocean,
or time with eternity? The only way, she showed in "Forever—is
composed of Nows—" (p 624), is by multiplication of the familiar
until it expands into the unimaginable. Infinitely extended, circuit
observations of days, months, and years could suggest divine experience. It was too easy, however, to become obsessed with
"Nows" rather than working for immortality as she meant to do,
preferring its "Slow Gold—but Everlasting—" to immediate rewards of temporal industry (p 406).

All of Emily Dickinson's recurring themes related directly and
profoundly to the central issue of immortality. She was not responding simply to the formulaic promise of her Christian culture
but to an instinctive internal need. To someone who habitually felt
deprived, immortality offered a restitution of loss. "Of Heaven
above the firmest proof / We fundamental know," she reminded
Higginson when his brother died, "Except for it's marauding
Hand / It had been Heaven below" (p 1205). For a woman so intently concerned with death, immortality overcame fears of annihilation. It mitigated the fear of dying, which she defined once in
a happy mood as "but our rapt attention / To Immortality" (p 7).
And yet, for someone so protective of her circuit existence with
its secure identity and its relatively controllable consciousness, immortality seemed an invasive and often threatening force, one that
she attempted to tame by raising hopeful questions: "Why should
we hurry—why indeed / When every way we fly / We are mo-
lested equally / by immortality" (p 1646) and "Is Immortality a
bane / That men are so oppressed?" (p 1728).

Dickinson's allegiance to her circuit even as she celebrated immortality has led readers over the years to define immortality on

her behalf in intracircumferential terms, thereby discounting the superhuman religious context of the word. Theodora Ward, for example, argued that the poet's use of this key term was more Greek than Christian, that both immortality and eternity meant that "wholeness of life contained in the great mystery of the inner world" that, in classical mythology, would have united her with the immortals.[3] But Dickinson, despite her modestly classical education, paid little attention to Greek deities or classical ideals of human fulfillment. Her letters and poems reveal a mind saturated instead with Christian imagery. Nor did she share the modern agnosticism to which Sharon Cameron confesses on behalf of many of the poet's critics who interpret her religious vocabulary in secular terms because, for many twentieth-century readers, "That there is no immortality is a state of affairs we accede to with comfortable sophistication, a loss we have most of us agreed upon."[4] There was nothing comfortably sophisticated about Emily Dickinson, nor did she set aside momentous questions so easily. In 1879, she uttered a sharp rejoinder to such dismissals, proclaiming, "Those not live yet / Who doubt to live again—" (P 1454). Already living and intending to keep on living, she accepted in this poem a version of the paired lives notion of her 1856 letter to Graves but only as a figure of speech that opened the way for more adequate similes demonstrating the unity of life seemingly divided by death. Rather than terminating one life or separating two, death functions here as the narrow stream of water uniting two larger bodies, as the drawbridge above the stream that links two shores on one road, and as a hyphen combining apparently disparate ideas in one concept. Time connects with immortality; it is neither subsumed by it nor eliminated. The person, however, lives on in a transformed mode as bodiless spirit or "Costumeless Consciousness." Yet it remains consciousness. The person retains the bulwark of identity. It was a condition that Dickinson anticipated and practiced even within the circuit, as we note in her comment to Higginson that "A Letter always feels to me like immortality because it is the mind alone without corporeal friend. Indebted in our talk to attitude and accent, there seems a spectral power in thought that walks alone—" (L 330). By the force of that spectral power of consciousness (even more brilliantly realized in her poems than in letters), she hoped to advance across the drawbridge from her limited circuit to the dazzling "Disk to be—." She focused attention on the "inlets" and "outlets" of the mind (P 1421), all of them offering perspective on immortality.

Dickinson cherished the idea of immortality, also, as a perpetuation of love. Indeed, she defined love in terms of infinity and timelessness, describing it as "anterior to Life—/ Posterior—to Death—/ Initial of Creation, and / The Exponent of Earth—" (P 917). It was a circumference-defying force, one that allowed her to sacrifice the corporeal aspects of friendship to its perpetuation in "Costumeless Consciousness" (P 1454), a condition she actually came to prefer in all but a few favored human relationships. As early as 1858 she had overcome her early disposition to clasp greedily at her friends and was able to offer a hopeful farewell to her neighbor, Mrs. Haven: "I know you will come again—if not today—*tomorrow*—if not tomorrow as we count—after the little interval we pass in lifetime here. Then we wont say 'Goodbye,' since immortality—makes the phrase quite obsolete" (L 192). Loving, knowing, being: To none of these did she anticipate cessation. The overwhelming impression of Emily Dickinson's writing is that she believed in immortality but wondered how to imagine or articulate it in human terms.[5]

The imagined projections of immortality transmitted to the poet from within her culture involved heaven, pictured in various ways suggested by biblical revelation and human notions of the ideal. Not surprisingly, Dickinson rejected most of the traditional views and often made them the butt of her ironic humor. The child persona behind which she so often hid when making unsettling observations served her in good stead for assaulting hackneyed presentations of heaven as some sort of glorified earth still somehow subject to societal hierarchies and to mundane routine. Pretending to inquire about this celestial refuge, she took advantage of the opportunity to denounce orderly New England habits.

> What is—"Paradise"—
> Who live there—
> Are they "Farmers"—
> Do they "hoe"—
> Do they know that this is "Amherst"—
> And that I—am coming—too—

Do they wear "new shoes"—in "Eden"—
Is it always pleasant—there—
Wont they scold us—when we're hungry—
Or tell God—how cross we are—

You are sure there's such a person
As "a Father"—in the sky—
So if I get lost—there—ever—
Or do what the Nurse calls "die"—
I shant walk the "Jasper"—barefoot—
Ransomed folks—wont laugh at me—
Maybe—"Eden" a'nt so lonesome
As New England used to be!

(P 215)

Obviously Amherst is no paradise for a timid child, nor has it conditioned her to anticipate boundless love and joy. The child dreads an eternity of correction and alienation. Not even the materialistic promise of new shoes brings comfort, given the usual restrictions on such finery below. Her child shows no more zeal for heaven than Huck Finn did although as anxious as he to escape from experienced constrictions. The speaker of "I never felt at Home—Below—" (P 413) asserts outright that "I dont like Paradise—/ Because it's Sunday—all the time—/ And Recess—never comes—" but sees no possibility of evading a coercive God.

Even when not denouncing heaven, Dickinson's child-speakers raised disturbing questions—especially by their habit of taking metaphorical language too literally. Thus, the speaker of "It troubled me as once I was—" (P 600) recalled her girlish fear of having heaven collapse upon the earth and crush her; she had been both confused and terrified by a spatial presentation of the cosmos in which heaven figured on a plane above the earth while the infernal regions presumably blazed below. Characteristically, however, the Dickinsonian speaker ignored the danger of tumbling into the abyss but worried instead about being flattened by celestial collapse. In "You're right—'the way *is* narrow'—" (P 234), also, the poet cultivated her childlike trick of quoting transmitted lore in seeming acquiescence even as she demonstrated her own helplessness to make sense of that tradition.

The technique served her well in "I think just how my shape

will rise—/ When I shall be *'forgiven'*—" (P 237), where both quotation marks and italicization designate derivative and as yet unassimilated language. The key word is, of course, *"forgiven."* Forgiven what? The speaker neither says nor seems to know. No sin is mentioned here, nor is there evidence even of unfocused guilt. The notion of forgiveness has been transmitted to her without its moral context. So has the spatial concept of heaven been imposed on her. She expects to rise out of sight until lifted into a new realm where she can parrot her uncomprehending thanks. The vagueness of the language in stanza three leaves the reader intentionally in doubt about the *"this"* of which she hopes to be relieved like the previous drifts of anguish, but the burden she hopes to escape may well be this fantasized heaven with its eternal suppression of independent thought and moral self-esteem. Rather than having her soul lifted up at the end, she drops it herself—presumably onto the earth. She exclaims exultantly that she has held it *"unshriven,"* unforgiven—perhaps in fact still innocent despite the negative assumptions of those who have tried to lift her aspirations skyward. Despite traditional theological lore, this speaker shows no sense of needing God's mercy and no real inclination toward a celestial home.

When she forsook the supposedly naive child role, Dickinson slashed ironically at paradisal notions that she felt degrading to her ideal of immortality. She cut away clichés in poems like "Is Heaven a Physician?" (P 1270), in which she undermined the metaphors that liken heaven to a doctor or a bank, and in "We pray—to Heaven—" (P 489), in which she denounced the folly of imagining paradise spatially as a place of refuge to which overburdened souls might fly. "Is Heaven a Place—a Sky—a Tree?" she asked, then answered her own question: "Location's narrow way is for Ourselves—/ Unto the Dead / There's no Geography—." Instead, there were "State—Endowal—Focus," not just in some penthouse of the universe but everywhere, presumably even here and now. "Where—Omnipresence—fly?" she asks, freshening the reader's perspective on God's presence within his creation. Even the one poem in which she claimed to have visited heaven gave Dickinson occasion to disturb the usual tall-tale extrapolations from dreams of worldly wealth by which deprived mortals fantasize golden streets, glittering mansions, and shining raiment (P 374). Ascribing value to the fragile, the evanescent, and the delicately beautiful rather than the grand (and appropriately expressing her values in the briefest of lines), Dickinson envisaged a minuscule paradise with "Duties—of Gossamer—/ And Eider—names—," but it was still an unsatisfying one in which, at best, she would be "Almost—contented." No sensate imagery, no concrete representation, could do anything but cheapen immortality.

Nor did hopes of eternal compensation satisfy the sense of loss within the beloved circuit. Her most logically structured poem, "I reason, Earth is short—" (P 301), demonstrated the failure of reason to buttress dreams of heavenly replenishment. Promised bliss failed to atone for absolute earthly anguish and the inevitability of loss. Science shared in the failure of reason. She even blamed it once for undermining traditional hopes of celestial relief, complaining that "What once was 'Heaven' / Is '*Zenith*' now—/ Where I proposed to go" (P 70). Reassuming her child persona here, she clung to hope for her naive vision of the protective, welcoming heaven in which she had actually ceased to believe. Many years later she returned in a happier frame of mind to the devastating effects of science on belief, commenting to Judge Lord that "Mrs Dr Stearns called to know if we didnt think it very shocking for Butler to 'liken himself to his Redeemer,' but we thought Darwin had thrown 'the Redeemer' away" (P 750). Secular knowledge, unfortunately, offered no substitutes for the wishes it was undermining.

Consequently, Dickinson continued to distrust science and logic as much as she questioned tradition, and she remained open to the possibility of "The Heaven, in which we hoped to pause / When Discipline was done / Untenable to Logic / But possibly the one—" (P 1293). The clearest proof she found "Of Paradise' existence" was death, "it's Bisecting / Messenger—" (P 1411). "Too much of Proof affronts Belief," she exclaimed in another poem in which she offered as evidence for immortality the instinctive movement toward it of living beings, the need for restitution, and the appropriateness of God's providing fitting enclosure for the saints already gone from earth (P 1228). The good in this life, then, served as a pledge for heaven—but also as a repudiation of its necessity except in cases of loss. When Lavinia returned from an 1873 visit with the Hollands, Emily wrote to her sister's hostess, "Vinnie says you are most illustrious and dwell in Paradise. I have never believed the latter to be a superhuman site" (L 391). She went on immediately to celebrate nature's putting on of incorruption that cast into doubt the dark belittlings of this world that her father and sister tolerated from their minister. "Eden, always eligible, is peculiarly so this noon," she noted, and Paradise might be in Amherst or Springfield as well as realms above. In joyful moods, she felt plenitude immediately, prompting her to suppose herself already in heaven and to assume it a fact "that Earth is Heaven—/ Whether Heaven is Heaven or not" (P 1408). The notion of heaven seemed to her at times a forbidding one, perversely denigrating bliss already known by comparison with something supposedly better so that Christians were expected to carry on "Immured the whole of Life / Within a magic Prison," reprimanding "the Happiness / That too competes with Heaven" (P 1601). Reluctant to see this world as "just the Primer—to a life—/ Unopened—rare—Upon the Shelf—," she preferred the primer to the promised book of life (P 418). When life seemed "too blissful" (in the phrase she liked to quote from Sue's friend, Kate Scott Anthon), Dickinson felt the need for nothing more (L 177).

The best moments seldom lasted (P 393), however, and the poet generalized once that "Lest this be Heaven indeed / An Obstacle is given / That always guages a Degree / Between Ourself and Heaven" (P 1043). Memory of bliss and anticipation of it served as inducements, so that Dickinson often envisaged heaven as a welcome prospect although she seldom conceived of it in terms of the traditional divine kingdom. Defining heaven subjectively as any unattainable goal, she linked it to fleeting earthly revelations such as "The Color, on the Cruising Cloud—/ The interdicted Land—/ Behind the Hill—the House behind—," to anything she wanted yet could not reach (P 239). The very existence of appetites in limited persons cursed with disappointments seemed to necessitate their eventual satisfaction.

Strongest among such appetites was that for love, and Dickinson's anticipations of heaven emphasized the intimate companionship of friends. It was not love of God that drew her there or any pious fantasy of resting in Abraham's bosom that inspired her hopes but the prospect of endless union with those she already loved within her circuit world. Thus, one of her poems gives us "Fleshless Lovers" meeting in heaven to affirm an eternal commitment necessarily hidden below (P 625), and one of her letters to

Judge Lord regrets Christ's denial of such fantasies: "—and in Heaven they neither woo nor are given in wooing—what an imperfect place!" (L 750). For the most part, however, she focused her hopes on nonerotic unions with the friends who made earthly existence comfortable. Essential figures within this community would be Dr. and Mrs. Holland, as their poet-friend often confided to them in the three decades of their association. As early as 1853 she was writing to the Hollands "Heaven is large—is it not? Life is short too, isn't it? Then when one is done, is there not another, and—and—then if God is willing, we are neighbors then" (L 133). A few years later she sketched her profile of heaven for them as an expansive, idyllic garden that she could share uninterruptedly with her friends.[6] It was deprivation on earth, she confessed, that prompted her longing for heaven; so there was an element of anger in her contemplation of God as celestial architect. Still, she admitted that "I should like to see what He *was* building for us, with no hammer, and no stone, and no journeyman either." Sending a flower to Elizabeth Holland in 1860, she looked forward to the day when "You and I, and Dr Holland, / Bloom Eternally! / Roses of a steadfast summer / In a steadfast land" (P 163). These were sentimental views of a pastoral retreat and not necessarily representative of the poet's later imaginings, which tended to grow more abstract. Heaven, she observed once, is "vast—as our Capacity—/ As fair—as our idea—" (P 370), and her ideas grew less conventional as she moved beyond the cheery fantasy of an early poem like "There is a morn by men unseen—" (P 24) and the biblical literalism of "Over and over, like a Tune—" (P 367) with its "Justified Processions" of celebrating saints. Throughout Emily Dickinson's life, the idea of heaven continued to beguile and entice her—continued also to intimidate her at times. Accustomed to renunciation and austerity, what would she make of "so much Joy" (P 172)? Immured within the magic prison of her temporal circuit (P 1601), she had grown so accustomed to the bars that those who had escaped to the other side struck her as similarly confined even though she felt them to be both free and jubilant. When Gilbert died, she exclaimed:

> Immured in Heaven!
> What a Cell!

> Let every Bondage be,
> Thou sweetest of the Universe,
> Like that which ravished thee!
> (P 1594)

And she looked forward to similar confinement herself. Never succeeding in formulating an adequate image of heaven, she still conceived of it as a sensorily imaginable expression of immortality. While rejecting conventional paradisal views as ludicrous, limiting, and illogical, she searched for more adequate representations of the mysteries outside circumference.

One reason for Dickinson's problem with envisaging heaven is that it was known to her as God's home, and her attitude toward God was a confused and troubling one. As with heaven, traditional lore led her to absurd suppositions she found it necessary to reject. She blamed distorted religious formation in childhood for adult defenses against the Deity.

> Who were "the Father and the Son"
> We pondered when a child,
> And what had they to do with us
> And when portentous told
>
> With inference appalling
> By Childhood fortified
> We thought, at least they are no worse
> Than they have been described.
>
> Who are "the Father and the Son"
> Did we demand Today
> "The Father and the Son" himself
> Would doubtless specify—
>
> But had they the felicity
> When we desired to know,
> We better Friends had been, perhaps,
> Than time ensue to be—
>
> We start—to learn that we believe
> But once—entirely—
> Belief, it does not fit so well
> When altered frequently—

> We blush, that Heaven if we achieve—
> Event ineffable—
> We shall have shunned until ashamed
> To own the Miracle—
> (P 1258)

Adult attempts to inculcate reverence had only engendered terror. Efforts to promote faith had promulgated cynicism. The appalled child recoiled from both God the Father and from Jesus. Yet the poem expresses a residual trust. The speaker feels that the persons of the Trinity might yet introduce themselves to her in later life even though she has discontinued her questioning. Childhood, Dickinson remarked elsewhere, is "earth's confiding time" (L 710). Faith not instilled then may never grow on this side of circumference. She blames God here even more than the human teachers whose harsh doctrines had resulted in her early and almost instinctive aversion to divinity. Principal responsibility for communication rested with him.

After her adolescent failure to experience conversion, Emily Dickinson tended to represent herself as an outsider to religion and as a dissenter against God. He had failed to reach out to her, and she often declared her reluctance to initiate interchange. When introducing herself to Higginson, she reported that her family were all religious "except me—and address an Eclipse, every morning—whom they call their 'Father'" (L 261).[7] To her they seemed to direct their faces to a cloud, which might have been obscuring Jehovah's radiant face but just as probably disguised some horror. It may have been the grimness of her parents' family devotions that gave her so negative an impression. Reminiscing late in life to Mrs. Holland after her husband's death, Dickinson recalled Dr. Holland's prayer on the first visit she and Lavinia had paid them—a prayer she remembered as "so simple, so believing" that it had introduced a different conception of God as sunshine rather than as cloud (L 731).

Generally, however, the poet reacted against the notion of God's paternity, denouncing him as an unfit parent in the remark "How many barefoot shiver I trust their Father knows who saw not fit to give them shoes" (L 207). God, then, compared unfavorably in parental solicitude even with stern Edward Dickinson, who not only clad his children but was making plans to start up fires that September night when his daughter remembered the freezing poor. When she addressed God as father, she did so with heavy irony.

> "Heavenly Father"—take to thee
> The supreme iniquity
> Fashioned by thy candid Hand
> In a moment contraband—
> Though to trust us—seem to us
> More respectful—"We are Dust"—
> We apologize to thee
> For thine own Duplicity—
> (P 1461)

Again he proved a harsh parent: vengeful, untrusting, uncommunicative. Her notions of God exaggerated the austere, grave, inexpressive qualities of Edward Dickinson's parental behavior.

Yet the squire provided security for his daughter. She looked to him for safety right up to his death in 1874.[8] If God the Father offered similar protection, she might feel indebted to him. Yet flawed teaching in childhood had undermined her confidence in a way that fastened upon her memory. As always in the experience of this woman with her heightened sensitivity to words and her alertness to tone, defective use of language inflicted lifelong pain. An 1877 letter to Higginson asked him, as a former clergyman, to explain a biblical expression to her in a way that might quiet fears aroused years before when, as a small girl, she had heard a minister demand at a funeral, "Is the Arm of the Lord shortened that it cannot save?" The preacher had emphasized the "cannot," and she confessed some thirty years later that "I mistook the accent for a doubt of Immortality and not daring to ask, it besets me still" (L 503). She need not have turned to Higginson for guidance, of course. No doubt she had long ago found the passage in Isaiah where the Lord speaks these words: "Wherefore, when I came, was there no man? when I called, was there none to answer? Is my hand shortened at all, that it cannot redeem? or have I no power to deliver? behold, at my rebuke I dry up the sea, I make the rivers a wilderness: their fish stinketh, because there is no water, and dieth for thirst" (Isaiah 50:2). It is a proud and powerful God who thunders here, not some celestial amputee. Even so, Dickinson was writing as late as 1882 about the mutilation of the divinity in whom she had been taught to trust; "God's Right Hand," she mourned, "is amputated now / And God cannot be found—" (P 1551). The anthropomorphic deity was all but dead to her, though she hardly found his disappearance liberating, observing instead that "The abdication of Belief / Makes the Behavior small—/ Better an ignis fatuus / Than no illume at all—." But the imaginary light, once quenched, could never be rekindled to the same intensity.

The religious tradition enjoined upon her at home, at school, and in church presented God to the poet as a cruel, jealous, all-powerful being. She enjoyed linking his reputed attributes ironically to criticize his seizure of persons she loved, as in these final stanzas of a farewell to a friend:

> If "God is Love" as he admits
> We think that he must be
> Because he is a "jealous God"
> He tells us certainly
>
> If "All is possible with" him
> As he besides concedes
> He will refund us finally
> Our confiscated Gods—
> (P 1260)

Those "confiscated Gods" included all persons she preferred to him, and there were many. God's jealousy of earthly attachments was one of his most striking attributes, to the point that Dickinson could ask Mrs. Todd rhetorically, within a year of her death, "Why should we censure Othello, when the Criterion Lover says, 'Thou shalt have no other Gods before Me'?" (L 1016). Not only was he jealous; he was cruel and indifferent to human pain. "It will never look kind to me," Dickinson announced to her Norcross cousins, "that God, who causes all, denies such little wishes. It could not hurt His glory, unless it were a lonesome kind. I 'most conclude it is" (L 234). Praying in one of her poems for a one-time "least Request," she addresses God euphemistically as "Sweet Deity" even while reproaching him inwardly as "Adamant" and "a God of Flint" (P 1076). She noted with dismay divine acquiescence in the destruction of beauty when frost beheads the flowers (P

1624) even though betraying amusement at her father's comeuppance from the family's gardener, Horace Church, who refused to hurry the harvesting process to save winter vegetables from frost but hid behind the pious excuse that "Squire, ef the Frost is the Lord's Will, I dont propose to stan in the way of it" (L 692). She hoped at the time of Church's death that "a nearer inspection of that 'Will' has left him with as ardent a bias in it's favor." For herself, she lived in constant apprehension of a jealous God's assault on whatever and whomever she loved, even anticipating Gilbert's loss in an 1879 letter to Mrs. Holland: "God's little Blond Blessing—we have long deemed you, and hope his so called 'Will'—will not compel him to revoke you. / The 'rectification of his Frontier,' costs the Earth too much—" (L 589). She wrote of God's garden depredations in "I had some things that I called mine—" (P 116), threatening to summon Lemuel Shaw, the Chief Justice of the Massachusetts Supreme Court, to her aid in filing a lawsuit against the Almighty. And she commented humorously on God's lack of response to Lavinia's desperate pleas for her drought-ravaged plantings, supposing that he was "too busy, getting 'angry with the Wicked—every Day'" (L 502).

Elsewhere the poet referred to her supposed father in heaven as a "Mastiff" (P 1317), although the successively gentler apostrophes "Burglar! Banker—Father!" of "I never lost as much but twice," (P 49) show her softening her expression of anger in hopes of wheedling restitution of yet another loss. God, then, might occasionally prove kind. He might even act paternal on occasion. But Dickinson remained conscious of his jealousy when confronted with the universal human tendency to play "with each other" rather than with him (P 1719). "The Maker's cordial visage, / However good to see," she observed in a comment on drowning, "Is shunned, we must admit it, / Like an adversity" (P 1718). So sharply aware of man's aversion to God (or to an anthropomorphic caricature of him), she contented herself with thinking of the divinity as "somewhat of a recluse" (L 551).

The dominant point to acknowledge in considering this poet's religious attitudes is that God was the most important person in Emily Dickinson's life.[9] Her relationship with him excelled all others in endurance and intensity. As the key to postcircumferential mysteries, he loomed before her as an irresistible force. God was awe; he was also love. Infinite and immortal, he transcended all human imagination. Yet her feelings toward him, despite her resistance to anthropomorphic paternal images, seem always to have been more filial than erotic; and as many commentators agree, her feelings toward God as father were inextricably intertwined with her complex emotional and volitional response to Edward Dickinson and all the other master figures with whom she populated her world. She was drawn to the power and safety God manifested. She reverenced awe.

In many ways, Emily Dickinson approached God more as her own father did than like any of her women acquaintances or typically orthodox Christians.[10] Her indifference to forgiveness, for example, mirrored the squire's unconsciousness of guilt. At the time of Edward Dickinson's conversion, his minister had reproached him for coming to God as a lawyer and ordered him onto his knees to confess himself a sinner. Yet he remained consistently legalistic in his relationship with divinity, dying with a dated title deed in his pocket that read "I hereby give myself to God."[11] His daughter, following a different but equally prideful profession, approached God not as sinner but as poet. Conscious of her gifts, including that of evading authority gracefully, she led off in the relationship with her sensitivity to natural revelation, her openness to intimations from beyond circumference, and her nearly magical skill with words. It was her eagerness for immortality and for eternal love that drew her toward her Creator, not fear or obedience. She looked to him as the fulfiller of yearnings. The God whom Dickinson loved, then, is better represented by the name "Awe" or by his own "I AM THAT I AM" (Exodus 3:14) than by any personal attributes. She felt free to quarrel with the jealous, angry, cruel figment of other people's imaginations because that figure was not the divinity she never stopped worshiping.

God's most enthralling aspect, so far as Dickinson was concerned, was his hidden quality. He was the sum of all mystery.

> Embarrassment of one another
> And God
> Is Revelation's limit,
> Aloud

Is nothing that is chief,
But still,
Divinity dwells under seal.
(P 662)

Being reclusive and "under seal," God eluded human searching—
a problem she confronted in "I know that He exists." (P 338), in
which the initial jollity of the celestial hide-and-seek game gives
way to fear either of God's indifference to the seeker, whom he
may simply leave to annihilation, or even worse of the supposed
hider's nonexistence, which makes a mockery of the quest. His
apartness troubled her, as she told Maria Whitney in 1883: "You
are like God. We pray to Him, and He answers 'No.' Then we
pray to Him to rescind the 'no,' and He don't answer at all, yet
'Seek and ye shall find' is the boon of faith" (L 830). The same
problems she encountered in trying to catch glimpses beyond circumference baffled her in her efforts to know the spirit presiding
over the mysterious force that attracted her.

Yet evidence of God's love for the circuit world provided an
incentive for Dickinson's search. Even though unable to find him
on the other side of circumference, she sometimes sensed his presence on her own side. While her pious neighbors gathered in
church to worship a distant deity, for example, she knew him to
be with her in the garden: "a noted Clergyman" whose sermon
was blessedly brief (P 324). When she gazed in admiration at the
sunset, she detected God within the crowd applauding those "far
Theatricals of Day" (P 595). She felt enough assurance of his love
for creation to declare that "No vacillating God / Ignited this
Abode / To put it out—" (P 1599), referring both to her beloved
earth and to specific persons (Bowles and Lord) whose loss she
mourned. When her mind misgave her about God's concern, she
questioned her thinking rather than his purposes in the supposition that "God made no act without a cause, / Nor heart without
an aim, / Our inference is premature, / Our premises to blame"
(P 1163).

God's immortality validated all others. He stood for the poet as
proof of enduring love and consciousness. Returning to the
whimsical image of his broken arm, she sometimes fantasized still
worse disasters to savor the irony of their impossibility. It would

take "The Funeral of God" (p 945), she asserted once, to erase a living thought (or a poem that breathes?), and truth could be expunged only on that impossible day when "Himself is borne away / From Mansion of the Universe / A lifeless Deity" (p 836). The very fact of her sending this latter poem to the serenely pious Dr. Holland reinforces its orthodox intent, as may its gathering in fascicle 7 with "How far is it to Heaven?" (p 929) and "Two Travellers perishing in Snow" (p 933).

Among God's beguiling mysteries none surpassed the wondrous multiplication of persons and identities within the Trinity. Dickinson enjoyed thinking of the multiple personalities of the Deity, his varied ways of wooing the soul that caused her to think of Jesus as John Alden courting the mortal Priscilla on behalf of the Father as Miles Standish, with the happy twist that "'Miles', and 'John Alden' were Synonyme—" so that the soul would unfailingly choose divinity (p 357). The indignant public response that greeted this poem when Mabel Loomis Todd first published it in the 2 April 1891 issue of the *Christian Register* and renewed itself with Martha Dickinson Bianchi's inclusion of it in *Further Poems* (1929) testifies to the heterodoxy of Dickinson's comic approach to one of the profoundest theological mysteries. But she could confront the riddle more directly also, as when she anticipated a "perfect—pauseless Monarchy—/ Whose Prince—is Son of None—/ Himself—Himself diversify—/ In Duplicate divine—" (p 721). The Holy Spirit, usually subordinated in her poetry to the awesome Father and loving Son, found recognition also in "Only God—detect the Sorrow—" (p 626), her tribute to God's respect for man. This was a complex God whom the poet worshiped, then, one to whom her responses were divided. It was the Father who captivated her imagination most as he presided over the realms beyond circumference and radiated an aura of power. But it was the Son she found most accessible, because he had entered the circuit and ennobled it.

Human efforts to exert a "Prognostic's Push" against circumference, even Dickinson's most inventive efforts, tended to result in frustration. For her, the barrier of death proved insuperable despite the attraction of the mysteries she intuited beyond it. But as I have demonstrated earlier with respect to conversion and sacraments, the barrier could be penetrated from the other side; and when it was, Jesus Christ was the most likely initiator of change. Grace dispensed through him permeated the divisions between the extracircumferential domain and the mortal circuit. Even more dramatically, Christ's actions as God in taking on human life, exposing himself to suffering, and triumphing over death established him as the one historical figure known to have shattered circumference. To Emily Dickinson, Christ's incarnation and historical existence enriched the finite human condition. As she told Higginson while he was mourning his wife in 1877, "To be human is more than to be divine, for when Christ was divine, he was uncontented till he had been human" (L 519). That same year she commented to another friend, "That the Divine has been human is at first an unheeded solace, but it shelters without our consent—" (L 523). Christ's humanity and consequent vulnerability to pain provided solace for her—especially at the time of her most intense emotional crisis, or just after it, in 1862 and 1863 and later in the final years of the 1870s and early 1880s when repeated losses of friends through death renewed her awareness of inevitable human grief.

Unlike the Father, awesome and remote, Jesus touched the poet as an intimate companion, sometimes even as a peer. Perhaps she had been influenced by Emerson's tribute to Raphael's painting of the Transfiguration with its accessible image of the Savior: "A calm benignant beauty shines over all this picture, and goes directly to the heart. It seems almost to call you by name. The sweet and sublime face of Jesus is beyond praise, yet how it disappoints all florid expectations! This familiar, simple, home-speaking countenance is as if one should meet a friend."[12] This was Dickinson's image of Jesus, too, at least her favored one. He was the only member of the Trinity with whom intimacy seemed possible; and when that intimacy failed her, when she felt that the Jesus Christ her friends loved didn't love her, she felt excruciating abandonment (L 39).

Generally, however, Dickinson's attitude toward Jesus was a more confident one. Unlike his remote Father hiding beyond circumference, Jesus had entered history actively, and she still envisaged him as a purposeful lover intently seeking out souls. She celebrated him once as the "Largest Lover" (P 573) and presented him elsewhere (P 317) as "Last—at the Knocker—/ And first—at the

Bell" when wooing his lady. She used biblical allusions to represent him as her gentle but persistent suitor.

"Unto Me?" I do not know you—
Where may be your House?
"I am Jesus—Late of Judea—
Now—of Paradise"—

Wagons—have you—to convey me?
This is far from Thence—

"Arms of Mine—sufficient Phaeton—
Trust Omnipotence"—

I am spotted—"I am Pardon"—
I am small—"The Least
Is esteemed in Heaven the Chiefest—
Occupy my House"—
(P 964)

Jesus, after all, understood anguish through direct experience, and it was his sorrow that drew Dickinson toward him in sympathetic fellowship. As she told a neighbor toward the end of her life, "When Jesus tells us about his Father, we distrust him. When he shows us his Home, we turn away, but when he confides to us that he is 'acquainted with Grief,' we listen, for that also is an Acquaintance of our own" (L 932). She culled from the Gospels examples of Christ's sufferings. His betrayal by his friends, especially Judas and Peter, impressed her profoundly as evidence of the God-man's isolation in grief. Someone so sensitive as she was to slights or withdrawals could only identify with Jesus as he cast a reproachful look at Peter the night of his arrest (P 203). She claimed to have shared her sovereign's dishonor (P 85). Dickinson was especially moved by reflection on Christ's hospitality toward the thief on Calvary, an episode to which she returned with hopeful appreciation in "Recollect the Face of me" (P 1305) and "'Remember me' implored the Thief!" (P 1180), in which she commemorated "this mightiest case / Of compensated Trust." The thief was to be Christ's guest in paradise. Dickinson liked the notion of being a welcome guest herself; it suited her ideals of friendship and her craving for snug security. So she remembered also the parable of the wedding guests summoned unexpectedly and prepared herself to be Christ's eventual guest in heaven (P 1262). As the friend of the apparently friendless and as a companion in grief, Jesus drew her toward him.

The crucifixion naturally impressed most deeply upon the poet the magnitude of willingly incurred divine suffering. Celebrated in "He gave away his Life—" (P 567), it was her preeminent example of Christ's love, as the resurrection was her strongest evidence for circumference-smashing force. In "One crown that no one seeks" (P 1735), she examined the paradox of voluntary agony, pointing out that the pain other men avoided was actively pursued by Christ, who "Its isolation coveted / Its stigma deified." Yet Dickinson's reflections on this climactic episode of salvation history were far from orthodox and seldom conventionally pious. Never did she give any evidence of valuing the atonement in any personal sense or of feeling guilt for the human sinfulness that prompted Christ's expiatory death. Nor would she accept responsibility for his sufferings. The doctrine of human depravity so stressed in Calvinist theology never directly influenced her self-image. Sometime in the final decade of her life, the poet recorded a pertinent childhood reminiscence in the draft of a letter: "We said she said Lord Jesus—receive my Spirit—We were put in separate rooms to expiate our temerity and thought how hateful Jesus must be to get us into trouble when we had done nothing but Crucify him and that before we were born—."[13] And a poem written at about the same time introduces a startling image of Jesus as "The Auctioneer of Parting" (P 1612), selling despair from the cross.

Dickinson showed much less interest in the crucifixion as a specific historical event related to salvation history from the Fall to the Apocalypse than she did in it as an example of more generalized human suffering. In "One Crucifixion is recorded—only—" (P 553), she presented Christ as a role model for other persons— notably herself—when forced to accept shame, isolation, and pain. "Gethsemane," she found, "Is but a Province—in the Being's Centre." Other poems from the early 1860s demonstrate the intensity of Emily Dickinson's interest in the crucifixion at the time she found herself most troubled and alone. In her prayer "Jesus! thy Crucifix" (P 225), she called on him to recognize "The smaller size" of hers; and in "I measure every Grief I meet" (P 561), she acknowledged her habit of noticing "the fashions—of the

Cross—/ And how they're mostly worn—/ Still fascinated to presume / That Some—are like My Own—." The speaker of "There came a Day at Summer's full," (P 322) tells how she and her lover "Each bound the Other's Crucifix—" as bond for their self-sacrificing love. The crucifix in this poem, however, witnesses to the hope of resurrection. Although a role model for suffering, Christ was also an example of triumphant martyrdom. By looking to him rather than more pitiful historical or literary figures as a precursor, the poet hinted at her confidence in eventual victory over the sufferings she endured.[14]

Jesus was important to the poet also as the divine validator of things she felt precious. For awareness of beauty, for example, "Our lord—thought no / Extravagance / To pay—a Cross—" (P 571). Christ's voluntary experience of death as well as human life constituted an endorsement in which other men and women could trust: "Life—is what we make it—/ Death—We do not know—/ Christ's acquaintance with Him / Justify Him—though—" (P 698). He had tested the seemingly fragile grounds of faith also and pronounced the bridge between humanity and the divine to be firm (P 1433).

Being no respecter of doctrines, however, the poet devoted surprisingly little attention to the two Christian dogmas most pertinent to her circumferential themes: the incarnation and the resurrection. Her Puritan heritage, with its deliberate subordination of Christmas as a holiday, tended to ignore the mystery of God's assuming human nature and entering the circuit world of mortality and finitude in the person of a homeless and persecuted infant. Absorbed as she was by her own problems of limitation and finitude, Emily Dickinson generally ignored the implications of Christmas. Within her world it was still a minor feast, distinctly inferior in emotional resonance to Thanksgiving and in zest of celebration to the county cattle fair. Mount Holyoke Female Seminary continued classes on Christmas, as did the Boston public schools in Austin's teaching days. The Dickinson family, which paid little attention to birthdays, downplayed Christ's as well except as an occasion for amusing children. Some of Emily's adolescent letters report on gifts left in her stocking, though she exclaimed in excited envy over Abiah Root's more bountiful celebration: "How magnificent the 'Christmas tree' must have been & what a grand time you must have had, so many of you!!!

Oh!!! I had a great many presents, Christmas, & New Year's holidays—both—but we had no such celebration of the former which you describe" (L 15).[15] No Christmas tree, no gathering of friends, and—more to the point—no church services to honor the day and draw out the mysteries of the incarnation that might later have stimulated poetic imagination.

From college days until after her father's death, Dickinson's letters made little or no reference to Christmas, though involvement with the growing family next door at the Evergreens and with the little friends of her niece and nephews brought frequent references late in Dickinson's life to Santa Claus, gifts, and friendly remembrance.[16] The closest she came to acknowledging the religious aspect of the occasion, however, was to entitle as "Christ's Birthday" a poem she thought of contributing to a charitable magazine concerned with aid to children in mission countries (P 1487). Journey imagery appears in it with reference to "The Road to Bethlehem" distant from Amherst "A rugged billion Miles," but nothing else confronts the awesome implications of Christ's simultaneous experience of circuit and ultracircumferential life.

So too with the theological import of Easter, a holiday Dickinson confessed herself likely to forget in a note of gratitude to a friend who remembered her dead father at the paschal season: "It is possible, dear friend, that the rising of the one we lost would have engrossed me to the exclusion of Christ's—but for your lovely admonition" (L 434). The one poem directly concerned with the wonder of Christ's rising from the dead commemorated Charles Wadsworth and suggested the possibility of human growth that might allow the person to develop beyond circuit boundaries and expand into the mysterious space outside: "Obtaining but our own Extent / In whatsoever Realm—/ 'Twas Christ's own personal Expanse / That bore him from the Tomb—" (P 1543). Given her attention to death and venturings beyond it, however, Dickinson seemed almost indifferent to Christ's movement out upon circumference, back into the circuit world in a translated condition, and then beyond circumference into the realm of infinity, immortality, and power from which he had come. It was Jesus within the mortal circuit and manifested as a suffering man who attracted her rather than the resurrected Lord.

In his human dimension, Christ served Emily Dickinson as

friend and role model. As her critics and biographers have observed, there appears to be a religious aspect to the poet's withdrawal from the world into the privacy of her chamber for the purpose of reflecting on her relationship to immortality, and it is easy to demonstrate that she found solace in the example of Christ's redemptive suffering.[17] Yet one must be careful not to overstate her identification with Jesus or even her affection for him. As a historical figure, he served as an inspiring example. But she found him less reliable as a postcircumferential strengthening force in her life. Even in 1862, when the image of the crucifixion recurred with particular force in her poems, Dickinson complained of the Savior's distance. The speaker of "He strained my faith—" (P 497) claims to have met every test of devotion only to be rejected or forgotten; while the speaker of "At least—to pray— is left—is left—" (P 502), grouped appropriately with "He strained my faith—" (P 497) and "I know that He exists." (P 338), finds the Son as elusive as his hidden Father. "Oh Jesus—in the Air—," she cries, "I know not which thy chamber is—/ I'm knocking—everywhere—." Even the worry about God's mutilated hand recurs with her fear that Jesus may have "no Arm for Me." Once beyond circumference, then, Jesus could not be depended upon to intervene within the circuit world again.

If one were to inquire about celestial beings to whom Emily Dickinson responded fondly, trustingly, and without tension, one would look to the angels in her letters and poems rather than to any trinitarian figure. Angels act in the Bible as divine messengers to man from immortality, and Dickinson seems to have regarded them as emissaries as well as friends. We see them in her poems welcoming heroes and sufferers to heaven and showing respect for persons neglected on earth. "Except to Heaven, she is nought," she wrote of a dead housewife, "Except for Angels—lone" (P 154). They watch over souls in breathless apprehension at critical moments of moral risk (P 139). They also figure as willing visitants to earth: the playmates who amused the child Emily in the woods when her parents warned of spooks and snakes (L 271) and the subtly disguised beggars she discerned "Smiling, as they request an alms—/ At some imposing door!" (P 117). She liked to think of them disguised as birds also, proof of the heavenly quality of natural epiphanies. Thus "Two Gabriels" appear in "Forever honored be the Tree" (P 1570), "registered in Nature's Book / As

Robins—Sire and Son—/ But Angels have that modest way / To screen them from Renown." The idea of such celestial visitants suited the poet's delight in surprises and confirmed her hope of interchange between circuit and postcircumferential realms. Like God admiring the sunset or Christ choosing human life, the angels served to validate her appreciation of ordinary gifts. As she reminded her niece when Martha was visiting friends in Springfield: "Who has not found the Heaven—below—/ Will fail of it above—/ For Angels rent the House next our's, / Wherever we remove—" (P 1544). Dickinson's angels, of course, were sentimental cherubs—not the warrior Michael or the cherubim driving Adam and Eve from Eden. Instead, she characterized them as heaven's children, instinctive friends of small, innocent persons below. She went so far in "God permits industrious Angels—" (P 231) as to fantasize these beings as fugitives from a celestial schoolhouse enjoying afternoon recess with New England youngsters before being called home at twilight. Friends and comforters only, her angels possessed no liberating power. They offered hope for companionship in heaven and counteracted the repelling force of awe, but they provided no real assistance in man's efforts to look or penetrate beyond circumference.

Angels might sometimes function as messengers *from* God, but Dickinson recognized the importance also of delivering messages *to* him—of maintaining communication across circumference. Prayer turned out to be the primary means of man's catching the Deity's attention and calling for his help. She had been given assurances of prayer's effectiveness, even memorable examples like the story of William Tell that she related as evidence that "God it is said replies in Person / When the cry is meant" (P 1152). So it is said, and so men wish to believe. When plunged too far into catastrophe for human rescue, the poet liked to think that "Prayer—remained—Our Side—" to summon help from "Our Old Neighbor—God—" (P 623), but her grouping of this poem near "I asked no other thing—" (P 621), about denial of prayer, raises doubts about God's response.

Several poems present a Dickinsonian child persona trying out the traditional lore about prayer only to encounter ironic surprises like those her child-speakers met in their attempts to make sense of transmitted teachings about God himself. The little girl who relates her story below finds that her timid requests have made her the joke of the universe.

> I meant to have but modest needs—
> Such as Content—and Heaven—
> Within my income—these could lie
> And Life and I—keep even—
>
> But since the last—included both—
> It would suffice my Prayer
> But just for One—to stipulate—
> And Grace would grant the Pair—
>
> And so—upon this wise—I prayed—
> Great Spirit—Give to me
> A Heaven not so large as Your's,
> But large enough—for me—
>
> A Smile suffused Jehovah's face—
> The Cherubim—withdrew—
> Grave Saints stole out to look at me—
> And showed their dimples—too—
>
> I left the Place, with all my might—
> I threw my Prayer away—
> The Quiet Ages picked it up—
> And Judgment—twinkled—too—
> That one so honest—be extant—
> It take the Tale for true—
> That "Whatsoever Ye shall ask—
> Itself be given You"—
>
> But I, grown shrewder—scan the Skies
> With a suspicious Air—
> As Children—swindled for the first
> All Swindlers—be—infer—
>
> (P 476)

Here we have a typically Dickinsonian persona: small, vulnerable, timid, and dependent. Habituated to making exclusions, she has trimmed the list of gifts she desires and now approaches her Father in apparent humility to cajole his help. But her efforts fail, as does her courage. The smiles on heavenly faces that originally encouraged her seem to freeze into grotesque masks. Nothing changes except within the speaker, who reacts cynically to her disappointment. Her loss of faith in God's responsiveness to prayer precludes her taking such a risk again.

Yet before indulging in pity for this frustrated child, we must recognize the mock humility and hidden blasphemy of her approach. She has been playing a good-little-girl game with God even before discovering that he has been tricking her. The prayer she offers is hardly a child's request; it is far too sophisticated, too abstract, and too arrogant. She is asking for heaven but not in the sense of salvation. It is a private heaven she demands in her beguiling way, "A Heaven not so large as Your's / But large enough—for me—." Examined closely, her prayer requests eternal isolation from God and everyone else. It is a selfish request, indeed an idolatrous one. No wonder God scorns it. And given the hollowness of the speaker's loving daughter pretense, it stands to reason that she would reject God after her failure. If God is a swindler, so is she; but he has gotten the better of her. This is less a poem about loss of faith than about replacement of manipulativeness by a less hopeful kind of cynicism.

A related poem, "I prayed, at first, a little Girl," (p 576), involves a child whose attempts to conform to the devotional practices she has been taught yield to independent application of golden-rule reasoning. Once she begins to think "How prayer would feel—to me—," she stops bothering or even insulting God by involving him in all her little problems. Although still longing for such supportive strength, she no longer expects it. She allows God his hidden dimensions and perhaps guards her own privacy as well. In general, Dickinson's poems discredit routine habits of prayer without seriously questioning the desirability of interchange. But like Huckleberry Finn, who discovered that you can no more "pray a lie" than pray down a fish line with hooks, the Dickinson persona found it useless to pray for trivial blessings and "perjury" to echo the language of obedient devotion, "'Father, thy will be done' today," when her own desires actually contradicted his (p 103).

The chief problem Emily Dickinson encountered with prayer as communication beyond circumference was the problem of audience. What evidence could she summon to prove that God was listening? Talking to him seemed "like writing a Note to the Sky—yearning and replyless—but Prayer has not an answer and yet how many pray!" (L 790). Did she even know whom to address? The desperate speaker of "I got so I could hear his name—" (P 293, quoted in full on page 25) thinks of herself as having business "with the Cloud," uncertain whether "any Power behind it, be, / Not subject to Despair—." She is consciously praying to an eclipse, as the poet suspected her family of doing inadvertently. With God hiding his face, man has no way of registering response to requests. At times, as in "Of Course—I prayed—" (P 376), the Dickinson speaker expresses anger at divine indifference. By creating her only to ignore the needs he implanted in her, God convicts himself of cruelty. Elsewhere, Dickinson demanded a definite answer to reiterated requests: "'Thou shalt not' is a kinder sword / Than from a disappointing God / 'Disciple, call again'" (P 1751). Yet God's behavior, as presented in her poems, can often be labeled rude—especially when he behaves like the sneering shopman of "I asked no other thing—" (P 621) who disparages the speaker's efforts to buy. Prayer as "the little implement" (P 437) designed by man to unlock the gates of immortality or at least pry a chink in the circumferential wall often failed of its purpose, mainly because of God's refusal to take an interest in the experiment but occasionally also because of man's clumsiness or insincerity in trying.

Despite several disclaimers to being a "Pagan" and therefore not in the habit of prayer, Dickinson continued the effort to communicate, and several of her poems may be classified as prayers in themselves (L 566; 976). In an early example, "Papa above!" (P 61), she hides behind figurative language to call for help. Ostensibly, she implores God's intervention in behalf of a mouse or rat about to fall victim to feline violence. But she confessed often elsewhere that she delighted in the triumphs of Lavinia's cats over rodent intruders (L 471). Presumably the speaker was identifying with the diminutive victim here and requesting her own salvation. But such salvation! It is an eternity of self-indulgence she anticipates, certainly not of worship or even of thanks: "Snug in seraphic Cupboards / To nibble all the day, / While unsuspecting Cycles / Wheel solemnly away!" (P 61).

A more earnest entreaty shows the speaker turning desperately to Christ, whom she admits to having forgotten earlier in favor of someone else whose heart she has been trying unsuccessfully to hold in hers but now entrusts to the Savior (P 217). The prayer reveals her need for Jesus in the midst of emotional crisis. To read the poem as it stands is to think of the speaker as resolving a conflict between human and divine loves by committing herself and her lover to Christ. Yet a prior variant gives quite a different impression. Instead of "the imperial Heart" she entrusts to the Lord, it is now "the departed Heart," so that this becomes a poem of mourning rather than romantic love. And she calls upon her "Father," not her "Savior," to express a desperate loneliness that drives her to renew communication. She feels isolated in the universe and wonders "Dost thou remember me?"—candidly distinguishing the other person's need from her own in apparent hope that God will refrain from visiting his anger with her upon the person she loves and for whom she solicits help.

Many years later, in 1877, Dickinson wrote a short prayer with variant lines that completely alter its meaning. In the copy sent to Sue, she wrote, "My Maker—let me be / Enamored most of thee—/ But nearer this / I more should miss—" (P 1403). But her two alternative versions change line two to "A Fence or two from thee—" or "A World or two from thee—," expressing a much more distant relationship. She was ironically praying for the chance to retain a circumferential barrier between herself and God even while keeping a sort of communication open. Again she was requesting a heaven of her own.

Not all prayers involve petition for blessings, although Dickinson's explicit references to prayer generally refer to such requests. There are complements to these, including prayers of adoration, of contrition, and of thanks. Some prayers are impassioned outcries to God without demands for help. Christ served as a model, showing many ways of addressing the Father, one of which she remembered when writing of "the Prayer / I knew so perfect— yesterday—/ That Scalding One—Sabacthini—" (P 313) that Christ had uttered from the cross: "My God, my God, why hast thou forsaken me?"[18] Often feeling abandoned herself and overwhelmed with suffering, the poet echoed her tortured Savior and the psalmist whom Jesus recalled. Another poem tells how the speaker found herself unable to mouth the formulas of prayer or even to assure herself of an audience. Having failed to articulate religious language, she confesses, "I worshipped—did not 'pray'—" (P 564), as though worship were not in itself a variety of prayer, a nobler one than petition. Open to God and in awe of him, the worshiper is more accepting of his messages than the glib talker assaulting God's ear. If one discounts the apparatus of prayer and looks instead to its substance, one finds prayerful utterance throughout Emily Dickinson's poems—especially her thankful celebrations of life, consciousness, and beauty, her reflections on evanescence and eternity, her probings at circumference to communicate with the force beyond it. Richard Sewall's suggestion to Millicent Todd Bingham about the contemplative, prayerful aspects of Dickinson's poetry locates her work in a tradition of Christian literature and demonstrates her closeness in spirit and purpose to her Puritan precursor, Edward Taylor.[19] Sewall speculated that the Amherst poet "wrote her poems in much the same spirit that her devout contemporaries prayed," performing a daily ritual of spiritual redirection and refreshment.

It is an odd fact that Dickinson wrote so few explicit prayer poems and that those few tend to be complicated with irony. She obviously found it difficult to talk directly *to* God, just as she found it awkward to talk *about* him. Yet her poems as a whole testify to a lifelong process of religious search and communicate a grateful, loving adoration she found it impossible to express adequately in the language her Calvinist culture gave her. God reached her indirectly through everything that she loved, and she responded indirectly through the magical associations of language. As she told Judge Lord, "It may surprise you I speak of God—I know him but a little, but Cupid taught Jehovah to many an untutored Mind—Witchcraft is wiser than we—" (L 562).

For her attentiveness to intuitions from immortality and her faculty for deciphering divine messages in natural processes, Emily Dickinson has often been described as a sort of mystic—as unorthodox in that sphere, however, as in any other. The directness of her experience of the divine even within the circuit world and her "power to project herself into an abstraction, beyond the hindering visible limitations surrounding her," encouraged her niece to apply such spiritual language to the aunt whom she recognized as distinguished for her "almost abnormal sensitiveness to apprehensions mortal or mystic."[20] Despite the misleading impression of otherworldliness such language sometimes conveys about a poet distinctly and jubilantly in love with this life, it serves a purpose in conveying a sense of the religious impulse motivating her response to beauty. This poet, who ignored church preaching, found "Bulletins all Day / From Immortality" (P 827) simply by opening her consciousness to the life around her that other people classified too roughly or simply ignored, finding in the pine tree by her window a possible "'Fellow / Of the Royal' Infinity" and responding eagerly to those "Apprehensions" she recognized as "God's introductions—/ To be hallowed—accordingly—" (P 797). "The Murmur of a Bee," she professed in another poem, "A Witchcraft—yieldeth me—" (P 155), and similar natural epiphanies conveyed an incommunicable closeness to God: "Take care— for God is here—/ That's all." Reverence and attentiveness manifest themselves in her poems, together with a characteristically Dickinsonian delight in sharing nature's secrets.

She never attained the ultimate goal of feeling at one with God, however; the ironic bent of her mind maintained excessive distance. Yet the intensity of Dickinson's response to natural revelation of indwelling divine power betrayed her yearning for such union and her recognition of its supernal origin. The very naturalness with which traditional religious or mystical terms come to mind with respect to Emily Dickinson alerts us to their inherent thrust at truth.[21]

There is, for instance, an ecstatic quality to Dickinson's poetry not explainable biographically, as Higginson mentally noted when startled by his reclusive friend's assertion that "I find ecstasy in living—the mere sense of living is joy enough" (L 342a). And despite the transience of such exalted experiences, there is ample evidence in her writing that she experienced the occasional "pivotal moments of revelation and insight—the moments of divine manifestation and human vision" that Albert Gelpi identifies as attributes of the New England tradition from the early Puritans, through Edwards kneeling in adoration on the forest floor, to Emerson, Thoreau, Whitman, and even Eliot.[22] Certainly the sensitivity revealed in the following poem bespeaks the same sort of momentary merger with divine power that left Emerson exultant on his bare common and Thoreau in awe before his sliding spring mud bank:

> In many and reportless places
> We feel a Joy—

Reportless, also, but sincere as Nature
Or Deity—

It comes, without a consternation—
Dissolves—the same—
But leaves a sumptuous Destitution—
Without a Name—

Profane it by a search—we cannot
It has no home—
Nor we who having once inhaled it—
Thereafter roam.
(P 1382)

It was the fleetingness of such glory that made the poet so conscious of her deprivation, that fired her longing for unbounded ecstasy beyond her mortal circuit. Intuitions of perfection reminded her that "The Love a Life can show Below / Is but a filament, I know, / Of that diviner thing" (P 673), which—in nature, music, and human affection—drew her toward circumference in hopes of finding and securing it: "'Tis this—invites—appalls—endows—/ Flits—glimmers—proves—dissolves—/ Returns—suggests—convicts—enchants—/ Then—flings in Paradise—."

Sometimes the heavenly gates did seem to open; sometimes Dickinson felt with stunning directness the force of divine love. In reporting such earthly intimations of immortality, she most often relied upon the language of music—most ethereal of the arts, most abstractly harmonious, and most traditionally associated with images of heaven. Thanking Mrs. Sweetser for her son's singing in the Homestead parlor, the poet remarked, "I had felt some uncertainty as to my qualification for the final Redemption, but the delightful Melody has entirely fitted me—" (L 920). A number of her poems suggest the effect of divine illuminations through reference to music or that harmony she celebrated as "Better—than Music! For I—who heard it—" (P 503). The wind song that delights her in "Of all the Sounds despatched abroad," (P 321) seems an opening into heaven with its "tufts of Tune—/ Permitted Gods, and me—." The speaker imagines that the music may even penetrate the grave, waking the dead to dance. Yet she pities those living persons insensitive to such beauty, unresponsive to her commonplace sources of ecstasy. In "Musicians wrestle everywhere—" (P 157), she feels surrounded by wondrous harmonies from beyond circumference, introducing the "'New life'." Music, of course, served as a metaphor for poetry, itself an inlet to ultracircumferential intimations.

Fortunately, such rapturous moments could occur in any place, at any moment; unfortunately, they could neither be predicted nor controlled—certainly not retained. Despite her compliment to Samuel Bowles that "You have the most triumphant Face out of Paradise—probably because you are there constantly, instead of ultimately—," Dickinson knew the impossibility of preserving momentary glimpses of heaven (L 489). Rather than triumphant, her face—like those of the personae who address us in her poems—was more likely to be doleful, stricken, surprised by loss. Deprivation of ecstasy caused pain even while providing incentive for further pushes of prognostication. "The Soul's Superior instants" (P 306) of "Mortal Abolition" from earthly limits served as "Eternity's disclosure / To favorites—a few—/ Of the Colossal substance / Of Immortality," but they lasted only briefly and were far less characteristic of her life than moments of renunciation or mourning. She understood, however, the value of such insights in motivating the circuit-bound person to press on against circumference.

> Did Our Best Moment last—
> 'Twould supersede the Heaven—
> A few—and they by Risk—procure—
> So this Sort—are not given—
>
> Except as stimulants—in
> Cases of Despair—
> Or Stupor—The Reserve—
> These Heavenly Moments are—
>
> A Grant of the Divine—
> That Certain as it Comes—
> Withdraws—and leaves the dazzled Soul
> In her unfurnished Rooms—
> (P 393)

It would be the soul dazzled by celestial radiance, then, who would be conscious of finitude, sensitive to the inadequacy of "unfurnished Rooms" to satisfy longings engendered by God as a means of enticing the soul to heaven. Dickinson eagerly took the risk of exposing herself to repeated painful reminders of her finitude and limitation—not because she thought contemptuously of herself but because she recognized her exceptional capacity for mystical insight and regarded herself, despite her lifelong conflict with the God of her fathers, as an especially promising candidate for heaven. Partaking of immortality—however briefly and tantalizingly—within her circuit world, she pushed against circumference for satisfaction of unquenchable longings.

10

"His Diameters"

The Unbounded Circle

THE CIRCLE imagery I have been elaborating throughout this book and especially in these three final chapters clarifies to us the metaphorical design by which Emily Dickinson fashioned her life through a sustained complex of inclinations, aversions, and choices. She thought of herself as a person with a distinctive identity and consciousness inhabiting the circle of mortal life. She felt at home there and reasonably happy. Were it not for the disappearances of people and experiences she loved into the mysterious area outside the circle and for intimations of glorious possibilities beyond its circumference, she might have been content. But a combination of deprivation and revelation drew Dickinson's attention to the boundary of mortal consciousness, instilling in her a fierce determination to find out what lay outside even while retaining the security of her familiar circuit. She used whatever means she could find to compensate for her limitations—chiefly imaginative means she derived from literary examples. By her reading and role playing, she tried out alternative lives and imagined herself inhabiting ampler circuits only to find that the satisfaction she craved lay outside *any* human circle.

Discovering that the circumferential barrier was the circle's primary point of interest, the poet concentrated her energy on that, attempting to explode the wall between the life she experienced and the immortality that alone could satisfy her need for permanent empowerment. That wall was death. All other barriers and transitions reminded her of death. Yet it was not circumference or death itself that attracted her but the likelihood of immortality beyond in the realm of awe, figured to her in the Christian vocabulary of God and heaven. The choices Emily Dickinson made in

her life, the emphases she placed in her poetry, and even the techniques she practiced in her prosody were all calculated to put her
on a collision course with circumference and either to catapult her
into the paradise she anticipated beyond it or to open her circuit
to enduring influxes of divinity. Unlike the Transcendentalists,
who identified growth of their personal identities and conscious-
nesses with participation in the Oversoul and who therefore valued individual expansion, Dickinson made a characteristic choice
in favor of intensifying limitation. She chose to diminish her circle
as a paradoxical strategy for attaining coveted power.

   Not that Dickinson held either her mortal identity or the natural
world of finite, evanescent beings in contempt. Far from it. As
she wrote to Mrs. Holland, "I trust we are grateful for the Life
that sees—and steps—and touches, if it is only the thrilling preface to supremer things—" (L 678). And she scoffed at the folly of
those who thought it pious to belabor the vanity of earthly satisfactions: "The worthlessness of Earthly things / The Ditty is that
Nature Sings—/ And then—enforces their delight / Till Synods
are inordinate—" (P 1373). "To have been made alive," she exclaimed to Maria Whitney, "is so chief a thing, all else inevitably
adds. Were it not riddled by partings, it were too divine" (L 860).
But it *was* riddled by partings, and she found constant reminders
that it was only the preface to supremer things. A thrilling preface, however—all the more so because the very fleetingness of
life's blessings provided constant incentive to clutch at them.

> Delight is as the flight—
> Or in the Ratio of it,
> As the Schools would say—
> The Rainbow's way—
> A Skein
> Flung colored, after Rain,
> Would suit as bright,
> Except that flight
> Were Aliment—
>
> "If it would last"
> I asked the East,
> When that Bent Stripe
> Struck up my childish
> Firmament—

> And I, for glee,
> Took Rainbows, as the common way,
> And empty Skies
> The Eccentricity—
>
> And so with Lives—
> And so with Butterflies—
> Seen magic—through the fright
> That they will cheat the sight—
> And Dower latitudes far on—
> Some sudden morn—
> Our portion—in the fashion—
> Done—
> (P 257)

Loss itself, then, and the prospect of death encouraged her to cherish everything she loved with the intensity of passion that vibrates throughout her writing.

Her mortal circle occupied a small space, however, in Dickinson's metaphorical design of the universe; beyond it extended endless, mysterious expanse. Just as the natural world could be absorbed within human consciousness, she recognized that divinity must comprehend both nature and humanity within its voluminous hold (P 1286). When she thought of herself within the grasp of "the Infinite," fantasized as a giant of geographical proportions with a Himalayan arm and Gibraltar in his hand, she decided to accept his mastery: "So trust him, Comrade—/ . . . / Eternity is ample, / And quick enough, if true" (P 350). Imagining herself as a tiny circle enveloped in space, she yet avoided hierarchical distinctions of merit in size. The moon's changes figured for her the importance of process in growth and contraction. It is movement between crescent and fullness that gives the moon its haunting degrees of shimmer.

> Which is the best—the Moon or the Crescent?
> Neither—said the Moon—
> That is best which is not—Achieve it—
> You efface the Sheen.
>
> Not of detention is Fruition—
> Shudder to attain.

Transport's decomposition follows—
He is Prism born.
(P 1315)

Process and change, growth and contraction, generate a beauty unattainable by stasis even of perfection. Human life, then, involved cyclic processes of expansion and retraction of the circuit, though the ultimate goal would be fullness. It was this changingly circumferential moon metaphor Dickinson chose in order to salute her little nephew at his death. "No crescent was this Creature—," she reminded his grieving mother, "He traveled from the Full—/ Such soar, but never set—" (L 868).

The choices that Emily Dickinson consistently made in her life—mostly negative choices—sharply diminished her circle. Rather than expanding upon the attachments that involve people actively within the circuit world, she restricted them. Rather than emphasizing temporal events, she ignored or belittled them. She narrowed her circuit to little more than the natural world of her garden, a moderate group of intimates with whom she was generally engaged in one-to-one relationships rather than communal friendship, and her own consciousness. It was a narrow world, deliberately so. By tightening the circle to the point that it barely enclosed her, she guaranteed a painful fit. She assured herself that she would always be pressing at the boundaries of mortality and consciousness. She made sure she could never forget circumference or miss any messages from beyond it. A poem Dickinson sent to her "Preceptor" as she was convalescing with an eye ailment in a Cambridge boardinghouse while Higginson led his black regiment into Civil War skirmishes enunciates her value system with startling clarity.

> The Only News I know
> Is Bulletins all Day
> From Immortality.
>
> The Only Shows I see—
> Tomorrow and Today—
> Perchance Eternity—
>
> The Only One I meet
> Is God—The Only Street—

Existence—This traversed

If Other News there be—
Or Admirabler Show—
I'll tell it You—
(P 827)

Higginson, on the other hand, occupied a much grander circle brightened with fewer of those "luminous flashes" he perceived as isolating his gnomic correspondent while they enriched her (L 330a). But Dickinson stood firm, even as deaths of those closest to her squeezed her circuit yet more tightly: "Take all away—/ The only thing worth larceny / Is left—the Immortality—" (P 1365).

I have laid stress on the circle's circumference because Emily Dickinson did. Because she made it her distinctive business, she focused her poetic insights with particular intensity on all kinds of transitions and barriers—especially the barrier of death. Loving the circle enclosed within her circuit, however, she valued its center also and made several revealing comments about the point one would think the opposite of circumference. Immortality lay outside circumference, as she generally conceived it, but eternity or forever at the center. "There is no first, or last, in Forever—," she assured Susan, "It is Centre, there, all the time—" (L 288). From this perspective, eternity emerges as a force concurrent with the circle as well as with the postcircumferential realm. Thus, Dickinson could correct false assumptions of disparity between this life and eternal duration in "The Blunder is in estimate" (P 1684), where she proclaims "He joins me in my Ramble / Divides abode with me / No Friend have I that so persists / As this Eternity." With eternity at the center of the circle and immortality without, time became unimportant except to those worldly agglomerative souls whose expanded circles left them free in personal space but generally out of touch with either center or circumference.

"Forever" lay at the center, and so did the Bible. Less than two years before her death, the poet observed to Mrs. Holland that "All grows strangely emphatic, and I think if I should see you again, I sh'd begin every sentence with 'I say unto you—' The Bible dealt with the Centre, not with the Circumference—" (L 950).[1] An interesting distinction, this—particularly in view of Dickinson's general identification of God as the force beyond circumference, the personal analogue of immortality. Presumably she was thinking of the Bible as the record and prediction of God's work in history from the Creation onward to the Second Coming. It narrates God's saving action in time, among men. Except for the book of Revelation and brief references to heaven elsewhere, Scripture offers divine perspective chiefly on the circuit world. God and eternity define the center of the circle, then, while awe and immortality entice beyond it. Viewed in such a way, the circle becomes an innate part of the vaster universe, not an alien capsule. The life to which the soul aspires has already begun because divinity is immanent within the circle as well as transcendent without it. Those "Bulletins all Day / From Immortality" (P 827) come from inside as well as outside. One who kept close to both center and circumference (easy to do in a constricted circle but an acrobatic feat in an ampler one) would be in steady contact with divine force.

"Time feels so vast that were it not" (P 802, quoted in full on page 18) presents most directly the advantage of the diminished circle with the awareness it necessarily fosters of amplitude beyond. Were she not reminded steadily of immortality, Dickinson acknowledges, she would limit her horizons to time. Credit for preventing circumference from engrossing her finity goes to God, who opens perspectives on infinity to her even within her circuit. He prepares her "By Processes of Size / For the Stupendous Vision / Of His Diameters—." Suddenly, linear images intrude upon the circle, slash across it, and intersect circumference to push outward into the domain of awe. The full extent of these diameters, of course, remains hidden although parts of them cut the otherwise only slightly permeable membrane of the circle. But cut they do, and it is worth our while to recall the linear images that manifest divine force in Dickinson's poetry. Most important, perhaps, is death itself—that "Bisecting Messenger" of paradise (P 1411). And there is the outward-thrusting force betrayed by nature even as it seems to fulfill and perfect the mortal circle: "The eager look—on Landscapes—/ As if they just repressed / Some Secret—that was pushing / Like Columns—in the Breast—" (P 627). How long can even the most circuit-bound heart withstand such battering rams? Even "The Dandelion's pallid tube" (P 1519) thrusts away circumference with its jubilant proclamation of life's triumph over death.

Anything that cuts can hurt, and God's diameters often appear in Dickinson poems as dreaded attackers of the circuit world, barricaded as it is to defend itself against invasion from without. The "Dirks of Melody" in the following poem pain the speaker with the unexpected and unwanted joy that forcibly prevents the soul from withdrawing into numb despair:

> One Joy of so much anguish
> Sweet nature has for me
> I shun it as I do Despair
> Or dear iniquity—
> Why Birds, a Summer morning
> Before the Quick of Day
> Should stab my ravished spirit
> With Dirks of Melody
> Is part of an inquiry
> That will receive reply
> When Flesh and Spirit sunder
> In Death's Immediately—
> (P 1420)

At this point, the speaker detects only the sharp point of God's diameter. Not until she too stands outside circumference will she behold the "Stupendous Vision" (P 802) that justifies immediate injury to the circuit. So, too, the melancholy inflicted by that famous "Slant of light" (P 258) reminds the poet of death as it cuts across circumference from immortality and orients her thoughts to possibilities beyond wintry stasis. God's diameters, then, inflict "Heavenly Hurt" that stings the circuit into recognition of whatever lies beyond it to aim such darts. So also with the slant of dazzling if unwelcome truth, which Dickinson likens to lightning's livid diameters (P 1129) that "dazzle gradually" lest they blind inhabitants of the circuit unaccustomed to the divine radiance without. All these linear thrusts bring messages from immortality.

Most central and most important of God's diameters are those that met at the center of historical time to form a cross, the crucifix that fused Christ's wondrous entry into the circuit with his even more dramatic egress. Christ's cross and the personal crosses Dickinson analogized to it bisected mortality, and they did so at the heart of human experience rather than beyond its periphery.

The sign of contradiction is the emblem of salvation. The outward-thrusting arms of the cross fling out beyond circumference.

One more image of God's diameters meeting at the center of the mortal circle to link finite man with immortality deserves consideration here: the asterisk symbol Dickinson began to use in the late 1860s but stressed heavily only in her final decade. A star-shaped juncture of diametrical lines creates a new circle of its own—one without visible circumference, without limits to its outward propulsion. As the printer's sign used to designate the dead on lists of names, it drew occasional attention in the poet's era as a symbol of ongoing life and remembrance. Barrett Wendell entitled one of his books *Stelligeri* in honor of those deceased Harvard alumni who dwell among the stars. It was an image that attracted Dickinson first in 1868, when she described the empty husk of a corpse as marked by "just an Asterisk" to represent the soul's escape (P 1135). She developed the image more fully in two elegies for Samuel Bowles—more accurately two drafts of one memorial poem (P 1525 and P 1616):

> Who abdicated Ambush
> And went the way of Dusk,
> And now against his subtle Name
> There stands an Asterisk
> As confident of him as we—
> Impregnable we are—
> The whole of Immortality
> Secreted in a Star.
> (P 1616)

After trying to ambush immortality by catching it unaware from the brink of circumference, Bowles has now followed the sun into "the land—the Sunset washes" (P 266), but the asterisk that, in circuit terms, points out his death gives visible evidence of a life force thrusting beyond mortal barriers into God's kingdom.

The poet returned to this idea again in an elegy for Judge Lord that she sent to his friend and executor, Benjamin Kimball.

> Go thy great way!
> The Stars thou meetst
> Are even as Thyself—

> For what are Stars but Asterisks
> To point a human Life?
> (P 1638)

The pilgrimage metaphor recurs here, especially pertinent now that motion and process themselves seem liberated to push endlessly into the unknown once the circumferential barrier has been displaced by the adventure of dying. One of the poet's two final poems—yet another elegy, this time for Helen Hunt Jackson—demonstrates Dickinson's continued attentiveness to this asterisk/star imagery within a month of her own death (P 1647). It was a glorious symbol for her, thrusting out as it did from the center of identity and consciousness into immortality and obliterating not the self but the obstacle of death. God's diameters and explosive human force merged and triumphed.

By narrowing her circle Dickinson positioned herself in constant direct contact with both center and circumference in a spot that would inevitably be pierced over and over by God's painful but liberating diameters. With her "narrow Hands" (indeed because of their narrowness), she gathered paradise in a way with which no giant could compete (P 657). Each deprivation and every negative choice contracted her circuit and brought her closer to immortality. The smallness of the poet's self-image and the exaggerated way in which she habitually restricted her claims to power or even to physical stature provide clues to her assault on the force that enclosed all human limitation and that she desperately wanted to penetrate. Because she considered herself "small, like the Wren," she positioned herself to share in God's glory. What she said of the spider, another neglected artist with whom she sometimes identified (P 1275), could be applied to her personally with her deliberate cultivation of limitation and loss as opportunities for spiritual insight. What Higginson may have guessed after editing her poems but probably never suspected in reading that ironically self-effacing description of herself she aimed at him in the summer of 1862 was Emily Dickinson's wonderful secret.

> Of Immortality
> *Her* Strategy
> Was Physiognomy.
> (P 1138)

Notes

1. "Could You Believe Me—Without?"

1 Thomas H. Johnson and Theodora Ward, *The Letters of Emily Dickinson*, 3 vols. (Cambridge, Mass.: Harvard University Press, Belknap Press, 1958), no. 268. Hereafter, letters are identified in the text by L and Johnson's number (e.g., L 268).

2 Jay Leyda, *The Years and Hours of Emily Dickinson*, 2 vols. (New Haven, Conn.: Yale University Press, 1960), II:357.

3 Ibid., 377. See also Millicent Todd Bingham, *Ancestors' Brocades: The Literary Debut of Emily Dickinson* (New York and London: Harper and Brothers, 1945), chap. 1.

4 Bingham, *Ancestors' Brocades*, p. 225; and Appendix I, "Emily Dickinson's Daguerreotype," from Millicent Todd Bingham, *Emily Dickinson's Home: Letters of Edward Dickinson and His Family* (New York: Harper and Brothers, 1955), pp. 519–522.

5 Leyda, *Years and Hours*, I:134.

6 Ibid., 132–133.

7 Lavinia reported to Austin, "Emilie's hair is cut off & shes very pretty." Bingham, *Emily Dickinson's Home*, p. 248; Leyda, *Years and Hours*, I:251. Thomas H. Johnson also identifies Dickinson as the "she with *curling hair!*" mentioned in her 1850 valentine (P 1): *The Poems of Emily Dickinson*, 3 vols. (Cambridge, Mass., and London: Harvard University Press, Belknap Press, 1955). Hereafter, poems are cited in the text according to Johnson's numbering system.

8 Bingham, *Emily Dickinson's Home*, p. 237.

9 Martha Dickinson Bianchi, *Emily Dickinson Face to Face: Unpublished Letters with Notes and Reminiscences* (Boston, Mass.: Houghton Mifflin, 1932), pp. 131–132.

10 Other delighted responses to photographs appear in many letters including one to Higginson in which she wrote, "Except your coming, I know no Gift so great—and in one extent, it exceeds that,—it is permanent" (L 477). See also letter 859 and Leyda, *Years and Hours*, II:378.

11   Leyda, *Years and Hours*, II:46.

12   Bianchi, *The Life and Letters of Emily Dickinson* (Boston, Mass.: Houghton Mifflin, 1924), p. 83.

13   Bingham, *Ancestors' Brocades*, pp. 224–227, 270–271.

14   Bingham, *Emily Dickinson's Home*, pp. 519–522.

15   Bianchi, *Emily Dickinson Face to Face*, pp. 15–16.

16   Leyda, *Years and Hours*, I:280 and II:480; Bianchi, *Emily Dickinson Face to Face*, p. 281.

17   Jean McClure Mudge, *Emily Dickinson and the Image of Home* (Amherst: University of Massachusetts Press, 1975), p. 19.

18   Bingham, *Emily Dickinson's Home*, p. 174.

19   Cf. Sandra M. Gilbert and Susan Gubar, *The Madwoman in the Attic: The Woman Writer and the Nineteenth-Century Literary Imagination* (New Haven, Conn., and London: Yale University Press, 1979), p. 587, and Mudge, *Emily Dickinson and the Image of Home*, pp. 18–19.

20   S. P. Rosenbaum, ed., *A Concordance to the Poems of Emily Dickinson* (Ithaca, N.Y.: Cornell University Press, 1964).

21   Prose Fragments (PF 103) in L, III, p. 927.

22   R. W. Franklin, *The Manuscript Books of Emily Dickinson*, 2 vols. (Cambridge, Mass., and London: Harvard University Press, Belknap Press, 1981), I:55–72.

23   Richard B. Sewall, *The Life of Emily Dickinson*, 2 vols. (New York: Farrar, Straus and Giroux, 1974), II:372.

24   Bingham, *Ancestors' Brocades*, pp. 166–167.

25   Ibid., 314–315.

26   Sewall, *The Life*, I:240.

27   For discussion of metaphorical design in the poems, see Inder Nath Kher, *The Landscape of Absence: Emily Dickinson's Poetry* (New Haven, Conn., and London: Yale University Press, 1974); Joanne Feit Diehl, *Dickinson and the Romantic Imagination* (Princeton, N.J.: Princeton University Press, 1981), p. 184; Sewall, *The Life*, I:239; Robert Weisbuch, *Emily Dickinson's Poetry* (Chicago, Ill., and London: University of Chicago Press, 1975); and Greg Johnson, "'A Pearl of Great Price': The Identity of Emily Dickinson," *ESQ* 26 (1980): 202–215. Dissenting from such interpretations is David Porter, who finds in ED no "life-centering angle of vision": *Dickinson: The Modern Idiom* (Cambridge, Mass., and London: Harvard University Press, 1981), p. 144.

28   Richard B. Sewall, "Introduction" in Richard B. Sewall, ed., *Emily Dickinson: A Collection of Critical Essays* (Englewood Cliffs, N.J.: Prentice-Hall, 1963), p. 8.

2. "The Wildest Word"

1   Leyda, *Years and Hours*, I:177–178. Sewall also presents this story, with reasons for doubting it, in *The Life*, II:419–422. A variant appears in Leyda, *Years and Hours*, II:478–479.

2   Leyda, *Years and Hours*, I:168.

3 Bianchi, *Life and Letters*, pp. 43–51; *Emily Dickinson Face to Face*, pp. 51–53.

4 Johnson, *Emily Dickinson: An Interpretive Biography* (Cambridge, Mass.: Harvard University Press, Belknap Press, 1955), pp. 76–84; George Frisbie Whicher, *This Was a Poet: A Critical Biography of Emily Dickinson* (1938; reprint ed., Ann Arbor: University of Michigan Press, 1957), pp. 99–112. See also Sewall, *The Life*, II: chap. 20; William R. Sherwood, *Circumference and Circumstance: Stages in the Mind and Art of Emily Dickinson* (New York and London: Columbia University Press, 1968), chap. 3; William H. Shurr, *The Marriage of Emily Dickinson: A Study of the Fascicles* (Lexington: University Press of Kentucky, 1983); and John Crowe Ransom, "Emily Dickinson: A Poet Restored," *Perspectives USA* (1956), reprinted in Sewall, ed., *Emily Dickinson: A Collection*, p. 98.

5 Ruth Miller, *The Poetry of Emily Dickinson* (Middletown, Conn.: Wesleyan University Press, 1968), esp. chaps. 5–7; David Higgins, *Portrait of Emily Dickinson: The Poet and Her Prose* (New Brunswick, N.J.: Rutgers University Press, 1967), chap. 4; and Sewall, *The Life*, II: chaps. 21–22.

6 Millicent Todd Bingham, *Emily Dickinson: A Revelation* (New York: Harper and Brothers, 1954). For reservations about the authenticity of documents published by Bingham, consult Anna Mary Wells, "ED Forgeries," *Dickinson Studies* 35 (1979): 12–16. Further attention to this relationship may be found in John Evangelist Walsh, *The Hidden Life of Emily Dickinson* (New York: Simon and Schuster, 1971).

7 Sewall, *The Life*, I:255.

8 Bingham, *Emily Dickinson's Home*, p. 413.

9 An early letter to Abiah Root makes sportive reference to maternity: "Twin loaves of bread have just been born into the world under my auspices—fine children—the image of their *mother*—and *here* my dear friend is the *glory*" (L 36).

10 Leyda, *Years and Hours*, I:213.

11 Ibid., II:76.

12 Ibid., 77.

13 Bingham, *Emily Dickinson's Home*, pp. 413–414.

14 Bingham, *Ancestors' Brocades*, p. 77.

15 Leyda, *Years and Hours*, II:76.

16 Accounts of such experiences appear in memoirs by MacGregor Jenkins, Gertrude Montague Graves, and an unidentified Amherst correspondent quoted in Leyda, *Years and Hours*, II:482–484.

17 Ibid., 357. See also Bingham, *Ancestors' Brocades*, p. 12, and Bianchi, *Emily Dickinson Face to Face*, pp. 34–35.

18 Bianchi, *Emily Dickinson Face to Face*, chap. 1, and MacGregor Jenkins, *Emily Dickinson: Friend and Neighbor* (Boston, Mass.: Little, Brown, 1930).

19 Leyda, *Years and Hours*, II:474–476; Sewall, *The Life*, II:610.

20 Sewall, *The Life*, II:448.

21 Consider, for example, Austin Warren, "Emily Dickinson," in Sewall, ed., *Emily Dickinson: A Collection*, pp. 113–115; Sherwood, *Circumference and Circumstance*, p. 152; and Gilbert and Gubar, *The Madwoman in the Attic*, pp. 613–621.

22   "Fire and Ice," in *The Poetry of Robert Frost* (New York: Holt, Rinehart and Winston, 1969), p. 220.

23   Noah Webster's *An American Dictionary of the English Language* (Springfield, Mass.: George and Charles Merriam, 1849) encouraged this use of the word *translation* by offering as the third of five meanings "the removal of a person to heaven without subjecting him to death" and by citing Hebrews 16 as an example of the verb *translate*: "By faith Enoch was *translated*, that he should not see death."

24   Genesis 5:24: "And Enoch walked with God: and he was not; for God took him." Dickinson focused attention on this text in poem 1342, thought by Johnson to be an elegy for her father.

25   Commenting on local gossip by "women who wore sensible stuff dresses" about her aunt's white costume, Bianchi concludes, "And the only person who never thought of it as a mystery was Emily herself, as she moved about her father's house and garden. They could no more approach her than they could make the moon come down and sit on their parlor sofas!" *Emily Dickinson Face to Face*, p. 37.

26   Leyda, *Years and Hours*, II:480–481.

27   Leyda, "Introduction," in *Years and Hours*, I:xxi.

28   The Reverend Jonathan L. Jenkins, in his memorial sermon for Edward Dickinson, suggested a close relationship between her father's religious views and ED's: "He had no great faith in ceremonies, in formulas of doctrine. He was free in his speech about religion, most unconventional in his practices. His religion was however most excellent and genuine." Sewall, *The Life*, I:68.

29   Leyda, *Years and Hours*, II:473.

30   Barbara Welter, *Dimity Convictions: The American Woman in the Nineteenth Century* (Athens: Ohio University Press, 1976).

31   L, III, PF 36.

32   See Barbara J. Williams, "A Room of Her Own: Emily Dickinson as Woman Artist," in Cheryl L. Brown and Karen Olson, eds., *Feminist Criticism: Essays on Theory, Poetry, and Prose* (Metuchen, N.J.: Scarecrow Press, 1978), pp. 69–91.

33   Jack L. Capps, *Emily Dickinson's Reading: 1836–1886* (Cambridge, Mass.: Harvard University Press, 1966). The clearest perspective on her literary habits, including her disposition to read "competitively and for companionship," may be found in Sewall, "Books and Reading," in *The Life*: II: chap. 28.

34   Ann Douglas, *The Feminization of American Culture* (New York: Alfred A. Knopf, 1977).

35   Emily Stipes Watts, *The Poetry of American Women from 1632 to 1945* (Austin: University of Texas Press, 1977), chaps. 3–5.

36   *Walden* may well be the closest parallel in American literature to Dickinson's assessment of values, and it resembles her work in its paradoxical application of Yankee economics to spiritual growth. "When a man dies he kicks the dust," Thoreau wrote in his chapter "Economy," and his neighbors buy the dust (even a dried tapeworm) at auctions. The Frost excerpt comes from

"New Hampshire," which contrasts New England pride in scarcity with a national zeal for surplus. Taylor had speculated in "Gods Selecting Love in the Decree" that colonial Yankees would have admired God's coach sent to carry the saints to heaven but would have rejected it as too expensive.

37 A 25 July 1878 editorial in the *Republican* suggested one of Helen Hunt Jackson's Amherst neighbors as Saxe Holm on the basis of subtle mystical questions found in the stories, morbidity, ideality, weirdness, interpolated poems "like strains of solemn music floating at night from some way-side church" with each thought "complete and rare, solemn with the solemnity of intense conviction." The domestic scenery to which the tales were limited, the smallness of the episodes, and the writer's humorlessness were all felt to point away from Mrs. Jackson as author and toward some reclusive woman whom the editorialist envisaged as "robed in white" like Hawthorne's Hilda. A later editorial note in the 3 August 1878 *Republican* terminated speculation with fact: "we happen to *know* that no person by the name of Dickinson is in any way responsible for the Saxe Holm stories." Leyda, *Years and Hours*, II:295–297.

38 Reviews of the *Poems* (1890) were mixed but surprisingly plentiful, as Klaus Lubbers demonstrates in *Emily Dickinson: The Critical Revolution* (Ann Arbor: University of Michigan Press, 1968), chap. 2. Reader response may be estimated by the rapid appearance of new printings—five editions between 12 November 1890 and February 1891, with a second volume in preparation.

39 Douglas, *The Feminization of American Culture.*

40 Leyda, *Years and Hours*, I:xxix–xxx.

3. *"An Enlarged Ability for Missing"*

1 Of these five poems, the two valentines were themselves verse-letters, while "There is another sky," (P 2) served as the conclusion of a letter to Austin (L 58) and was originally arranged as prose. "On this wondrous sea" (P 4) went as a letter to Susan Gilbert (L 105), while "I have a Bird in spring" (P 5) accompanied a letter to Susan (L 173).

2 Bingham, *Emily Dickinson's Home*, p. 148.

3 Johnson, *Emily Dickinson*, pp. 72–73; Sewall, *The Life*, II:400–403; Whicher, *This Was a Poet*, p. 93.

4 Miller, *The Poetry*, p. 173; Rebecca Patterson, *Emily Dickinson's Imagery* (Amherst: University of Massachusetts Press, 1979), p. 17.

5 Bianchi, *Emily Dickinson Face to Face*, pp. 65–66.

6 See Vivian R. Pollak, "Thirst and Starvation in Emily Dickinson's Poetry," *American Literature* 51 (1979): 33–49, for a fuller discussion of this theme.

7 I have adopted both of Dickinson's proposed variants here: "advertise" in line four and "one's" in line seven.

8 I analyze this parallel more explicitly in "Dickinson's Nobody and Ulysses' Noman: 'Then there's a pair of us?'" in *Dickinson Studies* 46 (1983): 9–14.

9 Deprivation, a dominant theme in ED's work, has received considerable critical attention starting with Richard Wilbur's seminal essay "Sumptuous

Destitution," in *Emily Dickinson: Three Views* (Amherst, Mass.: Amherst College Press, 1960), reprinted in Sewall, ed., *Emily Dickinson: A Collection*, p. 128. See also Albert Gelpi, *Emily Dickinson: The Mind of the Poet* (New York: W. W. Norton, 1965), p. 69; Johnson, "'A Pearl of Great Price'," pp. 202–203; John Cody, *After Great Pain: The Inner Life of Emily Dickinson* (Cambridge, Mass.: Harvard University Press, Belknap Press, 1971), chap. 2 and "Epilogue"; Barbara Mossberg, *Emily Dickinson: When a Writer Is a Daughter* (Bloomington: Indiana University Press, 1982); Vivian R. Pollak, *Dickinson: The Anxiety of Gender* (Ithaca, N.Y., and London: Cornell University Press, 1984); and Williams, "A Room of Her Own" p. 78.

10 I have adopted variant readings in lines five and six: "lurked" for "walked" and "stole" for "went," both tending to enliven the imagery.

4. *"The Precious Words"*

1 Capps, *Emily Dickinson's Reading*; Whicher, *This Was a Poet*, chaps. 9–12; Sewall, *The Life*, II: chap. 28.

2 Anderson, *Stairway of Surprise*, p. 78.

3 Prominent among works exploring literary influences on ED are the following: Diehl, *Dickinson and the Romantic Imagination*; Gelpi, *The Mind of the Poet*; Gilbert and Gubar, *The Madwoman in the Attic*; Margaret Homans, *Women Writers and Poetic Identity: Dorothy Wordsworth, Emily Brontë, and Emily Dickinson* (Princeton, N.J.: Princeton University Press, 1980); Karl Keller, *The Only Kangaroo among the Beauty: Emily Dickinson and America* (Baltimore, Md., and London: Johns Hopkins University Press, 1979); Hyatt Waggoner, *American Poets from the Puritans to the Present* (Boston, Mass.: Houghton Mifflin, 1968), chap. 7; and Watts, *The Poetry of American Women*.

4 Bianchi, *Emily Dickinson Face to Face*, pp. 138–139.

5 Johnson's note to letter 481 quotes Higginson writing about his friends' amusement with "my partially cracked poetess at Amherst."

6 My principal source for this overview of late eighteenth-century and early nineteenth-century New England Calvinism is Sydney E. Ahlstrom's *A Religious History of the American People* (New Haven, Conn., and London: Yale University Press, 1972), chaps. 25, 26, 37, 39.

7 Hawthorne, "The Custom House," *The Scarlet Letter*, ed., George Parsons Lathrop, Riverside ed., 12 vols. (Boston, Mass.: Houghton Mifflin, 1887), V:25.

8 Sewall, *The Life*, II:342–357.

9 *Aurora Leigh*, First Book, in *The Complete Poetical Works of Mrs. Browning*, ed., Harriet Waters Preston, Cambridge ed. (Boston, Mass.: Houghton Mifflin, 1900), p. 264.

10 Ibid., 266.

11 "Intellect," in *Emerson's Complete Works*, ed., J. E. Cabot, Riverside ed., 11 vols. (Boston, Mass.: Houghton Mifflin, 1886), II:320.

12 "The Prisoner of Chillon," in *The Complete Poetical Works of Byron*, ed., Paul

Elmer More, Cambridge ed. (Boston, Mass.: Houghton Mifflin, 1933), p. 405.

13 *The Poetical Works of Longfellow*, ed., Horace E. Scudder, Cambridge ed. (Boston, Mass.: Houghton Mifflin, 1975), pp. 110–111.

14 Ibid., 338–339.

15 The influence of *Aurora Leigh* on ED has been extensively studied recently by a number of authors: Diehl, *Dickinson and the Romantic Imagination*, chap. 1; Gilbert and Gubar, *The Madwoman in the Attic*, p. vi; and Walsh, *The Hidden Life of Emily Dickinson*.

16 *Aurora Leigh*, First Book, p. 255.

17 Leyda, *Years and Hours*, II:338.

18 *Aurora Leigh*, First Book, p. 261.

19 *Robert Browning: Poems and Plays*, ed., John Bryson, 5 vols. (London: J. M. Dent and Sons, 1906; reprinted., New York: Dutton, 1963), II:276.

20 Bianchi, *Emily Dickinson Face to Face*, p. 46.

21 *Robert Browning*, II:319.

5. *"I Play at Riches"*

1 Bingham, *Ancestors' Brocades*, p. 127.

2 Ibid., 35.

3 Ik Marvel (Donald G. Mitchell), "Sea-Coal and Anthracite," in *Reveries of a Bachelor: or, A Book of the Heart* (New York: Charles Scribner's Sons, 1884), pp. 43–44.

4 Martha Dickinson Bianchi, "My Surviving Aunt: Lavinia Dickinson," from her unpublished autobiography. This chapter appeared in *Prairie Schooner* 51 (Winter 1977/78): 325–344.

5 "Ode: Intimations of Immortality from Recollections of Early Childhood," in *The Poetical Works of William Wordsworth*, ed. E. De Selincourt and Helen Darbishire, 5 vols. (Oxford: Clarendon Press, 1958), IV:283.

6 For close study of this issue of ED's childish role, see Patterson, *Emily Dickinson's Imagery*, chap. 1 ("The Boy Emily"); Mossberg, *When a Writer Is a Daughter*; Cody, *After Great Pain*; and Dolores Dyer Lucas, *Emily Dickinson and Riddle* (DeKalb: Northern Illinois University Press, 1969), chap. 2.

7 Patterson links her discussion of the masculine titles ED appropriated with the boy-role analysis noted above, observing the virtual termination of both image clusters around 1865: *Emily Dickinson's Imagery*, pp. 16–17.

8 Ibid., 87, 215n. Patterson's version of the story differs in details from Tennyson's rendition—including the specific naming of Exeter, which he does not designate in "The Lord of Burleigh," in *The Complete Poetical Works of Tennyson*, ed., W. J. Rolfe, Cambridge ed. (Boston, Mass.: Houghton Mifflin, 1898), p. 107.

9 "The Beggar Maid" and "The Lord of Burleigh" form a cluster with "Lady Clare," also a poem on changed identity in relation to aristocratic status. Shakespeare's references in *Love's Labour's Lost*, *Richard II*, and *Romeo and*

Juliet to the legend of King Cophetua and the beggar would have reinforced the tale in ED's mind.

10 Austin apparently quoted Sue in wondering, "Is there anything in the 'mere relation of wife that gives you sometimes gloomy thoughts'—and if there is can I not say something that will relieve them. . . ." He urged, "Don't ever be discouraged, Sue, in thinking of 'a man's requirements'—I ask nothing but your love. . . ." This letter and other evidence of a troubled courtship appear in Cody's *After Great Pain*, pp. 206–215.

11 Mossberg, *When a Writer Is a Daughter*, pp. 173–174.

12 See Barton L. St. Armand, "Emily Dickinson's 'Babes in the Woods': A Ballad Reborn," *Journal of American Folklore* 90 (1977): 430–441.

13 Marvel, "Morning, Noon, and Evening," in *Reveries of a Bachelor*, pp. 171–173.

14 Clark Griffith, *The Long Shadow: Emily Dickinson's Tragic Poetry* (Princeton, N.J.: Princeton University Press, 1964), p. 155.

15 Characteristics of the sentimental literary tradition are discussed by Ann Douglas in *The Feminization of American Culture* and by Emily Stipes Watts in *The Poetry of American Women*. Commentary on the poet's gothic literary context appears in Gilbert and Gubar, *The Madwoman in the Attic*, pp. 585–586.

16 See Walsh, *The Hidden Life of Emily Dickinson*, esp. chaps. 3 and 4. Tables of alleged borrowings from Mrs. Browning appear in his notes, pp. 257–260; notes on borrowings from Charlotte Brontë and Lydia Maria Child appear on pp. 262–263. Walsh also assumes ED's virtual plagiarism from Emerson.

17 Anderson, *Stairway of Surprise*, p. 189.

18 "Love and Duty," in *The Complete Poetical Works of Tennyson*, pp. 85–87.

19 Thomas W. Ford, *Heaven Beguiles the Tired: Death in the Poetry of Emily Dickinson* (University: University of Alabama Press, 1966), p. 57.

20 Letter 11 described her visit to the dying Sophia, but ED did not actually witness this death. It was Lavinia, rather than Emily, who cared for their aunt, Lavinia Norcross, through her final sickness, and the Norcross cousins ministered in a similar way to their mutual cousin, Eliza Coleman. Edward Dickinson died alone in Boston. Aside from caring for her mother until her last moments in 1882, ED attended no deathbed between Sophia Holland's passing in 1844 and Gilbert Dickinson's in 1883. Poems written from the point of view of a watcher over the dying, therefore, should be classified as examples of her role playing.

21 See Ronald A. Sudol, "Elegy and Immortality: Emily Dickinson's 'Lay this Laurel on the One'," *ESQ* 26 (1980): 10–15.

22 Gilbert and Gubar, *The Madwoman in the Attic*, pp. 624–625.

23 R. W. Franklin, *The Editing of Emily Dickinson: A Reconsideration* (Madison, Milwaukee, and London: University of Wisconsin Press, 1967), pp. 40–46, and *The Manuscript Books*, I, pp. 533–560.

24 Several critics deal extensively with this issue: Diehl, *Dickinson and the Romantic Imagination*; Gilbert and Gubar, *The Madwoman in the Attic*, and Pollak, *The Anxiety of Gender*.

25 See especially Cody, *After Great Pain*, pp. 487–488

6. *"My Little Force Explodes"*

1   Anderson said that ED's "chief problem was control," *Stairway of Surprise*, p. 78; Sewall noted her early "problem of organization and coherence," *The Life*, I:240; Porter reads her request to Higginson as "pleading for his help to find control, to find some indwelling design by which her poetry might cohere," *The Modern Idiom*, p. 111. Not everyone agrees. According to Miller, ED's work "is a poetry of assemblage. Each single poem is complete; each fascicle is complete," *The Poetry*, p. 286; Archibald MacLeish finds tone rather than structure the controlling force in her poems, "The Private World," in Sewall, ed., *Emily Dickinson: A Collection*, p. 157.

2   She repeated this advice fifteen years after reading it in a letter to Higginson in which she reported, "Often, when troubled by entreaty, that paragraph of your's has saved me—" (L 488).

3   Johnson, in Appendix 9 to *The Poems of Emily Dickinson*, lists seven poems published in her lifetime, of which five appeared in the *Springfield Daily Republican* (numbers 3, 214, 216, 228, and 986). It is the last four of these that seem most likely to have been submitted by Sue to Samuel Bowles for publication. Poem 324 appeared in *The Round Table*, edited by Henry Sweetser and Charles Sweetser (distant members of the poet's family); and poem 67 was included by Helen Hunt Jackson in *A Masque of Poets: No Name Series* (Boston, Mass.: Roberts Brothers, 1878), p. 174. New discoveries by Karen Dandurand extend our knowledge of ED's publication history by showing that poem 35 also appeared in the *Republican*—perhaps contributed by Mary Haven—and by demonstrating that additional journals published ED's poems. Poems 228, 137, and 130 first appeared in *Drum Beat*, a wartime fund-raising paper of wide circulation. Poem 67 was published in the *Brooklyn Daily Union* long before Mrs. Jackson demanded it for her anthology. Two of these poems, numbers 137 and 228, were then reprinted in the *Republican*, and "Flowers—Well—if anybody" (P 137) was also selected for the *Boston Post*. These findings call attention to the role of the Reverend Richard Salter Storrs, Jr., editor of *Drum Beat*, as a significant figure in the poet's publication history; he and his wife were friends of Austin and Sue. Dandurand, "Another Dickinson Poem Published in Her Lifetime," *American Literature* 54 (1982): 434–437; "New Dickinson Civil War Publications," *American Literature* 56 (1984): 17–27.

4   Johnson, ed., *The Poems*, I:152–153.

5   Here is the alternative:

> Springs—shake the Seals—
> But the silence—stiffens—
> Frosts unhook—in the Northern Zones—
> Icicles—crawl—from Polar Caverns—
> Midnight in Marble—Refutes—the Suns—

6   See chap. 14 ("The Dickinson Rhetoric and the Structure of a Life") and Appendix I ("Vinnie as Stylist, Mimic, Reader, and Poet") in *The Life*, I:235–252.

7   Ibid., 155.

8 Bianchi, *Life and Letters*, p. 46.

9 Donald Thackrey, *Emily Dickinson's Approach to Poetry*, University of Nebraska Studies, new series, no. 13 (Lincoln: University of Nebraska Press, 1954), p. 17. William Sherwood writes of ED's "maximal use of limited resources" in *Circumference and Circumstance*, p. 17; Porter identifies compactness attained through "drastic elimination of discursive space" as her most inimitable feature in *The Modern Idiom*, p. 37; and Diehl describes her poems as "a kind of epitaphic monument" in *Dickinson and the Romantic Imagination*, p. 65. I have elsewhere applied New England economic thinking to ED's life and writing in "Doing Without: Dickinson as Yankee Woman Poet" in *Critical Essays on Emily Dickinson*, ed., Paul J. Ferlazzo (Boston, Mass.: G. K. Hall, 1984), pp. 205–223.

10 Franklin, "Introduction," in *The Manuscript Books*, p. xii.

11 Porter stresses the importance of approaching the poet through these scraps rather than through the orderly arrangement of poems we are accustomed to seeing on the printed page: *The Modern Idiom*, p. 2.

12 Editorial attempts to organize ED's poems constitute an enlightening story in themselves, though none has proven totally satisfactory as a design for the long-desired "reader's edition" that Johnson recommended. Mrs. Todd and Higginson arranged the poems thematically in four broad groups, also chosen by Bianchi for *Complete Poems* (1924): Life, Nature, Love, and Time and Eternity. For *Bolts of Melody* (1945) Bingham grouped the poems in twelve associational clusters arranged in climactic order to move from descriptive presentations of the natural world to philosophical poems on life's meaning. Johnson's three-volume, one-volume, and selected editions arrange the poems chronologically. Miller recommends a return to ED's own fascicle ordering, now possible through photographic reproduction of *The Manuscript Books* in Franklin's edition, though his volumes necessarily omit all those envelopes and kitchen scraps that interest Porter and reveal to us ED's composition habits in the last two decades of her life.

13 Conflicting arguments for fascicle cohesiveness and unified intention have been advanced by the following critics: Miller, *The Poetry*, p. 249; Martha Lindblom O'Keefe, "This Edifice: Studies in the Structure of the [13] Fascicles of the Poetry of Emily Dickinson," *Dickinson Studies* 42 (1982): 3–15; and Shurr, *The Marriage of Emily Dickinson*. The strongest dissent comes from David Porter in *The Modern Idiom*, p. 137.

14 Franklin, "Introduction" in *The Manuscript Books*, p. x.

15 Franklin dates poems 1729 and 1730 to circa 1858; poem 1737 to circa 1861, and poems 1710, 1712, 1725, 1727, 1739, and 1761 to circa 1862.

16 *The Poetical Works of Longfellow*, pp. 13–14.

17 I am indebted for this poem to Sewall's Appendix IV ("Popular Poetry: Selections from the *Springfield Republican*, 1858–62"), in *The Life*, II:742–750. Miss Burton's poem, published 12 July 1862, appears on page 746. For a less embarrassing example of moralistic poetry, consider Higginson's own poem "To Duty," as collected in Edmund Clarence Stedman, ed., *An American Anthology: 1787–1900* (Boston, Mass.: Houghton, Mifflin, 1900), p. 268.

18 "Of Being," in Ola Elizabeth Winslow, ed., *Jonathan Edwards: Basic Writings* (New York and Toronto: New American Library, 1966), p. 47.

19 Marvel, "Morning, Noon, and Evening," in *Reveries of a Bachelor*, pp. 206–207.

20 *Aurora Leigh*, Fifth Book, *The Poems of Elizabeth Barrett Browning*, p. 327.

21 Brita Lindberg-Seyersted, *The Voice of the Poet: Aspects of Style in the Poetry of Emily Dickinson* (Cambridge, Mass.: Harvard University Press, 1968), pp. 197–213. Also important for analysis of ED's poetic techniques are Sharon Cameron's *Lyric Time: Dickinson and the Limits of Genre* (Baltimore, Md., and London: Johns Hopkins University Press, 1979) and Porter's *The Modern Idiom*.

22 Johnson lists these in the variorum edition: "kindred," "fully," "free," "ample," "bounteous," "intimate," "affable," "affluent," and "gracious." Such lists appear often in drafts of ED's later poems, offering insight into her habits of composition.

23 Lindberg-Seyersted, *The Voice of the Poet*, pp. 234–237; Porter, *The Modern Idiom*, chap. 3.

24 I have adapted ED's variant for the last line of this poem, originally written "But we demand the Flame."

25 Leyda, *Years and Hours*, II:473.

26 Bianchi, *Life and Letters*, p. 44. Later in the same paragraph Bianchi comments that the quiet routine of the Homestead was "quite electric enough for her sensitive transmission."

7. *"Out upon Circumference"*

1 Leyda, *Years and Hours*, I:131.

2 Webster, *An American Dictionary*, p. 206.

3 Some critics emphasize the inwardness of the private circle of consciousness, bounded by circumference: Northrop Frye, *Fables of Identity: Studies in Poetic Mythology* (New York: Harcourt, Brace and World, 1963), pp. 199, 208–210; Griffith, *The Long Shadow*, p. 234; Sherwood, *Circumference and Circumstance*, pp. 218–223. Others stress the agglomerative, aspiring, outward-thrusting dimension of the term: Anderson, *Stairway of Surprise*, pp. 62–63; Gelpi, *The Mind of the Poet*, pp. 122–124; Cameron, *Lyric Time*, p. 135; Diehl, *Dickinson and the Romantic Imagination*, p. 166; Porter, *The Modern Idiom*, pp. 35, 181; and Wilbur, "Sumptuous Destitution," p. 133. Taking an intermediate position, Weisbuch deplores exaggerated attention to the word, then applies it both to a totally inclusive vision and to boundaries of thought: *Emily Dickinson's Poetry*, p. 117. Providing a diagram to illustrate her terminology, Miller presents the reader with two circles in vertical alignment—a small one representing the circuit world of the poet's consciousness and a large one representing the circumference world to which she aspired; the circles are linked by lines that cross at death. All the poems and fascicles, according to Miller, enact this process of juncture: *The Poetry*, pp. 234–246.

4   Diehl, *Dickinson and the Romantic Imagination*, p. 138, and Walsh, *The Hidden Life*, p. 260. Webster's *Dictionary* led ED to poetic uses of *circuit* and *circumference* by Shakespeare, Milton, and Dryden; while her *Cyclopaedia* reminded her of Sir Thomas Browne's metaphorical circle terminology. Waggoner, Gelpi, and others call attention to Emerson's essay "Circles" as a probable Dickinson source.

5   "Circles," in *Emerson's Complete Works*, II:281.

6   Porter reads the wife poems as representations of status changes and allegories of passage, all of them involving "a practicing of death": *The Modern Idiom*, pp. 195–209.

7   L, III, PF 49.

8   Sir Alexander Cockburn, whom Johnson and Ward identify in their commentary on this letter as lord chief justice of England and therefore "the epitome of awesome sedateness," was best known for two cases: the McNaghten murder trial in which he successfully defended Daniel McNaghten on grounds of insanity and formulated rules for legal responsibility, and the Tichborne case, in which he presided over the trial of a notorious impostor to a title and inheritance. ED could easily have associated this jurist, then, with insane situations and with efforts to regulate mankind's incorrigibly irregular behavior.

9   She speaks of this false awakening as "a delightful dream, out of which the Evil one bid me wake & again return to the world & its pleasures" (L 11). Edwards indicates the spiritual self-searching of Puritan youth while exercising unusual powers of discernment in distinguishing true from false conversion in the opening sentence of "Personal Narrative": "I had a variety of concerns and exercises about my soul, from my childhood; but I had two more remarkable seasons of awakening, before I met with that change, by which I was brought to those new dispositions, and that new sense of things, that I have since had": Winslow, ed., *Jonathan Edwards: Basic Writings*, p. 81. See also "A Treatise Concerning Religious Affections," in ibid., 184–195.

10   ED's bitterest letter, the famous "Sue—you can go or stay—" missive of 1854, probably resulted from Susan's pressure on her friend for religious conversion, a pressure she applied also to Austin during this period of their engagement. The poet wrote, "Sue—I have lived by this. It is the lingering emblem of the Heaven I once dreamed, and though if this is taken, I shall remain alone, and though in that last day, the Jesus Christ you love, remark he does not know me—there is a darker spirit will not disown it's child" (L 173).

11   "Days," in *Emerson's Complete Works*, IX:196. His speaker had neglected other offerings equally attractive to ED: "Bread, kingdoms, stars, and sky that holds them all."

12   Calvin's *Institutes* and *The Catechism of the Church of Geneva*, cited in E. Brooks Holifield, *The Covenant Sealed: The Development of Puritan Sacramental Theology in Old and New England, 1570–1720* (New Haven, Conn., and London: Yale University Press, 1974), p. 14.

13   Cameron identifies some of those two-way transformations represented by

ED's eucharistic imagery as those "from a semiotic to a semantic sphere, from unconscious to conscious, desire to language, instinct to awareness, difference to reference, logos to godhead and back to logos again": *Lyric Time*, p. 192.

14 Holifield, *The Covenant Sealed*, p. 215.

15 I have adopted ED's variant for the fourth line of this quatrain. The original reads "Like Chariots—in the Vest—."

8. *"Dying in Drama"*

1 Many critics have written thoughtfully on ED's responses to death, among them the following: Cameron, *Lyric Time*; Ford, *Heaven Beguiles the Tired*; Patterson, *Emily Dickinson's Imagery*; and Porter, *The Modern Idiom*.

2 Ford (in *Heaven Beguiles the Tired*, p. 155) and Griffith (in *The Long Shadow*, p. 121) both quote this passage as evidence of the speaker's envy of the dead woman's new knowledge, even though it obviously states reluctance to let this woman go while less valued persons remain alive. Consider this work sheet quatrain, written at about the same time: "Some Wretched creature, savior take / Who would exult to die / And leave for thy sweet mercy's sake / Another Hour to me" (P 1111). Jealousy of the dead woman exists implicitly in this poem but is not explicitly stated. Griffith elaborates on ED's desire for death as "the only real refuge from temporality" and change: *The Long Shadow*, p. 141.

3 L, III, PF 50.

4 Leyda, *Years and Hours*, II:475; Sewall, *The Life*, II:667.

5 See Weisbuch's explication of this poem in *Emily Dickinson's Poetry*, pp. 113–118, and Griffith, *The Long Shadow*, pp. 127–134, for analyses of the chaperon's role.

6 Leyda, *Years and Hours*, II:481. For commentary on ED's interest in heaven as the locus of lasting fame, see George Monteiro, "'Love & Fame' or 'What's a Heaven For?': Emily Dickinson's Teleology," *New England Quarterly* 51 (1978): 105–113.

7 According to Martha Dickinson Bianchi, "No one ever valued or fostered the fascination of a secret for a child as she did. When she wrote of my younger brother, 'Gilbert rejoiced in secrets. His young life was panting with them,' it was just as true of his Aunt Emily. She lent a contraband thrill to the slightest pretext." *Emily Dickinson Face to Face*, pp. 30–31.

8 Ibid., 174.

9. *"A Prognostic's Push"*

1 Bianchi, *Emily Dickinson Face to Face*, p. 70.

2 L, III, PF 53.

3 Theodora Van Wagenen Ward, *The Capsule of the Mind: Chapters in the Life of Emily Dickinson* (Cambridge, Mass.: Harvard University Press; London: Oxford University Press, 1961), pp. 34, 43.

4 Cameron, *Lyric Time*, p. 156.

5   For consideration of ED's vocabulary with differentiation among her usages over time of the words *immortality, eternity,* and *infinity,* see Robert W. Peckham, "This Colossal Substance," *Emily Dickinson Bulletin* 28 (1975): 112–123.

6   "My only sketch, profile, of Heaven is a large, blue sky, bluer and larger than the *biggest* I have seen in June, and in it are my friends—all of them—every one of them—those who are with me now, and those who were 'parted' as we walked, and 'snatched up to Heaven'" (L 185).

7   Only a few months before, however, ED had written to Bowles that "I pray for your sweet health—to 'Alla'—every morning" (L 241). As Anderson points out, the poet's ascription of religious feeling to all family members but herself "can only be taken as ironic inversion on the grand scale": *Stairway of Surprise,* p. 19.

8   In January 1875, ED wrote to Mrs. Holland, "Thank you for the Affection. It helps me up the Stairs at Night, where as I passed my Father's Door—I used to think was safety" (L 432).

9   Provocative consideration of ED's involvement with God, in particular the controversial issue of her love relationship with him, appears in the following: Griffith, *The Long Shadow,* p. 78; Keller, *The Only Kangaroo,* p. 66; MacLeish, "The Private World," p. 159; Sherwood, *Circumference and Circumstance,* p. 57; and Warren, "Emily Dickinson," p. 111.

10   For discussion of Edward Dickinson's conversion in 1850, when he was forty-seven years old, see Sewall, *The Life,* I:66–67.

11   Bianchi, *Emily Dickinson Face to Face,* p. 85.

12   "Art," in *Emerson's Complete Works,* II:337.

13   L, III, PF 51.

14   Porter discusses the Puritan typological mode of thinking that characterizes ED's crucifixion poems in *The Modern Idiom,* p. 167.

15   See also L 9, with its enumeration of her 1846 Christmas gifts from Santa Claus. Book inscriptions from the Dickinson library indicate that adult family members often exchanged gifts on New Year's Day (her father's birthday) rather than Christmas.

16   The most detailed of these letters regales little Sally Jenkins with reports on "the most beautiful Christmas on record" in 1880. In it ED describes gifts to all the household animals and concludes with reference to a floral tribute for her father's grave (L 682). See also her Christmas remembrances to Gilbert's friends after his death (L 876; 878; 956; 957; 958). ED seems always to have regarded Christmas as a festival for children.

17   Cf. Cecile W. Cary, "*The Mill on the Floss* as an Influence on Emily Dickinson," *Dickinson Studies* 36 (1979): 26–39; Miller, *The Poetry,* p. 112; Sewall, *The Life,* II:688–694; and Sherwood, *Circumference and Circumstance,* chap. 4.

18   Matthew 27:46. See also Psalm 22:1.

19   Bingham, *Emily Dickinson's Home,* p. 40.

20   Bianchi, *Emily Dickinson Face to Face,* p. xxii. Bianchi also reported "the aloofness from all time and place that was hers at will."

21   Valuable contributions to this discussion may be found in Louise Bogan, "A

Mystical Poet" in Sewall, ed., *Emily Dickinson: A Collection*; Steve Carter, "Emily Dickinson and Mysticism," *ESQ* 24 (1978); Kher, *The Landscape of Absence*, p. 23; Thackrey, *Emily Dickinson's Approach to Poetry*, pp. 32, 49; and Waggoner, *American Poets*, pp. 674–676. See also Walter Hesford's explication of "In snow thou comest" (P 1669) in *Dickinson Studies* 46 (1983): 15–19.

22 Gelpi, *The Mind of the Poet*, p. 76.

10. "His Diameters"

1 She may have been thinking of her father's manner of speech, as she described it earlier to the same correspondent: "'I say unto you,' Father would read at Prayers, with a militant Accent that would startle one" (L 432).

Index of First Lines

A Burdock—clawed by Gown— (229), 110

A Clock stopped—(287), 213

A Cloud withdrew from the Sky (895), 65–66

A curious Cloud surprised the Sky, (1710), 282n.15

A fuzzy fellow, without feet, (173), 169

A great Hope fell (1123), 64

A House upon the Hight (399), 123

A Light exists in Spring (812), 188

A little Bread—a crust—a crumb— (159), 59

A little East of Jordan, (59), 80, 138–139

A little overflowing word (1467), 148

A long—long Sleep—A famous—Sleep—(654), 213

A loss of something ever felt I— (959), 65

A Mien to move a Queen—(283), 12, 31

A narrow Fellow in the Grass (986), 98, 99, 281n.3

A Pit—but Heaven over it—(1712), 121–122, 282n.15

A poor—torn heart—a tattered heart—(78), 117, 208

A precious—mouldering pleasure—'tis—(371), 76

A Prison gets to be a friend—(652), 88

A Route of Evanescence (1463), 147

A science—so the Savans say, (100), 149

A Shady friend—for Torrid days— (278), 150

A single Clover Plank (1343), 164, 165, 170

A solemn thing—it was—I said— (271), 34–35

A Spider sewed at Night (1138), 144, 272

A Toad, can die of Light—(583), 222

A train went through a burial gate, (1761), 282n.15

A Wife—at Daybreak I shall be— (461), 174–175

A Word dropped careless on a Page (1261), 148, 150

A Word is dead (1212), 147, 150

A Word made Flesh is seldom (1651), 150, 191

Abraham to kill him (1317), 80, 244

Adrift! A little boat adrift! (30), 111

After all Birds have been investigated and laid aside—(1395), 147

After great pain, a formal feeling comes—(341), 87, 141

Again—his voice is at the door— (663), 118

All but Death, can be Adjusted— (749), 137

All the letters I can write (334), 150

Alone and in a Circumstance (1167), 63

Alone, I cannot be—(298), 75

Although I put away his life—(366), 29, 115

Ample make this Bed—(829), 201

An altered look about the hills—(140), 168

"And with what body do they come?"—(1492), 80

Apparently with no surprise (1624), 243–244

"Arcturus" is his other name—(70), 56, 237

Art thou the thing I wanted? (1282), 67

As by the dead we love to sit, (88), 66, 207

As if some little Arctic flower (180), 110

As the Starved Maelstrom laps the Navies (872), 67

As Watchers hang upon the East, (121), 200

At Half past Three, a single Bird (1084), 160

At last, to be identified! (174), 202

At least—to pray—is left—is left—(502), 253

Awake ye muses nine, sing me a strain divine, (1), 22, 198, 273n.7, 277n.1

Banish Air from Air—(854), 155–156

Be Mine the Doom—(845), 149

Because I could not stop for Death—(712), 123, 183, 216–219

Because that you are going (1260), 243

Bees are Black, with Gilt Surcingles—(1405), 146

Before I got my eye put out (327), 113

Before you thought of Spring (1465), 147

Behind Me—dips Eternity—(721), 163–164, 232, 247

Bereaved of all, I went abroad—(784), 66

Bereavement in their death to feel (645), 221

Better—than Music! For I—who heard it—(503), 36, 261

Blazing in Gold and quenching in Purple (228), 152, 167, 281n.3

By my Window have I for Scenery (797), 146, 260

Circumference thou Bride of Awe (1620), 194–195, 218

Cocoon above! Cocoon below! (129), 169

Conscious am I in my Chamber, (679), 137, 182

Contained in this short Life (1165), 84

Could live—did live—(43), 209

Crisis is a Hair (889), 177, 196

Dare you see a Soul at the White Heat? (365), 34

Death sets a Thing significant (360), 207, 213

Delayed till she had ceased to know—(58), 117

Delight is as the flight—(257), 265–266

Deprived of other Banquet, (773), 66

Did life's penurious length (1717), 152

Did Our Best Moment last—(393), 238, 262–263

Did you ever stand in a Cavern's Mouth—(590), 149

Do People moulder equally, (432), 223

Dont put up my Thread & Needle—(617), 179

Doubt Me! My Dim Companion! (275), 104

Drab Habitation of Whom? (893), 149

Drama's Vitallest Expression is the Common Day (741), 96, 137

Drowning is not so pitiful (1718), 244

Dust is the only Secret—(153), 224

Dying! Dying in the night! (158), 215

Elijah's Wagon knew no thill (1254), 37

Embarrassment of one another (662), 245–246

Essential Oils—are wrung—(675), 138

Except the Heaven had come so
near—(472), 183

Except to Heaven, she is nought.
(154), 253

Expanse cannot be lost—(1584), 231

Exultation is the going (76), 109

Faith—is the Pierless Bridge (915),
146

Fame is the one that does not stay—
(1475), 154, 220

Fame is the tint that Scholars leave
(866), 221

Fame's Boys and Girls, who never die
(1066), 220

Far from Love the Heavenly Father
(1021), 99

Finding is the first Act (870), 66

Fitter to see Him, I may be (968), 182

Flowers—Well—if anybody (137),
281n.3

For every Bird a Nest—(143), 12, 13

Forever at His side to walk—(246),
29, 108

Forever honored be the Tree (1570),
253–254

Forever—is composed of Nows—
(624), 232

Four Trees—upon a solitary Acre—
(742), 137

From Blank to Blank—(761), 60

From Cocoon forth a Butterfly (354),
150, 170

Further in Summer than the Birds
(1068), 63, 190–191

Given in Marriage unto Thee (817),
182

Glee—The great storm is over—
(619), 111, 139

Go thy great way! (1638), 271–272

God gave a Loaf to every Bird—
(791), 58

God is a distant—stately Lover—
(357), 247

God is indeed a jealous God—(1719),
244

God made no act without a cause,
(1163), 246

God permits industrious Angels—
(231), 63, 254

Going to Heaven! (79), 109, 110

Going to Him! Happy letter! (494),
148–149

Good Morning—Midnight—(425),
57

Had we our senses (1284), 113

He ate and drank the precious
Words—(1587), 73, 76, 93

He forgot—and I—remembered—
(203), 80, 249

He fumbles at your Soul (315), 150

He gave away his Life—(567), 250

He lived the Life of Ambush (1525),
271

He put the Belt around my life—
(273), 101

He scanned it—staggered—(1062),
116

He strained my faith—(497), 253

He told a homely tale (763), 99

He was my host—he was my guest,
(1721), 183

Heaven is so far of the Mind (370),
239

"Heaven"—is what I cannot reach!
(239), 59, 238

"Heavenly Father"—take to thee
(1461), 82, 242

Her final Summer was it—(795), 117,
207

Her—"last Poems"—(312), 91

Her Sweet turn to leave the Homestead (649), 116

Her sweet Weight on my Heart a
Night (518), 104

"Hope" is the thing with feathers—
(254), 151

How brittle are the Piers (1433), 251

How far is it to Heaven? (929), 247

How Human Nature dotes (1417),
228

How many times these low feet staggered—(187), 117, 213

How much the present moment
means (1380), 78

How the old Mountains drip with
  Sunset (291), 167
I am ashamed—I hide—(473), 103,
  174, 188
I asked no other thing—(621), 254,
  257
I breathed enough to take the Trick—
  (272), 35, 215
I bring an unaccustomed wine (132),
  204
I cannot buy it—'tis not sold—(840),
  67
I cannot dance upon my Toes—(326),
  130
I cannot live with You—(640), 27, 34
I cannot see my soul but know 'tis
  there (1262), 182, 250
I cautious, scanned my little life—
  (178), 66
I cried at Pity—not at Pain—(588),
  60, 99
I dreaded that first Robin, so, (348),
  102
I dwell in Possibility—(657), 272
I felt a Cleaving in my Mind—(937),
  178
I felt a Funeral, in my Brain, (280),
  141
I gave myself to Him—(580), 103
I got so I could hear his name—(293),
  25, 119, 129, 257
I had a guinea golden—(23), 63
I had been hungry, all the Years—
  (579), 58
I had not minded—Walls—(398), 123,
  161–162
I had some things that I called mine—
  (116), 63, 244
I had the Glory—that will do—(349),
  27, 45
I have a Bird in spring (5), 277n.1
I have a King, who does not speak—
  (103), 256
I hav'nt told my garden yet—(50),
  118
I heard a Fly buzz—when I died—
  (465), 219

I held a Jewel in my fingers—(245),
  63
I know lives, I could miss (372), 150
I know some lonely Houses off the
  Road (289), 94, 97
I know that He exists. (338), 246, 253
I learned—at least—what Home
  could be—(944), 105
I live with Him—I see His face—
  (463), 176
I lived on Dread—(770), 60, 122–123
I lost a World—the other day! (181),
  64
I meant to have but modest needs—
  (476), 254–256
I measure every Grief I meet (561),
  250–251
I met a King this afternoon! (166), 100
I never felt at Home—Below—(413),
  235
I never hear the word "escape" (77),
  109
I never lost as much but twice, (49),
  63, 97, 244
I often passed the village (51), 118
I play at Riches—to appease (801),
  96–97
I prayed, at first, a little Girl, (576),
  256
I read my sentence—steadily—(412),
  124–125
I reason, Earth is short—(301), 237
I saw no Way—The Heavens were
  stitched—(378), 195–197, 198
I see thee clearer for the Grave (1666),
  220
I shall know why—when Time is
  over—(193), 57
I should have been too glad, I see—
  (313), 163, 258
I should not dare to leave my friend,
  (205), 115, 204
I sometimes drop it, for a Quick—
  (708), 137
I started Early—Took my Dog—
  (520), 110–111, 112
I taste a liquor never brewed—(214),

152–153, 281n.3

I think I was enchanted (593), 75, 77, 192

I think just how my shape will rise—(237), 235–236

I think the Hemlock likes to stand (525), 34

I think To Live—may be a Bliss (646), 126–127

I thought that nature was enough (1286), 266

I tie my Hat—I crease my Shawl—(443), 121

I took my Power in my Hand—(540), 80

I took one Draught of Life—(1725), 282n.15

I tried to think a lonelier Thing (532), 55, 57

I was a Phebe—nothing more—(1009), 60

I was the slightest in the House—(486), 10, 60, 115–116

I went to Heaven (374), 32, 236–237

I went to thank Her—(363), 110

I would not paint—a picture—(505), 192

I Years had been from Home (609), 58

If ever the lid gets off my head (1727), 282n.15

If I can stop one Heart from breaking (919), 140

If I may have it, when it's dead, (577), 124

If I should cease to bring a Rose (56), 216

If I should'nt be alive (182), 118

If I'm lost—now—(256), 63

I'll tell you how the Sun rose—(318), 130

I'm ceded—I've stopped being Their's—(508), 45, 188–189

I'm Nobody! Who are you? (288), 61, 277n.8

I'm saying every day (373), 101

I'm sorry for the Dead—Today—(529), 116, 208, 218

I'm "wife"—I've finished that—(199), 103, 174

Immured in Heaven! (1594), 239–240

In falling Timbers buried—(614), 121

In many and reportless places (1382), 260–261

In rags mysterious as these (117), 253

In snow thou comest (1669), 287n.21

In Winter in my Room (1670), 179

Inconceivably solemn! (582), 35

Is Bliss then, such Abyss, (340), 109–110

Is Heaven a Physician? (1270), 236

Is Immortality a bane (1728), 232

It always felt to me—a wrong (597), 79

It ceased to hurt me, though so slow (584), 178

It did not surprise me—(39), 62

It dropped so low—in my Regard—(747), 137

It is easy to work when the soul is at play—(244), 150

It might be lonelier (405), 187–188

It tossed—and tossed—(723), 111

It troubled me as once I was—(600), 235

It was a quiet way—(1053), 183

It was not Death, for I stood up, (510), 87, 141

It was too late for Man—(623), 254

It would have starved a Gnat—(612), 58

It would never be Common—more—I said—(430), 63–64

It's Coming—the postponeless Creature—(390), 123

It's thoughts—and just One Heart—(495), 115, 187

I've dropped my Brain—My Soul is numb—(1046), 215, 216

I've got an arrow here. (1729), 282n.15

I've heard an Organ talk, sometimes—(183), 75, 143

I've known a Heaven, like a Tent—(243), 150

I've seen a Dying Eye (547), 212

Jesus! thy Crucifix (225), 250

Just lost, when I was saved! (160),
203–204

Just Once! Oh least Request! (1076),
243

Just so—Jesus—raps—(317), 248–249

Lay this Laurel on the One (1393),
117–118, 280n.21

Lest this be Heaven indeed (1043), 238

Let down the Bars, Oh Death—
(1065), 200–201

Let Us play Yesterday—(728), 58,
172, 173

"Lethe" in my flower, (1730), 282n.15

Life, and Death, and Giants—(706),
137

Life—is what we make it—(698), 251

Like her the Saints retire, (60), 200

Like Mighty Foot Lights—burned the
Red (595), 246

Love—is anterior to Life—(917), 234

Mama never forgets her birds, (164),
117

Me prove it now—Whoever doubt
(537), 119

Mine—by the Right of the White
Election! (528), 34, 35, 51, 139–140

Mine Enemy is growing old—(1509),
66

More Life—went out—when He
went (422), 150, 223

Most she touched me by her mute-
ness—(760), 60–61

Musicians wrestle everywhere—
(157), 261–262

Must be a Wo—(571), 251

My Cocoon tightens—Colors teaze—
(1099), 170

My first well Day—since many ill—
(574), 178

My Maker—let me be (1403), 258

My period had come for Prayer—
(564), 258–259

My Soul—accused me—And I
quailed—(753), 137

My wheel is in the dark! (10), 111

My Worthiness is all my Doubt—
(751), 137, 188

"Nature" is what we see—(668), 146

No Brigadier throughout the Year
(1561), 147

No Crowd that has occurred (515),
164

No matter—now—Sweet—(704),
101

No Notice gave She, but a Change—
(804), 106, 213

No Rack can torture me—(384), 87

No Romance sold unto (669), 75

Nobody knows this little Rose—(35),
281n.3

Not all die early, dying young—
(990), 222

Not any sunny tone (1674), 220

Not in this World to see his face—
(418), 239

Not "Revelation"—'tis—that waits,
(685), 228

Obtaining but our own Extent
(1543), 252

Of all the Souls that stand create—
(664), 24

Of all the Sounds despatched abroad,
(321), 131, 261

Of Course—I prayed—(376), 56, 257

Of Glory not a Beam is left (1647),
272

Of God we ask one favor, (1601), 82,
238, 239

Of Heaven above the firmest proof
(1205), 232

Of nearness to her sundered Things
(607), 207

Of Paradise' existence (1411), 237,
269

Of Paul and Silas it is said (1166), 80

Of the Heart that goes in, and closes
the Door (1098), 201, 218

Oh Shadow on the Grass, (1187), 185

On my volcano grows the Grass
(1677), 153

On such a night, or such a night,
(146), 60

On this long storm the Rainbow rose—(194), 212

On this wondrous sea (4), 277n.1

Once more, my now bewildered Dove (48), 111

One Blessing had I than the rest (756), 184

One crown that no one seeks (1735), 250

One Crucifixion is recorded—only—(553), 250

One Joy of so much anguish (1420), 178–179, 270

One need not be a Chamber—to be Haunted—(670), 120

One of the ones that Midas touched (1466), 147

One Year ago—jots what? (296), 25

Only God—detect the Sorrow—(626), 247

Our journey had advanced—(615), 202

Ourselves we do inter with sweet derision. (1144), 229

Ourselves were wed one summer—dear—(631), 104, 174

Over and over, like a Tune—(367), 239

Over the fence—(251), 59, 98

Pain—has an Element of Blank—(650), 177

Papa above! (61), 60, 257

Pass to thy Rendezvous of Light, (1564), 211

Perhaps you think me stooping (833), 190

Pigmy seraphs—gone astray—(138), 102

Pink—small—and punctual—(1332), 146

Poor little Heart! (192), 115

Prayer is the little implement (437), 257

Precious to Me—She still shall be—(727), 60

Presentiment—is that long Shadow—on the Lawn—(764), 146, 185

Promise This—When You be Dying—(648), 204

Publication—is the Auction (709), 43, 137, 146

Rearrange a "Wife's" affection! (1737), 107, 280n.11, 282n.15

Recollect the Face of me (1305), 80, 249

Rehearsal to Ourselves (379), 122

"Remember me" implored the Thief! (1180), 80, 249

Remorse—is Memory—awake—(744), 137, 146

Renunciation—is a piercing Virtue—(745), 27, 137, 146

Safe in their Alabaster Chambers—(216), 44, 129, 130, 131–133, 154, 196, 212, 218, 281nn.3–5

Savior! I've no one else to tell—(217), 257–258

Shall I take thee, the Poet said (1126), 24

She bore it till the simple veins (144), 208

She died—*this* was the way she died. (150), 117, 201

She lay as if at play (369), 117, 213

She rose to His Requirement—dropt (732), 105–106, 174

She staked her Feathers—Gained an Arc—(798), 18–19, 20, 170

"Sic transit gloria mundi," (3), 281n.3

Size circumscribes—it has no room (641), 162

Sleep is supposed to be (13), 179

Smiling back from Coronation (385), 101

So I pull my Stockings off (1201), 79–80, 98, 140

So much of Heaven has gone from Earth (1228), 237

So the Eyes accost—and sunder (752), 137

Some keep the Sabbath going to Church—(324), 246, 281n.3

Some say goodnight—at night—(1739), 282n.15

Some things that fly there be—(89),
170–171

Some, too fragile for winter winds
(141), 117

Some we see no more, Tenements of
Wonder (1221), 224

Some—Work for Immortality—
(406), 188, 232

Some Wretched creature, savior take
(1111), 285n.2

Somewhere upon the general Earth
(1231), 185

Soul, Wilt thou toss again? (139), 253

"Sown in dishonor"! (62), 80

Strong Draughts of Their Refreshing
Minds (711), 76

Success is counted sweetest (67),
281n.3

Such are the inlets of the mind—
(1421), 144, 234

Summer begins to have the look
(1682), 169

Suspense—is Hostiler than Death—
(705), 137

Sweet is the swamp with its secrets,
(1740), 98

Sweet Mountains—Ye tell Me no
lie—(722), 182

Take all away—(1365), 268

Take your Heaven further on—(388),
212

Talk with prudence to a Beggar (119),
67

Tell all the Truth but tell it slant—
(1129), 141, 270

Tell as a Marksman—were forgotten
(1152), 254

That after Horror—that 'twas us—
(286), 122

That first Day, when you praised Me,
Sweet, (659), 176

That it will never come again (1741),
150

That odd old man is dead a year—
(1130), 222

That short—potential stir (1307),
208–209

That Such have died enable Us
(1030), 223

That this should feel the need of
Death (1112), 222–223

The Admirations—and Contempts—
of time—(906), 222

The Auctioneer of Parting (1612), 250

The Bat is dun, with wrinkled
Wings—(1575), 146

The Beggar Lad—dies early—(717),
99

The Bible is an untold Volume (1545),
79

The Blunder is in estimate (1684), 268

The Bobolink is gone—the Rowdy of
the Meadow—(1591), 148

The butterfly obtains (1685), 170

The Butterfly's Assumption Gown
(1244), 170

The Child's faith is new—(637), 183

The Court is far away—(235), 100

The Dandelion's pallid tube (1519),
168–169, 269

The Day that I was crowned (356),
101

The distance that the dead have gone
(1742), 208

The Ditch is dear to the Drunken
man (1645), 153

The Drop, that wrestles in the Sea—
(284), 60

The face I carry with me—last—
(336), 27

The Face in evanescence lain (1490),
208

The Fact that Earth is Heaven—
(1408), 238

The farthest Thunder that I heard
(1581), 154

The fascinating chill that music leaves
(1480), 193

The feet of people walking home (7),
232

The first Day's Night had come—
(410), 124

The first We knew of Him was
Death—(1006), 220, 221

The gleam of an heroic Act (1687), 144

The going from a world we know (1603), 201–202

The Grace—Myself—might not obtain—(707), 137

The Grass so little has to do—(333), 151, 166

The Hollows round His eager Eyes (955), 99

The last Night that She lived (1100), 204–206, 285n.2

The Loneliness One dare not sound—(777), 120–121

The lonesome for they know not What—(262), 66, 172–173

The Love a Life can show Below (673), 261

The Malay—took the Pearl—(452), 102

The Martyr Poets—did not tell—(544), 221

The Missing All, prevented Me (985), 66

The Morning after Wo—(364), 150

The Murmur of a Bee (155), 260

The murmuring of Bees, has ceased (1115), 169

The Mushroom is the Elf of Plants—(1298), 146

The nearest Dream recedes—unrealized—(319), 59, 64, 130

The Night was wide, and furnished scant (589), 114–115

The only Ghost I ever saw (274), 123

The Only News I know (827), 165, 260, 267, 269

The Poets light but Lamps—(883), 221

The Rat is the concisest Tenant. (1356), 146

The Riddle we can guess (1222), 228–229

The Robin's my Criterion for Tune—(285), 111

The Rose did caper on her cheek—(208), 118

The saddest noise, the sweetest noise, (1764), 169

The Savior must have been (1487), 252

The Soul has Bandaged moments—(512), 125, 178

The Soul selects her own Society—(303), 31

The Soul unto itself (683), 56

The Soul's distinct connection (974), 154

The Soul's Superior instants (306), 144, 262

The Spider as an Artist (1275), 272

The Spirit lasts—but in what mode—(1576), 230–231

The Sun kept setting—setting—still (692), 215–216

The test of Love—is Death—(573), 248

The Things that never can come back, are several—(1515), 66–67

The things we thought that we should do (1293), 237

The Tint I cannot take—is best—(627), 193, 212, 269

The Trees like Tassels—hit—and swung—(606), 152

The waters chased him as he fled, (1749), 111–112

The Wind begun to knead the Grass—(824), 153–154

The Winters are so short—(403), 79

The World—stands—solemner—to me—(493), 27, 102, 174

The worthlessness of Earthly things (1373), 265

The Zeroes—taught us—Phosphorus—(689), 30–31

There came a Day at Summer's full, (322), 24, 113–114, 118, 124, 176, 251

There came a Wind like a Bugle—(1593), 154

There comes an hour when begging stops, (1751), 257

There is a finished feeling (856), 222

There is a morn by men unseen—
(24), 211–212, 239
There is a pain—so utter—(599), 141
There is a word (8), 221
There is another sky, (2), 277n.1
There is no Silence in the Earth—so
silent (1004), 135
There's a certain Slant of light, (258),
142–143, 270
There's been a Death, in the Opposite
House, (389), 98
These are the days when Birds come
back—(130), 168, 187, 281n.3
These are the Nights that Beetles
love—(1128), 122
These—saw Visions—(758), 212–213
These tested Our Horizon—(886),
200
"They have not chosen me," he said,
(85), 13–14, 80, 249
They leave us with the Infinite. (350),
266
They put Us far apart—(474), 123–
124
They say that "Time assuages"—
(686), 140–141
They shut me up in Prose—(613), 57,
58
This Consciousness that is aware
(822), 82, 208
This heart that broke so long—(145),
117
This is a Blossom of the Brain—
(945), 246–247
This is my letter to the World (441),
42
This—is the land—the Sunset
washes—(266), 166–167, 173, 182,
185, 196, 271
This Me—that walks and works—
must die, (1588), 231
This quiet Dust was Gentlemen and
Ladies (813), 213
This was a Poet—It is That (448), 138
This World is not Conclusion. (501),
227–228

Those—dying then, (1551), 242–243
Those fair—fictitious People—(499),
211–212
Those not live yet (1454), 161, 233,
234
Those who have been in the Grave the
longest—(922), 35, 208
Tho' I get home how late—how
late—(207), 110
Tho' my destiny be Fustian—(163),
239
Though the great Waters sleep,
(1599), 117, 246
Through lane it lay—thro' bramble—
(9), 110, 280n.12
Tie the Strings to my Life, My Lord,
(279), 110, 209
Time feels so vast that were it not
(802), 18, 19, 162, 269, 270
'Tis not that Dying hurts us so—
(335), 223
'Tis so appalling—it exhilirates (281),
125–126
'Tis so much joy! 'Tis so much joy!
(172), 210, 239
'Tis true—They shut me in the
Cold—(538), 60
Title divine—is mine! (1072), 102,
106, 171
To fill a Gap (546), 135
To hear an Oriole sing (526), 228
To know just how He suffered—
would be dear—(622), 206
To make a prairie it takes a clover and
one bee, (1755), 134
To my quick ear the Leaves—con-
ferred—(891), 122
To my small Hearth His fire came—
(638), 183
To pile like Thunder to it's close
(1247), 193
To put this World down, like a
Bundle—(527), 209
To the bright east she flies, (1573),
222
To venerate the simple days (57), 62

Too cold is this (1135), 271

Triumph—may be of several kinds—(455), 208

Trudging to Eden, looking backward, (1020), 99

Trust in the Unexpected—(555), 140

Truth—is as old as God—(836), 247

'Twas a long Parting—but the time (625), 238

'Twas Crisis—All the length had passed—(948), 205

'Twas just this time, last year, I died. (445), 116

'Twas like a Maelstrom, with a notch, (414), 125

'Twas such a little—little boat (107), 111

'Twas the old—road—through pain—(344), 207

'Twas warm—at first—like Us—(519), 212

Two Butterflies went out at Noon—(533), 144–145

Two Travellers perishing in Snow (933), 110, 247

Under the Light, yet under, (949), 213

Undue Significance a starving man attaches (439), 66

Unit, like Death, for Whom? (408), 224

Unto like Story—Trouble has enticed me—(295), 74–75

"Unto Me?" I do not know you—(964), 60, 249

Up Life's Hill with my little Bundle (1010), 57–58

Upon Concluded Lives (735), 201

Victory comes late—(690), 184

Volcanoes be in Sicily (1705), 153

Wait till the Majesty of Death (171), 100, 209

"Was not" was all the Statement. (1342), 276n.24

We Cover Thee—Sweet Face—(482), 208

We dont cry—Tim and I, (196), 57

We dream—it is good we are dreaming—(531), 214

We outgrow love, like other things (887), 28

We play at Paste—(320), 130

We pray—to Heaven—(489), 102, 151, 236

We talked as Girls do—(586), 116

We thirst at first—'tis Nature's Act—(726), 58, 144, 232

Went up a year this evening! (93), 208

What did They do since I saw Them? (900), 211

What if I say I shall not wait! (277), 209–210

What Inn is this (115), 123

What is—"Paradise"—(215), 56, 57, 234–235

What shall I do—it whimpers so—(186), 57, 140

What Soft—Cherubic Creatures—(401), 80, 150–151

When Bells stop ringing—Church—begins—(633), 151–152

When I count the seeds (40), 62, 169

When I have seen the Sun emerge (888), 99

When I was small, a Woman died—(596), 117

When they come back—if Blossoms do—(1080), 169

Where bells no more affright the morn—(112), 208

Where I have lost, I softer tread—(104), 65

Whether my bark went down at sea—(52), 64, 111

Which is the best—the Moon or the Crescent? (1315), 266–267

While it is alive (491), 187

Who abdicated Ambush (1616), 271

Who Court obtain within Himself (803), 19, 100

Who Giants know, with lesser Men (796), 18–19

Who has not found the Heaven—below—(1544), 254

Who were "the Father and the Son"
(1258), 240–241

Why—do they shut Me out of
Heaven? (248), 63

Why should we hurry—why indeed
(1646), 232

Wild Nights—Wild Nights! (249), 94,
108

You cannot make Remembrance grow
(1508), 220

You love me—you are sure—(156),
57

You said that I "was Great"—one
Day—(738), 25

You taught me Waiting with Myself—(740), 137

You'll know it—as you know 'tis
Noon—(420), 151

Your Riches—taught me—Poverty.
(299), 59, 64

Your thoughts dont have words every
day (1452), 148, 191, 283n.22

You're right—"the way is narrow"—
(234), 235

You've seen Balloons set—Hav'nt
You? (700), 150, 204

Index

Amherst Academy, 41, 48

Amherst College, 22

Amherst, Massachusetts: and ED folklore, 3, 20, 21–22, 29; as ironic prefigurement of heaven, 234–235, 238; remembrances of ED, 9; small-town provincialism 38–39

Anderson, Charles, 74, 113, 281n.1, 286n.7

Angels, 201, 211, 253–254

Anthon, Kate Scott Turner, 238

Art, penetrating circumference, 221

Asterisk, imagery of, 271–272

Atlantic Monthly, 44

Awe: as force beyond circumference, 161, 193–195; as foster mother, 120; identified with God, 244–245; as source of speculation, 228; yielding to possession, 202. *See also* Circumference; God

Barriers, as images of circumference, 200–201, 211, 226

Bianchi, Martha Dickinson (niece): comforted by ED, 57; describing ED, 8–9, 92, 154, 225, 259, 276n.25, 283n.26, 285n.7, 286n.20; as editor, 247, 282n.12; published ED portrait, 8; recipient of poem, 254; recollection of Austin, 6; source of Wadsworth love story, 23, 24

Bible: borrowing of stories from, 138–139; at the center, 268–269;

ED's favorite reading, 76–80; influence of scriptural criticism, 78–79; references to Enoch and Elijah, 35, 36–37; Genesis, 276n.24; Exodus, 245; 2 Kings, 36–37; Psalm 22, 286n.18; Isaiah, 242; Matthew, 286n.18; John, 13; 2 Corinthians, 143; Hebrews, 36; Revelation, 59. *See also* Myth, biblical

Bingham, Millicent Todd: account of ED portrait search, 8; childhood introduction to ED, 3; as editor, 282n.12; mentioned, 259

Bliss, Rev. Daniel, 100

Bolts of Melody, 282n.12

Boston Post, 281n.3

Bowdoin, Elbridge, 22

Bowles, Mary (Mrs. Samuel), 29, 220

Bowles, Samuel: death, 200, 201, 204, 206, 220, 226–227, 246; ED's description of, 262; as editor, 43, 281n.3; elegies for, 271; "Queen Recluse" comment, 30, 31, 32; recipient of letters, 12, 30–31, 262, 286n.7; recipient of poems, 106, 229; as reputed ED lover, 24, 28; in search of Higginson daguerreotype, 6

Bradstreet, Anne, 83

Brontë, Charlotte: as ED source, 280n.16; *Jane Eyre*, 113, 124

Brontë, Emily: poem read at ED funeral, 214–215; *Wuthering Heights*, 123, 124

Brontës, the, 41, 85
Brooklyn Daily Union, 281n.3
Browne, Sir Thomas, 163, 284n.4
Browning, Elizabeth Barrett: cited as favorite poet, 4; influence on ED, 75–76, 85, 95, 192, 280n.16; photographs of, 6–7; tribute to, 221; *Aurora Leigh*, 85, 90–91, 105, 113, 137, 140, 143, 163, 279n.15; mentioned, 21, 41
Browning, Robert: cited as favorite poet, 4; literary influence, 85, 91–92, 95; mentioned 21, 29, 41
Bryant, William Cullen, 202
Bunyan, John, 83
Burton, Matilda, 140
Byron, George Gordon, 86–88, 162, 196

Calvin, John, 187, 284n.12
Calvinism: conversion theology and psychology, 39–40, 180–184; doctrine, 10, 14, 250; language of, 259; as literary resource, 77, 80–84; perspective on death, 206, 211; sacramental theory, 191. *See also* Puritanism, Religion
Cameron, Sharon, 233, 284–285n.13
Capps, Jack L., 73
Carlo (dog), 4, 57, 88, 141, 221
Carlyle, Thomas, 6
Child, Lydia Maria, 280n.16
Christian Register, 247
Christian Union, 131, 132
Christmas, celebration of, 251–252, 286nn.15–16
Church, Horace, 244
Circle imagery, 159–161, 163, 264–272. *See also* Circumference
Circuit: claims of circuit world, 199–200, 204, 216–219; definition of, 161, 162; narrowing of, 267–268; protection of, 232–234. *See also* Circumference
Circumference: and awe, 194–197; defined as death, 164–165, 171, 199–224, 264–265, 268–269; as ED's

business, 16; God on the other side of, 18; imagery of, 159–197; as incentive to speculation, 225–263; interpretations of, 283n.3; theme of, 152; and translation, 37; unorthodox quest for, 68–69. *See also* Barriers; Circle imagery; Circuit; Death; Immortality
Civil War, 117, 130
Clark, Charles, 229
Clark, James, 229, 230
Clemens, Samuel. *See* Twain, Mark
Cockburn, Sir Alexander, 284n.8
Coleman, Eliza, 280n.20
Coleridge, Samuel Taylor, 84
Complete Poems, 282n.12
Cowan, Perez, 209, 223–224

Daguerreotype, 4–8
Dandurand, Karen, 281n.3
Darwin, Charles, 237
Davis, Aurelia Hinsdale, 22
Dead, the: influence of, across circumference, 219–223; as keepers of secrets, 212–215; as lures beyond circumference, 210–212, 223
Death: as circumference, 164–165, 171; as clarifier of life, 221–223; critical commentary on, 285n.1; personified, 217–219; as spur to supposition, 225–227; theme of, 116–118, 198–224. *See also* Circumference; Immortality
Deprivation: caused by death, 207–208; and heavenly compensation, 237; as a poetic theme, 62–69, 277–278n.9
Dickinson, Austin. *See* Dickinson, William Austin
Dickinson, Edward (father): death, 97, 146, 207, 226–227, 245, 252, 280n.20, 286n.16; ED's description of, 287n.1; elegy for, 117–118, 276n.24; as father, 4–6 passim, 22, 23, 29, 32, 51, 78, 241–242; identified with gothic roles, 120; poem addressed to, 179; political role, 21,

23, 100; prosaic views, 57, 95–96; religious concerns, 39, 245, 276n.28, 286n.10; mentioned, 86, 156, 200, 208, 244

Dickinson, Edward (nephew, Ned), 98

Dickinson, Emily Elizabeth: on art, 192–197; asterisk imagery, 271–272; attentiveness to dying, 204–206, 211, 212; barrier images, 200–201, 211, 226; choice of spinster role, 29–30; circle imagery, 159–161, 163, 264–272; circuit imagery, 161, 162; circumference theme, 19, 152, 159–197, 283n.3; compression of psychological states, 141–142; conflation of natural descriptions, 142–143; death theme, 116–118, 198–224, 285n.1; deprivation theme, 62–69, 277–278n.9; eccentric behavior, 16, 31, 37; editing of, 282n.12; education, 40–41; explosive imagery, 153–155; imagery of psychological transitions, 176–180; imagery of transitions in human life cycle, 171–176; implicit romantic narrative in poems, 23–27; interest in nature, 62–63, 166–171, 184–185, 200; language and rhetoric, 19, 133–134; letters (*see* Bowles, Mary; Bowles, Samuel; Clark, Charles; Cowan, Perez; Dickinson, Lavinia; Dickinson, Susan Gilbert; Dickinson, William Austin; Gilbert, Martha; Graves, John; Hale, Edward Everett; Haven, Mary; Higginson, Mary; Higginson, Thomas Wentworth; Holland, Elizabeth; Holland, Josiah Gilbert; Holland, Dr. and Mrs.; Humphrey, Jane; Jenkins, Sally; Lord, Otis Phillips; "Master"; Norcross, Frances and Louise; Norcross, Louise; Root, Abiah; Sweetser, Cornelia; Todd, Mabel Loomis; Turner, Clara Newman; and Whitney, Maria); letters as related to poems, 277n.1; letters as

stylistic workshop, 47–55; limitation theme, 56–62; madness theme, 124–126; marriage imagery, 26–27, 173–176; metaphorical life design, 16–20, 274n.27; moral distillation, 140–141; narrative foreshortening, 138–140; negative choices, 21–46, 267; poetics, 128–156; "Processes of Size" metaphor, 18–20, 269; quest or journey imagery, 17, 167–168, 201–204, 209–211, 272; radical insufficiency, 55–62; reading habits, 39, 41–42, 78–83, 278n.3, 279n.15; religious experiences, 77, 180–191, 225–263, 284n.9, 286nn.6, 9; resistance to publication, 42–44; responses to sexual restrictions, 40–42, 44–46; role playing, aristocrat, 99–102; role playing, bride, 102–108; role playing, child, 56–59, 97–99, 234–236, 237, 254–256, 279n.6; role playing, daisy, 14; role playing, dying person or corpse, 50, 213–219; role playing, gothic figures, 53–54, 120–126; role playing, Judah, 48; role playing, Khedive, 89; role playing, quester, 50, 65, 108–112; role playing, scholar, 15, 221; role playing, sentimental figures, 54, 114–119; role playing, Socrates, 14; role playing, watcher over the dying, 116–117, 280n.20; role-playing strategy, 19, 95–117; sacramental imagery, 148, 150, 185–191; self image, 3–11, 16–17, 19–20, 272; smallness theme, 272; stages of her writing, 145–148; stories about reputed lovers, 21–24, 28; sunset imagery, 166–167, 200, 218, 221; syntactic tightening, 148–152; verse forms, 143–145; white clothing signifying translation, 33–37; wren imagery, 9, 11–13, 19–20, 272

Dickinson, Emily Norcross (mother): death, 204, 223, 226–227, 280n.20; elegy for, 221–222; identified with sentimental roles, 120; as invalid,

199; mentioned by ED, 48; quoted by ED, 98; scandalized by religious speculation, 79

Dickinson, Gilbert (nephew): death, 201–202, 211, 212, 226–227, 231, 239, 244, 267, 280n.20, 286n16; described by ED, 285n.7

Dickinson, Lavinia Norcross (sister): comments on her own daguerreotype, 6; conversion, 39, 181, 182; as correspondent, 50; as exemplar of industriousness, 217; nursing ill aunt, 280n.20; physical comparison with ED, 9; projected visit to Boston, 51–52; quoted, 133; recipient of letter, 88; reputation as mimic, 96; shaping public image of ED, 3, 8, 9, 22, 28, 30, 31, 32, 94, 128, 159, 273n.7; subject of ED fantasy, 49–50; mentioned, 111, 199, 215, 237, 241, 244, 257

Dickinson, Martha. See Bianchi, Martha Dickinson

Dickinson, Susan Gilbert (Mrs. William Austin): conversion, 182, 284n.10; as "Dollie," 57, 118, 215; as editor, 44, 203–204; as editorial adviser, 131–133, 135, 152, 154; engagement to Austin, 52, 106, 280n.10; as literary confidante, 6, 23, 76; obituary for ED, 40, 154; and publication of ED poems, 281n.3; quoted, 224; recipient of letters, 10, 28, 48–49, 50, 52, 53, 55, 89, 168, 220, 224, 267, 268, 284n.10; recipient of poems, 106, 148, 258, 277n.1; mentioned, 138, 238, 281n.3

Dickinson, William Austin (brother): comment on photography, 6; conversion, 39; ED's concern for, 9; on ED's love life, 28; ED's relationship with, 51–52; on ED's role playing, 15–16; education, 41; engagement to Susan Gilbert, 52, 106, 280n.10, 284n.10; observation of sister's

withdrawal, 30; reaction to ED portraits, 8; recipient of letters, 9, 47–48, 49, 51–52, 52–53, 85–86, 92–93, 96, 114, 186; recipient of poem, 277n.1; religious speculation, 79; reticence about ED, 3; unhappy marriage, 29; westward inclination, 109; mentioned, 99, 114, 198, 207, 224, 251, 281n.3

Dickinson, William Cowper (cousin), 12

Diehl, Joanne Feit, 163, 282n.9

Donald, Rev. E. Winchester, 16, 31–32

Drum Beat, 281n.3

Dryden, John, 284n.4

Easter, awareness of, 252

Edwards, Rev. Jonathan: on conversion, 284n.9; quoted, 141; "Personal Narrative," 180, 181; mentioned, 81, 82, 260

Eliot, George: ED's interest in, 21; photograph on ED's wall, 8; responses to, 76, 85; mentioned, 192, 215

Eliot, Thomas Stearns, 260

Emerson, Ralph Waldo: as ED source, 280n.16, 284n.4; ED's responses to, 76, 85; on literary influence, 85; quoted on image of Christ, 248; "Circles," 160, 163, 166; "Days," 185, 284n.11; mentioned, 19, 41, 260

Emmons, Nathanael, 81

Eternity: at the center, 268; as endless time, 214, 218. See also Immortality

Fame, as radiance from beyond circumference, 220–221

Fascicles: numbers 33 and 34 examined, 183–184; organization of, 13, 135–138; question of cohesiveness, 282n.13

Ford, Emily Fowler (Mrs. Gordon Lester), 35–36, 37, 104

Ford, Thomas W., 285n.2
Fowler, Emily. *See* Ford, Emily Fowler
Franklin, Sir John, 109
Franklin, R. W.: dating of poems, 106, 282n.15; as editor, 13, 121, 135–136, 282n.12
French, Daniel Chester, 194–195
Frost, Robert, 34, 43, 276–277n.36
Frothingham, Octavius Brooks, 78
Fuller, Margaret, 19

Gelpi, Albert, 260
Gilbert, Martha (Mrs. John Williams Smith), 11
Gilbert, Susan. *See* Dickinson, Susan Gilbert
Gladden, Washington, 229–230
God: as agent of deprivation, 63; and circumference, 18, 162, 268–272; competitor with human love, 24; distance from, 132; ED's relationship with, 40, 240–247, 254–260, 286n.9; failure of communication with, 129; and fantasies of heaven, 238, 239; as keeper of secrets, 202, 223, 225; natural revelations of, 191; as object of speculation, 228, 231; quest for, 182; sacramentally involved with man, 187; source and owner of talent, 43. *See also* Jesus; Religion; Trinity
Gothic literary conventions, 120–126
Gould, George, 22–23, 29, 30
Graves, John, 28, 54–55, 225–226, 233
Griffith, Clark, 112, 285nn.2, 5

Hale, Rev. Edward Everett, 206
Hall, Mary Lee, 22, 23, 24, 28
Harvard, John, 194, 195
Harvard University, 194, 195, 271
Haven, Mary (Mrs. Joseph), 234, 281n.3
Hawthorne, Nathaniel: literary influence, 85; on women writers, 43; "The Custom-House," 83; *The*

House of the Seven Gables, 85–86; *The Marble Faun*, 82, 277n.37; *The Scarlet Letter*, 77, 86; mentioned, 39, 111, 112
Heaven, images of, 234–240
Higginson, Mary Channing (Mrs. Thomas Wentworth), 77, 134
Higginson, Thomas Wentworth: comments on ED, 9, 214–215, 278n.5; contrast with ED, 267–268; early correspondence with ED, 3–4; as editor, 43, 94, 151, 153, 282n.12; first visit to ED, 9, 17–18, 34; friends' reaction to ED, 77; invitation to Boston, 39; "Letter to a Young Contributor," 4, 281n.2; as literary preceptor, 15, 16, 41, 128–131, 281n.2; as poet, 282n.17; portrait sought by Bowles, 6; recipient of letters, 3–5, 9–10, 14–15, 16–17, 21, 48, 59, 87, 126, 128, 132, 141, 146, 206, 208, 217, 228, 233, 241, 242, 248, 273n.10, 281n.2; recipient of poems, 64, 147; mentioned, 31, 76, 97, 133, 145, 154, 159, 220, 221, 231, 232, 260, 272, 281n.1
Hitchcock, Edward, 83
Holland, Elizabeth (Mrs. Josiah Gilbert): daguerreotype, 6; recipient of letters, 6, 78, 122, 134, 150, 165–166, 184, 186, 201, 202, 211, 217, 237–238, 241, 244, 265, 268, 286n.8, 287n.1; recipient of poem, 67; wren image applied to, 11
Holland, Dr. Josiah Gilbert: death, 226–227, 241; as editor, 43; recipient of letter, 200; recipient of poem, 247
Holland, Dr. and Mrs. Josiah Gilbert: and fantasies of heaven, 239; recipients of letters, 14, 50, 239
Holland, Sophia, 116, 280n.20
Holy Spirit, the, 247
Hopkins, Samuel, 81
Humphrey, Jane (Mrs. William H. Wilkinson): recipient of letters, 29–

30, 50, 51, 181, 199, 214; mentioned, 199
Humphrey, Leonard, 10

Immortality: outside circumference, 268; as Death's chaperon, 218–219; as "Flood subject," 199, 223–224, 231–232; probings toward, 225–263. See also Circumference; Eternity; Religion
Independent, 203–204
Industriousness, as circuit value, 207, 208, 211, 217
Irving, Washington, 117

Jackson, Helen Hunt: death, 88; as ED editor, 281n.3; elegy for, 272; pressures ED to publish, 33; recipient of poems, 147; Saxe Holm stories, 43–44, 277n.37
Jason, 66
Jenkins, Rev. Jonathan L., 39, 276n.28
Jenkins, Sally, 286n.16
Jesus: as bridegroom, 175, 176; and circumference, 182, 247–253; as comforter, 60; crucifixion, 253, 270–271; as frustrated saint, 80; greeting the elect dead, 206, 209, 211, 215, 219; on his Apostles, 13–14; as initiator of conversion, 180; and the Lord's Supper, 189–190; love of, 185–186; promise of abrogated death, 223; schoolmaster image of, 57; Transfiguration, 37. See also God; Religion; Trinity
Johnson, Thomas H.: biographical speculation, 52; dating of poems, 27, 106; as editor, 17, 130, 136, 137, 217, 273n.7, 276n.24, 278n.5, 281n.3, 282n.12, 283n.22, 284n.8
Journey, imagery of, 201–204, 209–211, 272

Keats, John, 4, 84, 104
Keep, Wallace, 8
Kemble, Fanny, 95

Kimball, Benjamin, 220, 271

Larcom, Lucy, 42
Leyda, Jay, 5, 17, 38
Limitation, theme of: chosen pattern of constriction, 21–46; ED's use of, 19. See also Radical insufficiency; Smallness
Lindberg-Seyersted, Brita, 144
Longfellow, Henry Wadsworth: allusion to, 247; literary influence of "Pegasus in Pound," 85, 88–90; "The Wreck of the Hesperus," 111, 139; mentioned, 41
Lord, Otis Phillips: death, 220, 226–227, 246; elegy for, 117, 271–272; illness of, 229; recipient of letters, 21, 153, 237, 238–239, 259; romance with ED, 21, 24, 28; mentioned, 111
Lyon, Mary, 5, 41, 81

MacLeish, Archibald, 281n.1
Madness, theme of, 124–126
Maher, Margaret (Maggie), 5
Marriage, imagery of, 102–108, 173–176. See also Dickinson, Emily—role playing
Marvel, Ik (Donald Grant Mitchell): quoted, 143; storm narrative, 111; and translation, 35, 36, 37; *Reveries of a Bachelor*, 95; mentioned, 41, 84, 112, 122
"Master": recipient of letters, 10, 14, 82, 87, 167; uncertain identity of, 28
Mather, Cotton, 225
Melville, Herman, 34, 141, 229
Miller, Ruth, 281n.1, 282n.12, 283n.3
Milton, John, 284n.4
Mitchell, Donald Grant. See Marvel, Ik
Monteiro, George, 285n.6
Moral concerns, lack of emphasis on, 140–142, 236, 245
Mount Holyoke Female Seminary: academic regimen, 41, 159, 160,

251; conversion pressure, 81; daguerreotype craze, 5; and menagerie, 182

Mount Holyoke Journal, 5

Mysticism, approaches to, 259–263

Myth: Amherst, 3, 20, 21–22, 29; biblical, 79–80, 85; classical, 233 (*see also* Jason; Ulysses); ED's private myth, 20

Nature: natural epiphanies, 184–185; natural transitions as analogues to circumference, 166–171, 200; as source of loss, 62–63

Newton, Benjamin: death, 52, 206; as tutor, 41

Norcross, Frances and Louise (cousins): nursing ill cousin, 280n.20; recipients of letters, 172, 180, 192, 198, 201, 204, 223, 226, 243; recipients of poems, 117, 146, 147, 191

Norcross, Lavinia (aunt, Mrs. Loring): dying, 168, 280n.20; elegy for, 117; mentioned by ED, 53

Norcross, Louise, 11

Osgood, Frances, 42

Park, Rev. Edwards Amasa, 80

Parker, Theodore, 78

Patterson, Rebecca, 101, 279nn.7, 8

Peckham, Robert W., 286n.5

Poe, Edgar Allan, 76, 124

Poems (1890), 277n.38

Poems (1891), 94

Porter, David: on bride and wife poems, 174, 284n.6; on ED's style, 282nn.9, 11, 12; on lack of design in poems, 274n.27, 281n.1; on typological thinking, 286n.14

Prayer, attitude toward, 254–259

Psychological states, circumferential, 202

Puritanism: characteristics of, 225, 260, 286n.14; continuity in ED's imagination, 81–83; conversion

morphology, 180. *See also* Calvinism

Quest, imagery of. *See* Journey

Radical insufficiency, as a poetic theme, 56–62, 67–69. *See also* Limitation; Smallness

Religion: attitudes toward conversion, 180–184; church membership, 185–186; hopes to validate, 229–230; influence of religious reading, 77–84; private religious search, 68–69; sacraments, 73, 185–191. *See also* Bible; Calvinism; God; Jesus; Prayer

Root, Abiah (Mrs. Samuel W. Strong): conversion, 39; correspondence with ED, 9; recipient of letters, 9, 10, 48, 49, 180, 181, 214, 218, 251–252, 275n.9

Rosenbaum, S. P., 11

Round Table, 281n.3

Sacramental imagery, 148, 150, 185–191. *See also* God; Jesus; Religion

St. Armand, Barton L., 280n.12

Sand, George, 90

Sentimental literature: application of its conventions to ED's life, 29; ED's use of its conventions, 42, 114–119; suitability for young ladies, 41–42

Sewall, Richard B.: on Dickinson family rhetoric, 133; on ED's reading, 276n.33; on ED's role playing, 16, 17; on ED's style, 281n.1; rejection of misplaced pity, 19–20; on writing as prayer, 259; mentioned, 34, 73, 74

Sewall, Samuel, as analogizer, 225

Shakespeare, William: primary literary resource, 84, 95, 279–280n.9; reading club, 95; vocabulary, 284n.4; *Romeo and Juliet*, 13; mentioned, 41

Shaw, Lemuel, 244

Shelley, Percy Bysshe, 13, 84, 163
Sherwood, William, 282n.9
Sigourney, Lydia, 42
Smallness, theme of, 3–20, 272. *See also* Limitation; Radical insufficiency
Spofford, Harriet Prescott, 84
Springfield Daily Republican: conjectures on Saxe Holm authorship, 43, 277n.37; ED poems in, 131, 281n.3; editorial judgment, 44; typical contributors, 140
Storrs, Rev. Richard Salter, Jr., 281n.3
Stowe, Harriet Beecher, 42
Sudol, Ronald, 280n.21
Sunset imagery, 166–167, 200, 218, 221
Sweetser, Cornelia Peck (Mrs. John Howard), 261
Sweetser, Henry and Charles, 281n.3

Taggard, Genevieve, 22
Taylor, Edward, 43, 81, 259, 276–277n.36
Tennyson, Alfred Lord: as ED source, 279nn.8, 9; "The Lord of Burleigh," 101–102, 103; "Love and Duty," 113–114, 119; mentioned, 176
Thackrey, Donald, 134
Thoreau, Henry David, 39, 43, 260, 276n.36
Todd, Mabel Loomis: and Amherst folklore, 3, 22; distant relationship with ED, 3, 33; as editor, 35, 44, 63, 94, 131, 151, 153, 247, 282n.12; recipient of letter, 243; search for

ED portrait, 8; mentioned, 15–16, 28, 31
Tolman, Susan, 5
Transcendentalism, 265
Translation, imagery of, 35–38
Trinity, the, 247, 248. *See also* God; Jesus
Turner, Clara Newman, 185
Twain, Mark (Samuel Clemens), 98, 198, 235, 256

Ulysses, 62

Victoria, Queen, 102
Victorian literary conventions, 95, 112–114

Wadsworth, Rev. Charles: death, 226–227, 229, 230, 252; reputed ED lover, 23, 24, 28, 29, 30
Walsh, John Evangelist, 163, 280n.16
Ward, Theodora Van Wagenen: definition of immortality, 233; editor of *Letters*, 17, 217, 284n.8
Webster, Noah: *An American Dictionary*, 160, 276n.23, 284n.4
Weisbuch, Robert, 283n.3, 285n.5
Wells, Anna Mary, 275n.6
Wendell, Barrett, 271
Whicher, George Frisbie, 73
Whitman, Walt, 19, 260
Whitney, Maria, 246, 265
Wilbur, Richard, 277–278n.9
Wood, Abby (Mrs. Daniel Bliss), 39, 181
Wordsworth, William, 84, 96, 97, 172
Wren imagery, 272